Crafts Market Place

Where and How to Sell Your Crafts

Crafts Market Place

Where and How to Sell Your Crafts

Edited by Argie Manolis

BETTERWAY BOOKS
Cincinnati, Ohio

Other fine Betterway Books are available from your local bookstore
or direct from the publisher.

01 00 99 98 97   5 4 3 2 1

International Standard Serial Number: 1092-471X
International Standard Book Number: 1-55870-433-7

Production Editor: Tara Horton
Interior design: Sandy Kent
Cover design: Chad Planner
Cover photo: Erik Von Fisher/Blink
Photo on page 7: Kathy Caputo Ruzek

Betterway Books are available for sales promotions, premiums and
fund-raising use. Special editions or book excerpts can also be created to specification. For details, contact: Special Sales Manager,
F&W Publications, 1507 Dana Avenue, Cincinnati, Ohio 45207.

ACKNOWLEDGMENTS

Thanks to Tracey Herring, Nancy Mosher, Maria Nerius and Kathy Caputo Ruzek for sharing their craft expertise with the readers of this book.

Thanks to Carla Thomas for the time she spent helping to edit Part One, and to everyone who worked on the book, especially Barb Brown.

A special thanks to Nancy Mosher, Maria Nerius and Kathy Caputo Ruzek for their time, patience and support. As consultants, they spent hours collecting hundreds of addresses and looking over preliminary outlines and industry questionnaires. Their careful attention to the project during its early stages has made a huge difference.

Finally, a very special thanks to Tara Horton for going above and beyond her job description and keeping the book going through its many rough spots. Without her work, *Crafts Marketplace* never would have been finished!

ABOUT THE COVER

The vase and plate were hand crafted by Maddy Fraioli of Fraiolware.

The doll was created by Lisa Drumm of Don Drumm Studios & Gallery.

Eddie Reed is the crafter of the turned wood box.

Jim and Sue Aufderhaar of Basic Elements are the artists of the bead necklace.

CONTRIBUTORS

TRACEY HERRING is a doll and teddy bear artist who has also received several writing awards. Her work has been widely published. Tracey regularly judges doll shows and helps craftspeople with business concerns as a consultant, with special emphasis on show presentations and advertising. She wrote chapter seven.

NANCY MOSHER began NanCraft®, her professional craft business, in 1979. She offers business seminars and personal consulting for craftspeople. Her articles have been published in several craft-related magazines. She is on the Board of Directors of the Southwest Craft and Hobby Association and the Association of Craft and Creative Industries. She acted as a consultant for this book, and also wrote chapter two.

MARIA NERIUS is editor of *Craft Supply Magazine* and a columnist for *Craftrends* and *Crafts 'n Things*. A long-time writer and professional craftsperson, Maria shared her expertise as a consultant for the book. She also wrote chapters four and six.

KATHY CAPUTO RUZEK's successful professional craft business complements her success as a writer. Among the books she has written are *How to Start Making Money With Your Crafts* and *The Selling From Home Sourcebook*. Kathy shares her knowledge in chapters one, three and five. She also made significant contributions as a consultant for this book.

Table of Contents

Part Two
MARKET LISTINGS

Introduction

Welcome to *Crafts Marketplace*, the "Yellow Pages" for craftspeople who want to begin selling their work or to expand their current markets. This book is an extensive directory of craft markets in the United States and Canada, including everything from shows to catalogs, craft malls to galleries, and much, much more. It comes to you from Betterway Books, a division of F&W Publications. F&W Publications has been publishing directories for creative people since 1921. Our line of directories includes 15 books, from the ever-popular *Writer's Market* series for writers to the more specialized *The Teddy Bear Sourcebook* and *The Doll Sourcebook*.

Crafts Marketplace continues our commitment to directory publishing. For decades, our directories have allowed creative people to get the detailed information they need to help them choose markets for their work. You will find that our listings include everything you could possibly want to know about a given market. We sent thousands of questionnaires to markets across the United States and Canada, and those that responded are listed in this book. The information was provided by the owner or manager of the market listed and has been verified. Nevertheless, specific information is subject to change, as this book will be available for two years before it is revised and updated.

Defining the Craftsperson

The craft market is a diverse and widespread network of men and women creating products ranging from the $5 handmade gift item to sculptures costing more than $1,000. Consequently, defining the craftsperson is quite a challenge. Some craftspeople make inexpensive country crafts during their free time, and sell them at shows as time allows. Others are full time craftspeople with a diverse line of work. Still others concentrate on one medium or product.

This book is for craftspeople at any level, doing any kind of work, from the beginner who is experimenting with various products, to the established craftsperson with an extensive product line. The only requirement is the craftsperson must want to begin selling their work, or to expand their current markets. For the purposes of this book, a **craft** includes everything from the low-cost country and traditional crafts to the high-quality fine craft. Any item made by hand is considered a craft, with one exception. This exception is any flat work of art considered a piece of fine art, e.g., a painting or drawing. Markets for these types of work can be found in *Artist's and Graphic Designer's Market*, published by Writer's Digest Books.

The crafts we are talking about probably fall into one or more of the following general categories: fine crafts, home decor, wearable art, figurines, jewelry, dolls/stuffed animals/toys, miniatures/dollhouses, pottery/ceramics, wooden crafts, nature crafts/floral, paper products, leather crafts, stained glass items, baskets, needlework crafts, recycled crafts, hand blown glass items and sculpture. For the purposes of this book, a **craftsperson** is someone who makes and sells his or her crafts.

How can this book be aimed at such a diverse group of people? Simple. The detailed listings allow us to include information about the type and price range of crafts sold at each show, direct sales market or retail market listed. You will be able to tell, at a glance, whether or not your products will fit a particular market. Once you have narrowed the possibilities, you can read the detailed descriptions of the stores, or find out how a market or show is publicized, or learn about payment options. Finally, you will find information on how to approach the market about selling your work!

A Guide to Part One

Part one includes advice from industry experts on market research, financial considerations and promoting your business. Part one also addresses specific information on how to sell to the markets listed in this book. Industry experts Tracey Herring, Nancy Mosher, Maria Nerius and Kathy Caputo Ruzek will help you get started, if you are new to the craft business. They will also offer advice that even the experienced craftsperson can use.

A Guide to Part Two

Part two is the most important section of this book. It includes more than 575 listings of markets for craftspeople, with detailed information that will help you narrow down prospective markets and explain how to contact them. The market listings are divided into the following categories:

- *Craft shows* are listed in chapter eight. This chapter includes listings of both promoters and single shows. Listings identify shows as wholesale or retail, and include information about the show dates, times and locations. They also include attendance figures, admission cost, types of crafts sold and information about how the show is advertised or promoted to help you narrow your options. Finally, the listings include the type and number of spaces available, how much it costs to participate, and how to apply.
- *Direct sales* opportunities are listed in chapter nine. They include craft malls, co-ops and other markets. The listings include business hours and descriptions, types and price ranges of crafts sold. They also list how the market is promoted, the type and number of spaces available and how to apply for a space. Payment policies and responsibilities of the craftsperson are also included.
- *Resources for selling through the mail* are listed in chapter ten. They include catalogs that sell handmade crafts, resources for help in producing your own catalog/promotional materials, and other direct mail resources. Detailed information about types of products and costs are also included.
- *Places to sell wholesale* are listed in chapter eleven. They include retail stores selling crafts, galleries and other retail markets. Also included are listings of craft brokers and representatives who will sell your crafts for you. These listings include business hours, description of the markets, and types and price ranges of crafts sold. Information on how the market is promoted, business policies, where the buyer finds crafts for the shop, special programs and how to query is also included.

If information in a particular listing is missing, it is because the owner, manager or organizer of a particular market did not provide the information on his or her questionnaire.

A Guide to Part Three

Part three includes listings of resources that will help craftspeople in their businesses. The listings in chapter twelve are for business products, including packaging products, show equipment and computer products. Chapter thirteen lists services for craftspeople, including banking and accounting services, insurance services, legal services, Internet services, classes/workshops and other services. Chapter fourteen lists trade organizations for craftspeople, and chapter fifteen lists craft-related publications.

Finding a Listing

The listings in both parts two and three are divided by chapter according to the major category into which they fit (shows or retailers, for instance). In many cases, they are also subdivided within the chapter. The best way to start is by browsing through the chapters and choosing the types of sales opportunities you are interested in pursuing, if you do not already know.

If you are interested in finding listings in a particular geographical area, the geographical index in the back of the book lists markets by state. This is especially helpful when looking for shows in your area. The general index includes all the markets in alphabetical order, to help you find specific listings a second time.

The best way to find the right markets for your work, however, is to set time aside to skim through this book. Consider the following questions about your own product before you begin:

1. Define your product in terms of category and price range. Does it fit this market? The types and price ranges of products sold through each market are included in the listings, and these will prove to be your most important considerations. Let's say you sell wearable art in the $50-100 price range. You can automatically eliminate all markets with price ranges significantly above or below yours, and any markets that do not include wearable art. For instance, a craft mall with an average price range of $5-20 and a retail craft shop with mostly floral and wooden crafts would not be your ideal markets. Someone interested in high-quality wearable art would never think of looking for your product in these markets, so how could you expect to sell your work?
2. How many different craftspeople sell through this market? These figures are included in the listings.

Will you be one of 10, 100 or 500 craftspeople whose work will be sold through this market?

3. Check attendance figures for shows and promotional/advertising information for all markets. How many people will see your product?

4. Do you expect to face a great deal of competition within this market? The more types of products sold, the less direct competition you will face. On the other hand, more types of products means less focus, and you must decide if your customers are likely to see your product in a given market. A show with few vendors and a high attendance is not necessarily the best show for you if all the vendors have products very similar to your own, or if everyone attending is looking for a product completely diffferent from the ones you are selling.

5. Set a reasonable financial goal. How much profit can you reasonably expect to make after considering all the costs involved?

Ask these five questions each time you consider a particular market. Remember to return to part one for more detailed information about how to sell through the various markets! Chapter one will help you in product development and research as you choose the best markets for your work. Chapters four through seven will help you in your considerations of specific types of markets, with one chapter dedicated to each of the following: shows, direct mail, direct sales (in which the craftsperson sells directly to the final customer), and retailers (in which the craftsperson sells his or her work, at wholesale to a retailer, who then sells to the final buyer). It may be helpful to have your marker ready to highlight possible markets, and a pen to make notes in the margins, as you skim through this book.

Don't limit your search to the types of markets through which you currently sell your work. If you are an old hand at the show circuit, for instance, take time to browse through the direct sales and retailer listings.

I hope this book provides you with the information you need to start or continue your market search. Good luck, and happy crafting! 🌀

1

Selling Your Crafts

Getting Started: Developing a Product Line

BY KATHY CAPUTO RUZEK

The crafts marketplace is a vast and competitive arena. There are thousands of people out there doing the same thing that you are doing—making and selling crafts. Having an attractive product is just not enough to guarantee sales success. You need to have a knowledge of the market, including where your products fit into that marketplace and who your customers are. This information will provide you with the tools to produce a successful and competitive product line.

Many new craftspeople industriously produce a large inventory of products without having any idea if their products will sell or what their customers need or want. Craftspeople know what *they* like, and may assume their customers will have the same tastes. This doesn't always work, and new craftspeople often become dissatisfied with their sales and disillusioned about the crafts industry in general.

But this doesn't have to happen. Anyone can develop a product line that will sell. By evaluating your product ideas before you produce large quantities of inventory and by conducting sound market research, the products you make can enjoy healthy and long-lasting sales.

Market Research

Market research is finding out everything there is to know about who is buying what—as well as when and where—so you can make products people will want to buy. Tracking popular trends, evaluating your product in light of those trends, and targeting the correct consumer market for your products are all facets of market research.

Focusing on a National Market

To ensure consistently strong sales for the longest period of time, you must study the consumer marketplace, and not only locally. Many trends start on one coast of the United States and more across the country toward the opposite shore. Some trends have initial momentum but never gain enough consumer interest to flourish.

If you travel to other parts of the country on vacation, you should take special notice of what is selling at craft shows in the areas you visit. Maybe in a few months those products or that type of product will become popular in your own area. The inspiration for some of my best and most profitable craft ideas were found while I was traveling cross-country on vacation. I made notes, scribbled drawings, and brought these new ideas home, incorporating their flavor into my own work.

If you are not in a position to travel, then it is especially important for you to read not only craft magazines, but also fashion, decorating, economic and special interest magazines to keep your finger on the pulse of the consumer marketplace. As you read and observe, take notes of any recurring styles, products, trends, and attitudes. Eventually, a pattern will become evident, and you will be able to capitalize on it.

The idea for an Indian doll was conceived in 1987 while I was traveling through the Southwestern United States on vacation. Also on that trip, I passed through Oklahoma and first saw a mop doll. I found they were very popular in the West and Midwest. I combined both ideas (Indian and mop doll) into one product that sold very well.

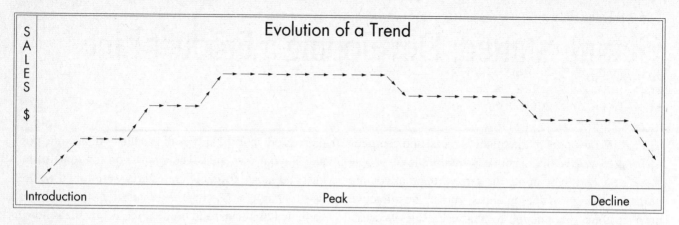

Fads, Trends and Timing

There is a BIG difference between a fad and a trend. A fad has no staying power. It reaches its peak very quickly and its drop in popularity is equally swift. By the time you hear of it or see it, the product's life cycle may already be in the latter part of the second stage, soon to be on the decline, and it will be too late for you to make any use of it. A trend evolves more slowly, taking a little time to pick up speed and usually years to reach the point of market saturation. The changes evoked by a trend have more to do with lifestyle and attitude rather than with one simple product. The "Pet Rock" was a very successful fad. Southwestern design is a popular trend.

Trends are slower to take hold, so proceed cautiously when you identify an up-and-coming trend. Make sure you don't introduce large quantities of the product too early into the marketplace. Test-market first before you go into mass production. You might find that you have to wait awhile before interest catches up in your area.

Fads are valuable to you if you can jump on the bandwagon immediately and the product itself fits well with your current product line. But don't abandon your current products to go into the fad merchandising business. It could be a very short career. Timing is very important here. If you can identify a fad *before* it reaches its peak, the product fits in well with your current product line, and you are aware that you are not making a life-long commitment to producing the product, then go ahead with it. Just be on a constant lookout for declines in sales, and don't produce what you may not be able to sell.

In the long run, it is much better to be cautious and follow trends rather than fads. Raw materials are expensive, and time is money. You would not want to waste either of these on a product or products that would not significantly increase your sales figures for years to come. Producing a product line that has general and (as much as possible) universal appeal is by far the safer route to travel. You can always incorporate some fadish pieces from time to time on a test market basis and still not jeopardize the integrity of your whole product line.

Do not ever be so secure in your product that you don't feel the need to add to it, delete from it, or try new things to enhance it. Time, trends and consumer tastes don't remain the same forever. You will have to change with them if you want to experience consistent success. Constantly re-evaluate your products in light of new market information to ensure that they will maintain at least their original appeal.

Product Evaluation

Now let's take a look at your products themselves. Presumably, you have already developed at least a prototype product line, even if you are not yet at the point of actively selling your crafts. Take each product individually, and ask yourself the following questions, "Is it neat?" "Is it complete?" "Is it unique?" These are the three basic features of a successful product. How do your products measure up? The discriminating consumers of today are looking for quality in their products. Amateur *homemade* crafts are a thing of the past. Professional quality *handmade* products are the ones that sell.

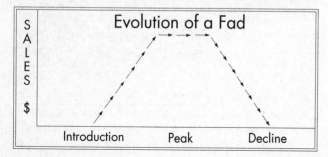

Is it *Neat*?

Visualize each product in a store setting. Would it look rough, primitive and out of place? Then you have some work to do to make it "store quality." Is it neatly finished with no glue showing, no threads hanging, no frayed edges? If it is, then the product has already passed the first test. Nothing less than that will do in today's competitive marketplace. It should be as professional a piece as you are capable of producing.

Is it *Complete*?

Your product should also be *complete.* There should be nothing that needs to be added to it to make it usable. A doll without a dress or a jewelry pendant without a chain (or at least the option to purchase one) are not complete products. They cannot be immediately utilized by the consumer. Look at your own product. Is there something you need to add to it? Is there anything that the customer will have to buy in order to use your product?

Is it *Unique*?

Your products should be unique to give yourself the much-needed market edge. They should have something special about them that very definitely states that they were *made by you*. Why take the time to craft a product that is already being mass-produced and sold everywhere from flea markets to department stores? You couldn't possibly compete. You might say that yours is "better," but in most cases it really won't matter. The very cost-conscious public will view yours as basically the same product—only more expensive.

Put your creative genius to work and find a way to make your products different from both mass-produced products and from those made by other craftspeople. Let it stand out in a crowd and show off your very special talents. Your customers' appreciation will be reflected in your sales dollars.

Five Questions to Ask Yourself If Your Product Isn't Selling

1. Is the size of my product the size my customers need?
2. Is a similar product being mass-produced at a much lower cost already?
3. Is my product available in the colors my customers want?
4. Am I displaying my products in the best possible way at shows? Am I showing through my display how my products will look in my customer's home?
5. Am I selling my products in the right places? Will the customers who want my products actually get the chance to see them?

The Three Basic Features of a Successful Product

1. Is it neat? There should be no loose threads hanging, glue showing, or raw or ragged edges. Eliminate imperfections except those deliberately designed to enhance its appeal.
2. Is it complete? No additional products should need to be purchased or attached to make your product usable.
3. Is it unique? Too many new craftspeople "borrow" ideas from others and from the common marketplace. There are still so many new products to discover, new techniques to perfect, new mediums with which to work, and new ideas to incorporate into your own work. Let your creativity shine through—not someone else's.

Finding Your Niche and Targeting Your Market

Most new craftspeople start out making crafts for themselves, their friends or for family members. Then, inevitably, someone asks, "Why don't you try to *sell* these?" Sound familiar? Encouraged by those close to them, new craftspeople blindly proceed into the crafts marketplace with products they are not even sure they can sell. If you *already* have a product line or have made some prototype products that you would like to try to sell, then you will need to find a niche for those products in the current marketplace.

When I first started making Christmas tree skirts, that was the only product I wanted to make. I really enjoyed designing them, and I loved to work with quality fabric. Encouraged by friends and family, I produced a substantial inventory and then went out and tried to sell them. Was I successful? No. Not initially. My first few craft show seasons were very disappointing. Why? Because I made what *I* liked in sizes and designs that would fit *my* needs. I just assumed that everyone else had the same tastes and needs that I had. I was wrong.

At this point, I could have easily become discouraged enough to give up crafting altogether. But there had to be a *reason* why my products weren't selling. So I conducted my own market research. I went to stores that sold my type of products and took note of the tree skirts for sale, writing down the color scheme, price, design and size of each. I bought magazines and books on home decor and Christmas decorating. I asked potential customers probing questions when I displayed my crafts at shows. Questions such as "What kind of Christmas tree do you usually buy?" "How large is it?" "What colors do you use to decorate it?" "What room is used to display your Christmas tree?" "Do you own your own home or live in an apartment?" I also made mental notes about my customer, including what she looked like, how she dressed, how old she was. I guesstimated her household income and other tidbits of information so I would know exactly *who* my customer was.

As it turned out, there were many reasons why my product wasn't selling. First of all, the *size* was wrong. Not everyone bought apartment-sized five-foot Christmas trees. Many people bought large, wider, live trees that required larger tree skirts than the ones I made. Others bought *huge* trees to accommodate cathedral ceilings in their homes. Still others used very small "tabletop" trees—I had no idea!

Second, tree skirts in the same size, fabric and design were already being *mass-produced* and were available at any general merchandise or department store for cheaper than I could make them.

Third, all my Christmas tree skirts were red, green and white. Not everyone used the same *colors* to decorate their homes for the holidays. Some people used metallics (gold and silver). Others liked to match the muted tones already found in their homes for a more formal effect—mauve, peach, mint, etc. Plaid was a popular Christmas fabric design. *Red* and especially red ruffles were preferred over any other color fabric for a tree skirt.

Fourth, I had not displayed my products properly. They were laid nicely on a table, but half the customers couldn't even tell what I was selling.

Fifth, I was not selling in the right places. The craft shows in which I participated were not for the upscale market that I needed for the type of product I was selling at the prices I needed to charge.

So, armed with all this new information, I set out to conquer the Christmas tree skirt market. I had found my niche—larger tree skirts in better fabrics for a more upscale market. I now knew who my customers were and what they needed, so I developed a plan to give it to them.

I added products that were larger, and very large to accommodate absolutely any size Christmas tree. I also used my leftover fabric to make small tabletop tree skirts and decorator accessories that matched my tree skirts. I varied the styles, fabric, designs, and colors to match every decor seen in the home decor magazines I read. I had display racks made to show off my products to their best advantage. (Even the average-sized products sold better because now my customers could *see* them.) And finally, I spent a little more money in entry fees to apply to the better craft shows in more upscale areas.

What happened after all these changes? Sales success. Finally! But I could have avoided two seasons of poor sales if I had taken the time to conduct my market research *before* I started making tons of product that almost no one wanted to buy. I could have also saved myself hundreds of dollars in raw materials. And if I had not finally asked some questions and done some research, I *never would have known* what it was that I did wrong. Market research led me to design an effective show display and sell products that my *customers* wanted to buy.

So, if you are already set on a particular craft or product line that you enjoy, do some investigating and test marketing before you produce large quantities. Know your customers. Ask them questions that will help you better meet their needs. Evaluate and adapt your products in light of what you have learned. The forms on the following pages will help you in this research. Form 1A will remind you of questions to ask your customers. Form 1B will help you ask the right questions as you develop new products. Use Form 1C to evaluate your product. You may want to photocopy these forms and keep them in a three-ring binder with other records. Sometimes even the smallest changes could make the difference between no sales and "Yo! Sales!" Analyze your product's market, and know where your product fits into that market. Find your niche! ❧

MARKET RESEARCH—*Customer Profile* (Check all that apply)

Gender: ☐ Male ☐ Female

Age: ☐ Child ☐ Teen ☐ 20-55 years ☐ Senior

Education: ☐ High School ☐ College

Annual Household
Income: ☐ under $20,000 ☐ $20,000–$30,000
☐ $30,000–$50,000 ☐ over $50,000

Occupation: ☐ Blue Collar ☐ Professional
☐ Self-Employed ☐ Other: _____

Decorative Tastes: _____

_____

_____

_____

_____

_____

_____

Reason for Purchase: for self? ☐ Yes ☐ No ☐ As a gift? For whom?
☐ Husband ☐ Wife ☐ Father ☐ Mother ☐ Sister
☐ Brother ☐ Son ☐ Daughter ☐ Grandfather ☐ Grandmother
☐ Male friend ☐ Female friend ☐ Other: _____

Questions I could ask my customers
to better target their needs:

1. "_____?"

2. "_____?"

3. "_____?"

4. "_____?"

5. "_____?"

6. "_____?"

7. "_____?"

Form 1A

MARKET RESEARCH—*General Market Information*

Special *interests* I have noticed that
are especially popular:

       1. _____

       2. _____

       3. _____

       4. _____

Possible up-and-coming *trends* I have
identified through my research:

       1. _____

       2. _____

       3. _____

       4. _____

Other observations:

       1. _____

       2. _____

       3. _____

       4. _____

How I can use this information to make my
current products more marketworthy:

       1. _____

       2. _____

       3. _____

       4. _____

Form 1B

MARKET RESEARCH—*Product Evaluation*
(Complete one for *each* product)

Is it *neat?* ☐ Yes ☐ Needs some work

Is it *complete?* ☐ Yes ☐ _____ needs to be added

Is it *unique?* ☐ Yes ☐ Not really

Is there something about it that says it was *made by me*?

☐ Yes ☐ Not really

What can I do to *personalize* this product? _____

_____

Have I seen mass-produced versions of this product? ☐ Yes ☐ No

Where? _____

How is my product *different* from
the mass-produced version?

1. _____

2. _____

3. _____

4. _____

How is my product *similar* to the
mass-produced version?

1. _____

2. _____

3. _____

4. _____

My Price: _____ Their Price: _____

Why the difference? _____

Form 1C

CHAPTER TWO

Financial Considerations for Your Craft Business

BY NANCY MOSHER

*W*hether you are hoping your handcrafted items will reap a second income or a new career, if you want to make money by selling your work, you need to treat your crafting as a business. This means taking the right steps to establish your business and learning to handle your finances. It means establishing a team of people who will help you make money with your crafts.

Establishing Your Business

As a professional craftsperson, you will probably choose to establish your business as a sole-proprietor. This is a one owner company, and the business income is recorded on supplementary forms and added to your personal income tax return. It is the simplest form of business—you reap all the profits, but you are also responsible for all its liabilities.

As the business grows, you may decide to incorporate your business or take on a partner. While this form of business makes taxes and other business considerations more complicated, you will have less liability and your personal income and property will not be at stake if something goes wrong. The business will become an entity unto itself.

As you establish your business, you will need to register it in the county, city, state or province under whatever rules your state or province has. After deciding on the name for your business, which then becomes your "Doing Business As" (DBA) or assumed name, you will register it with the county clerk.

There are many advantages to registering your DBA. If the business name has already been registered by someone else, then you cannot use it. If you register your name, no one can use it in your county. (To have exclusive use, you must register for a trademark with the U.S. office.) Finally, many banks require a DBA in order to establish a business checking account.

After you have registered your name, the next step is to apply for a state resale certificate from the state tax revenue office. This certificate provides you with the information on collection and payment to the state. You will have to pay income tax on all sales collected in the state in which you live. If you do craft shows outside your home state, then you must contact that state's revenue office concerning the collection and payment of sales tax due there. Some craft show promoters will provide you with the needed information and forms to make the job simple to accomplish.

From the very beginning, you will want to build a team of experts to perform special tasks for you and your business. Some you will use frequently and others only occasionally, but they are always good to have if needed. Bank personnel, a lawyer, a certified public accountant (CPA), and the sales representatives from whom you purchase your supplies are people with whom you want to build a relationship.

Bookkeeping and Accounting

Most craftspeople concern themselves with the product, marketing and perhaps the advertising facets of a business, but they neglect the book work that is often dreaded, ignored or misunderstood. The book work needed to keep track of your finances, income and expenses, inventory and trends is a vital part of keeping the business going. Record keeping is done not only for figuring the different kinds of taxes you need to pay but also for business analysis. These numbers are used to help in future planning and budgeting, or when borrowing money. Thus the better kept the statistics the better analysis and projections you can make.

In the beginning, your taxes and bookkeeping responsibilities will be fairly simple, but it is still important to be certain they are accurate. Your financial records will consist of an income and expense ledger and any other record tracking you might wish to do, which might include a running record of all craft shows and gross sales, average sales and number of customers. If you are selling your work in a craft mall, you might want to keep track of the rent/gross relationship in each one. Inventory tracking is an integral part of the business and necessary for tax figuring. You may wish to separate the different income avenues to see which is bringing in more profit.

Most tax departments consider crafting to be a cash-intensive business, so craft businesses are more likely to be audited. The more careful you are in recording all transactions, keeping all documentation and being consistent, the more advantageous it will be if you should be audited.

Your bookkeeping ledgers should include all the information you will need when filling out the tax forms, doing any analysis and constructing a budget. Recording every business expense not only lowers your income tax burden, but also helps you pinpoint where your money is being spent. As you are developing your expense ledger, some of the categories you might need will be craft supplies, office supplies, rents, travel, bank, dues, advertising, shipping/mail, books/periodicals and professional fees.

The income ledger will also need several columns to record the different kinds of business activity. The separation of taxable and nontaxable sales is needed when calculating the sales tax due to the state. You may wish to pay to your state tax office only the amount you collected. You may also want to separate the income by category to track which avenues are the most profitable. With both the income and the expense ledger you can create more columns if you have special needs you wish to track. It is easier to combine a couple of totals later than to try to separate numbers for two new subtotals.

Sample income and expense ledgers are provided for you on pages 18-25. Forms 2A and 2B are samples of completed income and expense ledgers. Forms 2C and 2D are blank versions of these ledgers. You may wish to photocopy these blank ledgers and keep them in a three-ring binder for your own use, or change them to fit your own needs.

An integral part of your bookkeeping is the use of a CPA. You are the expert in crafting, but you must rely on a CPA, the expert in finances and taxes, to help you at tax time and as other information is needed. Your CPA will save you time, money and aggravation. Hire a CPA who is familiar with both home-based and hand-crafted businesses. With rules changing yearly, your CPA can keep you apprised of what changes you need to make in your record keeping. He or she is an important part of your team, so be sure to find a CPA with whom you can have a comfortable working relationship.

Understanding Taxes

Taxes are one of those burdens—responsibilities—of being in business. With careful records, you will be paying only what is owed to the different agencies. As a sole-proprietor, your income taxes will be figured on special forms that will be attached to your personal income tax return. To start, you will need a Schedule C Profit and Loss and a Schedule SE Social Security form. Other forms you might need include Form 4562-Depreciation & Amortization and Form 8829-Business Use of Home. Your CPA will become even more valuable to your business as it grows and more tax forms become a part of the business' responsibilities. Some publications you can read on taxes are 587-Business Use of Your Home, 533-Self Employment Tax and 534-Depreciation. You can get these by calling 1-800-829-3676.

Each state has its own taxes on income, sales and personal property. The phone number for the state revenue office can be found in the special section of the phone book that lists all state offices. Learn about these different taxes that you will be obligated to pay so that you do not have a surprise. You do not want to get caught without the funds to pay for these obligations.

Your Business Bank Account

For the business to stand on its own and grow, it is best that you separate your personal and business money by using a business checking account. The IRS prefers this, and you will find it easier to keep track of your business money. In addition, a business check is sometimes required as proof of business legitimacy when filling out some financial forms or applications to business organizations. If you should wish to borrow money, the business checking account is an excellent reference source for your business and financial activity.

When opening a business account, shop for a bank just like you would when purchasing a new piece of equipment, looking for a new wholesale distributor or hiring your CPA. You will want to inquire about the costs of a business account. Don't be afraid to negotiate, especially if you already have a relationship with the bank. Also inquire about what is needed to provide your company with charge card capability. The bank personnel should make you feel good about doing business with them and should be interested in you as a customer.

Sometimes a large investment is in order for the business to grow or make changes. Having a good financial history, good records to back up your statements, and knowing some of the key personnel in the bank may be the difference in getting the loan.

Also, as your business grows, you may want to get a line of credit with your bank. This is like a revolving credit line that you can continually borrow from and pay off in short terms. With this account, you do not have to reapply for a loan. You have quick turnover for such things as purchasing raw goods. As soon as the product is sold, the loan is paid and the loan capability goes back to the original line of credit amount.

Pricing Your Craft

Pricing your craft is one of the most difficult parts of being in business. There are many things to consider besides the cost of raw goods and your time in making the product. In addition to all the tangible costs, the product must be one that is wanted by the shoppers, and

---

Your Professional Image

No matter how savvy you are in your financial pursuits, you will never succeed if you do not present yourself as a professional. Craftspeople have difficulty being accepted as "real" business people. There is a lack of respect for them, and they often feel they are at a disadvantage when in business negotiations with others. The other party may have the impression that you are a stay at home craftsperson trying to get a better deal rather than a legitimate businessperson making a business transaction. Your telephone calls, voice mail, correspondence, business references, financial responsibility, appearance and conversation all affect how you are treated.

When making phone calls, have all pertinent information ready. Write your questions down or have the receipt handy for reference if you are solving a problem. Eliminate any background noise that might interfere with the conversation.

A computer or a typewriter is the best way to handle all correspondence. Letterhead stationery will give a more professional presentation than a note scribbled on a scratch pad with Daffy Duck's picture.

In today's society of dressing more casually, it is easy to ignore the times that you should strive to look professional. Craftspeople spend many of their working hours in a studio or workshop in "work clothes." When working with customers, going to trade shows, or any number of other business situations, your personal appearance will greatly influence how you are accepted as a serious business person. Being as professional as you can in all aspects of your business will pay you many dividends!

---

the price must fit the perceived value of the product. Will the shopper pay that amount for it? Comparing the prices others are charging for similar products will help you decide if the price is right. If it is way out of line with the competition, you will need to reevaluate your price. Are you asking too much for your labor? Have you incorrectly figured your overhead? Have you purchased the raw materials at the lowest price possible?

The methods you use in determining the price of the product will also be influenced by your financial needs. Is this a part-time endeavor or your livelihood? James Dillehay's book *The Basic Guide to Selling Arts and Crafts* presents pricing in a different light than any other formula written. His approach, especially for those wishing to sell their work as a livelihood, includes how much money you will need to live for a year and what hourly wage you will need to gain that amount. You then figure all other expenses and come up with a yearly business gross. Finally, you must decide if your product will fit into those numbers and needs. *The Crafter's Guide to Pricing Your Work* by Dan Ramsey, published by Betterway Books, provides a detailed guide to this complicated business consideration.

No formula is going to work 100 percent of the time on every product made. The shopper and the competition will influence your price on each item. Trial and error is the best way to figure out the best price for your product.

Extending Credit and Collecting Payment

You must be willing to accept checks if you are going to sell your craft. On occasion that one dreaded thing happens: a check is returned for insufficient funds. Make sure you have a phone number on every check so you will be able to call the customer and make arrangements for this to be corrected. There may be a simple explanation, and the problem could be easily solved. If you are not successful, you can turn a check over to a collection agency or to the DA's office if you think it would be an effective way to get your money. Sometimes a bad check must be filed away and written off on your taxes.

As a beginner, you will have some other small considerations involving credit situations, so you will need to plan ahead and decide how you wish to handle them. If you do special orders, you will need to decide on the risk of doing the project and getting paid for it. You may want a percentage down or full payment in advance. Many of the craft malls have layaway plans, so

INCOME ACTIVITY

	MONTH (who income from)	1 SALE	2 TAXABLE SALE HOME-BASE	3 CRAFT SHOWS	4 CRAFT MALLS	5 WHOLESALE CONSIGNMENT TAX EXEMPT	6 OTHER TAX EXEMPT	
1	JANUARY							1
2	Crafter's Alley	200.00			200.00			2
3	Crafter's Mall	150.00			150.00			3
4	Peanut Patch—Wholesale	40.00				40.00		4
5	Girl Scouts	20.00					20.00	5
6	Crafter's Alley	100.00			100.00			6
7	Crafter's Mall	150.00			150.00			7
8	January Home-based sales	10.00	10.00					8
9	**JANUARY TOTALS**	670.00	10.00		600.00	40.00	20.00	9
10								10
11	FEBRUARY							11
12	Crafter's Alley	125.00			125.00			12
13	Crafter's Mall	145.00			145.00			13
14	Appleton, TX Craft Show	1400.00		1200.00		200.00		14
15	Crafter's Alley	150.00			150.00			15
16	Home-based City Craft Show	800.00	800.00					16
17	Crafter's Mall	125.00			125.00			17
18	February Home-based sales	50.00	40.00			10.00		18
19	**FEBRUARY TOTALS**	2795.00	840.00	1200.00	545.00	210.00		19
20								20
21	MARCH							21
22	Crafter's Alley	140.00			140.00			22
23	Crafter's Mall	100.00			100.00			23
24	Morton, OK Craft Show	1200.00						24
25	Crafter's Alley	105.00			105.00			25
26	West City, TX Craft Show	500.00		500.00				26
27	Crafter's Mall	195.00			195.00			27
28	March Home-based sales	45.00	40.00			5.00		28
29	**MARCH TOTALS**	2285.00	40.00	500.00	540.00	5.00		29
30								30
31								31
32								32
33								33

Form 2A

	7	8	9	10	11	12	13	14	
	RETURNED MERCHANDISE		SALES TAX COLLECTED				OUT OF STATE	OUT OF STATE SALES TAX	
1									1
2									2
3									3
4									4
5									5
6									6
7									7
8			.75						8
9			(.75)						9
10									10
11									11
12									12
13									13
14			84.00						14
15									15
16			60.00						16
17									17
18			2.95						18
19			(146.95)						19
20									20
21									21
22									22
23									23
24							1200.00	63.00	24
25									25
26			40.00						26
27									27
28									28
29			(40.00)				1200.00	(63.00)	29
30									30
31									31
32									32
33									33

Form 2A continued

EXPENSE ACTIVITY

		1	2	3	4	5	6	
	ITEM	COST	ADVERTISING PROMOTIONAL	BANK CHARGES	MOTEL	MEALS	OTHER TRAVEL	
1	JANUARY							1
2	The Floral Shop	25.00						2
3	Jane's Craft Supply	50.00						3
4	The Floral Shop	45.00						4
5	The Photo Place	9.00	9.00					5
6	Rents	195.00						6
7	Telephone	1.05						7
8	Bank Charges	9.25		9.25				8
9	**JANUARY TOTALS**	334.30	9.00	9.25				9
10								10
11	FEBRUARY							11
12	Appleton Show Expenses	125.25			75.00	50.00	Road toll .25	12
13	Display (lumber)	100.00						13
14	Donation (cash—Girl Scouts)	100.00						14
15	Stamps	5.00						15
16	Jane's Craft Supply	75.00						16
17	Book	18.00						17
18	Candy/Office K-Mart	10.00	1.00					18
19	Rents	195.00						19
20								20
21								21
22								22
23								23
24								24
25								25
26								26
27								27
28								28
29								29
30								30
31								31
32								32
33								33

Form 2B

	7	8	9	10	11	12	13	14	
	OFFICE SUPPLIES	DISPLAY	POSTAGE/ SHIPPING	TELEPHONE/ BOOTH RENT	BOOKS/ MAGAZINES	CRAFT SUPPLIES	LARGE EQUIPMENT	MISC. TAXES, DUES, DONATIONS, PROF. FEES (TAKEN OUT OF INVENTORY)	
1									1
2						25.00			2
3						50.00			3
4						45.00			4
5									5
6				Rent 195.00					6
7				Phone 1.05					7
8									8
9				Rent 195.00		120.00			9
10				Phone 1.05					10
11									11
12									12
13		100.00							13
14								donation 100.00	14
15			5.00						15
16						75.00		5.00	16
17					18.00				17
18	9.00								18
19				Rent 195.00					19
20									20
21									21
22									22
23									23
24									24
25									25
26									26
27									27
28									28
29									29
30									30
31									31
32									32
33									33

Form 2B continued

INCOME ACTIVITY

	1	2	3	4	5	6
MONTH (who income from)	**SALE**	**TAXABLE SALE HOME BASE**	**CRAFT SHOWS**	**CRAFT MALLS**	**WHOLESALE CONSIGNMENT TAX EXEMPT**	**OTHER TAX EXEMPT**
1						
2						
3						
4						
5						
6						
7						
8						
9						
10						
11						
12						
13						
14						
15						
16						
17						
18						
19						
20						
21						
22						
23						
24						
25						
26						
27						
28						
29						
30						
31						
32						
33						

Form 2C

	7	8	9	10	11	12	13	14	
	RETURNED MERCHANDISE		**SALES TAX COLLECTED**				**OUT OF STATE**	**OUT OF STATE SALES TAX**	
1									1
2									2
3									3
4									4
5									5
6									6
7									7
8									8
9									9
10									10
11									11
12									12
13									13
14									14
15									15
16									16
17									17
18									18
19									19
20									20
21									21
22									22
23									23
24									24
25									25
26									26
27									27
28									28
29									29
30									30
31									31
32									32
33									33

Form 2C continued

EXPENSE ACTIVITY

	ITEM	1 COST	2 ADVERTISING PROMOTIONAL	3 BANK CHARGES	4 MOTEL	5 MEALS	6 OTHER TRAVEL	
1								1
2								2
3								3
4								4
5								5
6								6
7								7
8								8
9								9
10								10
11								11
12								12
13								13
14								14
15								15
16								16
17								17
18								18
19								19
20								20
21								21
22								22
23								23
24								24
25								25
26								26
27								27
28								28
29								29
30								30
31								31
32								32
33								33

Form 2D

	7	8	9	10	11	12	13	14
	OFFICE SUPPLIES	**DISPLAY**	**POSTAGE/ SHIPPING**	**TELEPHONE/ BOOTH RENT**	**BOOKS/ MAGAZINES**	**CRAFT SUPPLIES**	**LARGE EQUIPMENT**	**MISC.** TAXES, DUES, DONATIONS, PROF. FEES (TAKEN OUT OF INVENTORY)
1								
2								
3								
4								
5								
6								
7								
8								
9								
10								
11								
12								
13								
14								
15								
16								
17								
18								
19								
20								
21								
22								
23								
24								
25								
26								
27								
28								
29								
30								
31								
32								
33								

Form 2D continued

you will have to decide if you are willing to wait for your money over several months of installments. Be sure to ask the mall owner how their plan works and inquire about what happens if the customer defaults.

If you intend to sell wholesale, then you must decide how to extend credit to your customer. Do not immediately extend credit to a business that you know nothing about. Have the first orders paid up front by cash, C.O.D. or even credit card. You may want to do all wholesale sales this way. If the time should come when you want to do this by credit, ask for references to establish trust in the business owner's ability to pay his or her bills. You might even check with the Better Business Bureau in the buyer's community to see if there are any complaints against the business owner.

Whatever you decide, plan carefully and know ahead of time how you are going to handle these transactions. Not only will it help you do a better job, but the customers who work with you will feel more confident in you and your ability to deliver your product.

Investing in a Business Computer

Should you have a computer for your business? This can be a tough question. The computer is a valuable tool for many things, but the first consideration in its purchase is usually bookkeeping and other record keeping. Bookkeeping in itself can be intimidating to the novice, so first get the bookkeeping skills down with paper and pencil, then consider using a computer. After developing the format for your ledgers, it will be easier to pick the kind of software you need.

The goals of your business will influence your decision to add a computer. It is a big investment to make if you do not take full advantage of it. A computer can make that dreaded inventory an easier job, whether it be keeping track of raw materials or finished goods. It will be easier to compare yearly or monthly statistics. Correspondence and mailing lists will look more professional. A program for making invoices and keeping track of other business will only benefit your business. You also can create some of your own signs, brochures and other promotional materials with a computer.

Craft show guides, trade organizations, craftspeople, consumers and supply houses are all going on the Internet, which is creating a new reason for investing in business computers. Getting a modem and hooking into an online service will also be a consideration.

The more you learn about running a business, the more questions you will have. Remember to call on your team of experts for help whenever you need it. Ultimately, organization and early consideration of all the business aspects of your craft will give you more time to do what you like best—creating your handmade craft!

Advertising, Publicity and Promotions

BY KATHY CAPUTO RUZEK

to advertise—to *announce,* to *declare*
to publicize—to *inflate,* to *enhance*
to promote—to *further* or *forward* a cause
—*Webster's Dictionary*

*I*n most cases, advertising and promoting your craft business is executed in a subtle manner. The very nature of *handmade* products lends itself more toward gentle selling than toward the razzmatazz marketing methods used to promote most mainstream products. But advertise you must, if you want your business to grow and flourish. There's absolutely no sense in taking the time and effort to produce a handmade craft if you are not planning to do all that you can to make the public aware of it.

Yet most new craftspeople don't give a second thought to promoting themselves or their products except by participating in craft shows. Even craft shows don't take full advantage of the opportunity to leave a lasting impression that may result in future sales. Craft shows are a good way to start promoting your products, but they can only provide you with limited market exposure. This is often not enough to sustain a healthy craft business. Newspaper advertising can also help boost your sales, while magazine advertisements will help you reach a more distant market.

Promoting Your Business for Free

Some of your most productive newspaper coverage will cost you nothing more than possibly the price of film processing and postage. This is good news to the new craftsperson who doesn't have tons of money to spend.

Local newspapers are always interested in publishing information about local people. You can help them out by supplying them with information about yourself and your craft business. I'm sure that if you browse through your own local newspaper, you will find feature articles and press releases about other local people starting new businesses, announcing an open house, or introducing new products or services. If you are just starting out, a feature article or press release might be the perfect way

to introduce yourself to the public. Both of these are *free* forms of newspaper advertising.

Local Newspaper Feature Articles
Before you contact any newspaper to ask them to write a story about you and your crafts business, you should prepare a concise list or "script" about yourself, how you got started, your crafts, your specialties, and your business in general. Make it as interesting as possible. Brag a little—but not too much. Don't forget to include information on any special training you have had in your particular craft, any awards you have received or special events in which you have participated as a member of the crafts or local community.

Once you have the facts written down in a logical sequence and in an interesting format, you are ready to contact the local media. Skim through your hometown newspaper for the name of the reporter who writes personal stories about local people or new business owners. Call the reporter and tell him or her about yourself and your craft business. Use your script in case you get flustered and so you won't forget to mention anything important. But don't make it sound like you are reading the information. Keep your voice lively but business-like.

Ask the reporter if he or she would like to do a feature article on you to help launch (or better publicize) your business. In some cases, the reporter might offer to come to your home or place of business to interview you, and may even bring a photographer to take photographs of you and your products. In other cases, the reporter may ask (or you could suggest) that you send a biography and profile of yourself and your company. Make sure that this profile and any newspaper articles written about you include information on how potential customers can contact you.

You may be asked to submit your own photographs. You should be prepared for this with good, clear, black and white photographs of you and your products. These should be uncluttered, centered and well focused. You might want to take the original photos in color and then have a photo lab reproduce them in black and white.

Script Format for Contacting Your Local Paper

Here is a basic script format you can use as a guide when writing your own script before contacting your local paper. First, call the newspaper. Ask for the reporter by name. If the reporter is not available, leave your name and number. If they answer the phone:

"Hi! My name is Farah Smith." (Identify yourself.)

"I live in Windsor on Montana Road." (Let the reporter know you are a local resident.)

"I was reading the Windsor Chronicle, and I noticed that you write feature stories about local businesses." (You subscribe to the newspaper.)

"Well, I've just started a business here in town and I thought you might be interested in writing an article about my business." (The reason for your call.)

"It's called Farah's Florals." (Your business name.)

"I make wedding arrangements, seasonal florals, swags, wall pieces—anything with flowers—dried and fresh. I grow most of the flowers I use in my own gardens." (The nature of your business.)

"You have to see my gardens and my showroom! They're just filled with flowers!" (Pique their interest.)

"I've been a member of the Windsor Garden Club for the past 20 years, since I was 16 years old. I just love to work with flowers!" (You have roots in the local community and sound excited about what you do.)

"Currently, I am the Garden Club's Chairman of Special Events. Did you attend the Daffodil Festival at Windsor High School in March? Well, we hosted that event, and I was its chairperson." (Add something important or interesting about yourself. Ask some questions so the conversation is not one-sided.)

"Do you know the Harringtons? Frank Harrington owns the drug store in town." (Mention that you know people in the community.)

"Well, I did the floral arrangements for their daughter Julie's wedding in May, and everyone just loved my work. I'm also doing the Markham wedding in December and The Windsor Community Church. Do you know the Markhams on Housan Road?" (Add something positive about your business, and continue to establish your roots in the community.)

"But I don't do only wedding florals. In fact, I have a whole line of florals. I especially like to do seasonal work like Christmas wreaths." (More about your business.)

"I'll be participating in a few local craft shows this season. Will you be covering the Windsor Community Church fair or the Junior Women's League Holiday Boutique? I'll be at both of those." (More interesting information about the future of your business and events of which they may not be aware.)

"If you have the time, I'd love for you to come to the house and see my work. Would you be interested?" (Ask the question and wait for an answer.)

This way, you can always have copies made in either color or black and white. If your original photos were taken with black and white film, there would be no way to convert them to color later on.

Whether the reporter comes to your home or you are asked to send the newspaper information will depend largely on how busy the reporter is and how actively he or she pursues this type of story lead. You have a much better chance for a feature article in a small local town newspaper than you would in a newspaper in a major city. It is not as easy to get free feature articles from newspapers in towns other than your own unless you participate in an event in that town. Local residents buy local newspapers to get local information about local people and events. If they wanted to have more far-reaching information, they would buy the *Wall Street Journal*. Small town reporters know this. But there *is* a way to get newspaper coverage in towns other than your own.

Craft Show Feature Articles

When you sign up for a craft show, send the show promoter a copy of your self-written biography, copies of any newspaper articles that have been written about you, a well-composed black and white photograph of you with your products, and a note giving the show producer permission to use this information in pre-show publicity articles. Many show promoters will take advantage of this offer, and you could see your name appearing in their local papers. This is a great way to increase your exposure at no additional cost. You may be able to reach areas that otherwise wouldn't be interested in featuring you in a story because you are not a local resident.

These feature articles are worth their weight in gold. When you participate in a craft show, display copies of any newspaper articles written about you in your show booth. Send copies to other show producers when you send out your show applications. Use the articles to publicize and promote your crafts business. You might find that customers and show producers alike will show more interest in you and your work because you have received prior publicity. Keep a copy of each feature article in a portfolio.

You might also find that people will recognize you after the article runs in the newspaper. They might stop you in a local store and ask more about your crafts and your company. They might look for you personally at craft shows. They might tell their friends about you. This kind of publicity is priceless.

Press Releases

Press releases are shorter than feature articles and sometimes don't include photographs, but they are still a valuable way to advertise your crafts business. If you send press releases to a newspaper, they may lead to the newspaper contacting you for an interview and feature article.

You can use a press release to announce the opening of your business, a special sale, or an open house, to introduce a new product or product line, to make the public aware of a local show in which you will participate, and to publicize any other interesting tidbits of information about your crafts business. Just make sure that the event is newsworthy from a reader's standpoint. If you constantly bombard the local media with press releases, they will lose their special value and the newspaper personnel will get tired of reading them. Save them for newsworthy information and interesting events. A sample press release is on page 28.

Newspaper Advertising

Most craftspeople don't use classified or display ads to advertise their products in newspapers, but they can be an effective way to gain consumer interest and increase sales.

Classified Ads

Classified ads are placed in a special section of the newspaper along with ads for "Real Estate For Sale" or "Help Wanted" and other such category headings. The format is short and to the point and includes about 15 to 25 words. Ask what classified category heading your newspaper offers. Some have special sections for "Crafts" or "Special Interest Products." Pick the one that you feel would best suit your market. If you offer a special seasonal product or service, a classified ad may be especially helpful in boosting your sales.

This is a very inexpensive way to advertise, but your ad will be listed along with hundreds of other similar-looking ads. To avoid the "look alike" syndrome, spend a few extra dollars to put the first line of your ad or any other important information in capital letters (no more than a line or two) and/or bold print to help it stand out. The newspaper may also offer some simple artwork or graphics that you can incorporate into your classified ad for a small additional charge. Artwork—even if it's just a few tiny holly leaves decorating a Christmas ad—will spark the reader's interest more than a few lines of unadorned print.

Customers also need *repeated* reinforcement of information. A classified ad, placed in one newspaper for one day, will probably not be worth the cost. Longer-running ads (for a week, or four consecutive weekends) are much more effective, and most newspapers offer special rates for them. On page 29 are samples of crafts-related classified ads.

Display Ads

Display advertisements are those square boxes of information peppered throughout the newspaper body itself. They are much more visible than classified ads because they are incorporated into the *body* of the publication rather than being bunched together at the *end* of the newspaper or in a special section with hundreds of other look-alike ads.

Display ads are also much more expensive than classified ads, but they offer you the opportunity to include a drawing or photograph of your product or your company logo within the confines of your ad space. This will catch the reader's attention more readily than a small, undecorated classified ad.

Magazine Advertising

Magazine advertising, for the most part, is more expensive than newspaper advertising, but magazines also reach a much broader geographic area. While your local newspaper may only have a readership of a few thousand local residents, one popular magazine may have a nationwide readership of tens of thousands. Be aware that magazine advertising is not limited to display ads.

PRESS RELEASE

For Immediate Release

Contact: Farah Smith   Date: September 22, 1997
185 Montana Rd.
Windsor, NY
(505)555-2948

Farah Smith Hosts Open House of Holiday Florals

Farah Smith of Farah's Flowers in Windsor, NY is hosting a Holiday Floral
Exhibit Open House in her home at 165 Montana Road on Friday, Saturday
and Sunday, October 9, 10 and 11 from 10 AM to 4 PM.

On exhibit and for sale will be dried and fresh floral arrangements for the
entire holiday season. Festive Fall and Halloween floral decorations,
Thanksgiving centerpieces and Christmas wreaths are just some of the
creations that will be on display. Farah also welcomes the opportunity to
design customer floral pieces to meet your needs.

If you would like to attend, please call Farah at (505)555-2948. Refreshments
will be served, and there will be a free raffle held for one of Farah's fabulous
Christmas wreaths.

Sample press release

Classified Marketplace

$25 dollars for 25 words

SERVICES

Calligraphy

Let us address your holiday envelopes, print your special announcements or custom design your wedding invitations. 13 years experience. No job too small.
(303)555-6059

Preserve Those Memories

Lovely custom decorated picture frames in the ancient art of Origami. Awards, wedding invitations, birth announcements, photographs—anything! Prices from $12.95.
(303)555-3947

It's Party Time!

We can help make your birthday, graduation, retirement party a success with Caricatures of your guests. $200 for 4 hours.

FUNNY FACES
(303)555-1717

Stencilling

Let us decorate your home with stencil borders and wood floor stencil designs. Reasonable prices. Kits for do-it-yourselfers available.
(303)555-4321 for catalog.

Holiday Collectibles, Inc.

Handpainted Holiday plates, figurines, Nativities, and Christmas Village pieces. Signed, numbered original limited editions. Saturday & Sunday only.
993 Windsor Road, Windsor.
(303)555-9123

FOR SALE

Pottery Tableware

Local potter has original handcrafted tableware for sale. Large selection of designs and coordinated pieces to grace your table.
Call (303)555-2123

Christmas Wreaths

Custom dried and fresh, greens and floral, holiday arrangements, centerpieces and decorations. Two week delivery. Prices start at $16.95.

FARAH'S FLORALS
(303)555-4455

Handmade Quilts perfect for gift-giving. King, queen, full, single. Matching sheets, pillowcases and pillowquilts in traditional and decorator prints and colors.

THE QUILT LADY
(303)555-6931

Hand Smocked children's holiday outfits in sizes 18 months to 14. Dresses and rompers. Custom made or ready to wear. Call for appointment.

PerfectKids
(303)555-6721

Christmas Tree Skirts

Large selection of sizes, designs and fabrics to match any decor. Custom orders our specialty. After 6PM M-F.

'Tis the Season
(303)555-2675

Handmade lifesized 3′ ANN & ANDY dolls. Great gift for kids and doll collectors. $42.
(303)555-4566

FOR SALE

Creative Candleworks

Handcrafted scented holiday candles. Also, candle centerpieces, sconces, assortment of decorative candleholders. Call M-F 10AM to 4PM. Wholesale welcome.
(303)555-7789

Open House
Gould Jewelry Design
Sterling Silver and 14K. Order custom work now for Christmas Delivery. M-Sat. 9AM-4PM.

945 Maryland Court, Windsor
(303)555-5858

Attention Gift Shops!

Local woodworker seeks outlet for small wood products. Pine and Oak cutting boards, jewelry boxes and more. Call (303)555-4453 for wholesale pricing.

Decorate Your Holiday Table

Handcrafted napkins, tablerunners, tablecloths. Wonderful selection. Come visit us. Windsor School Holiday Boutique, November 15, 10AM-4PM. Booth #27.

The Well-Dressed Table
(912)555-6690

Great Stocking Stuffers!

Adult and children's brain teasers, puzzles, games. Fun gifts for all. Great grab bag gifts. Prices $5 to $15.

Mind Benders
(303)555-8895

Classified ads

31

Some publications are also able to offer reasonably priced classified ad alternatives.

Craft Catalogs and Magazines

Some craftspeople sell their products through craft marketplace magazines and in crafts-for-sale sections of the major craft publications. But in many cases, the people who read these magazines are looking for projects that they can make instead of buying the products that the *craftspeople* make. They may be craftspeople looking for new product ideas or browsing to get a feel for popular trends in their particular medium. They may be people looking for a decorative or seasonal craft project to make themselves to enhance their own homes. The crafts advertised in these publications are there for the copying, though that was not the intent of the craftsperson when he or she placed the advertisement.

It is always important to keep in mind the consumer market you are trying to attract. Before you advertise anywhere, ask yourself, "Who will see this?" Will it be other craftspeople or the consumer? Remember that you are trying to attract the consumer. One way to gauge this is to notice where the magazine is sold. Many general craft publications are sold primarily in craft *supply* stores. What type of person frequents these stores? Those interested in making their *own* handcrafted products and purchasing the supplies to do so.

If you are going to advertise in craft publications targeted at amateur craftspeople, it might be a better choice to offer your craft products in *kit* form with instructions for the do-it-yourselfer to complete the project rather than selling a finished product. *Patterncrafts* is a catalog offering crafts kits for sale. Contact *Patterncrafts* at P.O. Box 25639, Colorado Springs, CO 80936-5639, (719)574-2007.

Consumer Craft Magazines

There are, however, a few crafts magazines that target the consumer and craft-loving home shopper rather than craftspeople. In these publications, your advertisement should include a photo of your product, description, price, sales tax and ordering information. The photographs are very important in this type of publication. Make sure yours are clear, focused and in color. Hiring a professional photographer might be a good idea.

It is *very* expensive to do this sort of advertising, but many craftspeople have had great success selling through this type of magazine. Remember that you will probably need some inventory on hand in case your advertisement receives a great response. Delivery usually takes 4-6 weeks. Check the publications section in this book and the magazine racks at your local book and craft stores for these magazines.

Special Interest Magazines

If you have a product or products that fit into a special interest niche, you might want to advertise in consumer magazines specific to that market. For example, if you make decorative artwork of dogs and cats, try advertising your products in pet magazines. If your products are educational toys for children, then try an educational publication such as a school and library magazine or a magazine that targets teachers. If you sell unique decorative products for the home, consider advertising in magazines such as *Better Homes and Gardens* or *Home Decorating*. These might work much better for you than a crafts marketplace magazine.

Coding Your Advertising

If you place several ads in several publications at one time, be sure to code each one so you will be able to tell which ads brought in which responses. This can be done in a number of different ways: By adding a suffix to your post office box number that indicates which newspaper generated the response; by changing the format of your return mailing address for each one (without changing the content); or by designating a different department number in each return address. If the ad calls for response by phone, you could simply *ask* the caller where he or she saw your advertisement. Coding is the only way that you will know which ads worked and which didn't.

Advertising has a two-fold purpose. On the one hand, it is used to gain new customers, and secondly, it is used to remind old customers that you are still around and desire their business. One thing is for sure, crafts advertising and promoting should be an ongoing endeavor. One piece of advertising placed in one magazine or newspaper will not get you the sales that you need to keep you busy and your business profitable. Take the time and make the effort to promote yourself and your business. The rewards will be reflected in increased sales and a healthier, more profitable crafts business!

Selling at Shows

BY MARIA NERIUS

The outdoor community art and craft show was the true start of the professional craft industry as we know it today. The market has changed drastically, but craft shows remain one of the most popular and profitable marketplaces for those selling handmade works.

Types of Shows

In order to choose the best shows at which to sell your crafts, you must be familiar with the different types of shows available to the craftsperson. Shows are divided into four major categories: wholesale or retail, and juried or non-juried.

Wholesale vs. Retail

First, you need to decide if you wish to sell directly to the final user by selling retail, or if you'd rather sell to an intermediate buyer, thereby placing your product in the hands of a wholesaler who will re-sell to the final buyer.

Retail shows are known to most of us as art and craft shows, but they can also include seasonal boutiques, church and community bazaars, and indoor or outdoor markets. At the retail show, you display your own work to sell directly to the end user, your consumer or buyer. The outdoor craft show is probably one of the oldest markets in our industry, and in modern times many of these shows have been moved indoors to shopping malls and convention centers.

Wholesale provides the professional craftsperson (PC) with an outlet for selling his or her goods in volume to a specific buyer at a specific time and at a specific price. As a PC, you have a certain amount of control over the marketplace. You can establish minimum buys to the wholesaler by quantity (product must be purchased by six, dozen, gross) or dollar value (minimum purchase of $25-$500). This allows you to better manage your cash flow and inventory.

Wholesale selling is normally done at trade shows or gift markets. These shows and marts are located throughout the country. Atlanta, Miami, Dallas, Los Angeles, San Francisco, Chicago, Columbus and New York City are home to the largest U.S. based gift marts.

Prices must be structured at the wholesale level, allowing the wholesaler to mark-up the goods.

Gift markets should be contacted for an exhibitor package. This package includes information about the exhibit fee, space allowances, and display requirements that will allow you to put your exhibit together.

Juried vs. Non-juried

One of the first questions many new professional craftspeople ask is "What is the difference between a juried and non-juried art and craft show?" The most basic difference is that participants are accepted into a non-juried show on a first-come, first-served basis. Craftspeople wishing to show their products at a non-juried event must complete an application and send a show fee. Once the spaces are filled, no more applications are taken. In some non-juried shows, your work will be placed beside imports and referred to as buy/sells. You may want to find out what types of products will be displayed at the show. The listings in this book include this information.

Juried shows, on the other hand, not only require an application and space fee, but also slides or photos of your work and booth. They may ask for a separate fee for "jurying." The jurying fee is usually required to pay for the judges' time to review your work and is non-refundable. The jurying process ensures quality workmanship and, in some cases, limits the number of crafts in a specific medium. For example, a juried show that has 100 spaces may allow 20 percent to ceramics and 20 percent to mixed media. The idea is to keep variety in the show place and to spread competition equally for the consumer dollar.

Choosing a Show

Choosing the best shows for yourself and your product will take some research. Finding shows in which to participate is the first challenge professional craftspeople face. This book makes it easy! There are 110 promoters and 73 single shows listed in this book. The show dates will change each year, but the listings provide detailed information about audience, type of products and application process to help you make your decisions.

Wholesale shows can also be found through calendars and advertisements located in industry trade journals. Retail or consumer shows can also be researched by networking with fellow professionals, calling your local chamber of commerce, or using periodicals referred to as show guides.

There are several bits of information you must consider when choosing whether or not to do a show. The list below will get you started:

- How much will it cost to exhibit at the show? What does this fee include? Don't forget about extras such as electricity, chairs, etc., if they are not included.
- How much will it cost to travel to the show? Will you be driving and bringing your work with you, or flying and having your work shipped? Consider all these costs.
- Consider the date and hours of the show. Does this show conflict with another show that would be more profitable for you? Are consumers likely to attend this show?
- Is this an annual or first-time event? If this is an annual event, talk to past participants if possible. How did they do at the show? Did they find it to be rewarding? If this is a first-time event, consider the organizer's experience, and the time and place. Would it be a risk for you to participate, or does it seem as if this will be a lasting show for years to come?
- Is this show organized by a group/community or a promoter? How experienced is the organizer?
- Who do you contact to request a show application?
- What is the deadline for submitting an application?
- Are slides or photos required for entry? Do you have the necessary materials?
- Which categories are allowed? Does your work fit these categories?
- Will your money be refunded if the show is canceled? Will the show be rescheduled if it rains?
- Can you make it to the rain date?
- Is this an indoor or outdoor show, or does it include both indoor and outdoor exhibits?
- Does the booth space have adequate electrical outlets?
- What was last year's show attendance?
- How is the show promoted and advertised?

Answers to these questions will help you determine if the show is right for you. If possible, visit the show before you attend as an exhibitor.

Preparing for a Show

Goals should be set for any show in which you are preparing to exhibit. Based on expected attendance, write down how much inventory you will take to the show, and a goal for what sales figures or orders you want to meet.

Decide on a policy for what methods of payment you will accept. If you decide to accept credit cards, you must contact a local bank or financial institution that works with small businesses or non-storefronts. Ask your local bank for advice on accepting personal checks as well. For more information on methods of payment, see chapter five.

What to Bring to a Show

Whether the show is for one day or three weeks, plan for your needs before, during and after the show is to take place. You will need to bring all of the following:

- All display items: tables, table covers, shelving, crates, tools needed to assemble display, chairs, and if allowed, ice chest/cooler
- Inventory: priced, packaged and ready to display
- Guest book: to build a mailing list
- Cash box: receipt book, plenty of coins and small bills, credit card slips/charge card imprinter, calculator, a state sales tax table and special order forms if applicable
- Needed extras: pens for writing checks, extra price tags, business cards, price list and brochures
- Repair kit: scissors, glue and a craft supply (small quantity) that you need to repair items.
- Special order forms if applicable
- A copy of your state sales tax license, if applicable
- If using a canopy, have a separate check list of all items necessary to set up your canopy including all tools required for assembly
- A hand cart to carry items if needed
- Some items to work on or demonstrate during the slow selling times at the show
- Snacks and beverages
- Weather gear: visor, hat, change of clothing, sunscreen, comfortable shoes

Leave at home small children, books, TV, radios and pets. Don't bring items with strong scents or loud sounds, as they will disturb surrounding exhibitors.

Keep up to date with the IRS on travel and business deductions. Keep a careful record of all expenses for each show, including travel costs and mileage, if driving. Expenses must be recorded and filed for each show. Advance planning pays for itself in the long run.

Your Display

Your display must immediately attract potential buyers. Displays can consist of simple to elaborate shelving units, tables (which should be covered), signs (if needed), or props. If doing an outdoor show, you may want to have a canopy to protect you, your items and the consumer from inclement weather. It is best to be prepared for anything.

An eye-catching display is important when selling to either a wholesale or retail customer. The average buyer at a show has around one to two hours to browse before they want to leave the show or take a break. That gives you anywhere from 6-12 seconds to get their attention before the buyer moves on to another booth or display. This is not much time, but if you plan your display carefully, you may end up getting their attention and keeping it long enough to make a sale.

Give the buyer plenty of room to move. Watch your traffic flow when designing your booth. A "U" or "L" shape is favored by most craftspeople. Most booth spaces are approximately $10' \times 10'$, so every available nook and cranny should be used efficiently.

Also remember you are going to have to transport, set-up, and break down your display many, many times. Try to make your display only a quarter of your available transportation space in a vehicle or when shipping. There are hundreds of different types of display tools from plastic risers to wood crates to wire backdrops. Visit a few shows before deciding on your needs. See what works and what doesn't before investing in any large items.

Special Themes

The most successful displays usually include a theme. The theme can be related to your craft. For example, a sewer or quilter might sprinkle notions like buttons, pin cushions, or thimbles within the pieces displayed or use a few toy sewing machines for added fun. A theme can also be based on the current season or an upcoming holiday, such as Christmas. Why just place tree ornaments on a table when ornaments would look much better on a small Christmas tree in your booth? Sprigs of garland, lights, a bowl of cinnamon potpourri, or wrapped presents will put your potential buyers in the holiday buying spirit. Be as creative in your displays as you are in your craft design.

Color

The careful use of color catches the eye and accents your work. Make sure color does not distract from your pieces. Experiment with your color choices so that your crafts stand out rather than blend into the display.

Signs and Props

Signs are valuable selling tools, but need to be clearly written, concise and readable from a distance. Avoid more than three to four words per line and use no more than three lines per sign. Props can work just as well as signs if your items need to be explained or demonstrated. Place plant sticks in a flower pot, hang bird feeders with seeds, sunglasses in eye cases, or a roll of paper towels on a holder. Never assume your buyer knows what an item is or how it works!

Meeting Your Buyers

Salesmanship is also part of your display. Unlike selling by mail or other methods, you will actually be meeting potential customers face to face, so you will be selling not only your product, but also yourself. Be prepared to answer questions about your products and yourself. Practice selling your product to family and friends. Have some opening lines in your head. Your closing pitch at a trade show should always ask for an order. At a retail show, you should ask if your customer would like to make a purchase. Have a positive attitude and a smile!

Pay attention to the body language of browsers. If the potential buyer is with a friend, you may need to sell to the friend just as much as to the interested browser. Place your craft in the buyer's hand. Ask questions. Smile and interact with everyone in your booth. And watch your own body language. Make eye contact, lean in close and talk about your craft with pride and enthusiasm. Be prepared to demonstrate how a product works. You may even want to work on a product at your booth to show the customer how much work is involved in making it. You know that you love what you do, so share it with your customers!

It is easy to get burned out at a show. If possible, schedule relief times for yourself. It's best to bring someone with you who is also familiar with your products and take turns running the booth. If all else fails, ask your neighbor to exchange a break time with you.

Many professional craftspeople feel they aren't good sales people. If you feel you are not cut out to sell your own work, hire someone who likes to sell to do it for you. The extra cost of an outside salesperson might increase your profits in the long run and leave you with more time to create new products.

Evaluating a Show

It's important to write a brief evaluation of each show in which you participate, especially if you are doing several shows a year. It will be difficult from year to year to remember whether a particular show was profitable, whether the organizers were helpful and courteous, and whether the buyers seemed enthusiastic about your work. Form 4A on page 35 will help you.

Finally, remember that no matter how well you prepare, everyone experiences poor sales once in awhile. Off sales often reflect bad weather, poor advertising, regional economics, or other factors, so don't give up!

The show business of arts and crafts keeps the craftsperson in touch with the buyer and the competition. Enjoy your time with your customers. Take every opportunity to network with your peers. If you are prepared for and enthusiastic about "doing" a show, the results should be positive and profitable! &

SHOW EVALUATION FORM

Show Name: _____

Sponsor: _____

Date of Show: _____

Location: _____

Is this an annual event? ☐ Yes   ☐ No   Number of shows to date: _____

Available parking for vendors: _____

Available parking for customers: _____

Mostly buyers, or browsers? _____

Customers were mostly: ☐ Men   ☐ Women

Age range of most customers: ☐ Children   ☐ Teenagers   ☐ 20-55   ☐ Seniors

Publicity was: ☐ Good   ☐ Fair   ☐ Average   ☐ Poor

Space number: _____

Size of space: _____

Space included: _____

Overall, space was: ☐ Good   ☐ Fair   ☐ Poor

Number of exhibitors: _____   Number of direct competitors: _____

Sponsor's attitude: _____

Other exhibitors' attitudes: _____

Shoppers' attitudes: _____

Weather and environment conditions: _____

Food available: _____

Total sales: _____   Number of items sold: _____

Total expenses: _____

Conclusion: _____

_____

_____

_____

CHAPTER FIVE

Selling Crafts Through the Mail

BY KATHY CAPUTO RUZEK

*M*ail order is fast becoming today's preferred selling and buying method. For much of mainstream America, mail order offers the choice without the hassle. Ordering merchandise from a catalog and having your products delivered directly to your home is an appealing option. For the busy two-income family, buying through the mail is simply a matter of convenience. For the rapidly growing "over 65" segment of our population, it is just physically more feasible.

For craftspeople, selling products through the mail is a convenient way to do business and allows for a more flexible work-at-home schedule. Except for mailing your sales literature and shipping orders, which you must do during your post office's regular business hours, most of your work can be done at almost any hour of the day or night. Once your offering is mailed, you are again free to devote your time to producing your craft, leaving the mailing to do its work.

Many craftspeople prefer selling via mail order over participating in craft shows or getting involved in other one-on-one selling situations. Some provide their customers with mail order services as a supplement to other selling activities. This is the best approach, at least until you are satisfied that you can cut it as a mail order entrepreneur.

Developing a Mailing List

If you sell at craft shows, then you should have already developed at least a core mailing list of your own. The name of each and every person who buys one of your products or expresses an interest in them should be added to your mailing list. You can further supplement your own list by trading customer names with other craftspeople selling like products or products targeting the same customer base. If you have a computer database, you can add names to your mailing list on a continuing basis, keeping track of how long they have been on the list and how many times they have ordered items. If someone has received several mailings and has never placed an order, take them off the list.

Developing a mailing list of your own will take some time. Another option would be to *rent* a pre-qualified customer mailing list from a list company. Names of mailing list companies and brokers can be found in the Yellow Pages of your local phone book under the heading "Mailing Lists." To order a mailing list that suits your products, draw a mental picture of your customer, including age (range), gender, marital status, income level, education, type of residence and hobbies. The more you know about your customer, the more targeted your mailing list will be and the better your response rate. The list company will then search the names in its files to meet the criteria you have decided constitutes your "perfect customer." They have the capabilities to tailor to a very well-defined mailing list and can search their files by hundreds of different criteria.

Generally speaking, mailing lists are not sold; they are rented. For $75 to $200 per thousand names, you will be allowed the one-time use of the mailing list. The names can be supplied to you either on self-stick labels, magnetic tape or computer diskettes. The names you receive are the property of the mailing list company. Any customer who responds to your offering would be a name you could keep and use again. Ownership of all others reverts back to the mailing list company. To ensure that you comply, mailing lists are "planted" with control names. If a control name receives more than one offering from someone who has only rented one-time use of the list, legal action is usually taken against the offending party, or reimbursement is expected.

Selecting Sales Literature

Any sales literature that you send to your customers should be professionally printed and produced, especially if it includes photographs. Don't make the mistake of using a color copier to reproduce color photographs of your crafts. The result will look unprofessional and will diminish the value of your sales literature. Product photographs should be sharp, centered and uncluttered. Each photograph used in your sales literature will greatly increase production costs, so consider doing one composite photograph of several products rather than individual photos of each product. Just make sure you can see each product and the composite photo is not too crowded. If you are going to the expense of professional printing, it might be wise to consider having your products professionally photographed, or at least photographed by someone who has knowledge of lighting and composition.

The weight and quality of the paper that you use also communicates different messages to your customers. High quality heavy glossy paper, though it may impress your customers, is very expensive and will increase your postage costs considerably. But if you are selling high priced merchandise, then you might still want to use expensive paper to further emphasize the value of your products. If you sell rustic country crafts or wood, then a rough, grainy off-white paper might convey the message better than bright white typing-grade paper. Consult a printing professional for paper options that best represent the message you are trying to convey, present a professional image, and keep your costs under control.

The layout of your sales literature should also be uncluttered. Too much print might discourage the reader. Say what you have to say, provide all the information that you need to provide, but keep it simple. Sometimes, less is more.

Color Catalogs

Printing a full-color catalog costs thousands of dollars. Unless you are willing to add to that expense the cost of buying a tried-and-true mailing list of people who purchase crafts, you will probably not get the initial response you expected. It might take years before you break even from your original investment.

Of course, every craftsperson who sells through mail order dreams of producing a hefty full-color catalog that will have customers absolutely drooling for the products it contains. But let's be realistic. First of all, would you have enough different products to fill such a catalog? Second, could you *afford* to produce such a catalog? Third, are you so confident in sales expectations that you would be sure to recover production costs *plus* make a substantial profit within a reasonable amount of time? And finally, if your catalog *were* very successful, would you be able to produce enough inventory to keep up with the orders it would generate? The chance that you answered yes to *all* of these questions is very slim. So let's focus on sales literature that will be more affordable and ideas that will be more manageable for someone starting out in the mail order industry.

Black and White Catalogs

This is a reasonable compromise if you are thinking of producing your own catalog and if your products could be well-represented by pen and ink drawings or black and white photographs. You might also consider incorporating one additional color to make your catalog more visually appealing. It would be worth the additional expense.

A catalog of product drawings can be both effective and charming, further emphasizing the handmade quality of your work. I have seen several such catalogs where the drawings in no way diminished, but actually *enhanced* the value of the catalog and its products. Black and white photographs are much less appealing, and the processing is more expensive.

One thousand $5\frac{1}{2} \times 8\frac{1}{2}$ black and white catalogs, folded, with two staples at the seam, can cost anywhere from $150 (for about 8 pages) to $800, depending on the number of pages involved. This would certainly be in your price range.

Sell Sheets

If you would like to try your hand at mail order using color photographs and without investing great sums of money, you might start by producing a simple sell sheet/order form combination featuring one full-color composite of several of your most popular products. This would only cost about $250 per thousand or $500 per 5,000 pieces to have professionally printed.

You could use them at crafts shows to provide paying customers with the opportunity to purchase additional products by mail. You could hand them out to indecisive customers who may decide after the show to order your products. You can also mail them to customers already on your mailing list.

Self-mailers

Self-mailers are an excellent choice for a new craftsperson just starting to break into the mail order business. Everything the customer needs (including the return envelope!) is incorporated into two sides of one sheet of paper. Self-mailers make it as convenient as possible for a customer to order your products. They are reasonably priced and are available in a wide variety of sizes and formats to accommodate advertising for one product or many products.

Nationwide Printing Inc., 5906 Jefferson St., Burlington, KY 41005, (800)872-2902, offers full service printing for self-mailers, booklets and other sales literature in a wide variety of formats. Other options are available in the listings in part two of this book.

Sending Your Literature

The postal service offers several choices for sending your printed literature at a reduced rate. The most commonly used are "bulk rate" and "first class pre-sort." For each you will be required to pay an annual postal permit fee of about $75, and your mailing must be sorted, banded and labeled according to specific postal regulations.

Each of these mailing methods has some advantages and disadvantages. Bulk rate offers a higher per-piece discount and a low minimum requirement of only 200 pieces. But bulk rate is also much slower than first class pre-sort, and if the mail is not deliverable as addressed for any reason, the sender is never notified. So you could conceivably be sending mail to someone who no longer lives at that address and never know it!

First class pre-sort delivery is faster and more expensive than bulk rate, but still costs less than regular mail. The minimum mailing requirement is also higher at 500 or more pieces per mailing. And the added advantage of first class presort is that the post office will notify you of customer address changes and undeliverable mail so you won't waste unnecessary postage. If the customer has moved and a "forwarding order" is in place, the post office will provide you with the new address and you can resend your sales literature. If the customer has left no forwarding address, remove their name from your mailing list.

Accepting Credit Cards

Much of the appeal of mail order buying revolves around customer convenience. Anything that you can do to make it easier for your customers to order your products will make them more likely to buy your products. Accepting credit card payments and providing a toll-free 800 number for orders and inquiries will greatly enhance your sales.

Years ago, credit card companies were reluctant to offer merchant account privileges to home businesses. But much to their credit, they have moved with the times and now realize that home businesses can be as viable and lucrative an enterprise as any storefront operation.

Any retail merchant will confirm that being able to accept at least one major credit card will increase your sales by about 25 percent. Visa, MasterCard, American Express and Discover Card are the four most widely-used credit cards and, frankly, I don't think any mail order business will have much hope for success unless at least one (more is better) credit card is accepted. Much of the lure of mail order buying is lost if the customer has to mail a check and wait two weeks for the check to clear before you ship their merchandise.

Credit card companies charge a fee of anywhere from 2.5 percent to 5 percent of your invoice amount. This is a small price to pay for offering your customer the convenience of shopping by credit card. You can apply for MasterCard and Visa through your local bank or by calling Superior Bank Card at (800)621-2794. For information on opening an American Express merchant account, call (800)528-5200. For Discover Card merchant accounts, the number to call is (800)347-6673.

Some credit card companies will take your application and credit references over the phone. Others will have a sales representative visit your place of business before making any judgment or accepting you as one of their merchants.

Providing 800 Numbers

Coupling credit card acceptance with the convenience of offering an 800 number for customers to call to ask questions about your products or to place orders will increase your sales even more. 800 number costs vary from one phone company to another, but typically there is an installation fee of about $50, plus a monthly charge of $5 to $10, plus the cost of the actual calls. Sometimes, they offer "specials" where the installation fee is waived. The rates for the calls themselves vary from 12 cents per minute to as much as 27 cents per minute. Some carriers offer discounted rates for off-peak hours, while others have a flat per-minute rate and offer discounts based on usage. Rates may also vary depending on the distance between caller and receiver and whether you order a "personal" 800 number or a "business" 800 number.

If you find an 800 number is out of your reach, then at least buy a facsimile (fax) machine to offer your customers another option for ordering. Fax machines run about $200 to $900, and you can use your current phone line for your fax transmissions.

Shipping and Packaging

There are many freight carriers capable of delivering your products, but UPS and the postal service are the two most commonly used. UPS will not ship to a post office box, so you will have to instruct your customers to provide their street address if shipping by UPS. You should also offer an express shipping option at a higher price, such as Federal Express or UPS Overnight, in case your customers need to receive their merchandise in a hurry.

How you package your products for mail order shipment is another important concern. There is no need to waste money on custom imprinted packaging. A nice, neat *new* box with a custom label looks just fine. Labels cost about $50 per thousand and can be ordered from any office supply store. Your product should not be left to float around in its carton either. Provide some inexpensive filler to keep it from hitting the sides of the box and possibly damaging it. The more fragile your products, the greater the risk you take by shipping them. Foam rubber, Styrofoam "peanuts," and bubblepack can all help reduce the risk, but if you have *very* fragile merchandise, you may have to look into custom packaging to protect it. However you ship and package your products, it will cost you money. Make sure that you pass this expense on to the customer. Don't forget to include the "hidden costs" for items such as tape and staples.

Handling Returns and Refunds

You are in a position to set any return and refund policies you choose. But the more fair your policies, the more confident your customers will feel when ordering from you. Take as an example the case of L.L. Bean Co., which offers a no-questions-asked return policy with full refund. Wouldn't you feel confident ordering from them? I know I do. Tell your customers *before* they purchase any merchandise if they can expect an exchange only, a credit or a complete refund (with or without shipping charges).

Evaluating Mail Order Expenses

Starting a mail order business can be a very expensive undertaking. You need money not only to buy raw materials for the products you produce but also to pay for postage, print sales literature, develop or rent a mailing list, and advertise—all before you see a dime from your investment. These expenses must be recouped in your product price, which may make mail order selling cost-prohibitive for some products. The price you would have to charge might then be more than the customer is willing to pay.

Before you jump into a career in mail order, do a preliminary cost investigation. Study successful mail order catalogs for some ideas as to wording, pricing, policies and composition. Draw a tentative format for your sales literature. Get quotes from several print shops. Prepare a cash forecast of expenses. Analyze how much you can raise your product's retail price to cover these expenses. Keep in mind that the mail order market will bear slightly higher prices than craft shows.

If you are not in the financial position to start a crafts mail order business on your own, why not try enlisting other craftspeople into a co-operative mail order business? All promotional expenses would be shared equally. Each craftsperson could package and ship his or her products separately, or you could set up a "packaging station" and combine orders. This would make your offering more interesting and diversified. Since you are sharing costs, you would be in a better position to afford a more professional presentation. You would also have the added benefit of combining mailing lists from all the craftspeople involved.

Give mail order a try on a small scale first. If you like it, and the customers like what you have to sell, mail order could very well become your primary method of selling! ❧

Direct Sales Opportunities

BY MARIA NERIUS

*D*irect sales markets are markets, besides retail shows and direct mail, through which you can sell your crafts directly to the final buyer. In this book, listings for these types of businesses, which include craft malls and co-ops, are included in the direct sales section. These markets vary a great deal. This chapter will cover some of the most common direct sales markets in order to give you ideas for additional sales methods you may not have considered.

Craft Malls

A craft mall is a retail craft outlet that showcases the work of many artists and craftspeople through rented spaces. The display spaces can vary in size from a single shelf to a larger open floor space. The vendor usually signs a contract for a specific amount of space for a specific amount of time, ranging from a monthly to a yearly lease. The vendor is responsible for setting the selling price of items and keeping the display stocked. The mall management is responsible for display, selling, collecting sales tax, and providing the vendor with a detailed sales report.

When selecting a craft mall, consider the following factors:

- Location of the craft mall. The best sales usually come from craft malls located in high traffic areas with high visibility from the road.
- Will your items sell well? In a craft mall, your craft may be competing with similar craft items, similar price ranges and similar quality of workmanship. Make sure your crafts will stand out in the crowd and not blend in with other similar items.
- Terms of the contract. Read all contracts carefully because of the legal commitments. Understand exactly what is expected of you as a vendor and what you expect from the mall management.
- Services provided by the mall. Not all craft malls are the same. Many provide services that entice the customers to come back. Check out the services for credit card sales, layaway and advertising promotions. There should be some services for the

vendors. Newsletters, display development, resource centers and vendor promotions add value to your investment in a craft mall.
- Remote service. This is a service for out-of-state or out-of-city vendors. The mall will accept shipments of crafts and set-up a display for the remote vendor. Usually an additional fee is charged for the remote service, but vendors have an opportunity to expand their sales area.

Craft Cooperatives

The main difference between a co-op and a craft mall is that the individuals whose work is sold in the co-op also have ownership of the co-op. A craft mall is run and operated by an owner or manager in conjunction with a paid sales staff. Each vendor in a co-op is expected to spend a certain amount of time working in the shop.

Another difference between a craft mall and a cooperative is that a co-op is normally juried. You will submit finished samples of your work for review by a committee of co-op members. Your craft will be judged on workmanship and originality. In most cases, if your work competes with the work of a current co-op member, you will not be allowed in the co-op. The co-op limits the number of craftspeople working in a specific medium. This is a great advantage to you. If your primary craft is quilts, for instance, you will probably be the only person selling quilts in the co-op.

Tips for Effective Co-op Sales

Change the theme of your display frequently to keep regular customers interested. For more information on setting up an attractive display, see the section on show displays in chapter four. Much of the information in that chapter will apply to co-op displays.

Low ticket items from $5-15 will sell most quickly and will more than likely cover rent and commission expenses. Make your own unique hang tags and keep a good supply of business cards with your display. It is also an excellent idea to post a brief bio and photo of yourself within your display for a personal touch.

If you have the option to work in the shop once or

twice a month, take advantage of the opportunity. Working on site will help you stay in contact with your buyer, see how a business operates with a storefront, and allow you to add inventory to your display. Consider all the same questions for selection of a co-op as you would a craft mall.

Consignment Sales

Consignment sales are different from those of a craft mall or co-op. In simple terms, the craftsperson allows a retailer to display the work, and when a sale is made, the craft professional will be paid. In most cases the retailer will add a percentage to the price of an item to make the shop's profit.

At all times during a consignment agreement, the craftsperson holds all ownership rights to their property. The retail shop should be responsible for damage or theft, however. In most cases, the craft professional has no control over the final selling price, how the work will be displayed, or how well the items will be explained or highlighted. This category of sales is one of the most controversial, with true horror stories of shops closing overnight to wonderful stories of very successful sales. Do your homework. Talk to other consignees within the shop.

There are several reasons to go into consignment sales. One is that it is better to have work on display somewhere rather than just stored in inventory. Unlike other markets, consignment markets require no rent, time or other expenditures that must be made in advance. In many cases, a shop will buy outright if the crafts are selling to the consumer.

Make sure there is a contract that states what is expected of both parties, even if you must write the contract yourself. Frequent calls to the shop should allow you to make sure you have enough inventory on the shelves to make this market worth the effort. Always tag the product with your company information. This way, future sales will come directly to your business.

The Internet

The Internet is a fairly new area open to the craft professional. This is the future marketplace that will enhance catalog, show and retail sales for all of us. The following websites are good examples of what can be expected of the Internet Craft Showcases:

- The Professional Crafter: http://www.procraft.com
- Craftnet Village: http://www.craftnet.org
- Craftweb: http: http://www.craftweb.com
- Artisan's Corner: http://www.esinet.net/ac.html
- Craft Supply Magazine: http://www.craftsupply.com

These are very established sites on the World Wide Web. Each one has a unique way of presenting the work of art and craft professionals. Some sites have up to a thousand visitors a day from all over the globe.

Also, try browsing the Web through the different search tools available by entering your specific craft, your specific craft supply needs, or the word crafts, art, professional crafter, marketing, selling and more. These tools will be especially helpful:

- Yahoo: http://www.yahoo.com
- Lycos: http://www.lycos.com
- WebCrawler: http://www.webcrawler.com
- InfoSeek: http://www2.infoseek.com
- DejaNews: http://www.dejanews.com

To become part of an Internet showcase or gallery, you will have two investments: programming time to set up your page at the site, which is normally an hourly charge, and a rental fee per month to maintain the page. Shop around, because pricing for both programming and rent vary greatly. See the listings for Internet services in chapter thirteen.

It also is very helpful for the professional craftsperson to have an e-mail address for inquiries. This means the professional craftsperson must become Internet savvy, which really is not that difficult or time consuming. The business must have a computer, modem and online service to participate with electronic mail.

Many artists and craftspeople have been very successful online. Many use the Internet as a growing tool to expand their customer base, build a mailing list and increase yearly sales. Catalogs, new product information, and newsletters can all be sent very inexpensively via electronic mail. It is also an excellent idea to participate in bulletin board services (areas where notes are posted—usually within an on-line service) and Newsgroups (notes posted from all over the world about specific topics such as quilting, pottery or dollmaking). There are commercial bulletin board services where products can be sold directly through the board.

The most successful craft professionals keep an eye on the future, stay aware of new marketplaces and marketing tools, and take risks every once in a while. The Internet is the future. Whether to network with fellow professionals or to sell your wares, keep up to date on what's happening on the Net.

Home Shows

A craft home show is like a Tupperware party for crafts. Craft professionals use the home show or home party in two different ways. The first is as the main avenue of sales. In this case, shows are continually booked in various individuals' homes to bring in income. As the main source of income, this market must be consistently promoted, and your sales area must expand for growth. The professional craftsperson will often hire others to book, prepare and sell at the home show.

The second use is as an additional source of income, with the home show scheduled either at a rented location or in the craftsperson's own home. If used for additional income, an annual or biannual craft home show is very easy to handle without additional sales help.

In either case, the city or county in which the home show is held must be notified in advance to make sure there are no city or county statues prohibiting the exchange of money within a private home for business reasons. Every state, city and county will vary. Most municipalities consider the annual or biannual home show with the same regard as a garage or estate sale. Most states require that sales tax be collected, and the city/county's main concern is traffic safety.

The professional craftsperson must consider location, date, hours, inventory, invitations or advertising, and parking facilities. Prepare the area much like an open house. Remove all personal property from show room areas and set up an area for bagging purchased supplies and exchanging money. Literally transform rooms into selling showcases. This marketplace really allows you to display your work as it can be used by your potential buyer. If an item is purchased, replace it immediately. Consider inviting other professionals with crafts of non-competing mediums to join in to broaden the craft appeal, share the expenses and add to your guest list.

Christmas boutiques are the most popular and successful of the home shows. Play music, light scented candles, decorate a tree with lights and your ornaments that are for sale, serve spiced punch and cookies, and hire a baby-sitter for the kids so mom or dad can browse without distractions. The idea is to invite the customer to bring a gift shopping list and stay awhile. Offer gift wrapping and handmade gift tags. Have an area of less expensive items so children can purchase gifts for loved ones. Offer a free ornament or percentage off one item if your buyer brings a new guest for your mailing list.

Tools of the Trade

To present yourself and your company in a professional light to all the markets mentioned in this chapter, you should always be able to provide up-to-date paperwork.

- State, city, or county licenses if applicable.
- A résumé, listing your name, contact address, contact numbers (phone, fax and e-mail), a photo of yourself and a photo of your work, a listing of shows and other markets in which you have participated, and a mission statement for your company.
- A portfolio, or a picture book of your work, accomplishments, awards and items for sale.
- Photos do not need to be professionally done; they just need to be clear. They should show different angles of the craft. Include measurements if the photos do not show proportions.
- Business cards. Make these unique to your company. They should include a business name, your name, your contact address and phone number.
- Letterhead, usually matching the business card. A must for all business and professional correspondence.
- Business checking account. There is NO business without one. It is highly recommended to have a business savings account as well. Do not use a personal savings or checking account and never mix personal and business moneys. Never borrow out of the business for personal reasons unless it is a true emergency.
- Copy of resale or tax collection certificate. Keep this on hand at all times when selling or making a sales presentation if your state collects sales tax.
- Copy of the supplier invoice and a copy of the customer invoice.

Personalize items on site. Consider teaching bow making or have another small craft for guests to make. This can be a fun and enjoyable celebration of crafting and being a professional, so show off! If held at the end of your fiscal year, there is the added bonus of reducing your inventory, making the inventory much easier to handle for the tax time ahead of you.

Keeping Your Options Open

There are so many different markets for the craft professional's work that an entire book could be written on any one of the marketplaces alone. This chapter has highlighted a few of the most popular and accessible markets. But there are other options: selling directly to a retailer, selling wholesale to a catalog sales outlet, organizing a craft fair, selling through cable TV shopping channels, showcasing in galleries, opening up a storefront, and many other possibilities.

Never limit your possibilities to expand, evaluate, change or even give up one market for another marketplace. Sometimes that means taking a risk, but most areas can be researched with the help of the Small Business Administration or other business consulting firms. Part of growing a business is to keep searching for new and exciting areas to promote and sell your unique crafts! ❧

Selling Your Crafts Wholesale

BY TRACEY HERRING

*Y*ou've been making unique crafts for quite some time now. You like the work you do, and so do those around you. You've sold your work at craft fairs in your area. Perhaps you've even been accepted into a local juried organization. Production isn't a problem for you, and you could easily make quality pieces in volumes that exceed your present sales. Maybe you're thinking it is time for you to expand your horizons, reach beyond your neighborhood. But how? Which is the right direction for you to take? Perhaps it's time to try wholesale!

Why Sell at Wholesale to a Retailer?

As discussed in chapter four, wholesale and retail are quite different. Retail is defined as "the selling of goods in small quantities, especially to the ultimate consumer." Wholesale is "the selling of goods in large bulk, especially for resale." In other words, when you sell at retail, you're selling directly to the consumer at full price. Wholesale, on the other hand, means you are selling large amounts of your product to a retailer or "middle man," so that he or she can in turn sell your craft work to the public. Since the retailer must also make a profit, he or she will buy your product at wholesale and sell it at a mark-up (retail).

You may wonder why you should sell your craft at wholesale to a retailer, often at 30, 40, even 50 percent or more off your retail prices, when you could directly to the customer at retail price. The answer is quite simple. If what you want to reach a greater number of buyers with your craft work, then sharing profits with a retailer is a small price to pay for the opportunity and the exposure. If you are able to make large numbers of a piece or pieces, selling wholesale to various retailers allows you to reach a much wider market. Retailers are able to present your work to people who otherwise might not have the opportunity to view your wonderful craftsmanship. They may display your work in their shops, or they may feature your craft at a show where they exhibit their wares to customers in another location. Often they will advertise in magazines or send photos to their customers. Keep in mind that besides the cost of the initial investment, the retailer takes on advertising costs, shipping and handling costs if the shop offers mail order, and the cost of displaying your work in an attractive way in their shops and at shows.

You will have to price your product differently when selling to a retailer. Your wholesale price should be no more than 30 percent below your retail price. While selling your work at wholesale to a retailer brings you less money per item, you will in fact make more money in the end, because your time will be spent creating items for actual orders you have already received. You will never have extra pieces left over, because each piece you make has already been sold.

Playing It Safe

When selling to retailers, remember to safeguard yourself. Don't let just anyone ask you for wholesale prices, claiming to be a shop owner. Require retailers to provide you with pictures of their shop, both inside and out, whenever possible. Request their *Sales and Use Tax Permit* or *Registration, Sellers Certificate* or *Business License*. Any valid business has at least one of these. Keep in mind that a business card or business letterhead can be printed from any computer and is not necessarily proof positive of a legitimate business. Don't be afraid to ask for C.O.D. or prepayment. Once a working relationship is established, you may feel comfortable changing this policy on a business to business basis.

Finding the Right Retailers

It will be important to familiarize yourself with the different retailers that sell products similar to yours. You must do your homework. Who are the retailers? What do they sell? In what price range do they deal? How do they attract customers? What is their customer base? Are they looking for a particular craft or product? How many artists do they currently represent? These are all important questions. To answer them, begin with this book! Let it be your lifeline. Read through the pages and you'll find that the answers to most of your questions are right in front of you!

The many craft magazines on the market will help you get a feel for the number and scope of retailers selling products in your medium. There is at least one magazine in each of the following fields: pottery, glass, fiber, jewelry, sculpture and metalwork. Before contacting a retailer, be sure your crafts are similar to the merchandise sold in that store. Retailer's advertisements will help you familiarize yourself with who's who in your market. If a gallery's ad features only work priced over $1,000, that's the market they're after. This certainly isn't the place for your one-of-a-kind hand-painted silk neckties. Your creations must mesh with the types of merchandise that a particular retailer carries and promotes, or they won't sell in that shop.

Remember, your work is a direct representation of you. You certainly don't want your fine crafts to become *shopworn* because they sit on a shelf too long. The shop or gallery owner will become frustrated, possibly blaming you because your work didn't sell, and certainly not wanting to purchase from you in the future. No one wins if this happens.

Once you have decided which market best fits your needs, find out how the various retailers attract prospective customers. Do they use magazine ads, newspaper ads, fliers, direct mail, walk-ins, shows, and opening nights for galleries? Do they use photographs in their ads? Are these ads full page or small, color or black and white? Is the craftsperson's name and the price included with each photo? If the shop or gallery offers walk-ins, shows or opening nights, how will your work be displayed? Knowing how you want your work presented makes selecting compatible retailers much easier. After all, you want advertising that is most beneficial to you and your craft work.

Contacting the Retailers

Now that you've targeted your market, how are you going to reach these retailers? Who do you contact? You're going to need names. Most of the listings in this chapter will include the name of the best person to contact. It will be important to reach the person who makes the buying decisions. You will not get the desired results if you end up dealing with an employee whose sole responsibility is to ring up purchases. Take time to learn the names of the people in charge. Using proper names instead of generalized salutations or a simple "Hello" in correspondence shows that you know who you are contacting, and will allow your work to stand out from the mass mailings they receive from others. Begin a file or database of these shops and their contact people.

Making Phone Calls
There are various avenues you can take to reach new retailers. Once you have established a list of store or gallery owners with whom you want to do business, it's time to choose the most beneficial avenue for you. One option is to contact the retailers via telephone. This, however, may not be your best choice because the retailer is unable to see your craft work over the phone. Also, you may not have his or her full attention because of customers in the shop or a call on another line.

Traveling to Shops and Galleries
Another option is traveling directly to various shops and galleries. This gives you an opportunity to view, first hand, how different retailers display other craftspeople's work. You meet the retailers face to face and can present your work in person. This sounds good, but it is quite costly and time consuming to travel across country, even across state, to meet with prospective buyers. If you have the time and the resources for this avenue, then it is certainly an excellent choice. If not, don't worry, there are other alternatives that are equally promising.

Advertising in Magazines
Placing advertisements in art and craft magazines is another possibility. This method presents your work to both retailers and individual buyers. The buyers might bring your advertisement to their favorite shop owner. It is wise to add the notation "Dealer Inquiries Invited" to your advertisement. Also, make sure you list specific descriptions such as "rare wood," "one-of-a-kind design," "each piece made entirely by the artisan," or "custom developed colors" as well as the price. Before placing an advertisement, make sure customers who are likely to purchase your type of work will be reading the magazine in which the ad appears. For more information on advertising, see chapter three. Like traveling, advertising is quite costly. You must also continue to purchase ad space, or your name and your wonderful craft pieces run the risk of being forgotten once the next issue comes out.

Co-op advertisements with craftspeople interested in a similar market can give you part of a larger overall advertisement at a more affordable cost. Also, consider asking the advertising manager at each magazine how you can reduce your per ad cost.

Contacting Retailers Via Direct Mail

Finally, consider direct mail as a means of reaching retailers. This route will probably give you the greatest payback for the least amount of money. If you choose direct mail, you should start with a letter of introduction explaining who you are and what you are offering. Include two to four good quality, clear photographs or slides showing samples of your work. Be sure to show the range of your abilities. As with advertising, be sure to include specific descriptions and prices. Much of the advice in chapter five will help you plan your strategy for direct mail to retailers as well as regular customers.

Photographing Your Work

Be sure the photos you send are as professional as possible. You can take them yourself in your own home if you choose to do so, but make sure they are well photographed. Pay attention to lighting and background. The background should be a plain, neutral color that allows your product to stand out. It should be draped behind and under your product for the best effect. It is also a good idea to photograph your products near a window, so that the light shines in onto the product from one direction. If you do not feel comfortable taking your own photographs, it might be worth it to invest in a professional photographer.

Follow-Up Contacts

It is a good practice to keep a record of which photos you send to each retailer. Use the database or filing system you started when you began contacting retailers for this purpose.

Once you have contacted the retailer by mail, follow up with a phone call approximately two weeks later. Repeat this process about a month or so later. Include new photographs of your best work. Remember, the squeaky wheel does get the grease. You may also want to get referrals from other craftspeople and retailers. Just because one retailer does not feel she can sell your work, doesn't mean that she doesn't know of another shop or gallery with the perfect collector base for your very impressive signature craft.

Selling at Trade Shows

Trade shows are open to retailers only. The public is rarely permitted to attend, and if they do, they usually cannot buy. Gift shows are held each year in most major cities throughout the country. Many state universities also sponsor regional product trade shows through their business development offices. The American Crafts Council is one major crafts organization sponsoring large shows for their membership. Shop and gallery owners usually attend juried craft shows in their area.

See chapter four for more advice on finding trade shows. Once you have identified the trade shows where you want to exhibit your work, get your name on their waiting list. These lists can be extensive. To move your name up on the list, your work must be something the organizers want in their show. Be more than just another name on their list. Send them photos of new pieces as they develop. Send photocopies of articles about you and your work. Make your name familiar. Show them that your work is evolving, changing and exciting. Show promoters want enthusiastic attendees too! This keeps exhibitors, as well as buyers, coming back.

Although trade shows, gift shows, craft fairs and festivals are an excellent way to present your work before the greatest number of retailers from across the country at one time, keep in mind that participation is costly. Expenses are not limited to the cost of booth rentals. Consider the back and side drapes, tables and table covers, risers, lighting and even chairs that can be added expenses.

Give careful consideration to these shows, particularly when starting out. Realize that you will be transporting your craft work from your studio to the show site. How will you be traveling to the show? Are you able to transport your craft pieces and your display with you or will you have to ship them? Where will you be staying? How much will you spend for food and hotel space? Will you be able to walk or take a free shuttle from your hotel each day, or must you also include the costs of public transportation or cabs? If you plan to drive your own vehicle, realize that parking is limited and the costs are high.

Gather these figures, total them and then talk to other craftspeople who have exhibited at these shows. Get their input. You can benefit from networking in every aspect of this business. If you can possibly attend these shows prior to making your decision, you will learn much valuable information.

There are distinct advantages to selling wholesale as opposed to retail, although your profit per item will be lower. When you are making your creations to fill an order, each piece has already been sold. Your efforts are more focused. You're selling the items you're making and your bank account should reflect this, as will the smile on your face!

2
Market Listings

CHAPTER EIGHT

Craft Shows

PRODUCERS/ PROMOTERS

Retail

ADVERTISING ALLIANCE, INC.
Karen Lundquist
P.O. Box 210
Little York, NJ 08834
Phone: (908)996-3036
Fax: (908)996-7768
First show: 1984
Shows per year: 14
Times of year: April-October
Location: Westfield, Union, Somerville, Cranford, Flemington, Red Bank, Ridgewood, Englewood and Raritan, NJ. Outdoor. On Main Street of Downtown area.
Duration: 1 day
Attendance: 25,000
Admission: Free
Categories: Fine crafts, wearable art, jewelry, miniatures/dollhouses, wooden crafts, paper products, stained glass items, needlework crafts, hand blown glass items, home decor, dolls/stuffed animals/toys, pottery/ceramics, nature crafts/floral, leather crafts, baskets, sculpture
Price range: $5-1,000
Advertising/Promotion: All media
Spaces available: 150-400 per show. 12' × 10' spaces. Vendors bring all their own display, tables, electricity, etc.
Cost of space: $90-100
Application process: Shows are juried. For consideration, provide photos or slides (3), written description of work. No charge to apply.
Additional information: Events are promoted as "NJ's Famous Family Fun Festivals" and always include a large variety of food, as well as children's activities: petting zoo, pony rides, moonwalk, etc. Approximately 75% of exhibitors are crafts or art.

AFFTON ARTS AND CRAFTS SHOWS
Affton School Mothers
Mary Anne Kornberger
P.O. Box 190236
St. Louis, MO 63119
Phone: (314)351-1948; (314)638-3214
First show: 1972
Shows per year: 2
Times of year: Second weekend in March; second weekend in November
Location: Affton High School, 8309 Mackenzie Rd., Affton. Indoor.
Duration: Sat-Sun 9-4
Attendance: 2,000
Admission: Free
Categories: Fine crafts, wearable art, jewelry, miniatures/dollhouses, wooden crafts, paper products, stained glass items, needlework crafts, hand blown glass items, home decor, figurines, dolls/stuffed animals/toys, pottery/ceramics, nature crafts/floral, leather crafts, baskets, recycled crafts, sculpture
Price range: $5-100
Advertising/Promotion: Signs on school property, local papers, fliers, cable TV, many craft guide books. $50-100 budget.
Spaces available: 200 per show. 9' × 5' spaces, some doubles available. Limited tables rent for $10 (best to bring own). Limited electric available for $5.
Cost of space: $55 for 2 days
Application process: Shows are juried. For consideration, provide catalog/promotional materials, photos (2-3). No charge to apply.
Additional information: Producer offers one of the oldest shows in the area and one of few that do not allow commercial items.

AMERICAN CONCERN FOR ARTISTRY AND CRAFTSMANSHIP
Sara Cogswell Wells
P.O. Box 650
Montclair, NJ 07042
Phone: (201)746-0091
Fax: (201)509-7739

First show: 1976
Shows per year: 2
Times of year: July and September
Location: Lincoln Center for the Performing Arts in New York City. Outdoor. Around the Fountain in Lincoln Center Plaza and in Damrosch Park between the Metropolitan Opera and New York State Theater.
Duration: 2 weekends per festival
Attendance: 250,000
Admission: Free
Categories: Fine crafts, wearable art, jewelry, wooden crafts, paper products, stained glass items, hand blown glass items, toys, pottery/ceramics, leather crafts, baskets, sculpture
Price range: $15-5,000
Advertising/Promotion: Spots on radio, ads in major craft periodicals, ads in major Metropolitan Area newspapers, posters in subway, train and many locations in New York City, extensive press mailings and full color postcard mailer for craft artist mailing list.
Spaces available: 170 per show. No equipment provided. 8' × 8', 10' × 7', 10' × 10', 15' × 7' and 15' × 10' spaces.
Cost of space: $435-855. Corner space is an additional $90.
Application process: Combination of invited and juried. For consideration, provide slides (5). No charge to apply.
Additional information: Producer offers 24 hour security, secure parking garage, booth signs, full color postcard invitations, food discounts, clear instructions, moderately priced accommodations arranged, printed program, entertainment, comprehensive promotions campaign.

AMERICAN COUNTRY SHOWS, INC.
Amber Meyer
P.O. Drawer E
Fredericksburg, TX 78624
Phone: (210)997-2774; (210)997-1013
Fax: (210)997-0453
Shows per year: 22

Times of year: February-December

Location: OH, TX, NE and OK. Indoor and outdoor. Convention centers, fair grounds.

Duration: 1 weekend

Attendance: 8,000-22,000

Admission: $4 adults; $2 seniors; under 12 free

Categories: Fine crafts, wearable art, jewelry, miniatures/dollhouses, wooden crafts, paper products, stained glass items, needlework crafts, home decor, figurines, dolls/stuffed animals/toys, pottery/ceramics, nature crafts/floral, baskets

Price range: $5 and up

Advertising/Promotion: All media print in surrounding areas—185 miles out, national magazines, TV and radio. $13,000 and up budget.

Spaces available: 100 per show. $10' \times 10'$, $10' \times 15'$, $10' \times 20'$, $10' \times 30'$ booths with back drops.

Cost of space: $350 and up

Application process: Shows are juried. For consideration, provide photos or slides (3-5). No charge to apply.

AMERICAN CRAFT COUNCIL

American Craft Enterprises
21 South Eltings Corner Rd.
Highland, New York 12528
Phone: (800)836-3470
Fax: (914)883-6130
First show: 1965
Shows per year: 9
Times of year: February-April, June, August, September, December
Location: Bellevue, WA; Baltimore, MD; Atlanta, GA; St. Paul, MN; West Springfield, MA; Columbus, OH; San Francisco, CA; Tampa, FL and Charlotte, NC. Indoor. Convention centers.
Duration: Varies
Attendance: Varies
Admission: Varies
Categories: Fine crafts, jewelry, wooden crafts, paper products, hand blown glass items, home decor, figurines, dolls/stuffed animals/toys, pottery/ceramics, leather crafts, baskets, sculpture, metal, fiber
Spaces available: Varies
Application process: Shows are juried. For consideration, provide slides (5). $20 charge to apply.

Additional information: Many wholesale buyers attend these retail shows.

AMERICAN SOCIETY OF ARTISTS, INC.

P.O. Box 1326
Palatine, IL 60078
Phone: (312)751-2500; (847)991-4748
First show: 1972
Shows per year: Approximately 20
Times of year: February-December
Location: Chicago and Chicago suburban area, St. Louis area and Cape Girardeau and other cities in Missouri. Indoor and outdoor. Malls, downtown areas, parks—a variety of locations.
Duration: 1-3 days
Admission: Free
Categories: Fine crafts, wearable art, jewelry, miniatures/dollhouses, wooden crafts, paper products, stained glass items, needlework crafts, hand blown glass items, home decor, figurines, dolls/stuffed animals/toys, pottery/ceramics, nature crafts/floral, leather crafts, baskets, recycled crafts, sculpture, graphics and a wide variety of work
Price range: Varies
Advertising/Promotion: Print and electronic media, banners, postcards, posters, fliers, bumper stickers. Budget varies.
Spaces available: 35-300 per show. Exhibitors supply their own display setups. Space sizes vary depending upon physical setting of a particular show. $8' \times 10'$, $10' \times 10'$, $5' \times 10'$, $6' \times 10'$, $5' \times 12'$, etc. Also double and extra ½ spaces available at most shows.
Cost of space: Varies depending upon the show; $35-150.
Application process: Shows are juried. For consideration, provide photos or slides (4 of work, 1 of display), résumé, written description of work, No. 10 SASE. No charge to apply.
Additional information: Each show is different. Each show has its own type of customers, and is geared to suit customers. Type of work, prices, etc. varies from show to show.

AMERICA'S ARTISTS PRESENT . . .

Doug Alexander, New Life Creations
1572 W. Euclid Ave.
DeLand, FL 32720
Phone: (904)734-4277
First show: 1987

Shows per year: 4-5
Times of year: April, July, August, November
Location: Orlando Belz Factory Outlet World, Orlando, FL. Indoor. Inside two indoor malls of the tourist shopping complex.
Duration: 6 days
Admission: Free
Categories: Fine crafts, wearable art, jewelry, wooden crafts, paper products, stained glass items, needlework crafts, hand blown glass items, home decor, figurines, dolls/stuffed animals/toys, pottery/ceramics, nature crafts/floral, leather crafts
Price range: $1-200
Advertising/Promotion: Print and radio
Spaces available: 70 per show. Minimum of $7' \times 12'$ spaces, electricity available, exhibitors must provide their displays.
Cost of space: $190
Application process: Dealers are accepted on a first-come, first-serve basis, as long as they fit the requirements of the show. For consideration, provide photos or slides and SASE.

ANTIOCH CENTER

Aubrey Williams
5307 Center Mall
Kansas City, MO 64119
Phone: (816)454-1200
Fax: (816)454-0661
First show: Early 1970s
Shows per year: 2
Times of year: May, November
Location: Within the common area of the shopping center at the above address. Indoor.
Duration: F-Sun
Attendance: 10,000-15,000
Admission: Free
Categories: Fine crafts, wearable art, jewelry, miniatures/dollhouses, wooden crafts, paper products, stained glass items, needlework crafts, hand blown glass items, home decor, figurines, dolls/stuffed animals/toys, pottery/ceramics, nature crafts/floral, leather crafts, baskets
Price range: $3-300
Advertising/Promotion: Metro newspaper (*Kansas City Star*), local paper (*Dispatch Tribune*), 2-3 radio stations, signing, mall event fliers, outdoor

signing. $5,000 per show budget.

Spaces available: 150-160 per show. 1, 2 and 3 8-ft. table arrangements; art panels, 2- to 8-panel arrangements; panel and table arrangements; 50 sq. ft., 100 sq. ft., 150 sq. ft. spaces.

Cost of space: Tables $45 each; panels $25 each; 50 sq. ft., $70; 100 sq. ft., $135; 150 sq. ft., $200.

Application process: Shows are juried. For consideration, provide photos or slides (3). Rental fee must be included.

Additional information: Electricity provided at no charge. No food vendors or outside exhibits allowed.

ART PROMOTION COUNSELORS

Lauretta Worstell and Barbara Francis
P.O. Box 776
Alamo, TX 78516
Phone/Fax: (210)787-6996
First show: 1973
Shows per year: 45
Times of year: January-November
Location: New Orleans, LA; Laredo, Victora, Texas City, Abilene, Midland, Odessa, San Angelo, Roswell, Wichita Falls, Richardson, Tyler, McAllen and Harlingen, TX. Indoor. In malls.
Duration: 4 days
Attendance: Mall traffic, varies
Admission: Free
Categories: Fine crafts, wearable art, jewelry, miniatures/dollhouses, wooden crafts, paper products, stained glass items, needlework crafts, hand blown glass items, home decor, figurines, dolls/stuffed animals/toys, pottery/ceramics, nature crafts/floral, leather crafts, baskets, sculpture
Price range: $3 and up
Advertising/Promotion: Newspaper, radio, TV
Spaces available: 30-60 per show. 10' × 10' or 8' × 12' booths. Single, 1½ and double spaces are available.
Cost of space: $160-170 single; $230-252.50 1½; $300-320 double
Application process: Past participants have first priority. Open tables are available on a first-come, first-serve basis. For consideration, provide photos or slides (3). No charge to apply.

ART VENTURES WEST

Jackie Spivey
3212 Gus Thomasson Rd.
Dallas, TX 75228
Phone: (972)279-7271
First show: 1967
Shows per year: 29-32
Times of year: January-October and first week of November
Location: TX, LA, MO, AR, NE, NM. Indoor. Common area of shopping malls.
Duration: 5 days
Attendance: Mall traffic
Admission: Free
Categories: Fine crafts, wearable art, jewelry, miniatures/dollhouses, wooden crafts, paper products, stained glass items, needlework crafts, hand blown glass items, home decor, figurines, dolls/stuffed animals/toys, pottery/ceramics, nature crafts/floral, leather crafts, baskets
Price range: 50¢ and up
Advertising/Promotion: Newspaper, radio, mall signs
Spaces available: 25-30 per show. 10' × 10', 10' × 15', 10' × 20' booths. Exhibitors provide own set up.
Cost of space: $175-350
Application process: Past participants have first priority. For consideration, provide photos or slides. No charge to apply.

ARTISAN PROMOTIONS, INC.

Florence E. Flynn
83 Mt. Vernon St.
Boston, MA 02108
Phone: (617)742-3973
Fax: (617)742-0025
First show: 1982
Shows per year: 5
Times of year: Mid-March; mid-April; mid-October; second and third weekends in November
Location: Valley Expo Center, Methuen, MA; World Trade Center, Boston, MA. Indoor. First class exhibition halls.
Duration: 3 days-1 weekend
Attendance: 21,000
Admission: $6
Categories: Fine crafts, wearable art, jewelry, miniatures/dollhouses, wooden crafts, paper products, stained glass items, needlework crafts, hand

blown glass items, home decor, dolls/stuffed animals/toys, pottery/ceramics, nature crafts/floral, leather crafts, baskets, sculpture
Price range: $3-1,500
Advertising/Promotion: Radio, major TV affiliates, newspapers, press releases, radio interviews, give-aways, poster and coupon distribution, direct mail. $50,000 per show budget.
Spaces available: 200-400. 10' × 10' booths.
Cost of space: $300-400
Application process: Shows are juried. For consideration, provide photos or slides (4). No charge to apply.

ARTISTS' & CRAFTSMEN'S EXCHANGE, INC.

Donna Cartwright
110 Pebble Beach Ln.
Williamsburg, VA 23185
Phone: (757)229-8191
Fax: (757)229-8191
First show: 1983
Shows per year: 20-24
Times of year: Year-round
Location: Williamsburg, Virginia Beach, Hampton, York County, Newport News and Glouster, VA. Indoor and outdoor. Malls, shopping centers.
Duration: 1 day or weekend
Admission: Free
Categories: Wearable art, jewelry, wooden crafts, stained glass items, needlework crafts, hand blown glass items, pottery/ceramics, nature crafts/floral, leather crafts, baskets
Price range: 25¢-$200
Advertising/Promotion: Radio, TV, newspapers, magazines, posters, banners, fliers. Budget varies.
Spaces available: Varies. 8' × 10' floor space.
Cost of space: Varies
Application process: Shows are juried. For consideration, provide photos (3 of work, plus 1 of display), sample of work, written description of work. No charge to apply.

ARTS & CRAFTS FESTIVALS, INC.

P.O. Box 412
Canton, CT 06019
Phone: (860)693-6335
Shows per year: 4
Times of year: June, August, December

Location: Spring Arts & Crafts Festival, Berlin, CT (June); Summer Arts & Crafts Festival, Berlin, CT (August); Christmas Crafts Expo I and II, Hartford, CT (December). Indoor and outdoor. Hartford Civic Center, Berlin Fairgrounds.

Duration: F-Sun

Attendance: 12,000-25,000

Admission: $5-6.50 adults, $4-5.50 seniors, children 14 and under free

Spaces available: 100-300 per show

Cost of space: $220-560

Application process: Shows are juried.

BEACH ART CENTER

JoAnne King

1515 Bay Palm Blvd.

Indian Rocks Beach, FL 33785

Phone: (813)596-4331

First show: 1976

Shows per year: 2

Times of year: Mid-April and November

Location: Kolb Park on Bay Palm Blvd. Outdoor.

Duration: Sun 9-5

Attendance: 5,000

Admission: Free

Categories: Fine crafts, wearable art, jewelry, wooden crafts, stained glass items, hand blown glass items, pottery/ceramics, nature crafts/floral, leather crafts, baskets, sculpture, fine art

Price range: $10-500

Advertising/Promotion: Art and craft magazines, area newspapers and magazines, radio and TV

Spaces available: 125 per show. 12′ × 12′ area in park. Some on grass, some on cement.

Cost of space: $45-50

Application process: Shows are juried. Send for application.

THE BIZARRE BAZAAR

Alice Siegel

P.O. Box 8330

Richmond, VA 23226

Phone: (804)288-9467

Fax: (804)673-9047

First show: 1975

Shows per year: 2

Times of year: First weekend in December and two weeks before Easter

Location: Virginia State Fairgrounds and the Richmond Centre in Richmond, VA. Indoor. Fairground exhibition buildings and exhibition center downtown.

Duration: 1 weekend 10-7

Attendance: 6,000-20,000

Admission: $4.50 adult, $1.50 child

Categories: Fine crafts, wearable art, jewelry, miniatures/dollhouses, wooden crafts, paper products, stained glass items, needlework crafts, hand blown glass items, home decor, figurines, dolls/stuffed animals/toys, pottery/ceramics, nature crafts/floral, leather crafts, baskets, sculpture

Price range: Upper end

Advertising/Promotion: TV, radio, magazines, trade journals, newspapers, client mailing list. Budget varies.

Spaces available: 250-440 per show. 10′ × 12′ or 10′ × 24′, 2 tables, 2 chairs, drapes and electricity ($25 extra).

Cost of space: $350-450 for standard booth and $300-400 for artist crafter booth.

Application process: Shows are juried. For consideration, provide photos or slides, catalog/promotional materials, list of shows participated in. No charge to apply.

Additional information: We provide a high quality marketplace featuring crafts, artists, mixed media, gourmet foods, decorator items and jewelry.

ELISE BLACKWELL

P.O. Box 745

Selma, AL 36702

Phone: (334)872-1026; (334)874-8044

Fax: (334)242-8428

First show: 1979

Shows per year: 3

Times of year: Second Saturday of May, second Saturday of October, first two full weeks of December

Location: Old Cahawba, Historic Water Avenue and Performing Art Centre in Selma, AL. Indoor and outdoor. Historic street along the Alabama River; the old town of Cahawba, Alabama's first permanent capital; indoor at the Performing Art Centre in Selma.

Duration: 1 day, 9-5; 2 weeks, 9-5 daily and Sun 1-5

Attendance: 4,500-30,000

Admission: $1-2; $3/car

Categories: Fine crafts, wearable art, jewelry, miniatures/dollhouses, wooden crafts, paper products, stained glass items, needlework crafts, hand blown glass items, home decor, figurines, dolls/stuffed animals/toys, pottery/ceramics, nature crafts/floral, leather crafts, baskets, sculpture

Price range: 25¢ to hundreds

Advertising/Promotion: State radio stations and TV stations, state newspapers, billboards, brochures distributed statewide. In crafts magazines and newsletters throughout the US. Several hundred-several thousand dollar per show budget.

Spaces available: 50-400 per show. 12′ × 12′ spaces.

Cost of space: $25-70

Application process: Shows are juried. For consideration, provide photos (1). Application fee buys the booth.

Additional information: Each of my shows has its own characteristics and requirements and was uniquely designed to complement the organization it benefits.

BOCA RATON MUSEUM OF ART

Marlene Pomeranz and Sue Zipper

801 W. Palmetto Park Rd.

Boca Raton, FL 33486

Phone: (407)392-2500

Fax: (407)391-6410

First show: 1986

Shows per year: 2

Times of year: Last full weekend in February and the weekend after Thanksgiving

Location: Boca Center, Military Trail and Town Center Rd., Boca Raton. Outdoor. At shopping center.

Duration: Sat and Sun

Attendance: 50,000

Categories: Fine crafts, jewelry, hand blown glass items, pottery/ceramics, leather crafts, baskets, sculpture

Price range: $25-25,000

Advertising/Promotion: Radio, newspapers, museum newsletter, fliers

Spaces available: 100-200. 10′ × 10′ space. Bring own tent, etc.

Cost of space: $200-275

Application process: Show is juried. For consideration, provide slides (3). $20-25 charge to apply.

Additional Information: The show in November is jewelry only.

BRISTOL RENAISSANCE FAIRE

Ruth and Bill Farnham
12550 120th Ave.
Kenosha, WI 53142-7337
Phone: (847)395-7773
Fax: (847)395-0547
First show: 1988
Shows per year: 1
Times of year: Last weekend in June through third weekend of August (9 weekends).
Location: At above address. Indoor and outdoor. 20 acre grounds with 170 shops, 9 stages, food and games. Elizabethan English Village.
Duration: 10-7 Sat-Sun
Attendance: 200,000
Admission: $14.95
Categories: Fine crafts, wearable art, jewelry, miniatures, wooden crafts, paper products, stained glass items, needlework crafts, hand blown glass items, home decor, figurines, dolls/ stuffed animals/toys, pottery/ceramics, nature crafts/floral, leather crafts, baskets, sculpture, metal crafts, no plastic
Price range: 25¢-$5,000
Advertising/Promotion: Advertise in Milwaukee, Chicago, 7 TV stations, 11 radio stations, all print media. $400,000 budget.
Spaces available: 170 per show. Permanent shops: sales areas vary, 15'-50' frontage. Some have storage, workshops, living quarters.
Cost of space: $900
Application process: Shows are juried. Shows are invitation only. For consideration, provide photos or slides, written description of work. No charge to apply.
Additional information: All applicants are in period, 16th century, costume. Workshops are required.

BUCKLER PROMOTIONS, INC.

1697 Doyle Rd.
Deltona, FL 32725
Phone: (407)860-0092
Fax: (407)860-6157
First show: 1989
Shows per year: 40
Times of year: January-November
Location: FL, GA, VA, NC, SC, MS, AL. Indoor and outdoor. Convention centers and fairgrounds.

Duration: Sat-Sun
Attendance: 10,000-20,000
Admission: Adults $3, children under 12 free
Categories: Fine crafts, wearable art, jewelry, miniatures/dollhouses, wooden crafts, paper products, stained glass items, needlework crafts, hand blown glass items, home decor, figurines, dolls/stuffed animals/toys, pottery/ceramics, nature crafts/floral, leather crafts, baskets, recycled crafts, sculpture, wire art, calligraphy
Price range: $1-500
Advertising/Promotion: Newspapers, billboards, road signs, radio, TV.
Spaces available: Booth spaces average 10'×10' to 12'×12'.
Cost of space: $102-155 per space; $10-35 electric; $10-22 per night parking for RVs.
Application process: Shows are juried. For consideration, provide photos or slides (3). No charge to apply.

CERAMIC SHOWS

Wilma C. Bonner
1825 Lehigh St.
Easton, PA 18042
Phone: (610)253-6761
First show: 1975
Shows per year: 9
Times of year: March, September, October
Location: Allentown, Easton, Stroudsburg, Bethlehem and Trexlertown, PA. Indoor. In malls.
Duration: 4 days, mall hours
Admission: Free
Categories: Pottery/ceramics
Price range: 50¢-$150
Advertising/Promotion: In local papers appropriate to the malls and in ceramic magazines.
Spaces available: 20 per show. 24' single space. Must furnish own skirted tables.
Cost of space: $100-150
Application process: Past participants have first priority. Open tables are available on a first-come, first-serve basis.
Additional information: Items for sale must be porcelain, ceramic, pottery or related supplies.

CHARLESTON CRAFTS, INC.

Regina Semko
38 Queen St.
Charleston, SC 29401
Phone: (803)723-2938
First show: 1979
Shows per year: 2
Times of year: Last weekend in May and first weekend in June.
Location: Indoor and outdoor. In tree-lined Wragg Square Park in downtown near the visitors center. In Galliard Auditorium downtown Charleston.
Duration: 3 days (Fri, Sat, Sun)
Attendance: Outdoor—7,000-10,000. Indoor—4,000-6,000
Admission: Adults $2-3, children and seniors $1
Categories: Fine crafts, wearable art, jewelry, wooden crafts, stained glass items, hand blown glass items, pottery, baskets, sculpture, weaving, photography, graphics, quilting
Price range: $10-5,000
Advertising/Promotion: Trade journals, national publications, local print and PR media, regional literature distribution, rack cards at 12 statewide welcome centers, regional galleries, mailing lists to local patrons and interior designers. 30% budget.
Spaces available: Outdoor—90, indoor—75 per show. 10'×10'. Outdoor show has no electricity, no tables or canopies available. Indoor spaces are draped and have electrical outlets.
Cost of space: Outdoor: $125; indoor: $215
Application process: Shows are juried. For consideration, provide slides (5) and written description of work. $10 charge to apply.

CHAUTAUQUA CRAFTS ALLIANCE

Devon Taylor
P.O. Box 89
Mayville, NY 14757-0089
Phone: (716)753-1851
First show: 1981
Shows per year: 2
Times of year: July and August
Location: Chautauqua, NY. Outdoor. In Bestor Plaza, Chautauqua Institution.
Duration: 3 days
Attendance: 12,000
Admission: Varies by year

Categories: Fine crafts, wearable art, jewelry, wooden crafts, paper products, stained glass items, hand blown glass items, dolls/stuffed animals/toys, pottery/ceramics, nature crafts/floral, leather crafts, baskets, sculpture

Price range: $2.50-6,000

Advertising/Promotion: New York state tourist brochures, newspapers, magazines and radio. Over $5,000 budget.

Spaces available: 67 per show. 10' × 10' booths.

Cost of space: $150

Application process: Shows are juried. For consideration, provide slides (4). $10 charge to apply.

Additional information: Send SASE for application.

CITY OF DES PERES RECREATION DEPT.

Ann Jacob
12325 Manchester Rd.
St. Louis, MO 63131-4316
Phone: (314)966-4252
Fax: (314)966-2607
First show: 1975
Shows per year: 2
Times of year: Second weekend in June and the first weekend in December
Location: Des Peres Park and Des Peres Center Community Building at the above address. Indoor and outdoor.
Duration: 1 weekend
Attendance: 3,000
Admission: Free
Categories: Fine crafts, wearable art, jewelry, wooden crafts, stained glass items, needlework crafts, hand blown glass items, home decor, dolls/stuffed animals/toys, pottery/ceramics, nature crafts/floral, leather crafts, baskets, painting, photographs
Price range: $5-400
Advertising/Promotion: Ads in local newspapers, radio, flier inserts, posters and mailers. $1,000-1,800 per show budget.
Spaces available: 50-90 per show. 8' × 5' and 12' × 12' spaces. Exhibitor must supply own hanging equipment.
Cost of space: $50 and $75
Application process: Shows are juried. For consideration, provide photos or slides (2-3). No charge to apply.
Additional information: Artist must be present both days. Application dead-

line for the June show is the last week in April; first week in October for the December show.

CITY OF KISSIMMEE

Wayne Larson
320 E. Monument Ave.
Kissimmee, FL 34741
Phone: (407)932-4050
Fax: (407)932-1958
First show: 1989
Shows per year: 2
Times of year: July 4 and second weekend in December
Location: Kissimmee lakefront park. Outdoor. Park with lake, playgrounds, walkway and gazebo.
Duration: 1 day, 12-8 or 10
Attendance: 15,000-25,000
Admission: Free
Categories: Fine crafts, wearable art, jewelry, miniatures/dollhouses, wooden crafts, paper products, stained glass items, needlework crafts, hand blown glass items, home decor, figurines, dolls/stuffed animals/toys, pottery/ceramics, nature crafts/floral, leather crafts, baskets, recycled crafts, sculpture
Price range: $1-100
Advertising/Promotion: TV, radio, newspaper, magazine, bill inserts, T-shirts, radio station sponsorship. $15,000-20,000 budget.
Spaces available: 200 per show. 10' × 10' space. Vendor must have canopy and supply own tables and chairs.
Cost of space: $25 per day
Application process: Dealers are accepted on a first-come, first-serve basis, as long as they fit the requirements of the show.
Additional information: City of Kissimmee events are included in the "Top 20 Events" by the Southeast Tourism Society.

COAST & COUNTRY SHOWS

Bruce Baratz
P.O. Box 4
New London, CT 06320
Phone: (860)442-7976
Fax: (860)442-1827
First show: 1977
Shows per year: 12

Times of year: February, March, July-December
Location: Simsbury, Willimantic, Hartford, Colchester, New London and Norwich, CT and the Greater-Boston area. Indoor and outdoor. Main street, malls, town green, high school gyms, hotel ballrooms.
Duration: 1-3 days; 9-5 daily, Sun 12-5
Attendance: 2,000-5,000
Admission: Free-$2
Categories: Fine crafts, wearable art, jewelry, miniatures/dollhouses, wooden crafts, paper products, stained glass items, needlework crafts, hand blown glass items, home decor, figurines, dolls/stuffed animals/toys, pottery/ceramics, nature crafts/floral, leather crafts, baskets, recycled crafts, sculpture
Price range: $5-200
Advertising/Promotion: Ads in weekly and daily newspapers, press releases to all media, posters, fliers, direct mailings, cable TV, radio ads, signs on public streets. 25-50% of gross booth fee income budget.
Spaces available: 50-150 per show. Tables available at hotels and malls, most spaces are 10' × 10'.
Cost of space: $50-150
Application process: Shows are juried. For consideration, provide photos or slides (3) and written description of work. No charge to apply.

CONRAD ENTERPRISES

Peggy Conrad
406 S. Ave. B
Canton, IL 61520-3019
Phone: (309)647-2742
First show: 1980
Shows per year: 2
Times of year: November and December
Location: Rock Island, IL, Qcca Expo Center (November); Peoria, IL, Exposition Gardens (December). Indoor.
Duration: 1 weekend
Attendance: 6,000-12,000
Admission: Free-$3
Categories: Fine crafts, wearable art, jewelry, miniatures/dollhouses, wooden crafts, paper products, stained glass items, needlework crafts, dolls/stuffed animals/toys, pottery/ceramics, nature crafts/floral, leather crafts, baskets

Price range: $5-200

Advertising/Promotion: Ads on TV, in newspapers (daily and weekly), fliers, on billboards.

Spaces available: 100-200 per show. Rock Island, 10½′ × 10′ and up; Peoria, 9′ × 10′ and up.

Cost of space: Rock Island, $100 and up; Peoria, $85 and up

Application process: Shows are juried. For consideration, provide photos (3) and written description of work. No charge to apply.

COUNTRY FOLK ART SHOWS, INC.

8393 E. Holly Rd.
Holly, MI 48442

Phone: (810)634-4151; (810)634-4153

Fax: (810)634-3718

First show: 1983

Shows per year: Over 50

Times of year: Year-round

Location: Nationwide. Indoor. Mostly on fairgrounds and convention centers and halls.

Duration: F 5-9, Sat 10-5, Sun 10-4

Attendance: 8,000

Admission: F $6; Sat and Sun $5

Categories: Fine crafts, wearable art, jewelry, miniatures/dollhouses, wooden crafts, paper products, stained glass items, needlework crafts, hand blown glass items, home decor, dolls/ stuffed animals/toys, pottery/ceramics, nature crafts/floral, leather crafts, baskets, ragrugs

Price range: $2-290 and up

Advertising/Promotion: Billboards, signs, print ads, TV, radio and mailing list for customers (postcards and show fliers); *Country Folk Art Magazine* and *Quick N Easy Magazine.* $10,000-25,000 budget.

Spaces available: 125-300 per show. Booth—(3-sided room setting) a minimum requirement of 6 ft. in height. Need a business/booth identification sign. Booth sizes: 10′ × 10′, 10′ × 15′, 10′ × 20′, 10′ × 25′, 10′ × 30′.

Cost of space: $350-450 for a 10′ × 10′ booth—good for all 3 days

Application process: Shows are juried. For consideration, provide photos (6), or sample of work, written description of work. $20 charge to apply.

Additional information: We are the lead-ing folk art craft shows in the nation featuring hundreds of outstanding artisans across the country. Country Folk also produces wholesale shows.

CRAFT PRODUCTIONS, INC.

Karen Yackley
119 E. Pomery St.
West Chicago, IL 60185

Phone: (708)231-8644

Fax: (708)231-8645

First show: 1985

Shows per year: 20

Times of year: January-December

Location: Northern Indiana; Southern Wisconsin and all around Chicago-land suburbs. Indoor and outdoor. At downtown festivals, indoor malls, outdoor shopping centers, fairgounds and colleges.

Duration: 2 or 3 days

Attendance: 4,000

Admission: Free-$3.50

Categories: Fine crafts, wearable art, jewelry, miniatures/dollhouses, wooden crafts, paper products, stained glass items, needlework crafts, hand blown glass items, home decor, figurines, dolls/stuffed animals/toys, pottery/ceramics, nature crafts/floral, leather crafts, baskets, recycled crafts, sculpture

Price range: $2-700

Advertising/Promotion: Large shows— 2,000 posters, 100,000 fliers, 2,000 direct mail to customers, newspapers ads in all local papers, TV advertising and radio. $1,000-25,000 budget.

Spaces available: 50-400 per show. 10′ × 5′ up to 10′ × 10′. No equipment available except electricity.

Cost of space: $50-175

Application process: Shows are juried. For consideration, provide photos or slides (3). No charge to apply.

CRAFT SHOW PROMOTIONS, INC.

Lillian Domzalski
302 Allen Ave.
West Chicago, IL 60185

Phone: (630)293-3637

Fax: (630)293-3679

First show: 1985

Shows per year: 20

Times of year: January-December

Location: Around Chicagoland suburbs. Indoor and outdoor. At downtown fes-tivals, indoor malls, outdoor shopping centers, fairgounds and colleges.

Duration: 2 or 3 days

Attendance: 4,000-9,000

Admission: Free-$3.50

Categories: Fine crafts, wearable art, jewelry, miniatures/dollhouses, wooden crafts, paper products, stained glass items, needlework crafts, hand blown glass items, home decor, figurines, dolls/stuffed animals/toys, pottery/ceramics, nature crafts/floral, leather crafts, baskets, recycled crafts, sculpture

Price range: $2-700

Advertising/Promotion: Large shows— 2,000 posters, 100,000 fliers, 2,000 direct mail to customers, newspapers ads in all local papers, TV advertising and radio.

Spaces available: 50-400 per show. 10′ × 5′ up to 10′ × 10′. No equipment available except electricity.

Cost of space: $50-175

Application process: Shows are juried. For consideration, provide photos or slides (3). No charge to apply.

CRAFT SHOWS BY LORIS

Loris Wiersig
4530 NW 16th
Oklahoma City, OK 73127

Phone: (405)943-3800; (405)946-1584

Fax: (405)943-3849

First show: 1982

Shows per year: 2

Times of year: Middle of March; the weekend before Thanksgiving

Location: Both shows held at the Oklahoma State Fairgrounds, NW 10th and May Avenue, Oklahoma City. Indoor.

Duration: 1 weekend

Attendance: 15,000

Admission: $4

Categories: Fine crafts, wearable art, jewelry, miniatures/dollhouses, wooden crafts, paper products, stained glass items, needlework crafts, hand blown glass items, home decor, dolls/ stuffed animals/toys, pottery/ceramics, nature crafts/floral, leather crafts, baskets, sculpture

Price range: $1-$100

Advertising/Promotion: Advertised in Oklahoma City area and outlying areas, 40 billboards, newspapers, 5-6

TV stations, 7-8 radio stations. $25,000 budget.

Spaces available: 300-350 per show. Booth spaces. 5′×10′; 8′×10′ and 10′×10′. Exhibitor furnishes own equipment. Pegboards, tables, chairs available to rent.

Cost of space: $130, $165

Application process: Past participants have first priority. Open tables are available on a first-come, first-serve basis.

CRAFTS AMERICA

Betsy Kubie
P.O. Box 603
Greens Farms, CT 06436
Phone/Fax: (203)254-0486
First show: 1988
Shows per year: 2
Times of year: September, November
Location: Washington craft show—Washington Convention Center, Washington, DC. Westchester craft show—Westchester County Center, White Plains, NY. Indoor. Both shows take place in exhibition hall space.
Duration: 3 day wekend (Fri-Sun)
Attendance: 10,000
Admission: $8/$7
Categories: Fine crafts, wearable art, jewelry, hand blown glass items, pottery/ceramics, leather crafts, baskets, wood, furniture, metal
Price range: $35-25,000
Advertising/Promotion: National/local newspapers, magazines, radio, direct mail
Spaces available: 120-160 per show. 10′×10′ and 10′×15′ spaces. Exhibitor must provide or rent from decorating service 8′ high enclosure (3 sides) to screen from neighboring exhibitors. Also, should bring good lighting, carpeting and any extras for display of work to be sold.
Cost of space: It varies from show to show (approx. $600-700 per 10′×10′ booth).
Application process: Shows are juried. For consideration, provide slides (5 of work and 1 of booth). $20 charge to apply.
Additional information: We are searching for very high quality contemporary crafts to bring together with a dis-

cerning buying public in an exclusive highend marketplace.

JIM CUSTER ENTERPRISES, INC.

Cheryl Custer-Branz
P.O. Box 14987
Spokane, WA 99214
Phone: (509)924-0588
First show: 1976
Shows per year: 3
Times of year: Second weekend in November, weekend before Thanksgiving and the first weekend in March
Location: Spokane Interstate Fairgrounds and TRAC Facilities, Pasco, WA. Indoor.
Duration: 1 weekend (3 days)
Attendance: 17,000
Admission: Adults $2.50-4, 12 and under free.
Categories: Fine crafts, wearable art, jewelry, miniatures/dollhouses, wooden crafts, paper products, stained glass items, needlework crafts, hand blown glass items, home decor, figurines, dolls/stuffed animals/toys, pottery/ceramics, nature crafts/floral, leather crafts, baskets, recycled crafts, sculpture. Must be handcrafted. No imports, kits or representatives.
Price range: All price ranges
Advertising/Promotion: Radio, TV, cable, newspaper, billboards, electronic signs, etc.
Spaces available: 150-275. 10′×10′ floor space. Tables are available for rent. Exhibitors supply their own booths, etc. Back and side drapes are also available for rent.
Cost of space: $200-310
Application process: Open spaces placed based on the need of the sale. Shows are juried. For consideration, provide photos or slides (2 of product, 1 of booth). No charge to apply.
Additional information: Prices are subject to change.

DAYLILY PROMOTIONS
ARTS & CRAFTS SHOWS

Linda C. Brzezinski
P.O. Box 3097
Ann Arbor, MI 48106
Phone/Fax: (313)971-7424
E-mail: daylily@ic.net
First show: 1985
Shows per year: 6-10

Times of year: March, April, June, September, October, November, December
Location: Ann Arbor, MI area. Indoor and outdoor. High schools, community colleges, festival facilities.
Duration: 1-2 days
Attendance: 3,000-8,000
Admission: $2; under 10 free
Categories: Fine crafts, wearable art, jewelry, miniatures/dollhouses, wooden crafts, paper products, stained glass items, needlework crafts, hand blown glass items, home decor, figurines, dolls/stuffed animals/toys, pottery/ceramics, nature crafts/floral, leather crafts, baskets, sculpture
Price range: $5-2,000
Advertising/Promotion: Newspaper and radio within a 30 mile radius (paid ads and press releases); fliers distributed by artists; postcards mailed directly to past customers; signs; listings and ads in showbooks; and through Internet site. $35,000 budget.
Spaces available: 100-150 per show. Booths 10′×5′, 10′×8′, 10′×10′. Chairs available for free; tables available for rent at some shows.
Cost of space: $40-100
Application process: Shows are juried. For consideration, provide photos or slides (4). No charge to apply.
Additional information: No kits or commercial products accepted. No imports.

EMPIRE STATE CRAFTS ALLIANCE

Megan G. White, executive director
320 Montgomery St.
Syracuse, NY 13202
Phone: (315)472-4245
Fax: (315)746-4069
E-mail: esca@escacraft.com
First show: 1981
Shows per year: 2
Times of year: July and November
Location: Corning and Syracuse, NY. Indoor and outdoor. The Corning Show takes place on Market St., a main downtown street. Syracuse Show takes place at the Onondaga County Convention Center in downtown Syracuse.
Duration: 1 weekend
Attendance: 3,000-40,000
Admission: Free-$3

Categories: Fine crafts, wearable art, jewelry, wooden crafts, stained glass items, needlework crafts, hand blown glass items, pottery/ceramics, leather crafts, baskets, sculpture

Price range: $5-1,000

Advertising/Promotion: Newspapers, radio, TV, craft show guide, the Internet

Spaces available: 100 per show. Booths of varying sizes from 10′ × 10′ to 10′ × 20′ are available at both shows.

Cost of space: $180-370 (ESCA members receive reduced rates)

Application process: Shows are juried. For consideration, provide slides (5). No charge to apply.

ERIE PROMOTIONS & EXPOS, INC.

Sharon Concilla
P.O. Box 174
North East, PA 16428
Phone: (814)725-3856; (814)868-3416
Fax: (814)725-3441
First show: 1993
Shows per year: 4
Times of year: April, May, June, October, November
Location: Eastwood Expo Center, Niles, OH; Valley View Expo Center, Brookfield, OH; Millcreek Mall and Erie Civic Center in Erie, PA. Indoor. Paid admission shows in a mall or expo center.
Duration: 1 weekend
Attendance: 2,500-13,000
Admission: $2-3
Categories: Fine crafts, wearable art, jewelry, miniatures/dollhouses, wooden crafts, paper products, stained glass items, needlework crafts, figurines, dolls/stuffed animals/toys, pottery/ceramics, nature crafts/floral, baskets
Price range: $5-500
Advertising/Promotion: Billboards, radio, TV, newspapers, trade publications, fliers, posters. $2,500-15,000 budget depending on show.
Spaces available: 100-200 per show. Booths (10′ × 10′ to 12′ × 8′) or table.
Cost of space: $45-200
Application process: Past participants have first priority. Open tables are available on a first-come, first-serve basis.

ESAU, INC.

Katie Parton
P.O. Box 50096
Knoxville, TN 37950
Phone: (423)588-1233; (800)588-3728
Fax: (423)588-6938
First show: 1990
Shows per year: 2
Times of year: October, February
Location: Jacob Building, Chilhowee Park, Knoxville, TN. Indoor. Fairgrounds.
Duration: 3 days
Attendance: 13,500
Admission: $4
Categories: Fine crafts, wearable art, jewelry, miniatures/dollhouses, wooden crafts, paper products, stained glass items, needlework crafts, hand blown glass items, home decor, figurines, dolls/stuffed animals/toys, pottery/ceramics, nature crafts/floral, leather crafts, baskets
Price range: $1-200
Advertising/Promotion: Trade magazines, billboards, newspaper, TV, radio and fliers
Spaces available: 300 per show. 9′ × 10′ and 10′ × 13′ booths; backdrop and electrical provided; tables and chairs can be rented.
Cost of space: $100-190
Application process: Past participants have first priority. Open tables are available on a first-come, first-serve basis.

EVENTS MANAGEMENT GROUP, INC.

Steve Jahnke and Linda Shell
P.O. Box 8845
Virginia Beach, VA 23450-8845
Phone: (757)486-0220
Fax: (757)486-7761
First show: 1982
Shows per year: 5
Times of year: January, April, November
Location: Virginia Beach Pavilion, Virginia Beach; Capital Expo Center, Chantilly, VA. Indoor.
Duration: 3 days (10-6)
Attendance: 8,000-18,000
Admission: $4-5
Categories: Fine crafts, wearable art, jewelry, miniatures/dollhouses, wooden crafts, paper products, stained glass items, needlework crafts, hand blown glass items, home decor, figu-

rines, dolls/stuffed animals/toys, pottery/ceramics, nature crafts/floral, leather crafts, baskets, recycled crafts, sculpture

Price range: $5-1,000

Advertising/Promotion: TV, newspapers, radio, direct mail, press releases, magazines

Spaces available: 175-400 per show. 10′ × 10′ or larger draped booths.

Cost of space: $200-425

Application process: Shows are juried. For consideration, provide photos or slides (3 of work, 1 of display). No charge to apply.

FAMILY FESTIVALS ASSOCIATION

Debbie and Dave Stoner
P.O. Box 166
Irwin, PA 15642
Phone/Fax: (412)863-4577
First show: 1992
Shows per year: 5
Times of year: May-November
Location: Uniontown, Greensburg and Washington, PA; Berea, OH. Indoor and outdoor.
Duration: 2 weekends (4 days)
Attendance: 25,000-33,000
Admission: $4/$3.50 adults, children ages 6-12 $1, under 6 free.
Categories: Fine crafts, wearable art, jewelry, miniatures/dollhouses, wooden crafts, paper products, stained glass items, needlework crafts, hand blown glass items, home decor, figurines, dolls/stuffed animals/toys, pottery/ceramics, nature crafts/floral, leather crafts, baskets, recycled crafts, sculpture
Price range: $3-4,000
Advertising/Promotion: Radio, newspaper, TV, posters, fliers, billboards, newsletter, postcards. $35,000-42,000 per show budget.
Spaces available: 150-165 per show. 10′ × 10′; 10′ × 20′ or 10′ × 30′. Will work with whatever space is needed. All fairgrounds have RV hookups and showers on site. Electric available on site.
Cost of space: $200-300 per 10′ × 10′ space
Application process: Shows are juried. For consideration, provide slides (1) or photos (3) of work and 1 of booth display set-up. No charge to apply.

FANTASMA PRODUCTIONS INC. OF FLORIDA

George Perley
2000 S. Dixie Hwy.
West Palm Beach, FL 33401
Phone: (561)832-6397
Fax: (561)832-2043
First show: 1974
Shows per year: 6
Times of year: February, March, April, July, September, November
Location: West Palm Beach, Ft. Lauderdale, Miami, Tampa and Jacksonville, FL. Indoor and outdoor. In fairgrounds, parks and main streets.
Duration: 1-8 days
Attendance: 40,000-95,000
Admission: Free-$8
Categories: Wearable art, jewelry, miniatures/dollhouses, wooden crafts, paper products, stained glass items, needlework crafts, hand blown glass items, home decor, figurines, dolls/stuffed animals/toys, pottery/ceramics, nature crafts/floral, leather crafts, baskets, recycled crafts, sculpture
Price range: $1-50
Advertising/Promotion: TV, radio, print, word of mouth
Spaces available: 40-100 per show. 10' × 10' spaces. They include 500 watts of electricity (in most shows). The vendor has the option of bringing a tent or just a table.
Cost of space: $100-200
Application process: Dealers are accepted on a first-come, first-serve basis, as long as they fit the requirements of the show.
Additional information: Each show is completely different. We mainly produce festivals, which means that we include a large food section, carnival rides (in some shows), music (national to local level), and a craft/commercial section.

GILMORE ENTERPRISES, INC.

Cara Dudley
1240 Oakland Ave.
Greensboro, NC 27403
Phone: (910)274-5550
Fax: (910)274-1084
First show: 1974
Shows per year: 10
Times of year: March, April, August-November
Location: Columbia, Greensboro, Myrtle Beach, Winston-Salem, NC; Richmond, Chantilly, Roanoke, VA. Indoor. Fairground buildings or convention centers.
Duration: 3 day weekend
Attendance: 25,000-45,000
Admission: $4-6
Categories: Fine crafts, wearable art, jewelry, wooden crafts, paper products, stained glass items, needlework crafts, hand blown glass items, dolls/stuffed animals/toys, pottery/ceramics, nature crafts/floral, leather crafts, baskets, sculpture
Price range: $1-25,000
Advertising/Promotion: Billboards, radio, TV, magazines, newspapers, direct mail
Spaces available: 200-500 per show. 8' × 10'; 8' × 15'; 8' × 20' curtained booth spaces.
Cost of space: $200-350
Application process: Shows are juried. For consideration, provide photos or slides. No charge to apply.

THE GLYNN ART ASSOCIATION

Kay Wayne
319 Mallory St. (or P.O. Box 20673)
St. Simon Island, GA 31522
Phone: (912)638-8770; (912)638-8771
Fax: (912)638-8770
First show: 1969
Shows per year: 5
Times of year: Last weekend in March; Memorial Day weekend; 4th of July weekend; second weekend in October; first weekend in December
Location: Ocean Front Neptune Park, St. Simons Island. Outdoor. Ocean front park adjacent to Main Street.
Duration: 1 weekend
Attendance: 10,000-20,000
Admission: Free
Categories: Fine crafts, wearable art, jewelry, miniatures/dollhouses, wooden crafts, paper products, stained glass items, needlework crafts, hand blown glass items, home decor, figurines, dolls/stuffed animals/toys, pottery/ceramics, nature crafts/floral, leather crafts, baskets, recycled crafts, sculpture
Price range: $1 to several thousand
Advertising/Promotion: Festival listing publications, local radio and TV, newspapers in Atlanta, Jacksonville and Savannah. $3,000 budget.
Spaces available: 50-200 per show. All spaces are 10' × 10'. Exhibitor provides own set up and display.
Cost of space: $75-90
Application process: Shows are juried. For consideration, provide photos or slides (3). Fine art show requires 5 slides.
Additional information: The Fine Art Show on Memorial Day is very strictly juried. The Arts & Craft Festival in October and in July is easier to get into. The other two shows are craft only.

GUILFORD HANDCRAFT CENTER

Patricia Seekamp
P.O. Box 589, 411 Church St.
Guilford, CT 06437
Phone: (203)453-5947
Fax: (203)453-6237
First show: 1957
Shows per year: 2
Times of year: Third week in July; November-December
Location: At the address above. Indoor and outdoor.
Duration: Th-Sat
Attendance: 20,000
Admission: $5 in July; free in November-December
Categories: Fine crafts, wearable art, jewelry, wooden crafts, stained glass items, needlework crafts, hand blown glass items, home decor, dolls/stuffed animals/toys, pottery/ceramics, leather crafts, baskets, metal
Price range: $10-3,000
Advertising/Promotion: Major tri-state newspaper, magazines; national craft magazines; newsletters; radio. $11,000 per show budget.
Spaces available: 135. 10' × 12' booths. Electricity and security, as well as tents for the outdoor show, are provided.
Cost of space: $360
Application process: Shows are juried. For consideration, provide slides (5) and written description of work. $5 charge to apply.

THE HANDMADE IN AMERICA SHOW

Gordon T. Gattone
251 Creekside Dr.
St. Augustine, FL 32086
Phone: (904)797-2600
Fax: (904)797-4357
E-mail: hia@mallshow.com
Website: http://www.mallshow.com
First show: 1970
Shows per year: 32
Times of year: Year round
Location: FL, NY, NJ, MD, CT, PA, OH.
   Indoor. Malls, enclosed shopping cen-
   ters and hotels.
Duration: 5 or 10 days
Admission: Free
Categories: Fine crafts, wearable art,
   jewelry, miniatures/dollhouses,
   wooden crafts, paper products, stained
   glass items, needlework crafts, hand
   blown glass items, home decor, figu-
   rines, dolls/stuffed animals/toys, pot-
   tery/ceramics, nature crafts/floral,
   leather crafts, baskets, recycled crafts,
   sculpture
Price range: $10-10,000
Advertising/Promotion: Radio, newspaper, some TV and Internet
Spaces available: 25-50 per show. As
   much space as needed is provided.
   Displays must meet criteria and are
   furnished by exhibitor.
Cost of space: $350-600
Application process: Shows are juried.
   For consideration, provide photos or
   slides (4 of product and one of display). No charge to apply.
Additional information: Each show is
   professional and well organized. No
   imports are allowed and you will not
   have to compete with manufactured or
   mass produced merchandise. Members receive a newsletter with updates,
   new shows and survey results on past
   show performance.

HARVEST FESTIVAL

Exhibit Sales Dept.
601 N. McDowell
Petaluma, CA 95454
Phone: (707)778-6300; (800)321-1213
   (outside California)
First show: 1972
Shows per year: 15
Times of year: September-December

Location: AZ, CA, OR, NV. Indoor.
   Convention centers.
Duration: F 12-8, Sat 10-8, Sun 10-6
Attendance: 15,000-20,000
Admission: Varies
Categories: Fine crafts, wearable art,
   jewelry, miniatures/dollhouses,
   wooden crafts, paper products, stained
   glass items, needlework crafts, hand
   blown glass items, home decor, dolls/
   stuffed animals/toys, pottery/ceram-
   ics, leather crafts, baskets, sculpture
Price range: $1-3,000
Advertising/Promotion: Major daily
   newspapers, radio and TV, direct mail,
   transit posters, exhibitor discount
   cards, promotional fliers, visitor and
   convention listings. $1 million/year
   budget.
Spaces available: 200-380 per show.
   10' × 10' to 10' × 20' spaces. Back
   drops and 500 watts electricity provided.
Cost of space: 10' × 10', $500 and up,
   depending on show
Application process: Shows are juried.
   For consideration, prodive photos or
   slides (6), sample of work if necessary
   and photo of booth and costume/work
   in progress. No charge to apply.
Additional information: Send for application and brochure.

HEART & HOME, INC.

Cliff and Linda Hale
P.O. Box 5146
Morton, IL 61550
Phone: (309)263-0932
First show: 1989
Shows per year: 7
Times of year: April, June, September,
   October, November
Location: Lincoln, Springfield and Peo-
   ria, IL. Indoor and outdoor. Peoria
   shows are held at the Exposition Gar-
   dens Youth Building, Springfield
   shows are held at The Illinois State
   Armory Building, and Lincoln shows
   are held at The Logan County Fair-
   grounds.
Duration: 1 weekend
Attendance: Varies
Admission: $3, children 12 and under
   free
Categories: Fine crafts, wearable art,
   jewelry, miniatures, wooden crafts,

stained glass items, needlework crafts,
   home decor, figurines (carvings),
   dolls (handmade only), pottery, nature
   crafts/floral, leather crafts, baskets,
   sculpture, furniture
Price range: From several dollars to
   $100 plus
Advertising/Promotion: TV, newspapers, radio, fliers, election size posters, large signs, show cards, trade
   journals, free listings wherever possible, direct mailings and any other
   means we can think of. All shows are
   advertised this intensively. Budget
   varies from show to show, but all
   money collected from dealers in the
   form of booth fees is spent on advertising and promoting the shows.
Spaces available: 70-100 per show.
   13' × 8' or 15' × 9'. Electric is available at a nominal price at all shows.
   Chairs are provided at no additional
   charge.
Cost of space: $90-205
Application process: Shows are juried.
   For consideration, provide photos (at
   least 4 of work and 1-2 of booth). Pictures should be clear and current! No
   charge to apply.
Additional information: Our shows are
   top quality shows featuring the very
   best dealers, artisans and folk artists
   we can find. We are also very choosy
   about the variety of the merchandise
   and try not to have too much of the
   same media at any show. No commer-
   cially produced merchandise allowed.

HEART IN HAND FOLK ART SHOWS, INC.

Liz Williams and Carol Jilk
P.O. Box 55
Youngsville, PA 16371
Phone: (814)723-2610; (814)563-4726
First show: 1979
Shows per year: 4
Times of year: March, September, Octo-
   ber, November
Location: Erie, Pittsfield and Mars, PA.
   Indoor and outdoor. Hotel ball-
   rooms—March, October and Novem-
   ber; fairgrounds—September
Duration: 1 weekend (10-5)
Attendance: 1,500-8,000
Admission: $3-4
Categories: Wearable art, jewelry, minia-
   tures/dollhouses, wooden crafts,

stained glass items, needlework crafts, home decor, dolls/stuffed animals/toys, pottery, nature crafts/floral, leather crafts, baskets, traditional folk art

Price range: $5-600

Advertising/Promotion: Newspaper, radio, fliers, trade magazines. All in locations near site. Mailings also done for each show.

Spaces available: 36-120 per show. 8′×10′ at hotel shows, tables available; 10′×12′ at fairgrounds.

Cost of space: $80-180

Application process: Shows are juried. For consideration, provide photos or slides (2 of work and 1 of booth set-up) and written description of work. No charge to apply.

Additional information: No commercial/imports; exhibitors dress in "country" attire.

HEARTLAND CREATIVE

Herbert Adler
16380 Chicago Ave.
Lansing, IL 60438

Phone: (708)895-3710

Fax: (708)895-3200

First show: 1969

Shows per year: Approximately 60

Times of year: January through mid-November

Location: IN, IL, WI, MI; occasionally IA and OH. Indoor and outdoor. Malls, plazas, parks.

Duration: 3-day weekends, mall hours (most shows)

Admission: Free

Categories: Fine crafts, jewelry, miniatures/dollhouses, wooden crafts, paper products, stained glass items, needlework crafts, hand blown glass items, figurines, dolls/stuffed animals/toys, pottery/ceramics, nature crafts/floral, leather crafts, baskets, sculpture

Price range: All ranges

Advertising/Promotion: Print, electronic, billboard. Average of $1,000 per show budget.

Spaces available: 10-100 per show. Booths—approximately 10′×10′—configuration varies due to available space.

Cost of space: $65-135

Application process: Shows are juried.

For consideration, provide photos or slides (3). No charge to apply.

SYLVIA HENRY EXHIBITS (SHE)

Sylvia Henry
7 Tyroconell Ave.
Massapequa Park, NY 11762

Phone: (516)795-2377; (516)795-5915

First show: 1974

Shows per year: 25

Times of year: Year-round

Location: Upstate NY: Kingston; Queens: Bayside, Jamaica; On Long Island: Hicksville, Huntington Station, Lynbrook, Massapequa Park; Hanover, Holyoke, Brockton, Kingston, MA; Trumbull, Milford Enfield, CT; Indoor and outdoor. Most shows are in malls. Other shows are street fairs, parks, Long Island railroad station.

Duration: 5 days in malls; 2 days outdoor shows

Admission: Free

Categories: Fine crafts, wearable art, jewelry, miniatures/dollhouses, wooden crafts, stained glass items, needlework crafts, hand blown glass items, home decor, dolls/stuffed animals/toys, pottery/ceramics, nature crafts/floral, leather crafts, baskets, sculpture

Price range: $5-hundreds

Advertising/Promotion: Newspapers, signs, posters, fliers, etc.

Spaces available: 30-60 per show. Outdoor shows 10′×10′; malls 12′×5′ and 6′ depth and 12′×10′ and 12′.

Cost of space: $90-200 single spaces

Application process: Shows are juried. For consideration, provide photos or slides (4 including display). No charge to apply.

HOWARD HEARTSFIELD GALLERY

Karla Heartsfield
220 Kings Hwy.
Haddonfield, NJ 08033

Phone: (609)428-7373

First show: 1992

Shows per year: 3

Times of year: Thanksgiving and first weekend of spring

Location: Philadelphia, PA. Indoor. In a historic building in a park.

Duration: 1 weekend

Attendance: 10,000

Admission: $4

Categories: Fine crafts, wearable art, jewelry, stained glass items, hand blown glass items, pottery/ceramics, leather crafts, sculputre

Price range: $10-2,000

Advertising/Promotion: TV, radio, newspapers, magazines, mailings

Spaces available: 76 per show. Booths.

Cost of space: $350

Application process: Show are juried. For consideration, provide photos or slides (3). $10 to apply.

HSI SHOW PRODUCTIONS

Patrick Buchen, president
P.O. Box 502797
Indianapolis, IN 46250

Phone: (317)576-9933

Fax: (317)576-9955

First show: 1949

Shows per year: 3

Times of year: March, November

Location: All shows are held at the Indiana State Fairgrounds, Indianapolis, IN, in Expo Hall, West and South pavilions. Indoor.

Duration: 9 days

Attendance: 60,000-85,000

Admission: $6; 12 and under free

Categories: Fine crafts, wearable art, jewelry, miniatures/dollhouses, wooden crafts, paper products, stained glass items, hand blown glass items, home decor, figurines, dolls/stuffed animals/toys, pottery/ceramics, nature crafts/floral, leather crafts, baskets, sculpture

Price range: $1-35,000

Advertising/Promotion: Advertised in area newspapers, radio and TV and in trade show publications. $100,000 budget.

Spaces available: 400. Booths 10′×10′ and up.

Cost of space: $575-700 for 10′×10′ booth

Application process: Shows are invitation only. No charge to apply.

HUFFMAN PRODUCTIONS, INC.

Jim and Donna Huffman
P.O. Box 184
Boys Town, NE 68010-0184

Phone: (402)331-2889

First show: 1983

Shows per year: 6

Times of year: October and November
Location: Sioux Falls, SD; Blaine and Shakopee, MN; Des Moines, IA; Omaha, NE; Chicago, IL. Indoor. In auditoriums.
Duration: 1 weekend
Attendance: 20,000-30,000
Admission: $6 adult; $5 seniors and children 6-12; under 6 free
Categories: Fine crafts, wearable art, jewelry, miniatures/dollhouses, wooden crafts, stained glass items, needlework crafts, home decor, figurines, dolls/stuffed animals/toys, pottery/ceramics, nature crafts/floral, leather crafts, baskets, sculpture
Price range: $5-1,000
Advertising/Promotion: Newspapers, Chamber of Commerce fliers, convention and tourist bureaus listings, TV, radio, discount coupons, posters
Spaces available: 300-400. 8′ × 11′ booths, curtained on 3 sides, no tables provided (so the exhibitors can be more creative with their displays).
Cost of space: $350-450
Application process: Shows are juried. For consideration, provide photos or slides (3). No charge to apply.
Additional information: All shows feature handmade arts and crafts with the actual artist or craftsman present. There are food booths and continuous entertainment.

I.B.S. SHOWS, INC.
Louis I. Shelley, CEM—Show Director
190 NE 199th St. (Ives Dairy Rd.), Suite 203
North Miami Beach, FL 33179-2918
Phone: (305)651-9530; (954)467-7799
Fax: (305)652-2568
First show: 1979
Shows per year: 3+
Times of year: June, December, March
Location: Miami Beach Convention Center adjacent to parking lots, garage parking, valet parking, meter parking. Near hotel district and major thoroughfares. Indoor. Miami Beach Convention Center. In the heart of the Art Deco area near Ocean Dr.
Duration: W-Sun
Attendance: 165,000+
Admission: Adult $3.50, multi-day $5, child 6-12 $1, under 6 free
Categories: Fine crafts, wearable art, jewelry, miniatures/dollhouses, wooden crafts, paper products, stained glass items, needlework crafts, hand blown glass items, home decor, figurines, dolls/stuffed animals/toys, pottery/ceramics, nature crafts/floral, leather crafts, baskets, recycled crafts, sculpture
Price range: $1-150,000
Advertising/Promotion: Newspapers (*The Miami Herald, Ft. Lauderdale Sun Sentinel, Welcome Magazine, Bienvenides, El Nuevo Herald*), out-of-town newspapers in Florida, national trade papers; TV major media buy on NBC, ABC, CBS and local independents; major radio stations (15 stations, AM and FM); outdoor advertising. $.5 million budget.
Spaces available: 1,200 per show. 10′ × 10′ inside booths or corner booths; 10′w × 18′d perimeter booths, block space all available for areas larger than 20′w × 80′d.
Cost of space: Inside booths $550, corner booths $650, perimeter booths $775, plus 6½% tax.
Application process: Past participants have first priority. Open booths are available on a first-come, first-serve basis.
Additional information: Many wholesale sellers and customers attend these retail shows.

JUPITER PRODUCTS
Bob and Judy Grove
P.O. Box 38
Denver, NC 28037
Phone: (704)483-6860
First show: 1985
Shows per year: 25-30
Times of year: March-November
Location: Malls in Niagra Falls, Rotterdam, Rochester, Clay, Binghamton, Albany, Massena, Syracuse, Buffalo, Kingston, Glens Falls and Clifton Park, NY. The Berkshire Mall in Pittsfield, MA. Indoor.
Duration: 5 or 10 days
Admission: Free
Categories: Fine crafts, wearable art, jewelry, miniatures/dollhouses, wooden crafts, paper products, stained glass items, needlework crafts, hand blown glass items, figurines, dolls, pottery/ceramics, nature crafts/floral, leather crafts, baskets, sculpture
Price range: $5 and up
Advertising/Promotion: Newspaper, radio, TV. Malls are paid to do the advertisement.
Spaces available: 40-100 per show (depending on size of mall). 8′ × 10′ single or 8′ × 20′ double. Crafters supply all their own set up.
Cost of space: $170-190 for single spaces (5 day shows)
Application process: Shows are juried. For consideration, provide photos or slides (3). No charge to apply.
Additional information: We promote all mall shows. Send for schedules and rules.

JUST PROMOTIONS
Chuck and Louise Whigham
P.O. Box 6130
Augusta, GA 30916-0331
Phone: (706)796-0331
Fax: (706)771-0696
Shows per year: 27
Times of year: May-December
Location: SC, NC, GA. Indoor. In malls.
Duration: Th-Sun
Attendance: Mall traffic
Admission: Free
Categories: Fine crafts, wearable art, jewelry, miniatures/dollhouses, wooden crafts, paper products, stained glass items, needlework crafts, hand blown glass items, home decor, figurines, dolls/stuffed animals/toys, pottery/ceramics, nature crafts/floral, leather crafts, baskets, recycled crafts, sculpture
Spaces available: 10′ × 10′ to 10′ × 15′ spaces, electricity available.
Cost of space: $110-440
Application process: Past participants have first priority. Open tables are available on a first-come, first-serve basis.

LAKERIDGE WINERY & VINEYARDS
Charles G. Cox
19239 U.S. 27 N.
Clermont, FL 34711
Phone: (352)394-8627
Fax: (352)394-7490
First show: 1990
Shows per year: 6
Times of year: February, June, August, November, December

Location: At above address, approximately 30 minutes from Orlando. Outdoor. Beside the winery—open area with trees, a stage, etc.
Duration: 1 weekend 10-5
Attendance: 8,000-16,000
Admission: Usually $2 donation to charity
Categories: Fine crafts, wearable art, wooden crafts, stained glass items, dolls/stuffed animals/toys, pottery/ceramics, nature crafts/floral, leather crafts, baskets
Price range: $1-500
Advertising/Promotion: 3 newspapers, 2 radio stations, 2 TV stations. $8,000 budget.
Spaces available: 120 per show. 10′×10′ spaces.
Cost of space: $60 including tax
Application process: Shows are juried. For consideration, provide photos or slides (3).
Additional information: All shows have a variety of entertainment.

M-PAC, INC.
Kirk McMinn
P.O. Box 1377
Middleburg, VA 20118
Phone: (540)338-5272
Fax: (540)338-7358
First show: 1991
Shows per year: 5
Times of year: March, August, September, November
Location: Patriot Center, Fairfax, VA; Bethesda, MD. Indoor and outdoor. Convention centers, arenas.
Duration: F-Sun
Attendance: 15,000
Admission: $5.50 for Patriot Center, others are free
Categories: Fine crafts, wearable art, jewelry, miniatures/dollhouses, wooden crafts, stained glass items, needlework crafts, hand blown glass items, home decor, dolls/stuffed animals/toys, pottery/ceramics, nature crafts/floral, leather crafts, baskets, sculpture, fine art
Price range: $10-2,000
Advertising/Promotion: *Washington Post*, local newspapers, radio, TV, press releases, calendar listings, direct mail. Budget varies.

Spaces available: 200-250 per show. 10′×10′ booth space; table/chairs provided by exhibitor.
Cost of space: $285-325
Application process: Shows are juried. For consideration, provide photos or slides (3 of work, 1 of display). No charge to apply.
Additional information: No buy-sell or imports allowed.

MARCHÉ ENTERPRISES, INC.
Marlene Penn, president
P.O. Box 1847
Wheaton, MD 20915
Phone: (301)681-7880
First show: 1977
Shows per year: 20
Times of year: February-October
Location: PA, VA. Indoor.
Duration: 4-5 days
Categories: Fine crafts, wearable art, jewelry, miniatures/dollhouses, wooden crafts, paper products, stained glass items, needlework crafts, home decor, figurines, dolls/stuffed animals/toys, pottery/ceramics, nature crafts/floral, leather crafts, baskets, sculpture
Price range: $5-1,000
Advertising/Promotion: Print
Spaces available: 38-75 per shows. Table tops, booths 10′×8′, 10′×6′, according to placement; also 1½ spaces to 2.
Cost of space: $150-200
Application process: Shows are juried. For consideration, provide photos or slides (3).

K.A. MASHURA PROMOTIONS
Karen Ann Mashura
8004 Monroe Ave.
Munster, IN 46321
Phone: (219)836-5079
First show: 1989
Shows per year: 2-3
Times of year: April and October
Location: Munster, IN. Indoor. High school, Expo Center and other locations.
Duration: 1 weekend, 10-4 and 10-3
Attendance: 3,500
Admission: $1 or free
Categories: Fine crafts, wearable art, jewelry, wooden crafts, needlework

crafts, dolls/stuffed animals/toys, pottery/ceramics, nature crafts/floral, baskets
Price range: $20-250
Advertising/Promotion: Posters, display ads, press releases, cable TV, radio, fliers. $3,000 budget.
Spaces available: 100-200. 8′×10′, 6′×12′, 10′×10′ spaces.
Cost of space: $70-100
Application process: Shows are juried. For consideration, provide photos (3 of work and 1 of display). No charge to apply.
Additional information: Judges give Ribbon Awards 1st, 2nd, 3rd Place in categories of "Fine Arts," "Fine Crafts" and "Crafts."

MILL AVENUE MERCHANT ASSOCIATION
520 S. Mill, Suite 201
Tempe, AZ 85281
Phone: (602)967-4877
Fax: (602)967-6638
Shows per year: 2
Times of year: March and December
Location: South Mill St., Tempe. Outdoor.
Duration: F-Sun, 10-6
Attendance: 250,000
Admission: Free
Categories: Fine crafts, wearable art, jewelry, wooden crafts, paper products, stained glass items, needlework crafts, hand blown glass items, toys, pottery/ceramics, nature crafts/floral, leather crafts, baskets, sculpture, weaving, metalwork
Price range: $5-3,000
Advertising/Promotion: Ads on TV, radio and in print
Spaces available: 600 per show. Rentals available of tables and 10′×10′ tent. 5′×10′, 5′×15′ and 10′×10′ booths. Electricity $25-110.
Cost of space: $260-405
Application process: Shows are juried. For consideration, provide slides (5 of work, 1 of booth display) and written description of work.
Additional information: We provide booth sitters, overnight security and limited parking. We are handicap accessible.

MOSSY CREEK BARNYARD FESTIVALS

Carolyn Chester
106 Anne Dr.
Warner Robins, GA 31093
Phone: (912)922-8265
First show: 1980
Shows per year: 2
Times of year: Third weekend in April and third weekend in October
Location: Four miles north of Perry, GA. Outdoor. In deep piney woods around old homestead buildings, terraced area with natural ampitheater.
Duration: Sat-Sun 10-6
Attendance: 15,000
Admission: $4 adults, $1 children
Categories: Fine crafts, wearable art, jewelry, miniatures/dollhouses, wooden crafts, paper products, stained glass items, needlework crafts, hand blown glass items, home decor, figurines, dolls/stuffed animals/toys, pottery/ceramics, nature crafts/floral, leather crafts, baskets, sculpture
Price range: $5-8,000
Advertising/Promotion: Billboards in middle Georgia and Atlanta area, ads in newspapers and 4 TV stations. 55,000 brochures semiannually distributed at Georgia Tourism visitor centers, travel shows in Florida and Atlanta area. Release sent to 250 newspapers and 20 national periodicals. Budget varies.
Spaces available: 150 per show. 12' × 12' outdoor spaces. Exhibitors provide own canopy and equipment.
Cost of space: $85
Application process: Shows are juried. For consideration, provide photos or slides and catalog/promotional materials. No charge to apply.

MOUNTAIN ARTISANS SHOW PROMOTIONS

Doris Humter
155 N. Womack St.
Franklin, NC 28734
Phone: (704)524-3405
First show: 1987
Shows per year: 2
Times of year: Mid-July and Thanksgiving weekend in November
Location: In the Macon County Community Building 441, south of Franklin, NC. Indoor.

Duration: 2 days
Attendance: 3,000
Admission: $1.50-2
Categories: Fine crafts, wearable art, jewelry, wooden crafts, stained glass items, needlework crafts, dolls/stuffed animals/toys, pottery/ceramics, nature crafts/floral, leather crafts, baskets, sculpture
Price range: $25-150
Advertising/Promotion: Ads in *Ronay Guide, Sunshine Artists, ABC Crafts Guide,* Chamber of Commerce fliers, Welcome Center literature, local papers, regional magazines and papers. $5,000 budget.
Spaces available: 40-70 per show. 10' × 10' spaces, some tables available with building.
Cost of space: $65-95
Application process: Shows are juried. For consideration, provide photos or slides (2). No charge to apply.
Additional information: Crafts must be original work by the artist. No imports, no dealers.

MOUNTAIN HERITAGE ARTS AND CRAFT FESTIVALS

Mary M. Via
P.O. Box 426
Charles Town, WV 25414
Phone: (800)624-0577; (304)725-2055
Fax: (304)728-8307
First show: 1972
Shows per year: 2
Times of year: Second full weekend in June and last full weekend in September
Location: Off U.S. Route 340 between Charles Town and Harpers Ferry in Jefferson County, WV, at San Michael's Park. Outdoor. In sparsely developed park. The park is in various stages of development. The festivals have been held at this location since 1976.
Duration: Fri-Sun 10-6
Attendance: 20-000-25,000
Admission: Adults, $5; children 6-17, $3; under 6 free
Categories: Fine crafts, wearable art, jewelry, wooden crafts, paper products, stained glass items, needlework crafts, hand blown glass items, home decor, figurines, dolls/stuffed animals/

toys, pottery/ceramics, nature crafts/floral, leather crafts, baskets, sculpture
Price range: $1.50-15,000
Advertising/Promotion: Newspapers, magazines, radio and TV. Mostly regional, some national magazine advertising
Spaces available: 190 per show. Most spaces are 8' × 16' under large tents, other sizes available.
Cost of space: $75 plus 15% commission
Application process: Shows are juried. Actual arts and crafts are juried and must be brought, not mailed. No charge to apply.

SALLY MYROM

300 N. Drew St.
Redwood Falls, MN 56283
Phone: (507)637-8473
First show: 1983
Shows per year: 2
Times of year: After Easter and before Mother's Day; Sunday following Thanksgiving
Location: Redwood Falls National Armory, north on Hwy. 101 and Redwood Valley School on Cook St. Indoor. In 100' × 70' open area of Armory, and commons area and hallways of school
Duration: Sun 10-4
Attendance: 1,000-3,000
Admission: Free. Food donations accepted.
Categories: Fine crafts, wearable art, jewelry, miniatures/dollhouses, wooden crafts, paper products, stained glass items, needlework crafts, hand blown glass items, home decor, figurines, dolls/stuffed animals/toys, pottery/ceramics, nature crafts/floral, leather crafts, baskets, recycled crafts, sculpture
Price range: $30-100
Advertising/Promotion: Posters, newspapers and shoppers, radio ads and talk shows, TV. $1,750 budget.
Spaces available: 70-150 per show. Open areas are marked off in dimensions of varying sizes. Tables can be rented. Chairs available at no charge.
Cost of space: 50¢ a square foot
Application process: Dealers are accepted on a first-come, first-serve ba-

sis, as long as they fit the requirements of the show.

Additional information: Area clubs help with food concessions and rent booths to hold fund raisers. Draw people from sixty miles around. Located by Jackpot Junction Casino.

MYSTIC COMMUNITY CENTER

Caroline Degenhardt
P.O. Box 526
Mystic, CT 06355
Phone: (860)536-3575
Fax: (860)536-2049
First show: 1985
Shows per year: 2
Times of year: Memorial Day weekend and the weekend before Thanksgiving
Location: Mystic Community Center, Harry Austin Dr., Mystic. Indoor and outdoor. Inside and on the grounds of a large community center.
Duration: Sat 10-5, Sun 11-4
Attendance: 3,000
Admission: $1-2
Categories: Fine crafts, wearable art, jewelry, wooden crafts, paper products, stained glass items, needlework crafts, hand blown glass items, home decor, figurines, dolls/stuffed animals/toys, pottery/ceramics, nature crafts/floral, leather crafts, baskets, recycled crafts, sculpture
Price range: $5-300
Advertising/Promotion: 7 newspapers, 200 posters, 3,000 postcards, 35 signs on streets and 4,000 newsletters. $6,000-8,000 budget.
Spaces available: 60-105 per show. 8′ × 10′ indoor spaces, 10′ × 10′ open air, outdoor spaces.
Cost of space: $100-125
Application process: Shows are juried. For consideration, provide photos or slides (3 of crafts and 1 of booth set up). No charge to apply.
Additional information: Lots of volunteer assistance available. Large shopping bags provided free to artists. Free use of facility (gym, pool, free weights, tennis and racquetball courts) during shows' off hours. Food available on site. Free RV camper space available.

NATIONAL CRAFTS LTD. (NCL)

Mary F. Clark, director
4845 Rumler Rd.
Chambersburg, PA 17201
Phone: (717)369-4810
Fax: (717)369-5001
First show: 1975
Shows per year: 2
Times of year: Weekend after Columbus Day (October); weekend after Mother's Day (May)
Location: Gaithersburg and Frederick, MD. Indoor and outdoor. Fairgrounds; in buildings and outside.
Duration: F-Sun 10-6
Attendance: 16,000-25,000
Admission: Adults $6, children under 12 free, $1 off coupons available
Categories: Fine crafts, wearable art, jewelry, wooden crafts, paper products, stained glass items, needlework crafts, hand blown glass items, home decor, dolls/stuffed animals/toys, pottery/ceramics, leather crafts, baskets, sculpture, folk art, metal, batik
Price range: All price ranges
Advertising/Promotion: All major media
Spaces available: 325-425 per show. Booths—both indoor/outdoor available; sizes—10′ × 8′, 10′ × 10′, 15′ × 15′; booths are set up and designed by the exhibitor. They must be professional in appearance, sturdy and safe. We do not provide display equipment. Outside booths may set up a tent, canopy, or other form of protection.
Cost of space: $390-780, inside; $300-600, outside
Application process: Shows are juried. For consideration, provide slides (5 of work, 1 of display). $10 charge per show to apply.
Additional information: Shows consistently rated as top craft events in the country and Maryland. Shows feature nationally-known musical entertainment.

NEW ENGLAND CRAFT EXPOSITION, INC.

Dick and Joanne Colello
Box 35
Norwell, MA 02061
Phone: (617)659-2837
First show: 1985
Shows per year: 3
Times of year: Fall

Location: Furnace Brook School, Marshfiled, MA; Holiday Inn Exhibition Hall, Boxboro, MA and Royal Plaza, Marlboro, MA. Indoor. In a hall.
Duration: 1 or 2 days, 10-4
Attendance: 4,000 per day
Admission: $2.50
Categories: Fine crafts, wearable art, jewelry, miniatures/dollhouses, wooden crafts, paper products, stained glass items, needlework crafts, hand blown glass items, home decor, figurines, dolls/stuffed animals/toys, pottery/ceramics, nature crafts/floral, leather crafts, baskets
Price range: $5-500
Advertising/Promotion: Local and regional newspapers, mailings, discount coupons
Spaces available: 100 per show. Booths and tables available for rent.
Cost of space: $90-100 per day
Application process: Shows are juried. For consideration, provide photos or slides (3). No charge to apply.

NORTH EAST PROMOTIONS, INC.

Kristie Gonsalves
274 Silas Deane Highway
Wethersfield, CT 06109
Phone: (860)529-2123
Fax: (860)529-2317
First show: 1983
Shows per year: 10
Times of year: January-March, August, November
Location: Danbury, Hartford and Groton, CT; Providence, RI. Indoor and outdoor. Take place in 3 civic center facilities and 1 fairground.
Duration: 1-4 days
Attendance: 10,000
Admission: $1-6
Categories: Fine crafts, wearable art, jewelry, miniatures/dollhouses, wooden crafts, paper products, needlework crafts, hand blown glass items, dolls/stuffed animals/toys, pottery/ceramics, nature crafts/floral, leather crafts, baskets, sculpture
Price range: $20 and up
Advertising/Promotion: Newspapers, TV, radio, industry publications. $10,000 budget.
Spaces available: 70-125 per show. 10′ × 10′ booth, booth provided at in-

door shows. Canopies may be used at outdoor events.

Cost of space: $125-400

Application process: Shows are juried. For consideration, provide photos or slides (4) and sample of work. No charge to apply.

Additional information: All shows are juried and have high quality items. Exhibitors taken on first come first serve basis, after past participants. Decision is made within two weeks of receiving application.

ODC ENTERPRISES

H. Stevens
1665 W. Fifth Ave.
Columbus, OH 43212
Phone: (614)486-7119
Fax: (614)486-7110
First show: 1977
Shows per year: 5
Times of year: June, November, December, February
Location: Indianapolis, IN; Cleveland, Cincinnati, Columbus, OH. Indoor and outdoor. Convention centers, expo halls.
Duration: 2-4 days
Attendance: 10-30,000
Admission: $5
Categories: Fine crafts, wearable art, jewelry, stained glass items, hand blown glass items, dolls/stuffed animals/toys, pottery/ceramics, leather crafts, baskets, sculpture
Price range: $10-1,000
Advertising/Promotion: Direct mail, print ads, radio, TV. $15,000-40,000 budget.
Spaces available: 200-400 per show. 10′×10′, 10′×15′, 10′×20′.
Cost of space: $200-400
Application process: Shows are juried. For consideration, provide slides (5). $10 charge to apply.

OLDE FASHION PROMOTIONS

Kevin Van Gundy
P.O. Box 1952
Grand Junction, CO 81502
Phone: (970)241-8008
First show: 1977
Shows per year: 10
Times of year: March, April, October-December
Location: CO, UT, NM. Indoor and out-

door. Primarily large event centers.
Duration: 1-2 days
Attendance: 5,000+
Admission: Free
Categories: Fine crafts, wearable art, jewelry, miniatures/dollhouses, wooden crafts, paper products, stained glass items, needlework crafts, hand blown glass items, home decor, figurines, dolls/stuffed animals/toys, pottery/ceramics, nature crafts/floral, leather crafts, baskets, recycled crafts, sculpture
Price range: $1-5,000
Advertising/Promotion: TV, radio, print, signs, direct mail. 25% of sales budget.
Spaces available: Average of 100 per show. 8′×10′ booths.
Cost of space: $49-249
Application process: Past participants have first priority. Open tables are available on a first-come, first-serve basis.
Additional information: These are fun and profitable shows.

PA DESIGNER CRAFTSMEN

Kristy Wasielewski
10 Stable Mill Trail
Richboro, PA 18954
Phone: (215)579-5997
Fax: (215)504-0650
E-mail: pacrafts@aol.com
First show: 1946
Shows per year: 6
Times of year: May-November
Location: Shawnee-on-the-Delaware, Lancaster, PA and Tyler State Park in Richboro, PA; Winterthur, DE. Indoor and outdoor. Mostly on fairgrounds, in parks. The Lancaster shows are held in a sports complex.
Duration: 2-4 days
Attendance: 20,000
Admission: $5
Categories: Fine crafts, wearable art, jewelry, miniatures/dollhouses, wooden crafts, paper products, stained glass items, hand blown glass items, figurines, dolls/stuffed animals/toys, pottery/ceramics, leather crafts, baskets, sculpture
Price range: Varies
Advertising/Promotion: Fliers, newspaper inserts, billboards
Spaces available: 100-300 per show.

8′×10′ or 10′×12′ spaces. Exhibitors must provide their own booth or tent with backdrop.
Cost of space: $175-350
Application process: Shows are juried. For consideration, provide slides (3).
Additional information: We are a non-profit organization and in order to participate in the shows a person must be a member of the Pennsylvania Guild of Craftsmen and pass a jury process. For information about the guild, please see the listing in the Trade Organizations chapter of this book.

PACIFIC FINE ART FESTIVALS

Judy Cunningham
P.O. Box 280
Pine Grove, CA 95665
Phone: (209)296-1195
Fax: (209)296-4395
First show: 1980
Shows per year: 25
Times of year: Last weekend of March through last weekend of October
Location: Brawley, Belmont, Menlo Park, San Francisco, Walnut Creek, Foster City, Monterey, Los Altos, Oakland, Tahoe and San Carlos, CA. Outdoor. In parks, downtown sidewalks, shopping area sidewalks and on closed streets.
Duration: 2 or 3 days
Attendance: 25,000
Admission: Most are free
Categories: Fine crafts, wearable art, jewelry, wooden crafts, paper products, stained glass items, hand blown glass items, home decor, figurines, dolls/stuffed animals/toys, pottery/ceramics, nature crafts/floral, leather crafts, baskets, recycled crafts, sculpture. Not all are accepted at all shows.
Price range: $10-10,000
Advertising/Promotion: Newspapers, magazines, theater screens, rapid transit video messages, radio, TV, posters, postcard invitations. Budget varies.
Spaces available: 25-300 per show. No equipment provided; only ground space.
Cost of space: $75-115, plus 10% or flat fee (at some) of $250
Application process: Shows are invitation only.

PRAIRIE FLOWER ASSOCIATES

Barbara Wynne and Janice Dunlop
P.O. Box 109
Webb City, MO 64870
Phone: (417)782-1780; (417)835-4683
First show: 1983
Shows per year: 13
Times of year: March, July-November
Location: Kansas City and St. Joseph, MO; Overland Park, KS; Westminster and Aurora, CO. Indoor. All are in malls.
Duration: Th-Sun
Admission: Free
Categories: Fine crafts, jewelry, miniatures/dollhouses, wooden crafts, paper products, stained glass items, needlework crafts, hand blown glass items, home decor, figurines, dolls/stuffed animals/toys, pottery/ceramics, nature crafts/floral, leather crafts, baskets, sculpture
Price range: Broad range
Advertising/Promotion: TV, radio and newspaper. Budget varies.
Spaces available: 50-100 per show. Smallest space is $10' \times 6'$. Larger availalbe in 5 ft. increments ($15' \times 6'$, $20' \times 6'$, etc). Exhibitor furnishes their own table or art screens.
Cost of space: Smallest booths range from $110-120.
Application process: Shows are juried. Number is liminted in each category. For consideration, provide photos (2 of work and 1 of display). No charge to apply.

PREMIER PROMOTIONS

Sally Kaczynski
197 Kenton Place
Hamburg, NY 14075-4309
Phone: (716)646-1583
Fax: (716)648-4912
E-mail: salkay@aol.com
First show: 1983
Shows per year: 5-6
Times of year: May, June, September, November
Location: Amherst, Orchard Park and Hanburg, NY. Indoor and outdoor. Site varies from parks and fairgrounds to museums and colleges.
Duration: 1 weekend
Attendance: 10,000
Admission: $3-5
Categories: Fine crafts, wearable art, jewelry, miniatures/dollhouses, wooden crafts, paper products, stained glass items, needlework crafts, home decor, figurines, dolls/stuffed animals/toys, pottery/ceramics, nature crafts/floral, leather crafts, baskets, sculpture
Price range: $1-1,000
Advertising/Promotion: Radio, TV, all print media, fliers, street signs, craft magazines. $10,000-30,000 budget.
Spaces available: 100-300 per show. All booths from $10' \times 6'$ to $10' \times 20'$.
Cost of space: $135-650
Application process: Shows are juried. For consideration, provide photos or slides (5) and written description of work. No charge to apply.
Additional information: We are committed to producing quality shows and bringing the best possible event to the public and profitabilities to our vendors.

QUALITY GIFT SHOWS

John Myers
619 Meadows Dr. E
Richland, WA 99352
Phone: (800)762-1101; (509)627-1854
Fax: (509)627-4995
First show: 1988
Shows per year: 3
Times of year: March and November
Location: Spokane and Kennewick, WA. Indoor. Convention centers.
Duration: 3 days
Attendance: 15,000-20,000
Admission: $4
Categories: Fine crafts, wearable art, jewelry, miniatures/dollhouses, wooden crafts, paper products, stained glass items, needlework crafts, hand blown glass items, home decor, figurines, dolls/stuffed animals/toys, pottery/ceramics, nature crafts/floral, leather crafts, baskets, recycled crafts, sculpture
Price range: $1-1,000
Advertising/Promotion: Radio, TV, billboards, newspapers, counter coupons. $30,000 (market dpeendant) budget.
Spaces available: 175 per show. Draped both sides and back (8' high), electricity, overhead light, and company sign, aisles carpeted.
Cost of space: $375-475
Application process: Shows are juried.
For condsideration, provide photos or slides (5). No charge to apply.
Additional information: Vendors are required to decorate booths with Christmas greenery and lights and be in a "turn-of-the-century" costume.

QUOTA INTERNATIONAL OF PORT ARUTHUR, TEXAS

Dot Lunceford
P.O. Box 2151
Port Arthur, TX 77643
Phone: (409)962-1725
Fax: (409)727-7226
First show: 1982
Shows per year: 2
Times of year: Second weekend in November and the weekend before Easter
Location: Port Arthur Civic Center. Indoor.
Duration: Sat-Sun
Attendance: 5,000
Admission: Free
Categories: Fine crafts, wearable art, jewelry, miniatures/dollhouses, wooden crafts, paper products, stained glass items, needlework crafts, home decor, figurines, dolls/stuffed animals/toys, pottery/ceramics, nature crafts/floral, leather crafts, baskets
Price range: $1 and up
Advertising/Promotion: Newspapers, TV, radio, crafters magazines, street banners, fliers. $800 budget.
Spaces available: 100-141 per show. $8' \times 10'$ and $10' \times 10'$; electricity on request. No backdrop provided. One table and all chairs provided.
Cost of space: $75-85
Application process: Shows are invitation only.

R&M PROMOTIONS, INC.

Judy Bartlett
P.O. Box 587
Quinton, VA 23141
Phone: (804)932-8721; (800)891-6971
Fax: (804)932-3886
First show: 1995
Shows per year: 5
Times of year: Spring and Fall
Location: Richmond and Hampton, VA. Indoor. Fairgrounds and coliseum.
Duration: 3 days
Attendance: 8,000-10,000
Admission: $4.50-5.50

Categories: Fine crafts, stained glass items, needlework crafts, hand blown glass items, home decor, figurines, pottery/ceramics, baskets, sculpture

Price range: $50 and up

Advertising/Promotion: Newsprint, radio and TV. Minimum of $20,000 budget.

Spaces available: 100 per show. $10' \times 8'$ and $10' \times 10'$ spaces.

Cost of space: $130-150

Application process: Shows are juried. For consideration, provide photos or slides (3) and written description of work. No charge to apply.

Additional information: All fine art and craft shows are held in conjunction with other shows, such as home shows, interior design shows, etc.

RENAISSANCE CRAFT TABLES

Barbara Baroff
541 Woodland Dr.
Radnor, PA 19087

Phone/Fax: (610)687-8535

First show: 1985

Shows per year: 12-20

Times of year: March-May and July-November

Location: Towsen, MD; Philadelphia, Willow Grove, Amblen and Valley Forge, PA; Haddonfield and Loveladies, NJ. Indoor and outdoor. Take place at malls, main streets art centers, synagogues and schools.

Duration: 2 or 3 day weekend

Attendance: Varies

Admission: Free to $6

Categories: Fine crafts, wearable art, jewelry, wooden crafts, paper products, stained glass items, hand blown glass items, home decor, figurines, dolls/stuffed animals/toys, pottery/ceramics, nature crafts/floral, leather crafts, baskets, recycled crafts, sculpture

Price range: $5-100

Advertising/Promotion: Direct mail, radio and print. Budget varies.

Spaces available: 50-200 per show. $10' \times 10'$ otudoor and $10' \times 8'$ indoor spaces.

Cost of space: $75-200

Application process: Shows are juried. For consideration, provide photos or slides (4). $10 charge to apply (for most shows).

Additional information: My shows vary greatly.

BILL RIGGINS PROMOTIONS, INC.

Linda Renfroe
1403 W. Glen Ave.
Peoria, IL 61614

Phone: (309)692-7238

Fax: (309)692-7254

First show: 1978

Shows per year: 40-60

Times of year: Year-round

Location: IL, IA, OK. Indoor and outdoor. Malls, convention centers, parks.

Duration: 2-3 days

Attendance: 2,000-10,000

Admission: Free-$2

Categories: Fine crafts, wearable art, jewelry, miniatures/dollhouses, wooden crafts, paper products, stained glass items, needlework crafts, hand blown glass items, home decor, figurines, dolls/stuffed animals/toys, pottery/ceramics, nature crafts/floral, leather crafts, baskets, recycled crafts, sculpture

Price range: $1-300

Advertising/Promotion: Direct mail, TV, newspaper, signage, fliers, public service announcements and show handouts. Budget depends on the size of the show.

Spaces available: 30-200 per show. We rent space only. Exhibitors provide their own display. Tables, electricity, skirting and chairs are available for rent at some convention centers.

Cost of space: Booths fees are $25-235 depending on location of show.

Application process: Shows are juried. For consideration, provide photos or slides (4), catalog/promotional materials and written description of work. No charge to apply.

COOKIE ROSE PRODUCTIONS

Cookie Rose
12 Evergreen Dr.
Sherman, CT 06784

Phone: (860)355-9080

First show: 1993

Shows per year: 8-12

Times of year: March-May, October-December

Location: Indoor. Banquet halls, conference centers, colleges, etc.

Duration: 1 day

Attendance: 1,500-2,000

Admission: $1, some shows free

Categories: Fine crafts, wearable art, jewelry, miniatures/dollhouses, wooden crafts, paper products, stained glass items, needlework crafts, hand blown glass items, home decor, figurines, dolls/stuffed animals/toys, pottery/ceramics, nature crafts/floral, leather crafts, baskets, recycled crafts, sculpture

Price range: $1-200, average $10

Advertising/Promotion: Major and local newspapers, posters in local area, over 5,000 hand-out coupons for admission given to local merchants. Budget varies with each show.

Spaces available: Average 50 per show. Average space size $8' \times 8'$. All spaces are open with electric available at additional cost. Tables and chairs available at some locations; must notify first before show.

Cost of space: $65-75 for $8' \times 8'$

Application process: Shows are juried. For consideration, provide photos or slides (1-2). No charge to apply.

ROSE SQUARED PRODUCTIONS, INC.

Howard Rose
12 Galaxy Ct.
Belle Mead, NJ 08502-3836

Phone: (908)874-5247

Fax: (908)874-7098

E-mail: hgrose@aol.com

First show: 1982

Shows per year: 8

Times of year: May, June, September, October

Location: Indoor and outdoor. Parks, downtowns.

Duration: 1 weekend

Attendance: 12,000

Admission: Free

Categories: Fine crafts, wearable art, jewelry, wooden crafts, paper products, stained glass items, hand blown glass items, home decor, dolls/stuffed animals/toys, pottery/ceramics, leather crafts, baskets, recycled crafts, sculpture

Price range: $20-500

Advertising/Promotion: 4-color postcards, direct mail, major newspapers (*New York Times, Star Ledger*), billboards. Budget varies.

Spaces available: 140 per show.
10′ × 12′ booths usually.

Cost of space: $210 approximately

Application process: Shows are juried.
For consideration, provide photos or
slides (4) and booth photo. No charge
to apply.

ST. ROBERT PARISH

Carolyn Zorn
626 Muirland Dr.
Flushing, MI 48433
Phone: (810)659-2501; (810)659-3293
First show: 1978
Shows per year: 2
Times of year: March and December
Location: The Activity Building at St.
Robert Parish on Henry St., down-
town, Flushing. Indoor.
Duration: Sat 9-4
Attendance: 1,000
Admission: Free
Categories: Fine crafts, wearable art,
jewelry, wooden crafts, paper prod-
ucts, stained glass items, hand blown
glass items, home decor, figurines,
dolls/stuffed animals/toys, pottery/ce-
ramics, nature crafts/floral, leather
crafts, baskets, sculpture
Price range: $5-200
Advertising/Promotion: Banner over
Main Street; church bulletins; all area
radio stations; TV, *Catholic Weekly*
newspaper; *Flint Journal*; *Flushing
Observer*; 5 free-standing wood signs
at street intersections. Budget varies.
Spaces available: 125 per show. 8′ table
and 2 chairs or 8′ × 5½′ space and 2
chairs.
Cost of space: $35
Application process: Past participants
have first priority. Open tables are
available on a first-come, first-serve
basis.
Additional information: We provide
hostesses, kitchen phone, restrooms,
speedy check-in tables. Set up time is
7-9AM only on day of show. Sponsored by St. Robert Council of Catholic Women.

SAVANNAH WATERFRONT ASSOCIATION

Rick Lott and Leslie Goethe
P.O. Box 572
Savannah, GA 31402
Phone: (912)234-0295
Fax: (912)234-4904

First show: 1960
Shows per year: 14
Times of year: March-December
Location: Riverfront Plaza, Savannah.
Outdoor.
Duration: Some 3 day, most 1 day
Attendance: 5-10,000 (1 day); 100,000-
400,000 (3 day)
Admission: Free
Categories: Fine crafts, wearable art,
jewelry, wooden crafts, stained glass
items, needlework crafts, hand blown
glass items, dolls/stuffed animals/
toys, pottery/ceramics, nature crafts/
floral, leather crafts, baskets, sculpture
Price range: $1-several hundred
Advertising/Promotion: Locally and regionally—Savannah, Atlanta, Chalr-
eston, Jacksonville, Columbia, Macon. $500-10,000 budget.
Spaces available: 80-100 per show. Provide space only (10′ × 10′); can acco-
modate tables and canopies.
Cost of space: $75 (1 day); $200 (3 day)
Application process: Dealers are accepted on a first-come, first-serve basis, as long as they fit the requirements
of the show.

JANN SEVERIT PROMOTIONS, INC.

Jann or Cara
P.O. Box 9
Freeburg, IL 62243
Phone: (618)539-3395
Fax: (618)539-4734
First show: 1982
Shows per year: 30
Times of year: Year-round
Location: IL, IA, WI, MO, KY. Indoor.
Convention centers, fairgrounds, expo
buildings, civic centers, schools.
Duration: 1 weekend
Attendance: 3,500-14,000
Admission: Free-$3
Categories: Fine crafts, wearable art,
jewelry, miniatures/dollhouses,
wooden crafts, paper products, stained
glass items, hand blown glass items,
home decor, dolls/stuffed animals/
toys, pottery/ceramics, nature crafts/
floral, leather crafts, baskets, sculpture
Price range: $5-300 and up
Advertising/Promotion: Radio, TV,
newspapers, postcards, posters, fliers,
billboards, signs, national publica-

tions. Budget depends on each show.
Spaces available: 70-350 per show.
Booth spaces. 8′ × 10′, 8′ × 15′,
8′ × 20′, 10′ × 10′, 10′ × 15′,
10′ × 20′.
Cost of space: $100-400
Application process: Shows are juried.
For consideration, provide photos or
slides (3). No charge to apply.

SHOWCASE PRODUCTIONS, INC.

Valerie Smith
P.O. Box 91369
Portland, OR 97291
Phone: (503)526-1080
Fax: (503)526-0685
First show: 1984
Shows per year: 4
Times of year: First weekends in May
and November
Location: Denver, CO; Portland and Eu-
gene, OR; Tulsa, OK; Ft. Wayne, IN;
Columbus, OH. Indoor. Shows are
held in the convention centers or simi-
lar facility.
Duration: 3-4 days
Attendance: 15,000-40,000
Admission: $4-6.50
Categories: Fine crafts, wearable art,
jewelry, miniatures/dollhouses,
wooden crafts, paper products, stained
glass items, needlework crafts, hand
blown glass items, home decor, figurines, dolls/stuffed animals/toys, pot-
tery/ceramics, nature crafts/floral,
leather crafts, baskets, sculpture
Price range: $2-800
Advertising/Promotion: Newspaper, TV,
fliers, trade publications, radio.
$60,000-85,000 budget.
Spaces available: 400 per show.
10′ × 10′ booth space with 8′ drapes,
back wall and 3′ sides.
Cost of space: Varies, no commission
Application process: Past participants
have first priority. Open booths are
available on a first-come, first-serve
basis, as long as they fit our requirements. For consideration, provide
photos or slides (3). No charge to
apply.

SHOWTIQUES, LTD.

Steven Tashman
P.O. Box 592
Jericho, NY 11753
Phone: (516)681-1176
First show: 1991

Shows per year: 30
Times of year: Year-round
Location: Long Island, NY. Indoor and outdoor. Main streets, parks, hotels, catering establishments, colleges.
Duration: 1 weekend, 11-6
Admission: Outdoor, free; indoor, $3.50 ($2.50 with coupons)
Categories: Fine crafts, wearable art, jewelry, miniatures/dollhouses, wooden crafts, paper products, stained glass items, needlework crafts, hand blown glass items, home decor, figurines, dolls/stuffed animals/toys, pottery/ceramics, nature crafts/floral, leather crafts, baskets, recycled crafts, sculpture
Price range: $5-500
Advertising/Promotion: Newspapers, radio, TV, posters/cards, signs, local publications, trade publications
Spaces available: 100+. Outdoor—booths 10'×10'; indoor—booths 10'×10' and 10'×8', chairs, tables, electricity.
Cost of space: Outdoor—$65 for one day; $100 for weekend. Indoor—$115-150.
Application process: Shows are juried. For consideration, provide photos or slides (3 of work and 1 of display). No charge to apply.

SOHO ANTIQUES FAIR, COLLECTIBLES & CRAFTS

P.O. Box 337
Garden City, NY 11530
Phone: (212)682-2000; (203)227-4858
Fax: (516)742-4424; (203)454-3576
First show: 1992
Shows per year: 52
Times of year: Year-round, every Saturday and Sunday
Location: Outdoor. The shows take place in a large corner parking lot at the corner of Broadway and Grand St. in New York City.
Duration: 1 weekend each, 9-5
Attendance: 8,000-10,000 per day
Admission: Free
Categories: Fine crafts, wearable art, jewelry, wooden crafts, paper products, home decor, figurines, dolls/stuffed animals/toys, pottery/ceramics, baskets, recycled crafts
Price range: $1-1,000
Advertising/Promotion: Sunshine Artist,

Newtown Bee, New York Times, Hudson Valley Antiquer, Treasure Chest, prior show promotional catalogue, City Guide-New York, various guide books for NY. Budget varies.
Spaces available: 80 per show. Approximately 8'×12', 12'×12', 20'×20'. Tables are available for rental at $10 per day.
Cost of space: Prices are per day, $70-120.
Application process: Dealers are accepted on a first-come, first-serve basis, as long as they fit the requirements of the show. Past participants have first priority. Open tables are available on a first-come, first-serve basis.

SUE STOOKEY

P.O. Box 65151
West Des Moines, IA 50265
Phone/Fax: (515)277-8958
First show: 1991
Shows per year: 11
Times of year: January-March, May, August-November.
Location: Living History Farms, South Ridge Mall and Merle Hay Mall, Des Moines; Westdale Mall, Cedar Rapids; North Grand Mall, Ames, IA. Indoor and outdoor.
Duration: 2-4 days
Admission: Free
Categories: Fine crafts, wearable art, jewelry, miniatures/dollhouses, wooden crafts, paper products, stained glass items, needlework crafts, home decor, dolls/stuffed animals/toys, pottery/ceramics, nature crafts/floral, leather crafts, baskets, sculpture
Price range: $10-300
Advertising/Promotion: Local newspapers, radio, 3 TV stations, fliers, press releases, posters
Spaces available: 100 per show. 10'×10' spaces.
Cost of space: $100-170
Application process: Shows are juried. For consideration, provide photos or slides (3 of work, 2 of display).

SUNBELT EXPO

Jill Bergeron
P.O. Box 28
Tifton, GA 31793
Phone: (912)387-7944
Fax: (912)387-7503

Shows per year: 2
Times of year: Second weekend in November and third weekend in March
Location: Spence Field, 290 G. Harper Blvd., Moultrie, GA. Indoor and outdoor. Has excellent exhibit areas in new buildings with paved parking and walking areas. Site of Sunbelt Ag Expo.
Duration: Sat 9-5, Sun 10-5
Attendance: 10,000-25,000
Admission: $3
Categories: Fine crafts, wearable art, jewelry, miniatures/dollhouses, wooden crafts, paper products, stained glass items, needlework crafts, home decor, figurines, dolls/stuffed animals/toys, pottery/ceramics, nature crafts/floral, leather crafts, baskets
Advertising/Promotion: TV, radio, newspapers, direct mail, posters, billboards.
Spaces available: 300-400 per show. Inside booths 10'×8'; outside booths 12'×12'.
Cost of space: $55
Application process: Shows are juried. For consideration, provide photos or slides (1-2). $55 charge (cost for exhibit space) to apply.
Additional information: Exhibitors always report very good sales and almost always return.

SWEET LAVENDER CREATIONS

Marcia E. Banholzer
28 Deerfield Lane
Upper Saddle River, NJ 07458
Phone: (201)327-8842
First show: 1986
Shows per year: 2
Times of year: March, April, November, December
Location: Goetschius House Museum, Upper Saddle River and Bishop House, Saddle River. Indoor. Booth sites are historic homes listed on the U.S. Historic Registry and located on Main thoroughfares.
Duration: Spring: 15-20 days; holiday: 25-32 days
Attendance: 400-1,000
Admission: $3 per ticket. Each ticket is good for 3 visits.
Categories: Fine crafts, wearable art, jewelry, miniatures/dollhouses, wooden crafts, paper products, stained

glass items, needlework crafts, hand blown glass items, home decor, figurines, dolls/stuffed animals/toys, pottery/ceramics, nature crafts/floral, baskets, recycled crafts, sculpture

Price range: $1-375

Advertising/Promotion: Publications such as *Crafts Marketplace*; 17 local newspapers and shoppers in a tri-state area; 6,000 invitations to customer mailing list, posters and fliers distributed throughout locale; show goer guides, etc. $2,800 per show budget.

Spaces available: All merchandise is taken on consignment. There are between 200 and 250 crafters represented at each show. We decorate the historic houses with merchandise taken from crafters.

Cost of space: $35 application fee; 25% commission on sales.

Application process: Shows are juried. For consideration, provide photos or slides, catalog/promotional materials and sample of work.

Additional information: The historic settings of the houses provide a very charming ambiance for the boutiques. We have a reputation for fine quality and creativity in the merchandise we offer to our client base.

TENNESSEE ASSOCIATION OF CRAFT ARTISTS

P.O. Box 120066
Nashville, TN 37212
Phone: (615)665-0502
First show: 1972
Shows per year: 3
Times of year: May, September, October
Location: Centennial Park, Nashville and Riverfront Parkway, Chattanooga. Outdoor.
Duration: F-Sun 10-6
Attendance: 12,000-45,000
Admission: Free-$5
Categories: Fine crafts, wearable art, jewelry
Price range: $15-500
Advertising/Promotion: Ads in newspapers, local bus bench boards, radio ads. $12,000 per show budget.
Spaces available: 100-170 per show. 12' × 12' and 12' × 18' spaces; no electricity; security; printed program with artists' addresses.
Cost of space: $250

Application process: Shows are juried. For consideration, provide slides (5). $15 charge to apply.

LINDA TOLEDO EVENT MANAGING

Linda Toledo
29630 Road 44
Visalia, CA 93291
Phone: (209)651-0706
Fax: (209)582-0854
First show: 1984
Shows per year: 3
Times of year: Weekend before Mother's Day, weekend before Halloween and Thanksgiving weekend
Location: Tulare Co. Fairgrounds, Tulare, and Kings Co. Fairgrounds, Hanford, CA. Indoor. Inside buildings of fairgrounds.
Duration: 3 days
Attendance: May—2,500; Oct—1,000; November—7,300
Admission: May and October $2; November $3
Categories: Fine crafts, wearable art, jewelry, miniatures/dollhouses, wooden crafts, paper products, stained glass items, needlework crafts, hand blown glass items, home decor, figurines, dolls/stuffed animals/toys, pottery/ceramics, nature crafts/floral, leather crafts, baskets
Price range: $3-500
Advertising/Promotion: Newspaper ads, radio, 4' × 8' road sings, 3M boards, fliers, counter cards, posters, TV. Budget depends on show—each show is different.
Spaces available: 200-250 per show. Sell in 10' × 10' increments.
Cost of space: $97.50-107.50
Application process: Dealers are accepted on a first-come, first-serve basis, as long as they fit the requirements of the show.
Additional information: I produce fine quality shows with very professional advertising. I have a staff of people who have been with me from the start and they are very good in helping me take very good care of our exhibitors and our visitors. We strive to run a very professional event and work on improvements constantly.

TOP NOTCH CRAFTS, INC.

April Ackerman
P.O. Box 689
Blairstown, NJ 07825
Phone: (908)362-5006
Fax: (908)362-5850
E-mail: topnotch@vitinc.com
First show: 1980
Shows per year: 25
Times of year: Year-round
Location: Embassy Suites hotels in Piscataway and Parsippany, NJ; Ledgewood Mall, Ledgewood, NJ; Phillipsburg Mall, Phillipsburg, NJ; Hackettstown Mall, Hackettstown, NJ; Blairstown St. Festival and 4th of July festival, Blairstown, NJ; Sugar Loaf, NY craft festivals. Indoor and outdoor. Hotels, malls, main streets.
Duration: Weekends
Attendance: Average 10,000
Admission: Free
Categories: Fine crafts, wearable art, jewelry, miniatures/dollhouses, wooden crafts, paper products, stained glass items, needlework crafts, hand blown glass items, home decor, figurines, dolls/stuffed animals/toys, pottery/ceramics, nature crafts/floral, leather crafts, baskets, recycled crafts, sculpture
Price range: $1-1,000
Advertising/Promotion: Regional newspapers, cable TV, radio, our craft directory, Internet. $100,000 budget.
Spaces available: 75-200 per show. Booths.
Cost of space: $50-425
Application process: Shows are juried. For consideration, provide photos or slides (3) and written description of work. No charge to apply.

TOWN OF OCCOQUAN CRAFT SHOWS

Bobbie Frank
P.O. Box 258
Occoquan, VA 22125
Phone: (703)491-2168
Fax: (703)491-4962
First show: 1969
Shows per year: 2
Times of year: First weekend in June and the last full weekend in September
Location: In the streets of the historic district of Occoquan. Outdoor. The tents are set up in the streets which are closed to vehicular traffic. Shuttle

buses run from satelite parking lots.

Duration: Sat-Sun 10-6

Attendance: 200,000

Admission: Free

Categories: Fine crafts, wearable art, jewelry, miniatures/dollhouses, wooden crafts, paper products, stained glass items, needlework crafts, hand blown glass items, home decor, figurines, dolls/stuffed animals/toys, pottery/ceramics, nature crafts/floral, leather crafts, baskets, recycled crafts, sculpture, fine art, photography

Price range: $5-300

Advertising/Promotion: The shows are heavily advertised in Washington, DC newspaper, Richmond newspapers and papers in VA, MD, and DC, TV, 3 radio stations, magazines (national and local).

Spaces available: 410 per show. 10' × 10' spaces.

Cost of space: $250

Application process: Shows are juried. For consideration, provide photos or slides (4) and written description of work. No charge to apply.

UNITED CRAFT ENTERPRISES

Cheryl Sherman

Box 326

Masonville, NY 13804

Phone: (607)265-3230

Fax: (607)265-3792

First show: 1980

Shows per year: 8

Times of year: March-May, September-December

Location: Pennsauken and Flemington, NJ; Wrightstown, and King of Prussia, PA; Syracuse, NY. Indoor and outdoor. Major fairgrounds or exhibit centers.

Duration: 2-3 days

Attendance: 25,000

Admission: $5

Categories: Fine crafts, wearable art, jewelry, miniatures/dollhouses, wooden crafts, paper products, stained glass items, needlework crafts, hand blown glass items, home decor, figurines, dolls/stuffed animals/toys, pottery/ceramics, nature crafts/floral, leather crafts, baskets, sculpture

Price range: $20-2,000

Advertising/Promotion: Newspapers,

magazines, radio, TV, billboard, direct mail

Spaces available: 200-300 per show. 8' × 10' or 10' × 10' booths.

Cost of space: $230-380

Application process: Shows are juried. For consideration, provide slides (5 of work and 1 of display). No charge to apply.

VERMONT CRAFT EXPO

Peggy Mowle

River Road, HCR 65

Killington, VT 05751

Phone: (802)422-3783

First show: 1981

Shows per year: 3

Times of year: Last weekend in July, first weekend in October and Thanksgiving weekend

Location: Pico Base Lodge and Resort (Rt. 4), Sunrise MT Lodge (Junctions 4 & 100) and Cortina Inn (Rt. 4), Killington, VT. Indoor and outdoor. Ski lodges, outdoor areas, courtyards, tent and greens. Thanksgiving weekend conference and banquet center.

Duration: 1 weekend

Attendance: 8,000

Admission: Free

Categories: Fine crafts, wearable art, jewelry, miniatures/dollhouses, wooden crafts, paper products, stained glass items, needlework crafts, hand blown glass items, home decor, dolls/stuffed animals/toys, pottery/ceramics, nature crafts/floral, leather crafts, baskets, sculpture

Price range: $5-150

Advertising/Promotion: Inserts in *MT Times Paper*, plus 2 other newspapers. Live remote for each show from a local radio station (radio station ads week of shows). 15,000 fliers and posters at all Welcome Centers and Chamber of Commerce and all tourist attractions in central VT, press releases mailed statewide to all newspapers, tourist papers and magazines. $4,000 budget.

Spaces available: 80 per show. Booth spaces from 8' × 6', 4' × 12', or 8' × 10', indoor; 10' × 10', outdoor; 10' × 6', tent.

Cost of space: $155-185

Application process: Shows are juried. For consideration, provide photos or

slides (5). $10 charge to apply (one-time only).

Additional information: Foilage show voted one of VT's top ten fall events by VT Chamber of Commerce two years in a row.

VIRGINIA CRAFT FESTIVALS

Sharon Pierce and Michael McCullough

P.O. Box 310

Cashtown, PA 17310

Phone: (717)337-3060

Fax: (717)337-3138

First show: 1986

Shows per year: 6

Times of year: March, April, June, August-October

Location: Annandale (DC area), Williamsburg, Virginia Beach, VA and Bethesda, MD. Indoor. College/school campus, convention center.

Duration: 1 weekend, 10-6

Attendance: 5,000

Admission: $5-6

Categories: Fine crafts, wearable art, jewelry, needlework crafts, home decor, baskets, sculpture, folk art (authentic)

Price range: $10-5,000

Advertising/Promotion: Direct mail (colored postcards); radio; newspaper—*Washington Post, Richmond Times, Virginia Pilot*; regional magazines. $10,000-12,000/show budget.

Spaces available: 100 per show. Booths—10' × 10', 10' × 15', 10' × 20'. All booths are piped and draped (neutral colors).

Cost of space: $300-900 (varies with show)

Application process: Shows are juried. For consideration, provide photos or slides (4) plus one of booth setup. $10 charge to apply.

Additional information: Shows are of traditional and contemporary work. April Williamsburg show—traditional and folk art only. September show (DC area)—clothing/jewelry/accessories.

VIRGINIA MOUNTAIN CRAFTS GUILD

Kathy Hudson

P.O. Box 1369

Salem, VA 24153

Phone: (540)389-6163

First show: 1978

Shows per year: 3

Times of year: April; Labor Day weekend; first weekend in November

Location: Salem Civic Center, Salem; Claytor Lake State Park, Dublin, VA. Indoor and outdoor.

Duration: 1 weekend

Attendance: 15,000

Admission: $2

Categories: Fine crafts, wearable art, jewelry, miniatures/dollhouses, wooden crafts, paper products, stained glass items, needlework crafts, hand blown glass items, home decor, figurines, dolls/stuffed animals/toys, pottery/ceramics, nature crafts/floral, leather crafts, baskets, sculpture

Price range: $1-1,000

Spaces available: 70-110 per show. 10'×10', 11'×11', 15'×10', 16½'×11', 20'×10', 22'×11'; electricity available.

Cost of space: Start at $115 and $140 for members of guild; and $140 and $165 for non-members.

Application process: Show are juried. For consideration, provide slides (5), one slide must be of booth. $5 charge to apply.

VIRGINIA SHOW PRODUCTIONS

Patricia Wagstaff

P.O. Box 305

Chase City, VA 23924

Phone: (804)372-3996

Shows per year: 3-4

Times of year: October, November, March

Location: Manassas and Richmond, VA. Indoor and outdoor. Held at the Prince William County Fairgrounds and The Manassas Armory, The Showplace Armory and The Showplace Exhibition Center.

Duration: 3-4 days

Attendance: 20,000-40,000

Categories: Fine crafts, wearable art, jewelry, miniatures/dollhouses, wooden crafts, paper products, stained glass items, needlework crafts, hand blown glass items, home decor, dolls/stuffed animals/toys, pottery/ceramics, nature crafts/floral, leather crafts, baskets, sculpture, ironwork, reproduction furniture

Advertising/Promotion: Newspapers, trade magazines, radio, direct mail, TV, billboards

Spaces available: 200-450 per show. 8'×10' indoor, 10'×10' outdoor spaces; 10'×10' booths.

Cost of space: $250-350

Application process: Shows are juried. For consideration, provide photos or slides. No charge to apply.

Additional information: There is no commission on sales. The shows have been rated in *Sunshine Artist Magazine*'s "The Nation's Top 200 Best Traditional Craft Shows." The 1995 Virginia Christmas Show was rated as the 4th Best Traditional Craft Show in the nation by *Sunshine Artist.*

WASHINGTON SQUARE OUTDOOR ART EXHIBIT, INC.

Margot J. Luftig, executive director

115 East 9th St., 7C

New York, NY 10003

Phone: (212)982-6255

Fax: (212)982-6256

First show: 1931

Shows per year: 2

Times of year: Memorial Day weekend and the following weekend. Labor Day weekend and the following weekend.

Location: Greenwich Village, New York City. Outdoor. On the streets of Greenwich Village, near Washington Square Park.

Duration: Each show 5 days; 2 weekends

Attendance: 250,000

Categories: Fine crafts, jewelry, wooden crafts, stained glass items, hand blown glass items, pottery/ceramics, leather crafts, sculpture

Advertising/Promotion: Advertised in the *New York Times*. Promoted in New York metropolitan area mass print and broadcast media, plus art and craft magazines, photography magazines and travel and tourist publications.

Spaces available: 250 per show. Booths are 10'×4½'.

Cost of space: $225

Application process: Shows are juried. For consideration, provide slides (5). $10 charge to apply.

WHALE'S EYE

John and Suzanne Rocanello

653 Orleans Rd., Box 153

N. Chatham, MA 02650

Phone: (508)945-3084

First show: 1973

Shows per year: 12

Times of year: July, August, September, November

Location: Chatham, Dennis and Yarmouth, MA. Outdoor. Chatham Main St.; Dennis Rte 6A, Dennisport Rte. 28; Yarmouth, Station Ave., D/Y Regional High

Duration: 2 days

Attendance: 2,000-5,000

Admission: Free

Categories: Fine crafts, wearable art, jewelry, wooden crafts, paper products, stained glass items, hand blown glass items, home decor, dolls/stuffed animals/toys, pottery/ceramics, nature crafts/floral, leather crafts, baskets, recycled crafts, sculpture

Price range: $10-500

Advertising/Promotion: Newspaper, radio, posters. $500 budget.

Spaces available: 50-100 per show. 10'×10'. Craftsmen supply own displays.

Cost of space: $60-110

Application process: Shows are juried. For consideration, provide photos or slides (6 or more), catalog/promotional materials and written description of work.

WISCONSIN FESTIVALS, INC.

Karie Bennett or Loring Talsky

9312 W. National Ave.

West Allis, WI 53227-1542

Phone: (414)321-2100

Fax: (414)321-4169

First show: 1969

Shows per year: 7

Times of year: March, April, July, September-December

Location: Wisconsin State Fair Park, 8100 W. Greenfield Ave., West Allis. Indoor. Fairgrounds' 3 building exhibit center.

Duration: 1 weekend

Attendance: 21,000

Admission: Adults $4, children 6-12 $1, under 6 free

Categories: Fine crafts, wearable art,

jewelry, miniatures/dollhouses, wooden crafts, paper products, stained glass items, needlework crafts, hand blown glass items, home decor, dolls/stuffed animals/toys, pottery/ceramics, nature crafts/floral, leather crafts, baskets, sculpture

Price range: $10-600

Advertising/Promotion: Wisconsin and Illinois areas newspapers, Chamber of Commerce, media ticket-give-aways, radio and TV, tour sites/centers, hotel/motel/restaurant associations, tour brochures, magazines, entertainment books, state tour publications and postcards/fliers/posters. $30,000 per show budget.

Spaces available: 400 per show. 10' × 10' spaces, electric, tables.

Cost of space: Varies

Application process: Shows are juried. For consideration, provide photos (5). Must be over 18 years to exhibit. No charge to apply.

Additional information: Family entertainment is also featured.

WISHING WELL PRODUCTIONS

Debra Giusti
P.O. Box 7040
Santa Rosa, CA 95407
Phone: (707)575-9355
Fax: (707)542-3845
First show: 1976
Shows per year: 2
Times of year: Second weekend in June, first 2 weekends of December
Location: The Sonoma County Fairgrounds in Santa Rosa. Indoor and outdoor.
Duration: 1 weekend
Attendance: 35,000
Admission: $4-10
Categories: Fine crafts, wearable art, jewelry, miniatures/dollhouses, wooden crafts, paper products, stained glass items, needlework crafts, hand blown glass items, home decor, figurines, dolls/stuffed animals/toys, pottery/ceramics, nature crafts/floral, leather crafts, baskets, recycled crafts, sculpture, environmental products, new age spiritual products
Price range: $1 to hundreds
Advertising/Promotion: TV, radio,

newspapers, magazines, posters, fliers, mailers, word of mouth

Spaces available: 200-over 500 per show. Booths only. Average size is 10' × 10', there are also 8' × 10' spaces available. Outdoor booths only have space. Tables, canopies and side walls are available for rental. Indoor booths can access electricity.

Cost of space: $35-750

Application process: Past participants have first priority, the rest are juried. For consideration, provide photos or slides (4) and written description of work.

Additional information: Ongoing entertainment throughout the faire, from local to national performers. Strolling vendors in costume and strolling musicians.

WOODWILL CORPORATION

Julianne R. Williams
P.O. Box 5186
Hauppauge, NY 11788
Phone: (516)234-4183
First show: 1970
Shows per year: 22
Times of year: February-November
Location: NY, NJ and CT. Indoor and outdoor. Malls, outdoor on main street and convention center.
Duration: 3-5 days
Admission: Free-$4
Categories: Fine crafts, jewelry, miniatures/dollhouses, wooden crafts, stained glass items, needlework crafts, home decor, dolls/stuffed animals/toys, pottery/ceramics, nature crafts/floral, leather crafts, baskets, sculpture
Price range: $5-4,500
Advertising/Promotion: Newspaper, radio, posters, mailing lists. For convention center—$22,000 budget; malls do the advertising for mall shows.
Spaces available: 60-350 per show. Malls: 12' × 4' to 5' deep, 12' × 8' to 10' deep, 24' × 4' to 5' deep; outdoor: 12' × 3' or 10' × 10'; convention center: 10' × 10', 10' × 15', 10' × 20', etc.
Cost of space: $75-300
Application process: Shows are juried. For consideration, provide photos (2). No charge to apply.

WSBA/WARM 103

Gina M. Koch
P.O. Box 910
York, PA 17402-0619
Phone: (717)764-1155; (717)393-1155
Fax: (717)252-4708; (717)252-0991
First show: 1984
Shows per year: 5
Times of year: February, April, July, October, December
Location: Memorial Hall, York Fairgrounds, 334 Carisle Rd., York. Indoor.
Duration: 1 day
Attendance: 4,000-7,000
Admission: $3
Categories: Fine crafts, wearable art, jewelry, miniatures/dollhouses, wooden crafts, paper products, stained glass items, needlework crafts, hand blown glass items, home decor, figurines, dolls/stuffed animals/toys, pottery/ceramics, nature crafts/floral, leather crafts, baskets, sculpture
Price range: $20-500
Advertising/Promotion: Craft magazines and publications, newspapers, radio, direct mail. Budget varies.
Spaces available: 250-325. 10' × 10' booth spaces; 10' × 20' spaces; tables and electric can be rented.
Cost of space: $85 for a 10' × 10'
Application process: Past participants have first priority. Open tables are available on a first-come, first-serve basis.

Wholesale

COUNTRY FOLK ART SHOWS, INC.

8393 E. Holly Rd.
Holly, MI 48442
Phone: (810)634-4151; (810)634-4153
Fax: (810)634-3718
First show: 1983
Shows per year: Over 50
Times of year: Year-round
Location: Nationwide. Indoor. Mostly on fairgrounds and convention centers and halls.
Duration: F 5-9, Sat 10-5, Sun 10-4
Attendance: 8,000
Admission: F $6; Sat and Sun $5
Categories: Fine crafts, wearable art, jewelry, miniatures/dollhouses, wooden crafts, paper products, stained

glass items, needlework crafts, hand blown glass items, home decor, dolls/stuffed animals/toys, pottery/ceramics, nature crafts/floral, leather crafts, baskets, ragrugs

Price range: $2-290 and up

Advertising/Promotion: Billboards, signs, print ads, TV, radio and mailing list for customers (postcards and show fliers); *Country Folk Art Magazine* and *Quick N Easy Magazine*. $10,000-25,000 budget.

Spaces available: 125-300. Booth—(3-sided room setting) a minimum requirement of 6 ft. in height. Need a business/booth identication sign. Booth sizes: 10′×10′, 10′×15′, 10′×20′, 10′×25′, 10′×30′.

Cost of space: $380-420 for a 10×10 booth—good for all 3 days

Application process: Shows are juried. For consideration, provide photos (6), sample of work, written description of work. $20 to apply.

Additional information: We are the leading folk art craft shows in the nation featuring hundreds of outstanding artisans across the country. Country Folk also produces retail shows.

HSI SHOW PRODUCTIONS

Patrick Buchen, president
P.O. Box 502797
Indianapolis, IN 46250

Phone: (317)576-9933

Fax: (317)576-9955

First show: 1949

Shows per year: 3

Times of year: September

Location: All shows are held at the Indiana State Fairgrounds, Indianapolis, IN, in Expo Hall, West and South pavilions. Indoor.

Duration: 1 day

Attendance: 3,000

Admission: $20 member of State Florist Assn., $30 non-member

Categories: Fine crafts, wearable art, jewelry, miniatures/dollhouses, wooden crafts, paper products, stained glass items, hand blown glass items, home decor, figurines, dolls/stuffed animals/toys, pottery/ceramics, nature crafts/floral, leather crafts, baskets, sculpture

Price range: $1-35,000

Advertising/Promotion: Advertised in area newspapers, radio and TV and in trade show publications. $100,000 budget.

Spaces available: 400. Booths 10′×10′ and up.

Cost of space: $400 for 10′×10′ booth

Application process: Shows are invitation only. No charge to apply.

Additional Information: HSI also produces retail shows.

OFFINGER MANAGEMENT CO.

Stephanie Sordelet
1100-H Brandywine Blvd.,
P.O. Box 2188
Zanesville, OH 43702-2188

Phone: (614)452-4541

Fax: (614)452-2552

First show: 1930

Shows per year: 27

Times of year: January-October

Location: Columbus, OH; Louisville, KY; Birmingham, England; Dusseldorf, Germany; Chicago, IL; Baltimore, MD; Mexico City, Mexico; Sydney, Australia; Anaheim, Pomona, CA; Philadelphia, PA; New York, NY; Las Vegas, NV. Indoor. Hotels and convention centers.

Duration: 3 days

Attendance: Varies by show: from 1,500-12,000

Categories: Fine crafts, wearable art, jewelry, miniatures/dollhouses, wooden crafts, paper products, stained glass items, needlework crafts, home decor, figurines, dolls/stuffed animals/toys, pottery/ceramics, nature crafts/floral, leather crafts, baskets, recycled crafts, holiday and seasonal items

Price range: Varies

Advertising/Promotion: Various trade publications. Budget varies.

Spaces available: Booths

Cost of space: Varies

Application process: Point system or first come, first served. Varies per show.

PHILADELPHIA MARKET OF AMERICAN CRAFT

Barbara Bateman
The Rosen Group
3000 Chestnut Ave., Suite 300
Baltimore, MD 21211

Phone: (410)889-2933

Fax: (410)889-1320

Shows per year: 2

Times of year: February and late July/early August

Location: Philadelphia, PA. Indoor. At the Pennsylvania Convention Center.

Duration: 4 days

Admission: $15 (includes subscription to *Niche* magazine)

Categories: Fine crafts, wearable art, jewelry, wooden crafts, paper products, stained glass items, hand blown glass items, home decor, pottery/ceramics, leather crafts, sculpture

Price range: $2-2,000

Advertising/Promotion: Craft publications, gift publications, jewelry publications, direct mail, promotional pieces and stickers provided to exhibitors

Spaces available: 1,500 per show. 10′×10′ and larger.

Cost of space: $1,065 and up

Application process: Shows are juried. For consideration, provide slides (5 of work, 1 of booth).

Additional information: Exhibitors are selected for the design, quality and uniqueness of the work to be shown, as well as for their ability to service wholesale accounts in a timely and professional manner.

WESTERN EXHIBITORS

Mary Jane Craig
2181 Greenwich St.
San Francisco, CA 94123

Phone: (415)346-6666

Fax: (415)346-4965

First show: 1986

Shows per year: 2

Times of year: January/February and August

Location: Seattle, WA. Indoor. Washington State Convention and Trade Center, downtown, central Seattle.

Duration: 4½ days, 9-6 and 9-12

Admission: Free

Categories: Fine crafts, wearable art, jewelry, miniatures/dollhouses, wooden crafts, paper products, stained glass items, needlework crafts, hand blown glass items, home decor, figurines, dolls/stuffed animals/toys, pottery/ceramics, nature crafts/floral, leather crafts, baskets, recycled crafts, sculpture

Price range: Wide range

Advertising/Promotion: Major gift and craft trade magazines. Extensive budget.

Spaces available: 80 per show. Booths include 8' draped tables, 2 chairs, carpet, 500 watt outlet, free transportation to and from shipping dock, booth sign, ad in show directory, promotional stickers and postcards.

Cost of space: $1,200

Application process: Shows are juried. For consideration, provide photos or slides, catalog materials and deposit.

WSBA/WARM 103

Gina M. Koch
P.O. Box 910
York, PA 17402-0619
Phone: (717)764-1155; (717)393-1155
Fax: (717)252-4708; (717)252-0991
First show: 1984
Shows per year: 2
Times of year: March, September
Location: Memorial Hall, York Fairgrounds, 334 Carisle Rd., York. Indoor.
Duration: 2 days
Attendance: 4,000-7,000
Admission: $3
Categories: Fine crafts, wearable art, jewelry, miniatures/dollhouses, wooden crafts, paper products, stained glass items, needlework crafts, hand blown glass items, home decor, figurines, dolls/stuffed animals/toys, pottery/ceramics, nature crafts/floral, leather crafts, baskets, sculpture
Price range: $20-500
Advertising/Promotion: Craft magazines and publications, newspapers, radio, direct mail. Budget varies.
Spaces available: 250-325. 10' × 10' booth spaces; 10' × 20' spaces; tables and electric can be rented.
Cost of space: $400 for a 10' × 10'
Application process: Past participants have first priority. Open tables are available ton a first-come, first-serve basis.
Additional Information: WSBA/WARM 103 also produces retail shows.

ORGANIZERS
Retail

ALLIED ARTS ANNUAL SIDEWALK SHOW

Allied Arts Association
Mr. and Mrs. Joseph P. Fleming, directors
171 Kranichwood St.
Richland, WA 99352
Phone: (509)627-0556
First show: 1950
Time of year: Last full weekend of July
Location: Beautiful Howard Amon Park on the Columbia River. Outdoor. A beautiful and pleasant atmosphere. In consideration of the artists, as this is high desert dry country, we follow the tree line in setting up booths.
Duration: F 9-9, Sat 9-7
Attendance: 45,000
Admission: Free
Categories: Fine crafts, wearable art, jewelry, miniatures/dollhouses, wooden crafts, paper products, stained glass items, hand blown glass items, home decor, figurines, dolls/stuffed animals/toys, pottery (hand thrown only, no greenware), nature crafts/floral, leather crafts, baskets, sculpture
Price range: $1-10,000
Advertising/Promotion: Besides listings in approximately 50 catalogs, directories etc., we use newspaper, reader boards, TV, radio and ads in community newsletters, etc. Also PSAs, since this is an annual fund raiser for our Art Center and we are a not-for-profit organization. We are also included in some of the national advertising with our Water Follies Events, and we do advertise out of the area. This show has a great annual following built over the many years.
Spaces available: 260 spaces (about 50 are shared so artists are actually about 315 each year). 15' × 15' are marked out on the grass. We have many single and end rows that allow some extra spreading out.
Cost of space: $20 registration fee, and 15% of sales commission.
Application process: Show is juried. For consideration, provide slides (7 of work, 1 of display) and general description of art/craft for jurors on registration card. $10 charge to apply.
Additional information: This show has consistently grown in sales. 1996

sales were over $490,000. As a non-profit group (95% of which are artists themselves), we try to accomodate and make things pleasant for the artists. We are very organized and do set definite rules, which we have found makes the show run very smoothly and minimizes any problems.

AMERICA'S LARGEST CHRISTMAS BAZAAR

Susan Martin Rice
4001 NE Halsey #5
Portland, OR 97232
Phone: (503)282-0974
Fax: (503)282-2953
First show: 1982
Time of year: Thanksgiving weekend and the following weekend
Location: Portland Expo Center, 2060 N. Marine Dr., Portland. Indoor. Over 5 acres indoors at the Portland Fairgrounds, 3 buildings, all attached.
Duration: 6 days: Thanksgiving weekend and following weekend
Attendance: 47,000
Admission: Adults $4, many discounts
Categories: Wearable art, jewelry, wooden crafts, paper products, stained glass items, needlework crafts, home decor, figurines, dolls/stuffed animals/toys, pottery/ceramics, nature crafts/floral, leather crafts, baskets, candles
Price range: $1-200
Advertising/Promotion: All major TV and radio stations, large newspapers (display ads), direct mail to 80,000 previous buyers, posters, exhibitors postcards (120,000). Involved in community projects (canned food drives, toy drive). Over $100,000 budget.
Spaces available: 1,150. Booths 10' × 10', larger in increments of 10'. They include 1 bare 8' table, 500 watts of electricity, chairs, cloth backdrop and booth signs.
Cost of space: $295 for 10'; deduct 5% if all products are 100% handcrafted.
Application process: Past participants have first priority, and any remaining tables are available on a first-come, first-serve basis.
Additional information: We have a huge selection of gifts, handcrafts, art, foods and novelties.

AMISH ACRES ARTS & CRAFTS FESTIVAL

Richard Pletcher
1600 West Market St.
Nappanee, IN 46550
Phone: (219)773-4188
Fax: (219)773-4180
First show: 1962
Time of year: Second full weekend in August
Location: Amish acres at the above address. Outdoor. On grass surrounding pond at Amish Acres Historic Farm.
Duration: Th-Sat 9-8, Sun 10-5
Attendance: 70,000
Admission: $5
Categories: Fine crafts, wearable art, jewelry, miniatures/dollhouses, wooden crafts, paper products, stained glass items, needlework crafts, hand blown glass items, home decor, figurines, dolls/stuffed animals/toys, pottery/ceramics, nature crafts/floral, leather crafts, baskets, recycled crafts, sculpture
Advertising/Promotion: 35 newspapers, 5 TV network stations, 3 cable companies, 20 radio stations, 500,000 brochures
Spaces available: 320. 12' × 15' booths.
Cost of space: $100 plus 10% commission
Application process: Show is juried. For consideration, provide slides (4). Request application. $100 charge (refundable).
Additional information: 32nd best traditional craftshow in US, according to *Sunshine Artist.*

ANDALUSIA B.P.W. ARTS AND CRAFTS SHOW

Glinda K. Simmons
Rt. 5, Box 983
Andalusia, AL 36420
Phone: (334)222-3365; (334)222-4121
Time of year: First Saturday in December
Location: Kiwanis Fair Ground facility on South bypass in Andalusia. Indoor.
Duration: Sat 9-4
Attendance: 350-400
Admission: $1 (6 years and under are free)
Categories: Fine crafts, wearable art, jewelry, miniatures/dollhouses, wooden crafts, paper products, stained glass items, needlework crafts, home decor, figurines, dolls/stuffed animals/toys, pottery/ceramics, nature crafts/floral, leather crafts, baskets
Price range: $1 and up
Advertising/Promotion: Local newspapers, TV stations and local radio stations. State handouts for craft shows in visitation centers.
Spaces available: 40-50. 10' × 10' with electricity if needed. No tables or backdrops furnished.
Cost of space: $30
Application process: Dealers are accepted on a first-come, first-serve basis, as long as they fit the requirements of the show.

ARKANSAS VALLEY ARTS AND CRAFTS FAIR

Roy Aday
P.O. Box 1122
Russellville, AR 72811
Phone: (501)229-4200
First show: 1970
Time of year: End of September or beginning of October
Location: John E. Tucker Coliseum, Arkansas Technical University. Indoor.
Duration: F-Sat 10-8, Sun 12-5
Attendance: 12,000
Admission: Free
Categories: Fine crafts, wearable art, jewelry, miniatures/dollhouses, wooden crafts, paper products, stained glass items, needlework crafts, hand blown glass items, home decor, figurines, dolls/stuffed animals/toys, pottery/ceramics, nature crafts/floral, leather crafts, baskets, sculpture
Price range: $1-100
Advertising/Promotion: Magazines, posters, radio, TV. $2,500 budget.
Spaces available: 188. Floor space.
Cost of space: $75
Application process: Show is juried. For consideration, provide photos or slides (3). No charge to apply.
Additional information: 95% returns.

ART & CRAFT BOUTIQUE

Sisterhood of Congregation Beth El/
Esther Dansky
1200 Fairfield Woods Rd.
Fairfield, CT 06432
Phone: (203)372-2208
Fax: (203)374-4962
First show: 1990
Time of year: Fall
Location: Congregation Beth El at above address. Indoor. Takes place in upwardly mobile suburban community. Main thoroughfare street.
Duration: Sun 10-4
Attendance: 1,600-1,700
Admission: $2
Categories: Fine crafts, wearable art, jewelry, wooden crafts, paper products, stained glass items, hand blown glass items, home decor, figurines, dolls/stuffed animals/toys, pottery/ceramics, nature crafts/floral, leather crafts, baskets, recycled crafts, sculpture
Price range: $10-500
Advertising/Promotion: Paid advertising in 20 newspapers; PSAs on radio and TV, calendar listings and press releases sent to over 200 publications; wooden sandwich boards, 150-200 directional signs, library displays of artisans work; press releases on individual crafters go to both Fairfield and New Haven counties. $2,500 budget.
Spaces available: 45. 8' × 8' booth space, table available for rent, and limited electricity and 2 chairs available at no charge.
Cost of space: $60
Application process: Show is juried and invitational. For consideration, provide photos or slides (3), catalog/promotional materials and written description of work. No charge to apply.
Additional information: No kits, crafts must be handmade by exhibitor, lunch is available, no commission.

ASSUMPTION COLLEGE VOLUNTEERS' CRAFT FAIR

Priscilla McGarry
Assumption College
500 Salisbury St.
Worcester, MA 01615-0005
Phone: (508)767-7203
Fax: (508)756-1780
First show: 1981
Time of year: First weekend in October
Location: Laska Gym, Assumption College. Indoor. On campus, in the gym.
Duration: Sat 9-5
Attendance: 4,000
Admission: $1

Categories: Fine crafts, wearable art, jewelry, miniatures/dollhouses, wooden crafts, paper products, stained glass items, needlework crafts, hand blown glass items, home decor, figurines, dolls/stuffed animals/toys, pottery/ceramics, nature crafts/floral, leather crafts, baskets, recycled crafts, sculpture

Price range: $5-100

Advertising/Promotion: All college brochures and quarterly magazines, local newspapers, banners, posters, local TV and radio station stations, local magazines

Spaces available: 85. 8' × 10' sizes spaces, 8' tables available to rent, electricity available.

Cost of space: $100

Application process: Show is juried. For consideration, provide photos (4) and catalog/promotional materials. No charge to apply.

AUDUBON HOLIDAY FAIR

Audubon Naturalist Society
Sara Jane Rodman
8940 Jones Mill Rd.
Chevy Chase, MD 20815
Phone: (301)652-9188, ext. 3020
First show: 1970
Time of year: First weekend of December
Location: At above address. Indoor and outdoor. 40 acre nature sanctuary in residential neighborhood. 20,000 sq. ft. of heated, carpeted tents on site around historic mansion headquarters.
Duration: F 7-10, Sat-Sun 10-5
Attendance: 5,000
Admission: $20 on Friday (under 12 $10); $5 on Saturday and Sunday (under 12 free)
Categories: Fine crafts, wearable art, jewelry, wooden crafts, paper products, stained glass items, needlework crafts, hand blown glass items, home decor, figurines, dolls/stuffed animals/toys, pottery/ceramics, nature crafts/floral, leather crafts, baskets, recycled crafts, sculpture
Price range: $1-1,000
Advertising/Promotion: Paid ads and direct event listings in area papers; radio PSAs; 50,000 promotional brochures and posters

Spaces available: 125. 8' × 8'; 10' × 12' booths.

Cost of space: $300-550

Application process: Show is juried. For consideration, provide photos or slides (5), catalog/promotional materials, written description of work and completed application. $10 charge to apply.

Additional information: Work is selected that fits organization's mission. Features children's crafts area, live animal exhibit, holiday greens sale, gourmet foods, music and entertainment.

BIRMINGHAM ART IN THE PARK

Common Ground
7 South Perry St.
Pontiac, MI 48342
Phone: (810)456-8150
Fax: (810)456-8147
First show: 1974
Time of year: First weekend in September
Location: Shain Park in downtown Birmingham. Outdoor. Between the library and municipal building. The surrounding streets are Bates, Martin, Merrill and Henrietta.
Duration: Sat 10-6, Sun 10-5
Attendance: 65,000-70,000
Admission: Free
Categories: Fine crafts, wearable art, jewelry, wooden crafts, paper products, stained glass items, hand blown glass items, pottery/ceramics, leather crafts, baskets, sculpture
Price range: $15-10,000
Advertising/Promotion: Free and paid media (print, radio and TV), trade publications, area stores, mailing to organization patrons and past show patrons. $13,000 budget.
Spaces available: 156. 10' × 10' booth space, no electricity.
Cost of space: $250
Application process: Show is juried. For consideration, provide slides only (5). $15 charge to apply.
Additional information: All proceeds from the show go to support the programs of Common Ground, a 24-hour crisis service center. Live entertainment both days, food vendors from area restaurants, children's art area.

BROWN COUNTY WINTER ARTS & CRAFT SHOW

Joan Haab
7965 E. Rinnie Seitz Rd.
Nashville, IN 47448
Phone: (812)988-7920
First show: 1984
Time of year: Thanksgiving weekend
Location: Seasons Lodge and Conference Center, US 46 West, Nashville, IN. Indoor.
Duration: F-Sat 10-5
Attendance: 1,700
Admission: $1
Categories: Fine crafts, wearable art, jewelry, miniatures/dollhouses, wooden crafts, paper products, stained glass items, needlework crafts, dolls/stuffed animals/toys, pottery/ceramics, nature crafts/floral, leather crafts, baskets, photography
Price range: $10-200
Advertising/Promotion: Local and Indianapolis newspapers, radio stations covering 75 mile area, craft magazines and *Midwest Living*, Indiana events and travel fliers, etc. $3,000 budget.
Spaces available: 45. Booth areas approximately 9' × 10', tables and electric available.
Cost of space: $70
Application process: Show is juried. For consideration, provide photos or slides (3). $70 charge to apply.
Additional information: Features locally made arts and crafts. High quality only. No kits or molds used.

CAPITOL HILL PEOPLE'S FAIR

Capitol Hill United Neighborhoods, Inc. (CHUN)
Judy McElwain
1490 Lafayette St., #201
Denver, CO 80218
Phone: (303)837-1839
Fax: (303)830-1782
First show: 1971
Time of year: First weekend in June
Location: Civic Center Park in downtown Denver, (Colfax and Broadway are the 2 cross streets). Outdoor. Large downtown park.
Duration: Sat 10-7, Sun 10-6
Attendance: 300,000
Categories: Fine crafts, wearable art,

jewelry, wooden crafts, paper products, stained glass items, needlework crafts, hand blown glass items, pottery/ceramics, nature crafts/floral, leather crafts, baskets, recycled crafts, sculpture

Price range: $10-200

Advertising/Promotion: Ads in *Denver Post* and *Rocky Mountain News*, coverage on all area radio and TV stations on days of event.

Spaces available: 350. 10′ × 10′ booth space. Exhibitor brings own booth or tables.

Cost of space: $265-300

Application process: Show is juried. For consideration, provide slides (4). No charge to apply.

Additional information: No commercial, manufactured or imported items. There are 500 booths on site and they include a mix of food, arts and crafts and entertainment on six stages. *Sunshine Artist* named this show #40 in Fine Arts and #52 in Fine Crafts in 1996.

CHASCO CRAFT SHOW

New Port Richey Community Cooperative, Inc.
P.O. Box 622
New Port Richey, FL 34656
Phone: (813)842-8066
Fax: (813)841-4575
First show: Mid 1970s
Time of year: Mid-March
Location: Orange Lake in downtown New Port Richey. Outdoor. By lake, around natural sector, next to park.
Duration: Sat 10-5, Sun 10-4
Attendance: 20,000
Admission: Free
Categories: Wearable art, jewelry, miniatures/dollhouses, wooden crafts, paper products, stained glass items, needlework crafts, hand blown glass items, home decor, figurines, dolls/stuffed animals/toys, pottery/ceramics, nature crafts/floral, leather crafts, baskets

Price range: $25-100

Advertising/Promotion: In newspaper, Fiesta program—this craft show is part of a 10-day heritage event, fliers, posters, TV, radio. Advertising budget is part of the $27,000 advertising budget for the Chasco Fiesta.

Spaces available: 100. 10′ × 10′ spaces only. No electricity, may bring quiet generator if necessary.

Cost of space: $60

Application process: A 700 mailing list, plus we solicit applications, then newspapers on first-come, first-serve basis.

Additional Information: Chasco has sponsored the Chasco Fiesta event since 1922.

CHERRY BLOSSOM ARTS & CRAFTS FAIR

Allen Freeman
794 Cherry St.
Macon, GA 31201
Phone: (912)751-7429
Fax: (912)751-7408
First show: 1995
Time of year: March
Location: Central City Park, Macon. Indoor and outdoor.
Duration: F-Sat 10-8, Sun 10-6
Attendance: 25,000
Admission: Free
Categories: Wearable art, jewelry, wooden crafts, paper products, stained glass items, needlework crafts, home decor, dolls/stuffed animals/toys, pottery/ceramics, nature crafts/floral, leather crafts, baskets, sculpture

Price range: $15-30

Advertising/Promotion: *Sunshine Artists* and *Ronay Guide*

Spaces available: 80-100. Provide your own booth. Space inside is 16′ × 16′, outside is 12′ × 10′.

Cost of space: Inside $70, outside $60

Application process: Show is juried. For consideration, provide photos and complete list of items to be sold. No charge to apply.

CLEVELAND'S CHRISTMAS CONNECTION, INC.

Donna Sanfilippo and Ginger Palmer
P.O. Box 45395
Westlake, OH 44145
Phone: (216)835-9627
Fax: (216)356-1091
First show: 1986
Time of year: The weekend before Thanksgiving
Location: International Exposition Center (IX), 6200 Riverside Dr., Brook Park, OH. Indoor. In exhibition hall.
Duration: F-Sat 10-10, Sun 10-6

Attendance: 60,000
Admission: $7.50
Categories: Fine crafts, wearable art, jewelry, miniatures/dollhouses, wooden crafts, paper products, stained glass items, needlework crafts, hand blown glass items, figurines, dolls/stuffed animals/toys, pottery/ceramics, nature crafts/floral, leather crafts, baskets

Price range: $25-500

Advertising/Promotion: Radio, TV, newspaper

Spaces available: 800. Booth space only.

Cost of space: $3-3.80 per sq. ft.

Application process: Dealers are accepted on a first-come, first-serve basis, as long as they fit the requirements of the show.

Additional information: Also feature entertainment, children's areas, free parking, food and demonstrations.

COLUMBUS ARTS FESTIVAL

Greater Columbus Arts Council
55 E. State St.
Columbus, OH 43215
Phone: (614)224-2606
Fax: (614)224-7461
First show: 1962
Time of year: First full weekend in June including Friday
Location: Downtown Riverfront, Columbus. Outdoor. Streets and parks along riverfront.
Duration: Th-Sat 11:30-10, Sun 11:30-7
Attendance: 500,000
Admission: Free
Categories: Fine crafts, wearable art, jewelry, wooden crafts, hand blown glass items, home decor, figurines, dolls/toys, pottery/ceramics, leather crafts, baskets, recycled crafts, sculpture

Advertising/Promotion: Radio, TV, local and regional print. Budget varies.

Spaces available: 300. 10′ × 10′ spaces. Artists can furnish own tent or have space in festival tent at no additional charge.

Cost of space: $330-400

Application process: Show is juried. For consideration, provide slides (4). One slide must be of booth or display. Must fill out prospectus. $15 charge to apply.

Additional information: The Columbus

Arts Festival is recognized as one of the best in the country in both fine art and fine craft.

CUMBERLAND COUNTY'S SUNDAY ON THE SQUARE

The Arts Council of Fayetteville/
Jodi Schoenbrun
P.O. Box 318
Fayetteville, NC 28302
Phone: (910)323-1776
Fax: (910)323-1727
First show: 1973
Time of year: Late April
Location: Downtown Fayetteville, Haystreet Commons. Outdoor.
Duration: Sun 12-6
Attendance: 65,000
Admission: Free
Categories: Fine crafts, wearable art, jewelry, miniatures/dollhouses, wooden crafts, paper products, stained glass items, needlework crafts, hand blown glass items, home decor, figurines, dolls/stuffed animals/toys, pottery/ceramics, nature crafts/floral, leather crafts, baskets, recycled crafts, sculpture
Advertising/Promotion: The festival has almost 20 media sponsors in addition to print articles and ads.
Spaces available: 150. 10′ × 10′ space, electricity and water available.
Cost of space: $60
Application process: Show is juried. For consideration, provide photos or slides. No charge to apply.
Additional information: This is Eastern North Carolina's oldest and largest outdoor multi-arts festival.

DEERFEST

Teri Finelli
1601 E. Hillsboro Blvd.
Deerfield Beach, Fl 33441
Phone: (954)427-1050
Fax: (954)427-1056
First show: 1983
Time of year: November
Location: Quite Waters Park, 6601 N. Powerline Rd., Deerfield Beach. Outdoor.
Duration: Fri 5-11, Sat 11-11, Sun 12-7
Attendance: 45,000
Admission: $1 per person or $5 carload
Categories: Fine crafts, wearable art, jewelry, miniatures/dollhouses,

wooden crafts, paper products, stained glass items, needlework crafts, hand blown glass items, home decor, figurines, dolls/stuffed animals/toys, pottery/ceramics, nature crafts/floral, leather crafts, baskets, recycled crafts, sculpture
Price range: $2-2,000
Advertising/Promotion: Radio, local cable, all area newspaper. $7,000 budget.
Spaces available: 200. Must have tent to display. Spaces are 10′ × 10′. Must bring table, chairs, tent, etc.
Cost of space: $126-190
Application process: Show is juried. For consideration, provide photos or slides (1) and written description of work. No charge to apply.

DELRAY AFFAIR

Greater Delray Beach Chamber of Commerce
Lynn Bafaloukos
64 SE Fifth Ave.
Delray Beach, FL 33487
Phone: (407)278-0424
Fax: (407)278-0555
E-mail: chamber@delraybeach.com
First show: 1962
Time of year: Weekend after Easter
Location: East Atlantic Ave. (between Swinton Ave. and the Intracoastal Waterway). Outdoor. Along Atlantic Ave.: 8 city blocks plus adjacent side streets, plazas and parks in downtown picturesque Delray Beach.
Duration: F-Sun 10-6
Attendance: 250,000+
Admission: Free
Categories: Fine crafts, wearable art, jewelry, miniatures/dollhouses, wooden crafts, paper products, stained glass items, needlework crafts, hand blown glass items, home decor, figurines, dolls/stuffed animals/toys, pottery/ceramics, nature crafts/floral, leather crafts, baskets, recycled crafts, sculpture
Price range: $5-5,000
Advertising/Promotion: TV, radio, cable, newspapers. $7,500 plus in-kind budget.
Spaces available: 500. 10′ × 10′ booths.
Cost of space: $300-750
Application process: Show is juried. For consideration, provide photos or

slides (4). $10 charge to apply.
Additional information: Fine art is also a very important component of the Delray Affair as well as entertainment continuously on three stages and a whole children's area complete with rides, games and art projects.

DONA ANA ARTS COUNCIL RENAISSANCE CRAFTFAIRE

Dona Ana Arts Council/Judith Finch
224 N. Campo
Las Cruces, NM 88001
Phone: (505)523-6403; (505)523-4286
First show: 1971
Time of year: First full weekend of November
Location: Young Park located at the intersection of Lohman and Walnut Streets, Las Cruces. Outdoor. The park is fenced for the event; the entire park is transformed into a Renaissance Village with artisans and entertainers located throughout the park.
Duration: Sat-Sun 10-5
Attendance: 50,000
Admission: $2 donation
Categories: Fine crafts, jewelry, wooden crafts, paper products, stained glass items, hand blown glass items, dolls/stuffed animals/toys, pottery/ceramics, nature crafts/floral, leather crafts, baskets, sculpture
Price range: $5-500
Advertising/Promotion: Show is widely advertisied in the area; print media, radio, TV, various craft magazines (*Sunshine Artists*), Renaissance magazines carry the show listing. $20,000 budget.
Spaces available: 160. Artist spaces are 10′ × 10′. Artists must provide their own booth structure and set-up, which must be decorated in accordance with the Renaissance theme.
Cost of space: $150
Application process: Show is juried. For consideration, provide slides (4). Slides must be labeled with artist's name, media; top of each slide must be indicated. $20 charge to apply.
Additional information: Artists are expected to dress in Renaissance attire. All arts must be handcrafted by the artists who must be present at the show. It is a family event with chil-

dren's activities, entertainment areas, and a wide variety of food booths.

DOWNTOWN FESTIVAL & ART SHOW

City of Gainesville Cultural Affairs
Linda Piper
P.O. Box 490-30
Gainesville, FL 32602
Phone: (352)334-2197
Fax: (352)334-2146
First show: 1981
Time of year: November
Location: Downtown Gainesville between the Community Plaza and the Hippodrome State Theatre on SE First St. Outdoor.
Duration: Sat-Sun 10-5
Attendance: 80,000
Admission: Free
Categories: Fine crafts, wearable art, jewelry, wooden crafts, stained glass items, hand blown glass items, pottery/ceramics, leather crafts, baskets, sculpture
Price range: $25-1,000
Advertising/Promotion: All local newspapers in over 7 counties. Local radio and TV. $9,000 budget.
Spaces available: 220. 12′ × 12′ spaces.
Cost of space: $90
Application process: Show is juried. For consideration, provide slides (4). $10 charge to apply.

FAIRHOPE ARTS & CRAFTS FESTIVAL

Eastern Shore Chamber of Commerce
Kimberly McKeough, Community Events Coordinator
327 Fairhope Ave.
Fairhope, AL 36532
Phone: (334)928-6387
Fax: (334)928-6389
First show: 1952
Time of year: Third weekend in March
Location: Downtown Fairhope. Outdoor. On main streets.
Duration: F-Sun 10-5
Attendance: 150,000
Admission: Free
Categories: Fine crafts, wearable art, miniatures/dollhouses, wooden crafts, paper products, stained glass items, needlework crafts, hand blown glass items, home decor, figurines, dolls/stuffed animals/toys, pottery/ceramics, nature crafts/floral, leather crafts,

baskets, recycled crafts, sculpture
Price range: $2.50-1,000
Advertising/Promotion: Local and regional newspapers, TV, radio and posters in local stores
Spaces available: Approximately 200. 10′ × 12′ booths.
Cost of space: $175
Application process: Show is juried. For consideration, provide slides (3). $25 charge to apply.
Additional information: Fine Art is also juried and accepted (approximately one half is art and one half is craft).

FESTIVAL IN THE PARK

City of Montgomery Parks: Recreation/
Kay McCreery
1010 Forest Ave.
Montgomery, AL 36106
Phone: (334)241-2300
Fax: (334)241-2301
First show: 1973
Time of year: October
Location: Oak Park, at above address. Outdoor. In a 40 acre city park.
Duration: Sat 9-5
Attendance: 25,000-30,000
Admission: Free
Categories: Fine crafts, wearable art, jewelry, wooden crafts, stained glass items, needlework crafts, hand blown glass items, figurines, dolls/stuffed animals/toys, pottery/ceramics, nature crafts/floral, leather crafts, baskets, sculpture, metal work, graphics, porcelain
Price range: $5-1,000
Advertising/Promotion: Newspaper, TV interviews, radio interviews, inserts in bank deposit envelopes, posters in local businesses, banners, A-frames (sings) at intersections. $1,500 budget.
Spaces available: 280. 12′ × 10′ spaces along a paved walkway, exhibitors provide their own tables/displays.
Cost of space: $50
Application process: Show is juried. For consideration, provide slides (3). No charge to apply.
Additional information: All items are handcrafted, no kits.

FESTIVAL OF THE ARTS

Mohave Artists and Crafters Guild
Sally Leibold
4696 So-Hi Blvd.
Kingman, AZ 86413
Phone: (520)565-3213
First show: 1978
Time of year: Mothers Day weekend
Location: Metcalfe Park, Kingman. Outdoor. Opposite the museum and The Chamber of Commerce. Adjacent to High School.
Duration: Sat 10-5, Sun 10-4
Attendance: 3,000-5,000
Admission: Free
Categories: Fine crafts, wearable art, jewelry, miniatures/dollhouses, wooden crafts, paper products, stained glass items, needlework crafts, hand blown glass items, dolls/stuffed animals/toys, pottery/ceramics, nature crafts/floral, leather crafts, baskets, recycled crafts, sculpture, blacksmith made objects
Price range: $5-600
Advertising/Promotion: Posters, handouts, mailings, newspapers, radio. $700 budget.
Spaces available: 100. 10′ × 12′ spaces. Grass and gravel, some shade and some sun, some electric available.
Cost of space: $35, plus a returnable $10 security deposit, $5 late fee after May 5th.
Application process: Dealers are accepted on a first-come, first-serve basis, as long as they fit the requirements of the show.
Additional information: We have an "Art for Youth" space where children can paint for free; live entertainment both days; blacksmithing demonstration.

FESTIVAL OF TREES

Jr. League of Daytona Beach
200 Orange Ave.
Daytona Beach, FL 32114
Phone: (904)253-1756
Fax: (904)239-6776
First show: 1992
Time of year: First full weekend in December
Location: Ocean Center, 101 N. Atlantic Ave., Daytona Beach. Indoor.
Duration: Th 7-10, F-Sat 10-9,

Sun 10-5
Attendance: 30,000
Admission: $1-5
Categories: Fine crafts, wearable art, jewelry, wooden crafts, stained glass items, needlework crafts, home decor, figurines, dolls/stuffed animals/toys, nature crafts/floral, baskets, Christmas related items
Price range: $1-350
Advertising/Promotion: TV (station co-sponsor); newspaper ads and special insert we purchase totally devoted to the festival, paper also does some feature stories on festival; radio spots
Spaces available: 55-60. 10' × 10' booths including electricity.
Cost of space: $295-350
Application process: Show is juried. For consideration, provide photos or slides (4). No charge to apply.
Additional information: No flea market items, but we do allow quality commercial Christmas related items.

FIRST NATIONS ART, INC. (YA'AT'EEH)

Robert L. Painter
P.O. Box 2825
Sarasota, FL 34230
Phone: (941)366-3309
First show: 1995
Time of year: The weekend before Thanksgiving
Location: Along the Bayfront, Ken Thompson Park, Sarasota. Outdoor.
Duration: F 7-10PM (artist reception/preview), Sat-Sun 9-5
Attendance: 10,000
Admission: $3 adults, $2 children
Categories: Fine crafts, wearable art, jewelry, wooden crafts, pottery/ceramics, leather crafts, baskets, sculpture
Price range: $5-10,000
Advertising/Promotion: Advertise in publications like *Southwest Art, American Indian Art, Native Peoples Magazine,* etc.; regional lifestyle publications; local and regional newspapers, TV and radio. $5,000 budget.
Spaces available: 75-95. 12' × 12' up to 25' wide canopy spaces. 9' × 12' big top spaces. Doubles available, table rentals available, chairs provided.
Cost of space: Free for regular booth space, $50 for double space.

Application process: Show is juried. For consideration, provide photos or slides (2), catalog/promotional materials and written description of work. $25 charge to apply.
Additional information: We have a $25 membership/application fee—those who are accepted pay no booth fee or commission. Additional fee ($50) for oversize space. We are a non-profit organization formed to help artists. We do separate fund raising to pay for the booth spaces.

FOX LAKE CHRISTMAS FESTIVAL OF CRAFTS

Brevard County Parks & Recreation, North Area
Charlotte Thomas and Phyllis Walz
475 N. Williams Ave.
Titusville, FL 32796
Phone: (407)264-5105
Fax: (407)264-6428
First show: 1993
Time of year: Third Saturday in November
Location: Fox Lake Park, 4400 Fox Lake Rd., Titusville. Outdoor. All crafters are located in park, either under one of our pavilions, have their own canopy or are out in the open.
Duration: Sat 8:30-4:30
Attendance: 10,000
Admission: Free
Categories: Wearable art, jewelry, miniatures/dollhouses, wooden crafts, paper products, stained glass items, needlework crafts, home decor, figurines, dolls/stuffed animals/toys, pottery/ceramics, nature crafts/floral, leather crafts, baskets
Price range: 50¢-$350
Advertising/Promotion: Banners across major highway and road signs; local cable TV and radio; in "Where the Shows Are," 32 local newspapers; individual crafters each put out signs in businesses. Budget varies.
Spaces available: 500. 8' picnic table top, 10' × 10' spaces. Picnic tables and a few spaces are under pavilion. All other spaces are throughout the park.
Cost of space: $15 plus 90¢ Florida sales tax.
Application process: Dealers are on a

first-come, first-serve basis, as long as they fit the requirements of the show.
Additional information: Fox Lake Park is a 34-acre park and lake in nature landscape area.

GALT FARM ANTIQUES & CRAFTS

Bev Kemper
534 Red Hill Rd.
Narvon, PA 17555
Phone: (717)768-7609
First show: 1991
Time of year: November
Location: American Legion Bldg., Honey Brook, PA. Indoor. Main street in small town, 5 minutes from Turnpike Exit #22
Duration: F-Sat 10-7, 2 weekends
Attendance: 1,200
Admission: Free
Categories: Fine crafts, wearable art, jewelry, wooden crafts, paper products, needlework crafts, home decor, dolls/stuffed animals/toys, pottery/ceramics, nature crafts/floral, baskets, sculpture, Christmas items
Price range: $3-3,000
Advertising/Promotion: *Antiques Weekly, Antique & Auction News, Rennigers, County Lines, Country Living Magazine;* Lancaster and Pottstown newpapers; *Tri County* and *Pennysaver* newspapers; specialty publications. $2,500 budget.
Spaces available: Consignment show. Setup is done by the manager. Items are mixed, no specific booths. Dealers not required to be present.
Cost of space: $30 registration, 20% of all sales
Application process: Show is juried. For consideration, provide photos (4-6), sample of work and written description of work. No charge to apply.
Additional information: Beautifully decorated room-like settings.

GILROY GARLIC FESTIVAL

Gilroy Garlic Festival Association, Inc.
P.O. Box 2311
Gilroy, CA 95021
Phone: (408)842-1625
Fax: (408)847-7337
First show: 1979
Time of year: Last full weekend of July
Location: Christmas Hill Park, Gilroy.

Outdoor. Held in city park. The site is about forty acres. The arts & crafts area is one part of our garlic food fair.

Duration: F-Sun 10-7, gates close at 6 daily

Attendance: 135,000

Admission: General $8, seniors and children 6-12, $4, under 6 free

Categories: Fine crafts, wearable art, jewelry, wooden crafts, paper products, stained glass items, needlework crafts, hand blown glass items, home decor, figurines, stuffed animals/toys, pottery/ceramics, nature crafts/floral, leather crafts, baskets, recycled crafts, sculpture

Price range: $15-200

Advertising/Promotion: Mail out brochures, press kits, radio and TV closer to the event. Receive national and international coverage.

Spaces available: 90-100 (this could increase). 10′ × 10′, 10′ × 15′, 10′ × 20′ booth.

Cost of space: $475, $550, $950

Application process: Show is juried. For consideration, provide photos (6). $10 charge to apply.

Additional information: Artist must be present all 3 days of festival. No exceptions. Interested artists should send a SASE in November or December to Gilroy Garlic Festival at the above address. Applications are mailed mid-January. Because we are an outdoor event, it can be dusty and sometimes breezy.

GOOD OLE SUMMERTIME ARTS & CRAFTS FAIR

Vickie Garner
117 Sunrise
Hot Springs, AR 71913-2811
Phone: (501)624-6494
E-mail: jgarner249@aol.com
First show: 1985
Time of year: July
Location: Hot Springs, AR convention auditorium, Malvern Ave. and Convention Blvd. Indoor.
Duration: Sat 10-6, Sun 11-5
Attendance: 20,000
Admission: Free
Categories: Fine crafts, wearable art, jewelry, miniatures/dollhouses, wooden crafts, stained glass items, needlework crafts, hand blown glass

items, home decor, figurines, dolls/stuffed animals/toys, pottery/ceramics, nature crafts/floral, leather crafts, baskets

Price range: $5-150

Advertising/Promotion: TV, radio, newspaper, Weekend-end Entertainment Guide, state tourist information centers. $6,000 budget.

Spaces available: 225. Booths 8′ × 10′. Free table and chairs.

Cost of space: $85

Application process: Show is juried. For consideration, provide photos or slides (2-3) and catalog/promotional materials. No charge to apply.

Additional information: No manufactured or buy/sell items. All booths are indoor and air-conditioned. Send SASE for application.

HARVEST HOLIDAY, FINE ARTS, CRAFTS & QUILT SHOW

Rocky River Senior Center/
Joyce Waltz-Umerley
21014 Hilliard Blvd.
Rocky River, OH 44116
Phone: (216)331-0600, ext. 247
Fax: (216)331-1304
First show: 1990
Time of year: Beginning of November
Location: Rocky River Senior Center, Rocky River City Hall Complex, corner of Hilliard and Wagar Roads. Indoor.
Duration: F-Sat, 10-5
Attendance: 2,300
Admission: $1.50, under 12 free
Categories: Fine crafts, wearable art, jewelry, miniatures/dollhouses, wooden crafts, paper products, stained glass items, hand blown glass items, home decor, dolls/stuffed animals/toys, nature crafts/floral, leather crafts, baskets
Price range: $2-100
Advertising/Promotion: Newsletter, local newspapers, cable TV, *Creative Ohio*, *Ohio Magazine*, bulk mailing (3,000), fliers, bulletin boards
Spaces available: 35. Sizes vary (8′ × 10′ space most common), includes one 8′ table and two chairs.
Cost of space: $40
Application process: Show is invitation only.

HARVEST MOON ARTS & CRAFTS SHOW

Mike Bowen
P.O. Box 2682
Statesboro, GA 30458
Phone: (912)489-5935
Fax: (912)489-6348
E-mail: mbowen@sunbelt.net
First show: 1995
Time of year: Second weekend of November
Location: Kiwanis Ogeechee Fairgrounds, Statesboro. Indoor and outdoor.
Duration: Sat 9-5, Sun 12-5
Attendance: 10,000
Admission: $2 adults, children under 12 free
Categories: Fine crafts, wearable art, jewelry, miniatures/dollhouses, wooden crafts, paper products, stained glass items, needlework crafts, hand blown glass items, home decor, figurines, dolls/stuffed animals/toys, pottery/ceramics, nature crafts/floral, leather crafts, baskets, recycled crafts, sculpture
Price range: $5-100
Advertising/Promotion: Radio, TV, newspaper. $5,000 budget.
Spaces available: 150. Booths or outside spaces 15′ × 15′.
Cost of space: $50-75
Application process: Past participants have first priority, and any remaining tables are available on a first-come, first-serve basis.

HOLIDAY ART FAIRE

Jan Hughes, director of programs
130 N. Morrison St.
Appleton, WI 54911
Phone: (414)733-4089
Fax: (414)733-4149
First show: 1996
Time of year: Weekend before Thanksgiving
Location: Indoor. Liberty Hall Banquet and Conference Center, Appleton, WI.
Duration: F 12-8, Sat-Sun 10-5
Admission: $3 adults, 12 and under free
Categories: Fine crafts, jewelry, wooden crafts, pottery/ceramics, leather crafts, baskets
Advertising/Promotion: Arts and crafts magazines, newspapers. $10,000 budget.

Spaces available: 75. 8' × 10' booths.

Cost of space: Members: $100, Non-members: $125

Application process: Show is juried. For consideration, provide photos or slides (4). $5 charge to apply.

Additional information: Holiday Art Faire is a holiday version of Art in the Park for artists and craftspersons whose work includes wearable art and items appropriate for holiday gift giving and decoration. Appleton Art Center draws on its 36 years of experience as presenter of the Fox Cities' largest summer art fair to bring you this fine art and craft holiday fair.

HOLIDAY CRAFTS FESTIVAL

Mystic Community Center
P.O. Box 526
Mystic, CT 06355
Phone: (860)536-3575; (860)536-2049
Fax: (860)536-2049
First show: 1988
Time of year: Weekend before Thanksgiving
Location: Mystic Community Center, Harry Austin Dr. (off Masons Island Rd.), Mystic. Indoor. 1 mile from busy downtown.
Duration: Sat 10-5, Sun 11-4
Attendance: 3,200
Admission: $1
Categories: Fine crafts, wearable art, jewelry, miniatures/dollhouses, wooden crafts, paper products, stained glass items, needlework crafts, hand blown glass items, home decor, figurines, dolls/stuffed animals/toys, pottery/ceramics, nature crafts/floral, leather crafts, baskets, recycled crafts, sculpture, stepping stones, mail boxes
Price range: $10-250
Advertising/Promotion: Newspaper ads in 4 newspapers, 35 large professional signs in area at key intersections, 2 large banners hung over 2 main streets, 2,100 postcards, fliers hung at all local libraries, community centers. $4,000 budget.
Spaces available: 58. 8' × 10' booths.
Cost of space: $125
Application process: Show is juried. For consideration, provide photos or slides (4) and written description of work. No charge to apply.
Additional information: We provide volunteers to assist with set up and break down; free, large shopping bags to event goers; offer on-site parking/camping free of charge with use of tennis, racquetball, pool, beach, free weights and Nautilus equipment as well.

HOLIDAY SHOPPER'S FAIR

Janice Cropper
4001 Coastal Hwy.
Ocean City, MD 21842
Phone: (410)289-8311
Fax: (410)289-0058
First show: 1982
Time of year: Thanksgiving weekend
Location: Ocean City Convention Center at above address. Indoor. There are 2 floors of shopping inside Ocean City Convention Center.
Duration: Fri 12-6, Sat 10-6, Sun 10-4
Attendance: 20,000
Admission: Free
Categories: Fine crafts, wearable art, jewelry, wooden crafts, paper products, stained glass items, needlework crafts, dolls/stuffed animals/toys, pottery/ceramics, nature crafts/floral, leather crafts, baskets
Price range: $3-500
Advertising/Promotion: Fliers, banners and newspapers.
Spaces available: 168. 10' × 6', 10' × 10', 10' × 8' booths, back and side drapes included; one 110 volt-500 watts electrical outlet; 1 undraped table, 2 chairs.
Cost of space: $145-260
Application process: Show is juried. For consideration, provide photos or slides (4 or 5) and written description of work. No charge to apply.

KENTUCKY APPLE FESTIVAL, INC.

Ray Tosti, chairman
P.O. Box 879
Paintsville, KY 41240
Phone: (606)789-4355; (606)788-1491
First show: 1962
Time of year: First weekend in October
Location: Downtown Paintsville. Outdoor. On the street and 2 large parking lots.
Duration: Th 6-9, F 8-9, Sat 8-6
Attendance: 50,000
Admission: Free
Categories: Fine crafts, wearable art, jewelry, miniatures/dollhouses, wooden crafts, paper products, stained glass items, needlework crafts, hand blown glass items, home decor, figurines, dolls/stuffed animals/toys, pottery/ceramics, nature crafts/floral, leather crafts, baskets
Price range: $5 and up
Advertising/Promotion: Print 40,000 brochures advertising festival. $6,000 budget.
Spaces available: 100. 10' × 10' booth spaces, electricity provided for free, security at nights.
Cost of space: $75
Application process: Show is juried. For consideration, provide photos or slides and sample of work. $75 charge to apply.
Additional information: Hospitality workers and refreshments provided for all vendors during the show.

KETNER'S MILL COUNTRY FAIR

Sally McDonald
P.O. Box 322
Lookout Mountain, TN 37350
Phone: (423)821-3238
First show: 1978
Time of year: October, the weekend after Columbus Day
Location: Ketner's Mill, Whitwell, TN. The 100-acre site is along the banks of the Sequatchie River. Outdoor.
Duration: Sat 9-6, Sun 10-5:30
Attendance: 20,000
Admission: $4
Categories: Fine crafts, wearable art, jewelry, wooden crafts, paper products, stained glass items, needlework crafts, hand blown glass items, home decor, dolls/stuffed animals/toys, pottery/ceramics, nature crafts/floral, leather crafts, baskets, recycled crafts, sculpture, fine art
Price range: $2-200
Advertising/Promotion: Newspaper, TV talk show artist appearances, brochure, bus banners, PSAs, radio promotion—passes given out as part of radio station "Weekend Getaway" giveaway.
Spaces available: 175. 15' × 15' grassy space, exhibitor provides tables and tent. There are fourteen 12' × 12' spaces in the sawmill, which is an

open pavilion next to the grist mill, right along the river.

Cost of space: $100

Application process: Show is juried. Past participants have first priority. For consideration, provide photos or slides (4). At least 1 photo should be of the entire display.

Additional information: The Ketner's Mill Fair is the major fund raiser for the maintenance of Ketner's Mill, which is on the National Register of Historic Places. There are a number of traditional crafts demonstrated. We try to maintain the historic ambiance.

LA JOLLA FESTIVAL OF THE ARTS AND FOOD FAIRE

Ross Ehrhardt
4130 La Jolla Village Dr., Suite 10717
La Jolla, CA 92037
Phone: (619)456-1268
First show: 1987
Time of year: Beginning of June
Location: La Jolla Country Day School, 9490 Genesee Ave., La Jolla. Outdoor. Takes place on a large grass athletic field of a private school.
Duration: Sat-Sun 10-5
Attendance: 18,000
Admission: $5
Categories: Fine crafts, jewelry, wooden sculpture, stained glass items (limited to 2), hand blown glass items, pottery/ceramics (signed only), sculpture
Price range: $100-10,000
Advertising/Promotion: Radio, cable TV, newspapers, magazines, posters, fliers, mailing list and artist mailing list. $50,000 budget.
Spaces available: 175. All artist spaces are 10′×20′ arranged in groups of 4 and larger free-standing booths if necessary.
Cost of space: $295
Application process: Show is juried. For consideration, provide photos (5), catalog/promotional materials, written description of work and résumé. $20 charge to apply.
Additional information: All proceeds fund 20 programs (sports, educational) for people with disabilities. Highly rated by *Art Source Book, Arts & Crafts Fair Guide* and *Sunshine Artists* magazine.

LEESBURG ART FESTIVAL

Linda Watts
P.O. Box 492857
Leesburg, FL 34749
Phone: (352)787-0000
Fax: (352)326-2902
First show: 1977
Time of year: Second weekend in March
Location: Venetian Gardens on Lake Harris, Dixie Ave. in Leesburg. Outdoor. Beautiful lakefront garden setting in a city park.
Duration: Sat-Sun 10-5
Attendance: 45,000
Admission: Free
Categories: Fine crafts, jewelry, pottery/ceramics, hand blown glass items, sculpture
Advertising/Promotion: Magazines, TV, radio, all regional art & craft publications. $2,000 budget.
Spaces available: 235. 12′×12′ booths.
Cost of space: $85
Application process: Show is juried. For consideration, provide slides (4). $15 charge to apply.

LOUISVILLE CHRISTMAS SHOW

Georgie Kelly
P.O. Box 66
Madison, IN 47250
Phone: (812)265-6100
First show: 1989
Time of year: Weekend before Thanksgiving
Location: Commonwealth Convention Center, Fourth and Market Sts., downtown Louisville, KY. Indoor.
Duration: Fri 11-7, Sat 10-6, Sun 12-5
Attendance: 13-15,000
Admission: $5; children under 10 free; $1 discount with canned food donation
Categories: Wearable art, jewelry, wooden crafts, paper products, stained glass items, needlework crafts, home decor, dolls/stuffed animals/toys, pottery/ceramics, nature crafts/floral, leather crafts, baskets, metal sculpture
Price range: $5-1,000
Advertising/Promotion: Newspaper, TV, radio, billboards, fliers and calendars of events
Spaces available: 290. Draped 10′×10′ space.
Cost of space: $225

Application process: Show is juried. For consideration, provide photos or slides (3 of work and 1 of display) and written description of work. No charge to apply.

MADISON CHAUTAUQUA

Madison Area CVB/Michelle Karst
301 E. Main St.
Madison, IN 47250
Phone: (812)265-2956
Fax: (812)273-3694
First show: 1971
Time of year: Fourth weekend in September
Location: Streets around Lanier Mansion and along the Ohio River. Outdoor. In Hisoric downtown Madison.
Duration: Sat-Sun 10-5
Attendance: 60,000-80,000
Categories: Fine crafts, wearable art, jewelry, miniatures/dollhouses, wooden crafts, paper products, stained glass items, needlework crafts, hand blown glass items, dolls/stuffed animals/toys, pottery/ceramics, nature crafts/floral, leather crafts, baskets, sculpture
Price range: $25-100
Advertising/Promotion: Newspapers, TV, billboards and radio in Ohio, Indiana and Kentucky. $20,000 budget.
Spaces available: 245. 10′×17′ spaces.
Cost of space: $50-200
Application process: Show is juried. For consideration, provide slides (4) and written description of work. $10 charge to apply.

THE MYSTICAL, MAGICAL MERRIMENT OF CHRISTMAS

Pulaski Parks and Recreation/Pat Wiser
P.O. Box 333
Pulaski, TN 38478
Phone: (615)363-4666
Fax: (615)363-3408
E-mail: reedept@usit.net
First show: 1993
Time of year: Weekend before Thanksgiving
Location: At above address. Indoor.
Duration: Sat 7-5, Sun 1-5
Attendance: 1,000
Admission: Free
Categories: Fine crafts, jewelry, miniatures/dollhouses, wooden crafts, nee-

dlework crafts, hand blown glass items, home decor, figurines, dolls/stuffed animals/toys, pottery/ceramics, nature crafts/floral, leather crafts, baskets, sculpture

Price range: $10-25

Advertising/Promotion: All local radio, TV, newspapers; out of town newspapers and radio; via the Internet

Spaces available: 45. 10′ × 10′ booth. Bring own tables; electric available.

Cost of space: $15

Application process: Past participants have first priority, and any remaining tables are available on a first-come, first-serve basis.

Additional Information: Also featured are antiques, gingerbread house contest, art gallery, Santa workshop.

NATIONAL ANNUAL SHRIMP FESTIVAL
Linda Mickelson and Kathy Danielson
P.O. Drawer 3869
Gulf Shores, AL 36547
Phone: (334)968-6904; (334)968-4237
Fax: (334)968-5332
First show: 1970
Time of year: Second full weekend of October
Location: Public beach area at the end of Hwy 59. Outdoor.
Duration: Th-Sat 10-10; Sun 10-6
Attendance: 250,000
Admission: Free
Categories: Fine crafts, wearable art, jewelry, miniatures/dollhouses, wooden crafts, stained glass items, hand blown glass items, pottery/ceramics, nature crafts/floral, sculpture
Spaces available: 10′ × 10′ booths
Application process: Show is juried. For consideration, provide slides (4). $20 charge to apply.
Additional information: We have music, food and a Children's Art Village for children to do hands-on art work.

PETERS VALLEY CRAFT FAIR
19 Kuhn Rd.
Layton, NJ 07851
Phone: (201)948-5200
Fax: (201)948-0011
E-mail: pvcrafts1@aol.com
First show: 1970
Time of year: Last full weekend in September

Location: Peters Valley Craft Center, Rt. 615, Layton. Outdoor. In a meadow overlooking the Kittatiny Moutains.
Duration: Sat 10-6, Sun 10-5
Attendance: 14,000
Admission: $5 adult, $4 senior
Categories: Fine crafts, wearable art, jewelry, wooden crafts, stained glass items, hand blown glass items, pottery/ceramics, leather crafts, baskets, sculpture
Price range: $25-500
Advertising/Promotion: Craft guild newsletters, *Crafts Report* magazine, various craft show guides. $1,500 budget.
Spaces available: 165. 10′ × 10′ space, tented space $75 extra. No electric. All tables, etc. provided by crafter.
Cost of space: $210
Application process: Show is juried. For consideration, provide slides (5). $15 charge to apply.

PINK PALACE CRAFTS FAIR
Friends of the Pink Palace Museum
3050 Central Ave.
Memphis, TN 38111
Phone: (901)320-6408
First show: 1972
Time of year: First weekend in October
Location: Audubon Park, Memphis. Outdoor.
Duration: Th 10-6, F 10-9, Sat-Sun 10-6
Attendance: 45,000
Admission: $5 adults, $3 child or senior; advance tickets sold for $4 adult, $2 child
Categories: Fine crafts, wearable art, jewelry, wooden crafts, stained glass items, needlework crafts, hand blown glass items, dolls/stuffed animals/toys, pottery/ceramics, nature crafts/floral, leather crafts, baskets, sculpture
Price range: $1-500
Advertising/Promotion: Billboards, outdoor bus stop signs, newspaper ads, PSAs on radio, TV promotional spot of 10, 20 and 30 seconds, 2 radio sponsors, insert in light, gas and water bills and fliers at grocery store sponsor. $20,000 budget.
Spaces available: 250. Booth space is 10′ × 12′, tables and chairs are avail-

able for rent, most all of exhibitors bring their own set-up.
Cost of space: $250-400
Application process: Show is juried. For consideration, provide slides (3 individual, 1 booth) and written description of work. $15 charge to apply. April 1 deadline for fine crafts, May 1 deadline for handicrafts.
Additional information: This event promotes the fine craftsman, the handicraft artisan and the demonstrating craftsmen. All proceeds benefit the Pink Palace Museum. Our fair is educational as well, with special exhibits. There are 4 days of continuous entertainment on 2 stages and a variety of ethnic and traditional foods. It's "A Memphis Tradition."

PRATER'S MILL COUNTRY FAIR
Judy Alderman and Melanie Chapman
848 Shugart Rd.
Dalton, GA 30720
Phone/Fax: (706)275-6455
First show: 1971
Time of year: Mother's Day weekend in May, Columbus Day weekend in October
Location: Historic Prater's Mill, 500 Prater's Mill Rd., Dalton. Outdoor. Rural setting: Grist Mill, country store, barn, others
Duration: 9-6
Attendance: 10,000
Admission: $4 adults, children 12 and under free
Categories: Fine crafts, wearable art, jewelry, miniatures/dollhouses, wooden crafts, paper products, stained glass items, needlework crafts, hand blown glass items, home decor, dolls/stuffed animals/toys, pottery/ceramics, nature crafts/floral, leather crafts, baskets, sculpture
Price range: Wide range
Advertising/Promotion: Newspapers, radio and TV within 200 mile radius. $20,000 budget.
Spaces available: 217. 15′ × 15′ space—no tables, tents, etc. provided.
Cost of space: $100
Application process: Show is juried. For consideration, provide photos or slides (3) and biographical material on artist. No charge to apply.

PRESENTATION UNDER THE PINES

Plantation Inn/Art Show Coordinator
P.O. Box 1116, 9301 W. Ft. Island Trail
Crystal River, FL 34423
Phone: (352)795-1856
Fax: (352)795-0074
First show: 1977
Time of year: Saturday after Thanksgiving
Location: Plantation Inn and Golf Resort, Crystal River. Outdoor.
Duration: Sat 10-4:30
Attendance: 10,000
Admission: Free
Categories: Fine crafts, wearable art, jewelry, wooden crafts, paper products, stained glass items, hand blown glass items, dolls/stuffed animals/toys, pottery/ceramics, leather crafts, baskets, sculpture
Advertising/Promotion: Directories/magazines, Florida newspapers and local radio
Spaces available: 150. Space not assigned nor limited in size.
Cost of space: $50
Application process: Show is juried. For consideration, provide photos or slides (3 of craft, plus 1 of display). No charge to apply.

ST. JAMES COURT ART SHOW

St. James Court Neighborhood
Association
Susan Coleman
P.O. Box 3804
Louisville, KY 40201
Phone: (502)635-1842
Fax: (502)635-1296
First show: 1956
Time of year: First full weekend in October
Location: In historical Old Louisville on St. James Court. Outdoor. A historical/preservation residential area. St. James Court is the heart of the show. It branches out from there to surrounding residential streets and courts.
Duration: F-Sat 10-6, Sun 10-5
Attendance: 300,000+
Admission: Free
Categories: Fine crafts, wearable art, jewelry, wooden crafts, paper products, hand blown glass items, pottery/ceramics, leather crafts, sculpture,

kites, "egg" art, kaleidoscopes, fiber (textiles), metal
Price range: $5-3,500
Advertising/Promotion: Many national publications, particularly *Sunsine Artist*, *Art Fair Sourcebook*, etc. Locally, it is advertised via TV, radio and print media and promoted through Convention and Visitors Bureau.
Spaces available: 350+. Open areas of ground/sidewalk approximately 12′ × 12′. Exhibitors responsible for own setup (booth, tent, tables, etc.)
Cost of space: $350-425, depending on location
Application process: Show is juried. For consideration, provide slides (3). $15 charge to apply.
Additional information: This show's emphasis is on *fine* crafts. Please note that there are actually 5 shows operating under the same umbrella name, all executed by different old Louisville neighborhood associations. The information above is for the St. James Court portion of the show *only*, the oldest and largest portion.

ST. JOHNS RIVER FESTIVAL

Sam Silvernell
400 E. First St.
Sanford, FL 32771
Phone: (407)322-2212
Fax: (407)322-8160
First show: 1943
Time of year: First weekend in March
Location: Ft. Mellon Park, Sanford. Outdoor.
Duration: 2 days
Attendance: 5,000-10,000
Admission: Free
Categories: Fine crafts, wearable art, jewelry, wooden crafts, paper products, stained glass items, needlework crafts, dolls/stuffed animals/toys, pottery/ceramics, nature crafts/floral, leather crafts, baskets, sculpture, paintings
Spaces available: 90-100
Application process: Show is juried. For consideration, provide photos or slides (3), sample of work and written description of work.

SHADYSIDE SUMMER ARTS FESTIVAL

Ed D'Alessandro
P.O. Box 10139
Pittsburgh, PA 15232
Phone: (412)681-2809
Fax: (412)681-1226
First show: 1970
Time of year: August
Location: The Walnut St. Commercial District in Pittsburgh. Outdoor. The district has over 140 upscale retail shops with ajoining residential area.
Duration: F-Sun
Attendance: 250,000
Admission: Free
Categories: Fine crafts, wearable art, jewelry, miniatures/dollhouses, wooden crafts, paper products, stained glass items, needlework crafts, hand blown glass items, home decor, dolls/stuffed animals/toys, pottery/ceramics, nature crafts/floral, leather crafts, baskets, recycled crafts, sculpture, furniture
Price range: $5-10,000
Advertising/Promotion: Radio, TV, area and festival newspapers, direct mail. Over $30,000 budget.
Spaces available: 200. 10′ × 10′ and 10′ × 20′ booths (side-by-side or walk through); tables, chairs and electricity available.
Cost of space: $395
Application process: Show is juried. For consideration, provide slides (5) and written description of work. $15 charge to apply.
Additional information: Artist party to meet eachother; booth sales attendants; restaurant discounts for artists; artist hotel services; booth sitters; overnight security; artist parking lot 150′ from show area; special individual security for large sums of money and valuables. *Sunshine Artist* named this festival in their 1996 200 Best Fine Arts, Fine Crafts and Traditional Crafts Shows issue.

SHAKER WOODS FESTIVAL

Sue and Sam Ferguson
46000 New England Square
New Waterford, OH 44445
Phone: (330)457-7615
Fax: (330)457-1533
First show: 1983

Time of year: Second, third and fourth weekends in August

Location: Off St. 7, on County Line Rd., Columbiana, OH. Outdoor. In a woods.

Duration: Sat-Sun 10-6

Attendance: 100,000

Admission: $4.50 adults, 12 and under free

Categories: Wearable art, jewelry, miniatures/dollhouses, wooden crafts, paper products, stained glass items, needlework crafts, hand blown glass items, home decor, dolls/stuffed animals/toys, pottery/ceramics, nature crafts/floral, leather crafts, baskets, sculpture, weaving, soops, tatting, wood carvers, candles, more

Price range: $10-500

Advertising/Promotion: Newspaper (Cleveland, Youngstown, Akron, Pittsburgh, West Virginia and local), radio, TV, billboards, fliers. $25,000 and up budget.

Spaces available: 200. 10' × 12' and 15' × 18' spaces. Booths must be built by exhibitor.

Cost of space: $395-595

Application process: Show is juried. For consideration, provide photos or slides (3), sample of work, SASE and written description of work. No charge to apply.

Additional information: Our show is a juried invitational accepting quality work which must be made by exhibitor. Must demonstrate work and be in a Shaker 18th Century period costume.

SOUTH MIAMI ART & CRAFT FEST

Red/Sunset Merchants Association
Wanda Hammon
5854 S. Dixie Hwy.
South Miami, FL 33143
Phone: (305)558-1758; (305)666-6647
Fax: (305)666-0554; (305)271-7944
First show: 1984
Time of year: Last weekend in February
Location: Sunset Dr. in downtown South Miami. Outdoor. On a main street.
Duration: Sat-Sun 9-6
Attendance: 60,000
Admission: Free
Categories: Fine crafts, jewelry, wooden crafts, stained glass items, hand blown glass items, pottery/ceramics, baskets

Price range: Varied from medium to high end

Advertising/Promotion: TV, radio, newspapers, banners, posters. Budget varies.

Spaces available: 195. 10' × 10' booths.

Cost of space: $175

Application process: Show is juried. For consideration, provide slides (3 of work and 1 of display). No charge to apply.

Additional information: The show has a food court, music and entertainment and a hands on children's area.

SPRING FESTIVAL OF THE ARTS

Arts Council of Oklahoma City
400 W. California
Oklahoma City, OK 73102
Phone: (405)270-4848
Fax: (405)270-4888
First show: 1967
Time of year: End of April
Location: Festival Plaza, West California Street, Myriad Gardens, Oklahoma City. Outdoor. Takes place at a closed plaza, surrounding city streets and the adjacent conservatory/greenhouse and gardens.
Duration: T-Sat 11-9, Sun 11-5
Attendance: 750,000
Admission: Free
Categories: Fine crafts, wearable art, jewelry, pottery, sculpture. Show is mainly fine arts.
Price range: $5-25,000
Advertising/Promotion: Advertised on local and regional radio, newspaper, TV and magazines; extensive poster distribution in Oklahoma City metro area; national magazines; Bravo television network
Spaces available: 144. Tents are divided into 4 sections. Electric available. Booth sitters available. Sales are from central cashier.
Application process: Show is juried. For consideration, request application. $150 charge to apply.
Additional information: 20% commission goes to presenting organizion.

STARVING ARTIST ART SHOW®

Little Church of La Villita/Cleo Edmunds
508 Paseo de La Villita
San Antonio, TX 78205
Phone: (210)226-3593
First show: 1963

Time of year: The first weekend in April
Location: Downtown San Antonio La Villita and the Paseo del Rio (riverwalk). Outdoor. The historic district of La Villita (one square block) river walk from Hilton Hotel to old main library on one side (south), from Arneson River Theater to old main library on other side (north).
Duration: Sat-Sun 10AM-dark
Attendance: 36,000
Admission: $3, 12 and under free with adults
Categories: Fine crafts, wearable art, jewelry, miniatures/dollhouses, wooden crafts, paper products, stained glass items, needlework crafts, hand blown glass items, home decor, figurines, dolls/stuffed animals/toys, pottery/ceramics, nature crafts/floral, leather crafts, baskets, recycled crafts, sculpture
Price range: $100 limit
Advertising/Promotion: Art & frame shops (San Antonio, TX); street banners (San Antonio, TX), newspapers (San Antonio and other cities of Texas); *Sunshine Artist*, *Where It's At*, *The Network*, *S.A.C.*, *Southern Living*, *Texas Highways*, Southwestern Bell telephone (S.A.) directory, and many other publications
Spaces available: 800. 10' × 6' and 10' × 10' spaces for booths or tables. No equipment available.
Cost of space: $20 plus 10% sales
Application process: Past participants have first priority and any remaining tables are available on a first-come, first-serve basis.
Additional information: Please, no commercial items for resale, original arts and crafts only, no nudes or objectional material.

STOCKTON ASPARAGUS FESTIVAL ARTS & CRAFTS SHOW

Stockton Arts Commission/Vince Perrin, executive director
425 N. El Dorado St.
Stockton, CA 95202
Phone: (209)937-7488
Fax: (209)937-7149
E-mail: stkarts@inreach.com
First show: 1985
Time of year: Last full weekend in April
Location: Oak Grove Regional Park, at

the northeast corner of the intersection of Eight Mile Rd. and Interstate 5. Outdoor. Show is on the north side of a lake in the middle of a grassy park surrounded by a grove of large oak trees.

Duration: F-Sun, 10-7

Attendance: 100,000

Admission: $6

Categories: Fine crafts, wearable art, jewelry, miniatures/dollhouses, wooden crafts, paper products, stained glass items, needlework crafts, hand blown glass items, home decor, figurines, dolls/stuffed animals/toys, pottery/ceramics, nature crafts/floral, leather crafts, baskets, sculpture, photographs

Price range: $5-500

Advertising/Promotion: Print and broadcast media, billboards, through agricultural organizations, vendor postcards mailed to clients. $46,000 budget.

Spaces available: 115. Booths 10′×10′ under six large tents with no sides; booths face out, providing interior storage. Corner and double booths on request. No electricity. Adjacent vendor parking.

Cost of space: $300 for 3 days

Application process: Show is juried. $10 charge to apply.

Additional information: For our arts and crafts vendors we provide complimentary coffee, tea, fruit and doughnuts every morning; twice-a-day delivery to booths of food from Asparagus Alley; private vendor-only rest rooms and rest area; telephone for credit card checks; booth-sitting volunteers; money-changing service; shuttle of large items to buyer's car; discounts at area motels and hotels.

STOWE FLOWER FESTIVAL CRAFT SHOW

Stowe Area Association/Diane Wood
1652 Mountain Rd.
Stowe, VT 05672

Fax: (802)253-5159

E-mail: whiskrest@aol.com

First show: 1991

Time of year: Last weekend in June

Location: Whiskers Field, Mountain Rd., Stowe. Outdoor. Show takes place in a tent off the main road of this resort town. Part of the Stowe Flower Festival (40 events).

Duration: Sat-Sun 10-5

Attendance: 4,000-5,000

Admission: Free

Categories: Fine craft, wearable art, wooden crafts, paper products, hand blown glass items, pottery/ceramics, nature crafts/floral, baskets, sculpture, only flower and garden related items

Price range: $10-2,000

Advertising/Promotion: Direct mailing of 150,000 pieces in "Stowe" promotions; NY and Boston flower show booths; local radio and newspapers; posters

Spaces available: 100. Booth space only; 9′×10′ and 10′×10′; spaces on outer edge may go 10′×10′ out from the tent.

Cost of space: $100

Application process: Show is juried. For consideration, provide photos or slides (2). No charge to apply.

Additional information: Part of the Stowe Flower Festival which has 40 events. Craft fair accepts only flower and garden related crafts. Stowe is a popular resort town.

THE SUN VALLEY ARTS & CRAFTS FESTIVAL

Sun Valley Center for the Arts & Humanities
Sally Brock
P.O. Box 656
Sun Valley, ID 83353

Phone: (208)726-9491

Fax: (208)726-2344

First show: 1968

Time of year: August

Location: The soccer field of the Sun Valley Company Resort in Sun Valley. Outdoor. It is on a level, grassy field on the resort property of Sun Valley Company; adjacent to lodge, shops and recreational facilities.

Duration: F 10-6, Sat 10-6, Sun 10-5

Attendance: 2,000 daily

Admission: Free

Categories: Fine crafts, wearable art, jewelry, paper products, hand blown glass items, home decor, dolls/stuffed animals/toys, pottery/ceramics, leather crafts, baskets, recycled crafts, sculpture

Price range: $2,000-5,000

Advertising/Promotion: Advertised locally, regionally in newspapers, on radio. Through announcements sent to all of the S.V. Center for the Arts & Humanities membership. Banner on Main Street during week of festival, vacation planning guides sent out by Sun Valley Chamber of Commerce. $1,000 budget.

Spaces available: 140. Artists may rent either a 10′×10′ or a 10′×20′ space. They are responsible for their own booth, which must be attractive and sturdy, as well as any display items.

Cost of space: $250-400

Application process: Show is juried. For consideration, provide slides (5). $15 charge to apply.

TEMPLE TERRACE COMMUNITY ARTS FESTIVAL

Temple Terrace Art League
P.O. Box 291266
Temple Terrace, FL 33687

First show: 1973

Time of year: Second weekend in November

Location: Riverhills Park, Temple Terrace. Outdoor. Along the banks of the Hillsborough River.

Duration: Sat-Sun 10-4

Attendance: 200,000

Admission: Free

Categories: Fine crafts, wearable art, jewelry, wooden crafts, stained glass items, hand blown glass items, pottery/ceramics, sculpture

Price range: $3 and up

Advertising/Promotion: Newspapers—4 county area regional and national trade publications, local radio and TV. Budget varies.

Spaces available: 150. 10′×10′ outdoor spaces.

Cost of space: $80

Application process: Show is juried. For consideration, provide photos or slides (5). $80 charge to apply.

Additional information: Send an SASE for application. Application must be returned by September 1.

TULSA ARTS & CRAFTS FALL FESTIVAL

Donna Gibbs, exhibitor coordinator
P.O. Box 54424
Tulsa, OK 74155

Phone: (918)743-4311

First show: 1982

Time of year: First weekend in November

Location: Exposition Center at Expo Square (Fairgrounds), 21st and Yale, Tulsa. Indoor. Show is held inside the largest facility on the Tulsa fairgrounds.

Duration: F 10-8, Sat 9-6, Sun 12-6

Attendance: 15,000-20,000

Admission: $2

Categories: Fine crafts, wearable art, jewelry, miniatures/dollhouses, wooden crafts, stained glass items, needlework crafts, hand blown glass items, dolls/stuffed animals/toys, pottery/ceramics, nature crafts/floral, leather crafts, baskets, sculpture

Price range: $1-25,000

Advertising/Promotion: Metropolitan newspapers, expressway marquees, TV, periodicals, calendars, direct mail, radio, etc. Posters and fliers are distributed throughout area. Exhibitors are given an advertising summary at the show.

Spaces available: 200. Draped booths that are 10′ × 10′ with free electricity. Exhibitor may rent more than one space.

Cost of space: $125 plus 10% commission for 10′ × 10′

Application process: Show is juried. For consideration, provide slides (4). No charge to apply.

Additional information: Sponsor of show is Tulsa Arts & Crafts, Inc., an Oklahoma nonprofit corporation. Proceeds of show are given to selected charities. Exhibitors are provided with a hospitality room throughout the show. Boothsitters are available for short periods. Public enters facility from both sides, so exhibitors do not need to be concerned about right-handed crowds. There is not a bad location in the facility.

UPTOWN ART FAIR

Cari DeWall
3013 Holmes Ave. S.
Minneapolis, MN 55408
Phone: (612)823-4581
Fax: (612)825-6304
First show: 1963
Time of year: First weekend of August
Location: Hennepin and Lake St., Minneapolis. Outdoor. A business community and grassy park property in the uptown, adjacent to 2 Minneapolis Lakes.

Duration: F-Sun 10-dusk

Attendance: 350,000

Admission: Free

Categories: Wearable art, jewelry, stained glass items, hand blown glass items, pottery/ceramics, baskets, sculpture, paintings, drawings, photography

Price range: $25-3,000

Advertising/Promotion: Radio, TV, newspaper, magazines. $30,000 budget.

Spaces available: 525. 10′ × 10′ spaces.

Cost of space: $250-350

Application process: Show is juried. For consideration, provide slides (4). $20 charge to apply.

VALLEY FORGE PRESENTS A CRAFT EXTRAVAGANZA

Rose Brein Finkel and Arleen Strauss
P.O. Box 535
Devault, PA 19432
Phone: (610)827-1505
Fax: (610)640-2332
First show: 1996
Time of year: October
Location: Valley Forge Convention Center, King of Prussia, PA. Indoor.

Duration: 4 days

Categories: Fine crafts, wearable art, jewelry, miniatures/dollhouses, wooden crafts, paper products, stained glass items, needlework crafts, hand blown glass items, home decor, figurines, dolls/stuffed animals/toys, pottery/ceramics, nature crafts/floral, leather crafts, baskets, recycled crafts, sculpture

Price range: $5-5,000

Advertising/Promotion: Radio, direct mail, newspapers, magazines, fliers, posters. $20,000 budget.

Spaces available: 100. 8′ × 8′, 8′ × 10′, 10′ × 10′ and 10′ × 20′ spaces. Electricity, draped tables are available for rent. Exhibitors bring own booth, display, fixtures, lighting, etc.

Cost of space: $300 and up

Application process: Show is juried. For consideration, provide photos or slides (3 of craft, 1 of booth) and completed application. $10 charge to apply.

Additional information: The show offers the first 2 days for retail to the public, and the next 2 days for wholesale cash and carry for trade customers.

WESLEYAN POTTERS ANNUAL EXHIBIT AND SALE

Melissa Schilke
350 S. Main St. (Rt. 17)
Middletown, CT 06457
Phone: (860)347-5925; (860)344-0039
Fax: (860)347-5925
First show: 1955
Time of year: 2 weeks following Thanksgiving
Location: 350 S. Main St., (Rt. 17), Middletown, CT at the Pottery Studios. Indoor. The studios at Wesleyan Potters Craft Center.

Duration: 2 weeks beginning on a Saturday and ending on Sunday. Open 10-6 daily, Th-F 10-9.

Attendance: 10,000

Admission: Free

Categories: Fine crafts, wearable art, jewelry, wooden crafts, paper products, stained glass items, hand blown glass items, dolls/stuffed animals/toys, pottery/ceramics, leather crafts, baskets, sculpture, weaving

Price range: $2-2,000

Advertising/Promotion: Newspapers: *Hartford Courant, New London Day, New Haven Register, Middletown Press, Hartford & New Haven Advocate*, public radio; fliers mailed to 8,000 homes. $7,000 budget.

Spaces available: This is a gallery setting. Members of the Wesleyan Potters man the show. All work is on consignment.

Application process: Show is juried. For consideration, provide 3 samples of work. No charge to apply.

WONDERFUL WORLD OF OHIO

Karen Thomas
840 Lafayette Dr.
Akron, OH 44303
Phone: (303)867-2603
First show: 1966
Time of year: First 4 days including a weekend in October
Location: Stan Hywet Hall and Gardens, 714 N. Portage Path, Akron. Indoor and outdoor. Private home and grounds of the late F.A. Sieberling.

Duration: Th-Sun 10-5
Attendance: 20,000
Admission: $5
Categories: Fine crafts, wearable art, jewelry, wooden crafts, stained glass items, needlework crafts, hand blown glass items, dolls/stuffed animals/ toys, pottery/ceramics, nature crafts/ floral, leather crafts, baskets
Price range: $25-500
Advertising/Promotion: Local newspapers, fliers, TV
Spaces available: 25-30. Booths only. Each space is 10′ × 10′.
Cost of space: $400-450
Application process: Show is juried. For consideration, provide photos or slides (6) and sample of work. Personal screening advised. No charge to apply.
Additional information: Exhibitor must dress in Renaissance costume. Costume contest held. Monetary prizes (5). Be willing to donate an item for a raffle.

WOODSTOCK ARTS & CRAFTS FESTIVAL

Ruth Milstein
11831 NW 25th St.
Plantation, FL 33323
Phone: (954)370-8651
E-mail: rsnm@aol.com
First show: 1980
Time of year: First weekend in December
Location: Welleby Park, NW 44th St. and Hiatus Rd., Sunrise, FL. Outdoor. In a park.
Duration: Sat-Sun 9-5
Attendance: 30,000-40,000
Admission: $2 or 4 cans of food
Categories: Fine crafts, wearable art, jewelry, wooden crafts, stained glass items, needlework crafts, hand blown glass items, home decor, figurines, dolls/stuffed animals/toys, pottery/ceramics, nature crafts/floral, leather crafts, baskets, sculpture
Advertising/Promotion: Radio, signs on roadways, newspaper ads
Spaces available: 350. Booths, bring own set-up.
Cost of space: $175
Application process: Past participants have first priority, and any remaining tables are available on a first-come,

first-serve basis. Must provide photos or slides, but show is not juried.

YE MERRY OLDE CHRISTMAS FAIRE

Pauline Breidenbach
1418 San Rafael NE
Albuquerque, NM 87122
Phone: (505)856-1970
First show: 1990
Time of year: Thanksgiving weekend and first weekend in December
Location: Lujan Complex, New Mexico State Fairgrounds, Albuquerque. Indoor.
Duration: F-Sun
Attendance: 25,000
Admission: $4, children free
Categories: Fine crafts, wearable art, jewelry, miniatures/dollhouses, wooden crafts, paper products, stained glass items, needlework crafts, hand blown glass items, home decor, figurines, dolls/stuffed animals/toys, pottery/ceramics, nature crafts/floral, leather crafts, baskets, recycled crafts, collectibles, gifts
Price range: $10-1,000
Advertising/Promotion: TV, radio, newspaper, direct mail, city bus panels, fliers, media sponsors. $80,000 budget.
Spaces available: 250. 10′ × 10′ booths, pipe and curtain on 3 sides. Larger sizes available.
Cost of space: $295 +
Application process: Dealers are accepted on a first-come, first-serve basis, as long as they fit the requirements of the show. Products must be approved by Standards Committee.
Additional information: Show is set amid Old English Village Scenes. All exhibitors are strongly encouraged to wear costumes. Awards for best costumes and booths.

Wholesale

THE CORAL GABLES INTERNATIONAL FESTIVAL OF CRAFT ARTS, INC.

Pat Lowenstein
2100 Salzedo St., Suite 303
Coral Gables, FL 33134
Phone: (305)445-9973
Fax: (305)444-4754
First show: 1992

Time of year: Second weekend of November
Location: Downtown Coral Gables, on the streets of Ponce de Leon Blvd. and Alhambra Plaza. Outdoor. Central business district of the international city of Coral Gables in the heart of Miami.
Duration: Sat-Sun 10-6
Attendance: 75,000-100,000
Admission: Free
Categories: Fine crafts, wearable art, jewelry, miniatures/dollhouses, wooden crafts, paper products, stained glass items, needlework crafts, hand blown glass items, home decor, figurines, dolls/stuffed animals/toys, pottery/ceramics, nature crafts/floral, leather crafts, baskets, sculpture
Price range: $25-100
Advertising/Promotion: 9 radio stations, 6 TV stations, 5 local newspapers, on a billboard at a major intersection, on bus, Tri-Rail and Metro Rail stations and cars
Spaces available: 300. Booth spaces 10′ × 10′ and 10′ × 20′ are available with tables and chairs for rent.
Cost of space: 10′ × 10′ space is $200, 10′ × 20′ is $400.
Application process: Show is juried. $25 charge to apply.
Additional information: The Coral Gables International Festival of Craft Arts, Inc., (CGIFCA) is one of South Florida's most unique and entertaining cultural events. The two-day event features indigenous art ranging from song, dance, culinary culture, storytelling, folk art, traditional and contemporary craft art from North, Central, South America, Islands of the Bahamas, Caribbean, countries from Asia, Africa, Europe and highlights new countries each year.

POWERS' CROSSROADS COUNTRY FAIR & ART FESTIVAL

Coweta Festivals, Inc./Dee Dee Bauer, festival director and Dann Jackson, director of promotions
P.O. Box 899
Newnan, GA 30264
Phone: (770)253-2011
Fax: (770)253-8180
E-mail: cowetafest@aol.com

First show: 1971

Time of year: Labor Day weekend

Location: Historic Powers' plantation festival site. 10 miles west of Newnan, GA on GA Hwy. 34. Outdoor. Festival takes place under the spreading oaks of the Powers' Plantation, rolling terrain and heavily wooded.

Duration: Sat-M 9-6

Attendance: 60,000-70,000

Admission: $5 adults, $2 children (4-12), discounts for senior citizens and military

Categories: Fine crafts, wearable art, jewelry, miniatures/dollhouses, wooden crafts, paper products, stained glass items, needlework crafts, hand blown glass items, dolls/stuffed animals/toys, pottery/ceramics, nature crafts/floral, leather crafts, baskets, sculpture.

Price range: $1-5,000

Advertising/Promotion: TV—all Atlanta markets and Macon and Columbus, GA; billboards in metro Atlanta; radio spots, TV talk shows; 50,000 brochures, 3 major news releases before the festival; feature articles throughout Georgia. $40,000 budget.

Spaces available: 300. Raw ground along wooded paths. Exhibitor provides total display. 10'×10' and 10'×15' spaces available. Spaces vary in depth.

Cost of space: $150-200

Application process: Show is juried. For consideration, provide slides (5). $20 charge to apply.

Additional information: The festival features the work of 300 exhibitors from across America, continuous entertainment, and working demonstrations of actual farm life cica 1850. Our festival is basically ⅓ fine art; ⅓ fine craft and ⅓ traditional craft.

SHADYSIDE SUMMER ARTS FESTIVAL

Ed D'Alessandro

P.O. Box 10139

Pittsburgh, PA 15232

Phone: (412)681-2809

Fax: (412)681-1226

First show: 1970

Time of year: August

Location: The Walnut St. Commercial District in Pittsburgh. Outdoor. The district has over 140 upscale retail shops with ajoining residential area.

Duration: F-Sun

Attendance: 250,000

Admission: Free

Categories: Fine crafts, wearable art, jewelry, miniatures/dollhouses, wooden crafts, paper products, stained glass items, needlework crafts, hand blown glass items, home decor, dolls/stuffed animals/toys, pottery/ceramics, nature crafts/floral, leather crafts, baskets, recycled crafts, sculpture, furniture

Price range: $5-10,000

Advertising/Promotion: Radio, TV, area and festival newspapers, direct mail. Over $30,000 budget.

Spaces available: 200. 10'×10' and 10'×20' booths (side-by-side or walk through); tables, chairs and electricity available.

Cost of space: $395

Application process: Show is juried. For consideration, provide slides (5) and written description of work. $15 charge to apply.

Additional information: Artist party to meet eachother; booth sales attendants; restaurant discounts for artist; artist hotel services; booth sitters; overnight security; artist parking 150' from show area; special individual security for large sums of money and valuables. *Sunshine Artist* named this festival in their 1996 200 Best Fine Arts, Fine Crafts and Traditional Crafts Shows issue.

VALLEY FORGE PRESENTS A CRAFT EXTRAVAGANZA

Rose Brein Finkel and Arleen Strauss

P.O. Box 535

Devault, PA 19432

Phone: (610)827-1505

Fax: (610)640-2332

First show: 1995

Time of year: October

Location: Valley Forge Convention Center, King of Prussia, PA. Indoor.

Duration: 4 days

Categories: Fine crafts, wearable art, jewelry, miniatures/dollhouses, wooden crafts, paper products, stained glass items, needlework crafts, hand blown glass items, home decor, figurines, dolls/stuffed animals/toys, pottery/ceramics, nature crafts/floral, leather crafts, baskets, recycled crafts, sculpture

Price range: $5-5,000

Advertising/Promotion: Radio, direct mail, newspapers, magazines, fliers, posters. $20,000 budget.

Spaces available: 100. 8'×8', 8'×10', 10'×10' and 10'×20' spaces. Electricity, draped tables are available for rent. Exhibitors bring own booth, display, fixtures, lighting, etc.

Cost of space: $300-500

Application process: Show is juried. For consideration, provide photos or slides (3 of craft, 1 of booth) and completed application. $10 charge to apply.

Additional information: The show offers the first 2 days for retail to the public, and the next 2 days for wholesale cash and carry for trade customers.

CHAPTER NINE
Direct Sales

CRAFT MALLS, CO-OPS AND OTHER MARKETS

AMISH ACRES
Richard Pletcher
1600 W. Market St.
Nappanee, IN 46550
Phone: (219)773-4188; (800)800-4942
Fax: (219)773-4180
Type of business: Craft mall
In business since: 1969
Hours: 10-5 daily
Description of business: Amish Acres vendors have the potential privilege of displaying in up to eight distinct shops (Amish Acres, The Cow Shed, The Nappanee Collection, The House Across the Street, The Stone House Christmas Shop, The School Belfry, The Inn at Amish Acres and The Nappanee Inn) within the same complex with single management and accounting. Upon acceptance through a rigorous jurying process, experienced personnel accept vendor's merchandise priced with Amish Acres' own tags at the shop door, integrate and display it in its best light.
Categories: Fine crafts, wearable art, jewelry, miniatures/dollhouses, wooden crafts, paper products, stained glass items, needlework crafts, hand blown glass items, home decor, figurines, dolls/stuffed animals/toys, pottery/ceramics, nature crafts/floral, leather crafts, baskets, recycled crafts
More about products: Country/Amish flavor, rustic, folk, school themes, cow themes, high quality
Price range: $1-500
Advertising/Promotion: 35 newspapers (*Chicago Tribune* plus Detroit, Indianapolis and local), group tour business
Spaces available: Unlimited amount of inventory. Merchandise is not set up in booth presentation. Each vendor's items are displayed by Amish Acres in their best light.
Cost of space: Commission on products sold in lieu of space rental

Application process: For consideration, provide photos or slides (4-6), written description of work, request information packet.
Contract: Length of contract varies. Amish Acres reserves the right to not accept any merchandise in the jurying process based on quality and appropriateness. Craftsperson is paid monthly.
Out-of-town requirements: Accepts work by local or out-of-town craftspeople. We have a warehouse at which to receive any size product, boxed to large furniture items.
Craftsperson's responsibilities: Crafter must get crafts to location. If desired, can send out a monthly printout of what has sold.

ARTISANS CRAFT MALL
Yvette Kraemer
4305 E. Hwy. 377
Granbury, TX 76049
Phone: (817)573-8083
Type of business: Craft mall
In business since: 1989
Hours: 10-6 daily
Description of business: Unique tourist mall in quaint tourist town within 30 minutes of Dallas/Ft. Worth. Friendly atmosphere, great prices, excellent variety of *quality* crafts.
Types of products: Hand crafted items and greeting cards, soda shop, gift bags, tourist items
Categories: Fine crafts, wearable art, jewelry, miniatures/dollhouses, wooden crafts, stained glass items, needlework crafts, home decor, figurines, dolls/stuffed animals/toys, pottery/ceramics, nature crafts/floral, leather crafts, baskets, recycled crafts
Price range: 25¢-$750
Advertising/Promotion: All motel/hotels in area, local newspaper, tourist bureau, special sales and promos, *Friends & Neighbors*, Ft. Worth *Star Telegram*. $5,000-6,000/year budget.
Spaces available: 200. 4′×4′ and multi-

ples of 4′×4′s (4′×8′, 4′×12′, etc.). Back wall is 6′ tall pegboard of each booth.
Cost of space: $50 per month for 6 month lease, $60 per month for 3 month lease. 3+ booths get 15% discount.
Contract: Length of contract is 3 months or 6 months. After initial contract, month to month. Craftsperson is paid every other week.
Out-of-town requirements: Accepts work by local or out-of-town craftspeople.
Craftsperson's responsibilities: Crafter must get crafts to location and keep track of stock. Crafter must set up display. Mall provides central checkout and individual vendor numbers.

ARTISANS VILLAGE
Susan
182 N. Village Ct.
San Dimas, CA 91773
Phone: (909)394-0505
Type of Business: Craft mall
In business since: 1993
Hours: M-F 10-8, Sat 10-7, Sun 10-6
Description of business: Artisan's Village is a craft mall with a unique combination of individual booths and blended display areas that offer a wide variety of hand crafted items, popular collectibles and other items for home decorating and gift giving.
Types of products: Hand crafted items and collectibles: porcelain items, cards and giftwrap
Categories: Fine crafts, wearable art, jewelry, miniatures/dollhouses, wooden crafts, paper products, needlework crafts, hand blown glass items, home decor, figurines, dolls/stuffed animals/toys, pottery/ceramics, nature crafts/floral, leather crafts, baskets, recycled crafts, sculpture
Price range: $1-350
Advertising/Promotion: Community newspapers in surrounding areas, ads in and donations to area school and

community functions. $12,000-15,000/year budget.

Spaces available: 200. From a single shelf (3'w × 24"d) to end panel (3'w × 8'h × 12"d) to a minimum booth of 3'w × 3'd with 8' back wall. Blended option is about an "end panel's" worth.

Cost of space: Shelves—$30 or $35, end panels—$55 to $70, booths—$85 start, blended—$48 month

Application process: For consideration, provide photos, sample of work, catalog/promotional materials and written description of work.

Contract: Length of contract is 2 months initial, month to month thereafter. Rent own area—4% from net sales to advertising pool; blended—9%. Credit card purchases carry the bank's surcharge. Craftsperson is paid twice a month.

Out-of-town requirements: Accepts work by local or out-of-town craftspeople. Crafters must use provided bar code tags (3¢ each). Items must be tagged before shipping. Blended—no additional charge. Own booth—$15-25 first time set up. Plus $5-15 a month for remote restocking.

Craftsperson's responsibilities: Crafter must get crafts to location, keep track of stock and set up display except for blended and remote restockers. Merchandise sold by staff. Only hand crafted or embellished (50%) accepted.

BAY HEAD COUNTRY ACCENTS CHRISTMAS BOUTIQUE

Elaine Flannelly
P.O. Box 192
Bay Head, NJ 08742
Phone: (908)899-6398; (908)899-9251
Type of business: Consignment Christmas boutique
In business since: 1980
Hours: November, 9:30-5:30 daily
Description of business: We represent 250 crafters from over 30 states at present. All are juried with no exception; very few duplications. A mailing list of over 7,000 and a selling space of 3,000 sq. ft. enables us to be very successful for our crafters.
Types of products: Hand crafted items and jewelry and antiques.

Categories: Jewelry, wooden crafts, paper products, stained glass items, hand blown glass items, home decor, figurines, dolls/toys, pottery/ceramics, nature crafts/floral, baskets
Price range: $5-1,000
Advertising/Promotion: Local newspapers and TV, state magazines and 7,000 cards mailed. $12,000/year budget.
Spaces available: We decorate and display crafter's items ourselves.
Cost of space: $40 registration; 25% commission on all items sold
Application process: For consideration, provide photos or slides (6), sample of work and written description of work.
Contract: Length of contract is 1 month. Craftsperson is paid at the end of the show.
Out-of-town requirements: Acccpts work by local or out-of-town craftspeople. Crafter pays all shipping costs if mailed to us including insurance.
Craftsperson's responsibilities: Crafter must get crafts to location. We keep crafter informed of stock. Merchandise is sold by staff.

BROOKLINE ARTS CENTER

Isabella Frost
86 Mammouth St.
Brookline, MA 02146
Phone: (617)566-5715; (617)566-5212
Fax: (617)738-8760
Type of business: Non-profit organization with juried showcase
In business since: 1965
Hours: December, 12-6
Types of products: Hand crafted items only
Categories: Fine crafts, wearable art, jewelry, miniatures/dollhouses, wooden crafts, paper products, stained glass items, hand blown glass items, home decor, dolls/stuffed animals/toys, pottery/ceramics, nature crafts/floral, leather crafts, baskets, sculpture
Price range: $1.50-2,000
Advertising/Promotion: Local papers
Spaces available: 65-80. Gallery style setting, no booths.
Cost of space: $15 jury fee
Application process: For consideration, provide photos or slides (5) and written description of work.

Contract: Length of contract is 3 weeks. Once accepted we ask for a $50 refundable deposit to hold spot in show. Money is returned at end of show. Craftsperson is paid after the show.
Out-of-town requirements: Accepts work by local or out-of-town craftspeople. Must pay UPS fees to ship to us and have it sent back to them.
Craftsperson's responsibilities: Crafter must get crafts to location. We keep extensive inventory and track all items. Gallery sets up. Must sign an insurance wiaver, waiving BAC of any problems.

BUNNY HUTCH GIFTS

Lee Pooley
3401 Cleveland Ave.
Santa Rosa, CA 95403
Phone: (707)578-5881
Type of business: Co-op
In business since: 1989
Hours: T-Sat 10-5
Description of business: Craft mall. We sell country and Victorian crafts. Almost anything cute or pretty.
Types of products: Hand crafted items only
Categories: Wooden crafts, paper products, stained glass items, needlework crafts, home decor, figurines, dolls/stuffed animals/toys, pottery/ceramics, nature crafts/floral, sculpture
Price range: $5-300
Advertising/Promotion: Newspapers, mailing list, fliers.
Spaces available: All crafts are mixed with no limit.
Cost of space: $75 per month or $55 and 10%
Application process: For consideration, provide photos (3), sample of work and catalog/promotional materials.
Contract: Length of contract is monthly—no time limit. Craftsperson is paid the 10th of each month.
Out-of-town requirements: Accepts work by local or out-of-town craftspeople. Must pay own freight. No fee for stocking.
Craftsperson's responsibilities: Crafter must get crafts to location. Crafter will receive price tag back each month. Mall provides central checkout.

CHRISTMAS AT THE CABIN

Janice J. Brizius
251 Cotswold Place
Gahanna, OH 43230
Phone: (614)471-1141; (513)365-1388
Type of business: Consignment house
In business since: 1981
Hours: November-December, W-Sun 10-6
Description of business: Authentic old log cabin featuring the works of 50 nationwide crafters. Entire cabin is "decorated" with the arts/crafts. Artisans need not be present.
Types of products: Hand crafted items only
Categories: Fine crafts, wearable art, jewelry, miniatures/dollhouses, wooden crafts, paper products, stained glass items, needlework crafts, home decor, figurines, dolls/stuffed animals/toys, pottery/ceramics, nature crafts/floral, leather crafts, baskets, sculpture
More about products: Items that "look right" in the cabin setting sell best.
Price range: $1-2,000
Advertising/Promotion: Local news media, *Happenings in the Hills* and *Country Living* magazines and through "1-800-BUCKEYE" travel network
Spaces available: 50 artists accepted. No booths—entire cabin is "decorated" with the crafts.
Cost of space: A 25% commission is charged, plus a $10 advertising fee.
Application process: For consideration, provide photos or slides, sample of work, written description of work, price list and SASE for return of photos/samples.
Contract: Length of contract is during the November/December show. Craftsperson is paid at the conclusion of show.
Out-of-town requirements: Accepts work by local or out-of-town craftsperson. Crafters pay for UPS charges (both ways).
Craftsperson's responsibilities: Crafter must get crafts to location. Cabin personnel keeps track of inventory and calls for restocking. Merchandise is combined with all others. Items remaining at close of show are returned.

Crafter is paid for all items sold less a 25% commission.

COMMONWHEIL ARTISTS COOPERATIVE

Penny Whalen
102 Canon Ave.
Maniton Springs, CO 80829
Phone: (719)685-1008
Type of business: Co-op
In business since: 1972
Hours: 10-6 daily, year-round except 10-8 Memorial Day through Labor Day and Thanksgiving through New Year's.
Types of products: Hand crafted items only.
Categories: Fine crafts, wearable art, jewelry, wooden crafts, paper products, stained glass items, needlework crafts, hand blown glass items, home decor, pottery/ceramics, nature crafts/floral, leather crafts, baskets, sculpture
Price range: $1.50-2,500
Out-of-town requirements: Accepts work by local craftspeople only.
Craftsperson's responsibilities: Crafter must set up display.

COOMERS INC.

Kasey Tuttle
6012 Reef Point Lane
Fort Worth, TX 76135-2056
Phone: (817)237-4588
Fax: (817)237-4875
Type of business: Craft mall
In business since: 1988
Hours: M-Sat 10-6, Sun 12-6
Description of business: Coomers has 30 stores located in 9 states: AZ, CO, GA, IL, IN, KS, MO, OH, TX and still growing. We are the largest retailer of American handmade crafts created by hundreds of crafters from around the nation.
Types of products: Hand crafted items only
Categories: Fine crafts, wearable art, jewelry, miniatures/dollhouses, wooden crafts, paper products, stained glass items, needlework crafts, hand blown glass items, home decor, figurines, dolls/stuffed animals/toys, pottery/ceramics, nature crafts/floral, leather crafts, baskets, recycled crafts, sculpture
More about products: The main require-

ments are that the crafts are handmade and that they are made in America.
Price range: All ranges
Advertising/Promotion: Newspapers, trade publications, some radio and TV
Spaces available: Varies
Cost of space: $49-195, prices vary per store
Application process: For consideration, provide sample of work and written description of work.
Contract: Length of contract is 6 months. Craftsperson is paid every 2 weeks.
Out-of-town requirements: Accepts work by local or out-of-town craftspeople.
Craftsperson's responsibilities: Crafter must get crafts to location. We have a National Crafter Network program in effect. It includes decoration of booth and display of crafts to crafter's specs, photo of booth and monitoring of booths for effective display and sales. Shipment stocked and displayed within 24 hours. Weekly printout of sales with quarterly picture of booth. There is a charge if a crafter needs someone to set up their booth. We operate and market your business for you. Our friendly sales staff will provide your customers with excellent customer service and an enjoyable shopping experience.

COOPER STREET CRAFT MALL

Kim York and Steve Ashmore
1701 S. Cooper
Arlington, TX 76010
Phone: (817)261-3184; (800)653-1130
Fax: (817)861-4470
Type of business: Craft mall
In business since: 1990
Hours: M-W, F, Sat 10-6, Th 10-8, Sun 12-5
Description of business: Cooper Street Craft Mall is located in one of the fastest growing markets in the country. Over 500,000 people live in the trade area. Cooper Street Craft Mall has sold over $4 million worth of arts and crafts since its opening. Dealers need only select the amount of space they need, price their items and we'll do the rest. The mission of Cooper Street Craft Mall is to create a quality shopping experience for its customers that

results in maximum sales success for its dealers.

Categories: Fine crafts, wearable art, jewelry, miniatures, wooden crafts, paper products, stained glass items, needlework crafts, hand blown glass items, home decor, figurines, dolls/stuffed animals/toys, pottery/ceramics, nature crafts/floral, baskets, recycled crafts, sculpture

Price range: $1-250

Advertising/Promotion: Billboards, direct mail, newspaper, radio, TV. $50,000/year budget.

Spaces available: 330. 3′ × 4′ to 5′ × 10′. Fully constructed of ¼ inch pegboard.

Cost of space: Booth fees are $5 per foot per month and $10 a month advertising fee.

Application process: For consideration, provide photos.

Contract: Length of contract is 6 months. Dealer who is in 2 or more of our malls receives up to a 15% discount on booth fees. Craftsperson is paid twice monthly.

Out-of-town requirements: Accepts work by local or out-of-town craftspeople. Each mall has an employee assigned to help remote dealers. No additional fee for remote dealers.

Craftsperson's responsibilities: Crafter must get crafts to location. We provide detail listing of all items sold. We would be glad to set up display for remote dealers. Mall provides central computerized checkout. Mall reserves the right to disallow any merchandise at its sole discretion.

Additional information: State of the art security system including security tags and closed circuit cameras.

COTTAGE CRAFTERS CRAFT & ANTIQUE MALL

Margaret Rodgers
4636 Broadway
Allentown, PA 18104
Phone: (610)366-9222
Fax: (610)366-9223
E-mail: cottagecrafters@aol.com
Type of business: Craft and antique mall
In business since: 1993
Hours: M-F 10-8, Sat 10-6
Types of products: Hand crafted items

and antiques, furniture and collectibles

Categories: Fine crafts, wearable art, jewelry, miniatures/dollhouses, wooden crafts, paper products, stained glass items, needlework crafts, hand blown glass items, home decor, figurines, dolls/stuffed animals/toys, pottery/ceramics, nature crafts/floral, leather crafts, baskets, recycled crafts, sculpture

Price range: $1-2,000

Advertising/Promotion: TV, radio, billboards, local newspapers, fliers, brochures. $70,000/year budget.

Spaces available: 400. 1′ × 3′ × 6′h to 4′ × 8′ × 6′h; also large areas— 10′ × 8′, 12′ × 15′, etc.

Cost of space: 2′ × 4′ × 6′h is $80/month, $30 initial one time set-up fee, commission 5% of sales (for advertising)

Application process: For consideration, provide photos or slides and sample of work.

Contract: Length of contract is 6 months. Craftsperson is paid once a month.

Out-of-town requirements: Accepts work by local or out-of-town craftspeople. Free stocking service, will fax sales data weekly.

Craftsperson's responsibilities: Crafter must get crafts to location, keep track of stock and set up display unless crafter is out of area.

COUNTRY CRAFTS MALL

Linda Wright, manager
110 N. Bickford
El Reno, OK 73036
Phone: (405)262-4311
Type of business: Craft mall
In business since: 1990
Hours: M-Sat 10-5, Sun 1-5
Description of business: Country Crafts Mall has a tea room and adjoining antique mall where one can shop for hours and enjoy a relaxing lunch. It's located in historic downtown El Reno.
Types of products: Hand crafted items and bags, tissue paper, candles and collectibles
Categories: Fine crafts, wearable art, jewelry, miniatures/dollhouses, wooden crafts, paper products, stained glass items, needlework crafts, hand blown glass items, home decor, figu-

rines, dolls/stuffed animals/toys, pottery/ceramics, nature crafts/floral, leather crafts, baskets, recycled crafts, sculpture

Price range: $1-400

Advertising/Promotion: Interstate signs, newspapers, fliers. $10,000/year budget.

Spaces available: 100. 5′ × 5′ and up

Cost of space: Upstairs: $25 and up; downstairs: $50 and up

Application process: For consideration, provide photos (1) and written description of work.

Contract: Length of contract is 6 months. Required: a one 4-hour work day that can be waived for out of state dealers. Craftsperson is paid once monthly.

Out-of-town requirements: Accepts work by local or out-of-town craftspeople. A one time only set up fee is required to get booth set up and stocked, after that stocking is done free.

Craftsperson's responsibilities: Crafter must get crafts to location and set up display unless they are out of state. Clerks are provided.

COUNTRYSIDE CRAFT MALL & ANTIQUES I

35323 Plymouth Rd.
Livonia, MI 48150
Phone: (313)513-2577
Fax: (313)513-8984
Type of business: Craft mall
In business since: 1993
Hours: M-W, F 10-6; Th, Sat 10-8; Sun 11-5
Description of business: The largest seller of dealer made hand crafted items in the Midwest. Over 26,000 sq. ft. of arts, crafts, antiques and collectibles. Quality and customer satisfaction are our strongest points.
Types of products: Hand crafted items and antiques and collectibles
Categories: Fine crafts, wearable art, jewelry, miniatures/dollhouses, wooden crafts, paper products, stained glass items, needlework crafts, hand blown glass items, home decor, figurines, dolls/stuffed animals/toys, pottery/ceramics, nature crafts/floral, leather crafts, baskets
Price range: 50¢-$2,000
Advertising/Promotion: TV, news-

papers, the *Country Register*, billboards, grocery store carts, coupon mailers and direct mail

Spaces available: Varies (sometimes a waiting list). Pegboard booths 6′ high (5′3″ high in Livonia) painted white; 1′ × 2′ to 5′ × 8′ and larger spaces

Cost of space: $50-330 plus 8% of sales

Application process: For consideration, provide photos (3), catalog/promotional materials and written description of work.

Contract: Length of contract is 6 or 12 months. Craftsperson is paid twice a month.

Out-of-town requirements: Accepts work by local or out-of-town craftspeople. No charge for booth set up unless there are extra special needs; we provide photographs several times a year; crafts must be pre-coded and priced.

Craftsperson's responsibilities: Crafter must get crafts to location and keep track of stock. Trained staff manages the sales. If electric is needed there is a $30 one time fee.

Additional information: Please see the listings below for other locations.

COUNTRYSIDE CRAFT MALL & ANTIQUES II
40700 Van Dyke
Sterling Heights, MI 48313
Phone: (810)977-1633
Fax: (810)977-6625
Type of business: Craft mall
In business since: 1994
Hours: M-W, F 10-6; Th, Sat 10-8; Sun 11-5
Description of business: Over 30,000 sq. ft. Please see the above listing for more information.

COUNTRYSIDE CRAFT MALL & ANTIQUES III
1154 E. West Maple
Walled Lake, MI 48390
Phone: (810)926-8650
Fax: (810)926-8652
Type of business: Craft mall
In business since: 1996
Hours: M-W, F 10-6; Th, Sat 10-8; Sun 11-5
Description of business: Over 24,000 sq. ft. Please see the above listing for more information.

COUNTRYSIDE CRAFT MALL & ANTIQUES IV
4333 Miller Rd.
Flint, MI 48507
Phone: (810)230-0885
Fax: (810)230-0969
Type of business: Craft mall
In business since: 1996
Hours: M-W, F 10-6; Th, Sat 10-8; Sun 11-5
Description of business: Great location across from the Genesee Valley Mall. Please see the above listing for more information.

THE CRAFT CENTER AT CAMELOT VILLAGE
Mark and Tierney Beck
Rt. 9 West
Bennington, VT 05201
Phone/Fax: (802)447-0228
Type of business: Craft mall
In business since: 1993
Hours: 9:30-5:30 daily
Description of business: Owned and operated by professional crafters. The Craft Center is guided from the "crafter's perspective." Heavy tourism year round particularly from the Albany Capital region visit the noted complex of shops and attractions in a group of restored barns.
Categories: Fine crafts, wearable art, jewelry, miniatures/dollhouses, wooden crafts, paper products, stained glass items, needlework crafts, hand blown glass items, home decor, figurines, dolls/stuffed animals/toys, pottery/ceramics, nature crafts/floral, leather crafts, baskets, recycled crafts, sculpture
Price range: $1-2,000
Advertising/Promotion: TV, regional magazines, newspapers, tourist publications, signage and special events
Spaces available: 250. From 3′w × 2′d × 5′h floor display to 20′w × 2′d × 7′h wall space. All shelving and some fixtures supplied. All displays constructed of rough-cut pine. No pegboard allowed. No tacky. Lockable jewelry cases available with adjustable shelving. All hardware provided.
Cost of space: $30 per month to custom pricing for booth larger than 6′
Application process: For consideration, provide photos or slides (4), catalog/

promotional materials and written description of work.
Contract: Length of contract is 4 months minimum. Month to month after initial 4 months. Craftsperson is paid monthly.
Out-of-town requirements: Accepts work by local or out-of-town craftspeople. No charge for stocking or booth set-up.
Craftsperson's responsibilities: Crafter must get crafts to location. "Center" staff will do all merchandising and set up at no charge if desired. Merchandise is sold direct to customer in a retail environment.
Additional information: The Craft Center is part of Camelot Village, considered one of New England's most noted complexes, housed in a group of restored barns. The Center also houses Granite Lake Pottery Boutique and International Herbs.

THE CRAFT GALLERY
Ralph Lee
7524 Bosque Blvd., Suite I
Waco, TX 76712
Phone: (817)751-0693
Type of business: Craft mall
In business since: 1993
Hours: M-Sat 10-6, Sun 1-5
Description of business: We often hear about how the craft business is not what it used to be. Well not in Waco! We have opened the first arts and crafts mall in Waco; therefore, our 8,000 sq. ft. store is a brand new concept for Waco and they are eating it alive. We have the sales to prove it. We are still seeing growth of over 20%. If you want crafts in Waco, then you come to the Craft Gallery.
Types of products: Hand crafted items and antiques
Categories: Fine crafts, wearable art, jewelry, miniatures/dollhouses, wooden crafts, paper products, stained glass items, needlework crafts, hand blown glass items, home decor, figurines, dolls/stuffed animals/toys, pottery/ceramics, nature crafts/floral, leather crafts, baskets, recycled crafts, sculpture
Price range: 25¢-$500
Advertising/Promotion: TV, 4 different newspapers, radio, billboards, with 5

different boards on all major highways and interstates in Waco, direct mail—coupons and giveaways. $31,000/year budget.

Spaces available: 235. We have spaces ranging from a 2′×3′ to 4′×12′. All booths are a 3 sided peg board.

Cost of space: $40-130 for a craft booth.

Contract: Length of contract is 6 months. There are no work days. No check or credit card charges. We pay all the sales tax. You pay the first and last month's rent when you move in. There is a 5% commission on all items sold. Craftsperson is paid once a month.

Out-of-town requirements: Accepts work by local or out-of-town craftspeople. The crafter is responsible for shipping us the items and we will stock their booth the day we receive the merchandise at no charge to the vendor.

Craftsperson's responsibilities: Crafter must get crafts to location and keep track of stock. We provide a professional sales staff and a central cash register.

Additional information: We have a state-of-the-art security system to help prevent theft.

CRAFTER'S ALLEY

Gail James
5313 Sunrise Blvd.
Fair Oaks, CA 95628
Phone: (916)863-0797
Type of business: Craft mall
In business since: 1992
Hours: M-Sat 10-6, Sun 11-5. Extended holiday hours. Private shopping hours by appointment.
Description of business: Delightful bit of whimsey and country and the charm of hand fashioned Victorian gifts and florals. Hand blown glass and wood carvings with nostalgic collectibles, award winning local artists.
Types of products: Hand crafted items and Yankee candles, Thomas Kincaid prints
Categories: Fine crafts, wearable art, jewelry, miniatures/dollhouses, wooden crafts, paper products, stained glass items, needlework crafts, hand blown glass items, home decor, figurines, dolls/stuffed animals/toys, pottery/ceramics, nature crafts/floral,

leather crafts, baskets, recycled crafts, sculpture

Price range: $1-2,500

Advertising/Promotion: Sacramento Magazine, Sacto Visitor's Bureau Magazine, Country Register, Village News, TV, $3,500/year budget.

Spaces available: 150. Jewelry cases to 10′×10′ rooms (4′×4′, 4′×6′, 4′×8′). We have 7,000 sq. ft.

Cost of space: 4′×4′ is $125, 15% of sales and 4 hours a month of volunteer work or $20

Application process: For consideration, provide photos or slides, sample of work and catalog/promotional materials.

Contract: Length of contract is 3 months. Keep a full booth, sharing OK (no subletting). Full security system: cameras and electronic detectors (tags) at no cost. Craftsperson is paid every 2 weeks.

Out-of-town requirements: Accepts work by local or out-of-town craftspeople. Crafter pays shipping. We stock at no extra charge.

Craftsperson's responsibilities: Crafter must get crafts to location, keep track of stock and set up display. Management will set up by arrangement. Space decor/design on approval.

Additional information: Crafters Alley is in a beautiful open shopping center. Well maintained common area. Heavy traffic through the center, Sacramento's busiest intersection. Next to Trader Joes & Chili's.

THE CRAFTER'S BASKET

Pat Pellicciotti and Richard Henry
2826 Dekalb Pike, Northtowne Plaza
E. Norriton, PA 19401-1823
Phone: (610)275-5664
Type of business: Craft mall
In business since: 1996
Hours: M-Sat 10-8, Sun 12-5
Description of business: A totally unique gift shopping experience with all handcrafted merchandise by local crafters and artisans, including custom hand crafted furniture.
Types of products: Hand crafted items only.
Categories: Fine crafts, wearable art, jewelry, miniatures/dollhouses, wooden crafts, paper products, stained

glass items, needlework crafts, home decor, figurines, dolls/stuffed animals/toys, pottery/ceramics, nature crafts/floral, leather crafts, baskets, recycled crafts, sculpture, hand crafted furniture

Price range: $2-1,200

Advertising/Promotion: Local and county newspapers, cable TV access channels, fliers at craft shows. $3,000/year budget.

Spaces available: 164. Spaces range from 3′ wide to 6′ wide, all 5′ tall and 2′ deep. Wall spaces are 8′ tall. All are totally peg board.

Cost of space: $65-120 per month

Application process: For consideration, provide photos or slides (3-5) and sample of work.

Contract: Length of contract is 3 months (initial lease only), 6 months and 1 year. No commission on sales. $10 set up fee (one time). Craftsperson is paid monthly.

Out-of-town requirements: Accepts work by local or out-of-town craftspeople.

Craftsperson's responsibilities: After crafter initially sets up his/her booth, will accept and stock their booth via mail at no charge. Crafter pays all shipping charges. Crafter must get crafts to location. Crafter may decorate their booth as they like. Crafter must keep track of stock. Will notify crafter if stock is low. Crafter must set up display. Owners/management sells merchandise.

THE CRAFTER'S HEART GIFT SHOPPE & MALL

Harold and Tisha Todd
114 W. Main
Ada, OK 74820
Phone: (405)436-3727; (405)436-2410
Fax: (405)436-2410
Type of business: Craft mall
In business since: 1992
Hours: T-Sat 10-5
Description of business: Known as "Ada's Little Ozark." Visit the "Bear Barn," The Porch & Pantry, the Amish Marketplace, Town Square and The Piddlin Place Room & Board. Sit under a real 10′ Sycamore tree by the Blacksmith shop. Our main goal is to stock quality crafters.

Categories: Fine crafts, wearable art, miniatures/dollhouses, wooden crafts, paper products, stained glass items, needlework crafts, figurines, dolls/stuffed animals/toys, pottery/ceramics, nature crafts/floral, baskets, recycled crafts, sculpture

Price range: $1-600

Advertising/Promotion: Radio, TV, cable, newsletter

Spaces available: 80. Wall space $3' \times 6'$ to $8' \times 10'$. The space is peg as old wood. We try to customize for crafters.

Cost of space: $25-60, then reduced on larger space

Application process: For consideration, provide photos (2), sample of work and written description of work. Phone calls are also welcome.

Contract: Beginning contract on a 3 month lease, thereafter month by month. 30 days notice of intent to move.

Out-of-town requirements: Accepts work by local or out-of-town craftspeople.

Craftsperson's responsibilities: If items are mailed or shipped, we will stock and decorate booth and keep it appealing. We will not charge a stocking fee. We would like for the crafter to keep an inventory of their products although we will be glad to give an inventory check if requested. Merchandise is sold through the mall salesperson and floor clerks. We ask that the booth be replenished as products are sold.

Additional information: We also have a country/Victorian gift shop, all under one roof—5,000 sq. ft. of shopping.

CRAFTERS MALL OF BETHANY

Kay Barnes
6748 NW 39
Bethany, OK 73008
Phone: (405)495-2444; (405)495-2463
Fax: (405)943-4417
Type of business: Craft mall
In business since: 1991
Hours: M-Sat 10-6
Description of business: The mall is located in a sleepy suburb of greater Oklahoma City, on historic Route 66. It is part of the old downtown, with brick sidewalk, fluted light posts,

granite benches and flower beds. The mall is located at a traffic light with daily vehicle count exceeding 25,000.

Types of products: Hand crafted items and market items that supporting of the crafts industry

Categories: Wearable art, jewelry, miniatures/dollhouses, wooden crafts, paper products, stained glass items, needlework crafts, home decor, figurines, dolls/stuffed animals/toys, pottery/ceramics, nature crafts/floral, baskets, recycled crafts, calligraphy

Price range: 99¢-$90

Advertising/Promotion: Newspaper (circulation 350,000), TV (1 million viewers)

Spaces available: 150. Smallest is $4'd \times 5'w \times 6'h$. Limited number of booths are $2'd \times 6'h \times 8'w$, we will make any $4'$ deep booth as wide as needed.

Cost of space: $4'd \times 5'w \times 6'h$ is $80. No additional fees.

Contract: Length of contract is 6 months. Craftsperson is paid monthly.

Out-of-town requirements: Accepts work by local or out-of-town craftspeople. $2 per quarter hour increment working in "remote" craftsperson booth.

Craftsperson's responsibilities: Crafter must get crafts to location. Must have very detailed description and photo for the mall to do original set-up. Central cash register and tracking provided. Quarter inch peg board supplied by mall, floor covering required.

CRAFTERS MARKET

Linda Greenhaw
9120 E. 31st St., Suite C
Tulsa, OK 74145
Phone: (918)622-0512
Type of business: Craft mall and gift shop
In business since: 1991
Hours: M-W, F-Sat 10-6, Th 10-7, Sun 1-5
Description of business: The mall has 250 booths of quality crafts. We honor Discover, Visa and MasterCard.
Types of products: Hand crafted items and other items on approval
Categories: Wearable art, jewelry, miniatures/dollhouses, wooden crafts, stained glass items, needlework crafts,

home decor, figurines, dolls/stuffed animals/toys, pottery/ceramics, nature crafts/floral, candles

Price range: 50¢-$200

Advertising/Promotion: TV, newspaper, Preview, *Neighbors and Friends*. $10,000/year budget.

Spaces available: 250. $1' \times 2'$ to $4' \times 16'$, all spaces are peg board.

Cost of space: $20-240. No commission on 6 month lease. 1 time $25 booth fee. 3% charge fee on credit cards only.

Application process: For consideration, provide photos or slides.

Contract: Length of contract is 6 month lease with a 30-day notice; after 6 months, lease vendor is on a month-to month basis. Craftsperson is paid monthly.

Out-of-town requirements: Accepts work by local or out-of-town craftspeople. No extra charge for restocking.

Craftsperson's responsibilities: Crafter must get crafts to location and keep track of stock. We do give a print out of what was sold at end of month. Crafter must set up display. We have store employees who work the store.

CRAFTERS' MARKET OF MINNESOTA, INC. I

Ron Handevidt
1959 W. Burnsville Pkwy.
Burnsville, MN 55337
Phone: (612)890-2288
Type of business: Craft mall
In business since: 1991
Hours: M-F 10-9, Sat 10-5, Sun 12-5
Description of business: Crafters' Market of Minnesota is made up of two of the Minneapolis area's premier craft malls. Over 400 crafters participate in these individual craft display settings. They are a must see for any visitor to our area who appreciates the handiwork of fine craftspeople.
Types of products: Hand crafted items only.
Categories: Fine crafts, wearable art, jewelry, miniatures/dollhouses, wooden crafts, stained glass items, hand blown glass items, home decor, dolls/stuffed animals/toys, pottery/ceramics, nature crafts/floral, leather crafts, baskets, recycled crafts

Price range: 50¢-$400

Advertising/Promotion: Billboards, show directories, local print, tourism groups and magazines, hotel/motel brochure program, cable TV. $20,000/year budget.

Spaces available: 400. Fixtures are made of slatwall. Crafter can display on 3 walls and floor area of each display. Displays start with endcaps (4′ × 6′ flat surface). Then sizes start at 4′w × 32″d × 4½′h and increase in increments of 1 ft. all the way up to large furniture displays. 17,000 total sq. ft.

Cost of space: $40-250 and 5% of the sales.

Application process: For consideration, provide photos

Contract: Length of contract is 4 months. Craftsperson is paid once a month.

Out-of-town requirements: Accepts work by local or out-of-town craftspeople. Crafter can ship to us as they see fit. There is no re-stocking fee.

Craftsperson's responsibilities: Crafter must get crafts to location. Crafter receives a sales report with each check of what has sold. Local crafters set up their own displays. Crafters from farther away may ship merchandise to us and we will set up the display and restock for them. Crafter is responsible for all shelving and display materials. Hardware is available for purchase through the mall.

Additional information: See the listing below for a second location.

CRAFTERS' MARKET OF MINNESOTA, INC. II
Ron Handevidt
12500 Plaza Dr.
Eden Prairie, MN 55344
Phone: (612)829-0830
Type of business: Craft mall
In business since: 1991
Hours: M-F 10-9, Sat 10-5, Sun 12-5
Description of business: See the above listing for more information.

CRAFTER'S MARKETPLACE
Amy Couden
1403 W. Glen Ave.
Peoria, IL 61614
Phone: (309)692-7238
Fax: (309)692-7254
Type of business: Craft mall

In business since: 1994

Hours: M-Th 10-7, F-Sat 10-8, Sun 11-5

Description of business: Craft mall. Bright and contemporary with a 7,000 sq. ft. showroom.

Types of products: Hand crafted items and some selected and juried commercial items and gourmet food

Categories: Fine crafts, wearable art, jewelry, miniatures/dollhouses, wooden crafts, paper products, stained glass items, needlework crafts, hand blown glass items, home decor, figurines, dolls/stuffed animals/toys, pottery/ceramics, nature crafts/floral, leather crafts, baskets, recycled crafts, sculpture

More about products: Country, Southwestern, Victorian, contemporary, primitive, folk and whimiscal styles

Price range: $5-500

Advertising/Promotion: Regular TV ads with professional jingle; regular newspaper ads; direct customer mailings (9,000 +); local billboards; marketing to convention attendees; radio; special give aways and sale promotions; signage; Internet; public service announcements; promotional handouts at our craft shows; ads in visitor's guides; member of convention and visitor's bureau and Chamber of Commerce. $30,000/year budget.

Spaces available: 20. Sizes: 1′, 2′, 3′ and 4′-deep spaces, minimum of 4′ in width.

Cost of space: $21-170 per month and 10% commission (covers everything); 28% consignment also available

Application process: For consideration, provide photos or slides (4-5), written description of work and catalog/promotional materials.

Contract: Length of contract is 3 months, 6 months, or 12 months. Crafter must provide an additional 10% off to customer up to 12 days a year. The craftsperson is paid twice a month (15th and end of month).

Out-of-town requirements: Accepts work by local or out-of-town craftspeople. Products should be shipped to us, set-up is free. Products shipped back to exhibitor are charged shipping and handling fee.

Craftsperson's responsibilities: Crafter

must get crafts to location, keep track of stock and set up display.

Additional information: No work-day requirements; no refunds or exchanges on items sold; decorating service available (booth).

CRAFTERS MINI MALL, INC.
Bill Ihrer
116 W. Tyler St.
Longview, TX 75601
Phone: (903)758-7713
Fax: (903)753-0585
Type of business: Craft mall
In business since: 1990
Description of business: A retail outlet for crafters wanting to sell their products. Space is rented to the crafter for displaying their product.

Types of products: Hand crafted items only.

Categories: Fine crafts, wearable art, jewelry, miniatures/dollhouses, wooden crafts, paper products, stained glass items, needlework crafts, hand blown glass items, home decor, figurines, dolls/stuffed animals/toys, pottery/ceramics, nature crafts/floral, leather crafts, baskets, recycled crafts, sculpture

Price range: $1-800

Advertising/Promotion: Newspapers and trade magazines

Spaces available: 160

Application process: For consideration, provide photos (2-3).

Contract: Length of contract is 6 months. Craftsperson is paid monthly.

Out-of-town requirements: Accepts work by local or out-of-town craftspeople.

Craftsperson's responsibilities: Crafter must get crafts to location, keep track of stock and set up display. Store will behappy to set up if out of town or in a hurry. Merchandise sold by staff.

Additional information: There are three other locations: 2 in Tyler, TX and 1 in Shreveport, LA.

CRAFTER'S SHOWCASE I
Tracy Polczynski
10704 W. Oklahoma Ave.
West Allis, WI 53227
Phone: (414)327-0440; (800)483-0400
Fax: (414)327-6300
Type of business: Craft mall

In business since: 1992

Hours: M-W 10-6, Th-F 10-9, Sat-Sun 10-5

Description of business: Crafter's Showcase is the Midwest's largest collection of crafters offering 1,000 display booths in three Milwaukee area locations. Each store location is anchored by major retail chains, supplying high traffic and sales volume. Customers enjoy the friendly and helpful sales staff and the new merchandise arriving daily. The state of the art security system keeps a watchful eye on crafters' merchandise. This allows crafters to enjoy more time making crafts and less time selling.

Types of products: Hand crafted items only.

Categories: Wearable art, jewelry, miniatures/dollhouses, wooden crafts, paper products, stained glass items, needlework crafts, hand blown glass items, home decor, figurines, dolls/stuffed animals/toys, pottery/ceramics, nature crafts/floral, leather crafts, baskets

Price range: $1-120

Advertising/Promotion: Local/national newspapers and magazines, radio, billboards, restaurant placemats, bag stuffers, craft fairs

Spaces available: Average of 15-50. A variety of spaces are available ranging from 1′ × 3′ to 6′ × 6.5′

Cost of space: $50-245 a month depending on booth size and location. A 5% handling fee is also charged to cover the costs of staffing, advertising, supplies, etc.

Application process: Call or write for information.

Contract: Length of contract is 6 months or 12 months. Craftsperson is paid monthly.

Out-of-town requirements: Accepts work by local or out-of-town craftspeople. Crafters are required to supply shelving and/or display hooks. If the crafter wants the booth set up in a specific way, the crafter needs to send a diagram. There is no extra charge for set-up.

Craftsperson's responsibilities: Crafter must get crafts to location. If a crafter is in more than one location, the crafter can ship to one store, and the merchandise will be transferred to other locations. Crafter must keep track of stock. Mall provides central checkout.

Additional information: See listings below for other locations.

CRAFTER'S SHOWCASE II

Tracy Polczynski
N88 W15443 Main St.
Menomonee Falls, WI 53501

Phone: (414)250-0440

Fax: (414)250-0401

Type of business: Craft mall

In business since: 1993

Description of business: See the above listing for more information.

CRAFTER'S SHOWCASE III

Tracy Polczynski
The Manchester Mall
220 Oak St.
Grafton, WI 53024

Phone: (414)376-0440

Fax: (414)376-0401

Type of business: Craft mall

In business since: 1995

Description of business: See the above listing for more information.

THE CRAFTERS' VILLAGE

27548 Ynez Rd., Suite I-1
Temecula, CA 92591

Phone: (909)699-1936

Type of business: Craft mall

In business since: 1992

Hours: M-F 10-6, Sat 10-5, Sun 11-4, with extended holiday hours

Description of business: Family owned and operated. There are no work hours required. We have a magnetic checkpoint security system at entrance. There is no charge for credit card services, bad checks, or over-the-phone sales reports. Store is completely computerized.

Categories: Fine crafts, wearable art, jewelry, miniatures/dollhouses, wooden crafts, paper products, stained glass items, needlework crafts, hand blown glass items, home decor, figurines, dolls/stuffed animals/toys, pottery/ceramics, nature crafts/floral, leather crafts, baskets, recycled crafts, sculpture

Price range: $5-25

Advertising/Promotion: Local news-

paper fliers, *Craftmaster, Craft Supply*, sponsor local events, monthly $50 shopping spree giveaway, fliers sent to craft shows and boutiques, etc.

Spaces available: 150. Small wall spaces, glass cases up front, 1′ × 2′ up to 4′ × 6′ booths. All booths are bottom one half solid and top one half white lattice. All have power for individual lighting.

Cost of space: Booths are from $10.50 to $20.50 per sq. ft. Stores takes between 5% and 10% of monthly gross. No additional charges.

Application process: For consideration, provide photos and sample of work (whatever crafter feels is a good sample).

Contract: Length of contract is 3 or 6 months. Craftsperson is paid once a month.

Out-of-town requirements: Accepts work by local or out-of-town craftspeople. No charge for stocking or set up. All set-up materials must be provided by the crafter.

Craftsperson's responsibilities: Crafter must get crafts to location, keep track of stock and set up display unless the crafter is out of town.

CRAFTS AT THE MARKET PLACE

Albert Gomez
P.O. Box 252
West Creek, NJ 08092

Phone: (609)492-5060; (609)296-5480

Type of business: Craft mall

In business since: 1985

Hours: Open April-October, in season hours, June-August, 10-10

Description of business: Crafts at the Market Place allows artists to have a store space in a super prime summer location. Long Beach Island is a prime tourist market that draws an affluent population from all over the East Coast.

Types of products: Hand crafted items and herbs, calendars, books

Categories: Fine crafts, wearable art, jewelry, miniatures/dollhouses, wooden crafts, paper products, stained glass items, needlework crafts, hand blown glass items, home decor, figurines, dolls/stuffed animals/toys, pottery/ceramics, nature crafts/floral, leather crafts, baskets, recycled crafts, sculpture

Price range: $2-350

Advertising/Promotion: *Crafts Report* and Rosen show. $5,000/year budget.

Spaces available: 100. 1,000 sq. ft. prime summer retail space. Spaces are used by nature and size of craft work.

Cost of space: Free. Artist sets up his wholesale cost, we set mark-up based on market. Artist is guaranteed their price on sold goods.

Application process: For consideration, provide photos or slides (6), catalog/promotional materials and wholesale price list.

Contract: Length of contract is 6 months. Craftsperson is paid monthly.

Out-of-town requirements: Accepts work by local or out-of-town craftspeople. Artists may be responsible for all shipping costs (depends on category of contract).

Craftsperson's responsibilities: Crafter must get crafts to location. Monthly statement included with payment check. Setting up of display depends on the category of contract they participate in. We provide a sales staff with 3 register computerized terminals.

Additional information: Application is juried.

CRAFTWORKS

Donna Wright and Carol Dowling
3 Pierce St.
Northboro, MA 01532
Phone: (508)393-9435
Type of business: Co-op
In business since: 1979
Hours: 10-6 daily
Description of business: Craftworks is an artisan co-operative formed to provide a retail outlet for local artisans to market their handcrafts year round. All merchandise is hand crafted. Special orders are accepted and provide customers an opportunity to purchase one-of-a-kind items.
Types of products: Hand crafted items only.
Categories: Fine crafts, wearable art, jewelry, miniatures/dollhouses, wooden crafts, paper products, stained glass items, needlework crafts, hand blown glass items, home decor, figu-

rines, dolls/stuffed animals/toys, pottery/ceramics, nature crafts/floral, leather crafts, baskets, sculpture

Price range: $2-500

Advertising/Promotion: Ads in *Worcester Telegram* and *Gazette, Weekly Record*, handouts in shop, direct mail, cable. $3,000/year budget.

Spaces available: Our shop space is 1,500 sq. ft. Since we are a true cooperative, space is used for a craft as needed, and crafts are integrated to complement each other.

Cost of space: Monthly fee of $60 and work commitment of 12-20 hours a month per person.

Application process: Write to receive an application. For consideration, provide sample of work, written description of work and application to join and go through jury process.

Contract: Length of contract is 6 months. Security deposit refunded after commitment is fulfilled. Members of Craftworks participate in daily operation of shop, serve on committees, on board and at special events. Artisans must be able to participate in person. (We do not have consignment available.) Artisans are limited to one craft area. Craftsperson is paid once a month.

Out-of-town requirements: Accepts work by local craftspeople only.

Craftsperson's responsibilities: Crafter must keep track of stock.

CRAFTY HAMLET

Bob DiPalma
519 Cleveland St., #101
Clearwater, FL 34615
Phone: (813)447-3097; (800)313-6773
Type of business: Craft mall
In business since: 1993
Hours: 10-7 daily
Description of business: Boutique features work from more than 60 crafters, both domestic and international. It is located in downtown Clearwater with free parking and easy access to bus routes.
Types of products: Hand crafted items and gold plated pewter, marcasite jewelry
Categories: Fine crafts, wearable art, jewelry, miniatures/dollhouses, wooden crafts, paper products, stained

glass items, needlework crafts, home decor, figurines, dolls/stuffed animals/toys, pottery/ceramics, nature crafts/floral, baskets, recycled crafts, sculpture

Price range: $1-1,800

Advertising/Promotion: Local newspapers, direct handout, displays at other businesses. $1,500/year budget.

Spaces available: With inventory coding system, combining different crafters to match similar items. Has a store layout instead of seperate booths.

Cost of space: $20 per month fee plus 20% after the product is sold. If a credit card charge, 4% will be charged against the sale.

Application process: Always seeking crafter with unique products. For consideration, provide sample of work, catalog/promotional materials and written descritpion of work.

Contract: Length of contract is 3 months minimum, then one-month notice. $5 account set up fee. Craftsperson is paid monthly.

Out-of-town requirements: Accepts work by local or out-of-town craftspeople. Craftspeople who live out of town pay the shipment charge for sending merchandise to us. No additional charges.

Craftsperson's responsibilities: Crafter must get crafts to location. All stock is computerized—every month a list of items sold will be sent to the crafter. Crafter must do all the store decorations. Crafters are responsible for breakage. Mall handles all sales and advertisement.

THE DUSTY ATTIC I

Sharon Paul and Stefanie Wofford
3330 N. Galloway Ave.
Mesquite, TX 75150
Phone: (972)613-5093
Fax: (972)613-5097
Type of business: Craft and antique mall
In business since: 1991
Hours: M-W, F-Sat 10-6, Th 10-8, Sun 1-5
Description of business: The mall has over 500 antiques and craft dealers selling some of the best quality antiques and crafts in the US. The mall also features an old fashion general store, café and tea room.

Types of products: Hand crafted items and antiques and collectibles.

Categories: Fine crafts, wearable art, jewelry, miniatures/dollhouses, wooden crafts, paper products, stained glass items, needlework crafts, hand blown glass items, home decor, figurines, dolls/stuffed animals/toys, pottery/ceramics, nature crafts/floral, leather crafts, baskets, recycled crafts, sculpture

Price range: $1-1,000

Advertising/Promotion: TV, newspaper, direct mail and trade journals. $60,000/year budget.

Spaces available: Waiting list. 1'-5' to 5' × 10'

Cost of space: $55-200, depends on size, plus 5% commission on all sales.

Application process: For consideration, provide photos.

Contract: Length of contract is 6 months. Craftsperson is paid twice a month.

Out-of-town requirements: Accepts work by local or out-of-town craftspeople. Price the merchandise and ship it, we place it in your booth at no charge.

Craftsperson's responsibilities: Crafter must get crafts to location. Twice a month a printout of what sold along with check is sent to dealer. Dealer may call in or request fax in between pay periods.

Additional information: See the listing below for a second location.

THE DUSTY ATTIC II

Sharon Paul and Stefanie Wofford
2853 Central Dr.
Bedford, TX 76021
Phone: (817)355-1375
Fax: (972)613-5097
Type of business: Craft and antique mall
In business since: 1991
Hours: M-W, F, Sat 10-6, Th 10-8, Sun 1-5
Description of business: See the above listing for more information.

THE EMPORIUM AT BIG TOWN

Joe and Irene Willis
950 Big Town Mall
Mesquite, TX 75149
Phone: (214)320-2222
Type of business: Craft and antique mall and tea room

In business since: 1992

Hours: M-Sat 10-8, Sun 12-5:30

Types of products: Hand crafted items, new and consignment furniture and antiques

Categories: Fine crafts, wearable art, jewelry, miniatures/dollhouses, wooden crafts, paper products, stained glass items, needlework crafts, hand blown glass items, home decor, figurines, dolls/stuffed animals/toys, pottery/ceramics, nature crafts/floral, leather crafts, baskets, recycled crafts, sculpture

Price range: $1 and up

Advertising/Promotion: Billboards, *Neighbors & Friends, Antique Traveler*, direct mail

Spaces available: 36,000 sq. ft.

Application process: For consideration, provide photos, sample of work and written description of work.

Contract: Length of contract is 6 months. Craftsperson is paid twice a month.

Out-of-town requirements: Accepts work by local or out-of-town craftspeople. No charges for out of town stocking.

Craftsperson's responsibilities: Crafter must get crafts to location, keep track of stock and set up display.

FIRST CAPITAL CRAFT MALL, INC.

Darla Mummey
400 Chamber Dr.
Chillicothe, OH 45601
Phone: (614)773-0099
Fax: (614)775-8127
Type of business: Craft mall
In business since: 1995
Hours: M-Sat 10-7, Sun 12-6
Description of business: A beautiful building and location designed and constructed specifically for the display and market of quality handmade treasures. You will find all the traditional characteristics of a craft mall and much more! First Capital Craft Mall is laid out in a gallery, or maze layout, ensuring customers see each display. Booth locators, or wooden nickels, are located at each booth allowing the customer to take one and find their way back to items they like! In the "Four Season's Gallery," crafter's items are displayed in actual settings, such as the Christmas Living Room or the Spring Porch. The "Another Season in Time Antiques": section enhances the concept that the handcrafted items which are sold here are items that can be treasured and appreciated for years to come!

Types of products: Craft section is all partially or solely handcrafted, but we have added a small antique section: "Another Season In Time."

Categories: Fine crafts, wearable art, jewelry, miniatures/dollhouses, wooden crafts, paper products, stained glass items, needlework crafts, hand blown glass items, home decor, figurines, dolls/stuffed animals/toys, pottery/ceramics, nature crafts/floral, leather crafts, baskets, recycled crafts, sculpture, furniture (Amish style), wrought iton products

Price range: 50¢-$250

Advertising/Promotion: *The Country Register*, local radio, newspapers, magazines, surrounding are TV (network and cable), 2 billboards on St. Rt. 23, *Ohio Pass, Ohio Magazine, Tecumesh!* brochures, Chillicothe-Ross County Visitor's Guide, brochures—hotels, roadside rests, etc., airplane banner, balloon release, Weekend Anniversary Celebration, Christmas in July Celebration, Christmas Open House.

Spaces available: 220. $25-220 range from end cap wall spaces to large corner booths—can customize per requirements. All booths are made with ¼" tempered peg board and have stained/wooden caps finishing the dividers between the booths. Our spaces are layed out in a gallery, or maze, layout, ensuring customers pass all displays.

Cost of space: $50 deposit, monthly rental fee, 5% commission on sales.

Application process: For consideration, provide photos and sample of work.

Contract: Length of contract is 6 months. Items offered for sale must be partially or solely hand crafted by the person leasing the space. Checks and a sales statement are printed at the close of business on the 15th and last day of each month.

Out-of-town requirements: Accepts work by local or out-of-town craftspeople. Offers a free remote program.

We will stock your booth at no additional cost.

Craftsperson's responsibilities: Crafter must get crafts to location. A detailed sales report is sent with each check. We also call/fax if inventory gets low between checks. Crafter must set up display unless the crafter chooses the remote program. Merchandise is entered into the computer and our employees handle sales, customer service, and do booth inventories four times a day to straighten and rearrange booth displays so it looks like it was just set up. Must stay within designated boundaries, painting and decorating is permitted with management approval.

THE GALLERY AT CEDAR HOLLOW

Rose Brein Finkel
2447 Yellow Springs Rd.
Malvern, PA 19355
Phone: (610)640-ARTS
Fax: (610)640-2332
Type of business: Gallery
In business since: 1992
Hours: T-Sat 11-5, Sun 1-4; Seasonal hours are longer
Categories: Fine crafts, wearable art, jewelry, miniatures, wooden crafts, paper products, stained glass items, needlework crafts, hand blown glass items, home decor, figurines, dolls/stuffed animals/toys, pottery/ceramics, nature crafts/floral, leather crafts, baskets, recycled crafts, sculpture, fiberarts, gourmet crafts, candles, metal work, folk art
More about products: Fine contemporary crafts and original art. Large assortment of all types of hand crafted jewelry. Women's and children's apparel and accessories.
Price range: $5-2,500
Advertising/Promotion: All local newspapers, Philadelphia papers and others within 50 miles of gallery. Magazine, radio, craft show calendar, Internet. $15,000-20,000/year budget.
Spaces available: Wearable room, pottery room, jewelry room, fine art room, special exhibition room for changing theme shows, fiber arts and floral room, and many more areas for other types of work.
Cost of space: Jury/processing fee of

$18-25 (higher at Christmas); yearly membership fees; 40/60 commission is $75/year, working members get higher commissions and lower fees.
Application process: For consideration, provide photos or slides (3), SASE and written description of work.
Contract: Length of contract is either 2 months for special exhibitions or 1 year for 40/60. Ongoing for 50/50. Special exhibit—work must remain until end of show. No shop worn items. Everything must be in top condition. Craftsperson is paid monthly.
Out-of-town requirements: Accepts work by local or out-of-town craftspeople. Return/shipping is COD. Everyting must be tagged or labeled and inventory list enclosed. Numbering item must be done as required on application.
Craftsperson's responsibilities: Crafter must get crafts to location. A printout of monthly sales is included with check. Owner, working members, and several employees man the gallery and sell the work. Local exhibitors are requested to attend "Meet the Artisan" receptions for openings.
Additional information: Gallery has several outdoor shows spring-fall. Anyone may apply—limited space. Gallery consignors get a discount on space fees. No commission. Send SASE for forms.

GRANNY'S ATTIC

Joni Short
201 E. Main
Ada, OK 74820
Phone: (405)436-4241
Type of business: Craft and antique mall
In business since: 1993
Hours: T-Sat 10-5
Description of business: Granny's Attic is located in a two-story home built in 1917. Seven rooms are filled with crafts and antiques from all over Oklahoma. Crafts are selected from more than 50 crafters in this area. Joni makes her Victorian lampshades right in the store.
Types of products: Hand crafted items and gifts and candles.
Categories: Fine crafts, wearable art, jewelry, wooden crafts, paper products, stained glass items, needlework

crafts, home decor, figurines, dolls/stuffed animals/toys, pottery/ceramics, nature crafts/floral, leather crafts, baskets, recycled crafts, sculpture, handmade Victorian lampshades
Price range: 50¢-$400
Advertising/Promotion: Local newspapers, radio and area maps. $250/year budget.
Spaces available: 50+. Most booths are 3' × 2' with 8' ceiling. Newest is contract space, combined crafts to make a special look.
Cost of space: Most space is $25 a month, special areas are $30 and up.
Application process: For consideration, provide sample of work.
Contract: Length of contract is 30 days. Craftsperson is paid first of each month.
Out-of-town requirements: Accepts work by local or out-of-town craftspeople.
Craftsperson's responsibilities: Crafter must get crafts to location. Crafters are responsible for shipping. There is no charge for set up, just monthly rent. Crafter must keep track of stock and provide someone on location to sell merchandise.

THE HAND CRAFTERS BARN

Chuck Guilbeault, owner and Paula Stratton, manager
Main St., Route 16, P.O. Box 2060
North Conway, NH 03860
Phone: (603)356-8996
Fax: (603)356-4766
Type of business: Craft mall
In business since: 1989
Hours: Winter hours 9-5 daily, Summer hours 9-8 daily
Description of business: The Hand Crafters Barn is an 18th century landmark post and beam building renting display booths to 300 artists and artisans. It is a quality, juried facility open year yound in a major four season tourist economy. It is a unique, highly-visible property featuring award-winning gardens. Various booth sizes are available to suit the tenant's needs. It occupies a curb-side location on the major tourist artery. The property is owned and operated by indviduals with extensive retail and marketing background.

Types of products: Hand crafted items only.

Categories: Wearable art, jewelry, miniatures/dollhouses, wooden crafts, paper products, stained glass items, hand blown glass items, home decor, dolls/stuffed animals/toys, pottery/ceramics, nature crafts/floral, leather crafts, baskets, sculpture

Price range: $5-1,500

Advertising/Promotion: Member of Mt. Washington Valley Area Attractions Assoc., advertise in their visitors guides; member of Mt. Washington Valley Chamber Commerce, advertise in their publications and New Hampshire Dept. of Tourism publication; various resort map and guide publications, local and regional newspapers. $10,000-15,000/year budget.

Spaces available: 300. Various booth sizes available. Typical booth size is $2'd \times 6'8''h \times 5'w$; wooden walls and shelves; art lamps available; custom stain available.

Cost of space: $80-180 per month depending on size; 4% of total MasterCard/Visa sales; 2% of cash/check sales.

Application process: For consideration, provide photos or slides, sample of work and catalog/promotional materials.

Contract: Length of contract is 6 months. Craftsperson is paid monthly.

Out-of-town requirements: Accepts work by local or out-of-town craftspeople. Stock room space is available at no charge; UPS shipments are accepted for restocking at no charge; booth set up at no charge; $25 fee for custom carpentry.

Craftsperson's responsibilities: Crafter must get crafts to location. Computerized inventory system: monthly sales summary generated; salesfigures available daily; fax service available weekly at $5 per month charge. Booth set-up and design services available at no charge. All tenants use same item tagging system with a central check out.

Additional information: Will ship customer purchases via UPS if so desired at no charge to tenant for packing time and shipping materials utilized.

HANDCRAFTER'S HAVEN

Cheryl Zielke
40 Main St. N.
Woodbury, CT 06798

Phone: (203)263-2111; (203)266-4824

Type of business: Store front offering 3,000 sq. ft.

In business since: 1992

Hours: 10-5 daily

Description of business: We will sell your treasured hand crafted items in our unique shop located among the antique shops and historical sites of picturesque Woodbury. Over 150 artisans on display with sound customer base.

Types of products: Hand crafted items and cards and decorative flags

Categories: Fine crafts, wearable art, jewelry, miniatures, wooden crafts, stained glass items, needlework crafts, home decor, dolls/stuffed animals/toys, pottery/ceramics, nature crafts/floral, baskets

Price range: 25¢-$200

Advertising/Promotion: 6 local newspapers covering Connecticut, *The Craft Digest*, local restaurant placemats, special edition newspaper inserts, brochures, town guides.

Spaces available: Varies day to day. $2'w \times 12''d \times 6'h$—$65/month; $2.5'w \times 12''d \times 6'h$—$75/month; $3'w \times 12''d \times 6'h$—$85/month; $4'w \times 24''d \times 6'h$—$110/month; wall lattice $3.5' \times 5.5'$—$35/month; $4'w \times 12''d \times 12''h$ shelf—$35/month; customized areas are also availale as materials are avaialble. No commissions/percentages taken; monthly rent only.

Application process: For consideration, provide photos or slides, sample of work and catalog/promotional materials.

Contract: Length of contract is 6 months. Craftsperson is paid monthly.

Out-of-town requirements: Accepts work by local or out-of-town craftspeople. UPS shipment gladly accepted with no extra cost for set-up fees. Shipping and handling charges responsibility of crafters.

Craftsperson's responsibilities: Crafter must keep track of stock. Out of state artisans are welcome to ship products and we will set up—local artisans expected to do own display. We provide computerized system with each artisan having code for proper reimbursement.

HOMESPUN CRAFT & ANTIQUE MALL

Patty Mink
5729 Little Rock Rd. SW
Tumwater, WA 98512

Phone: (360)943-5194

Fax: (360)943-0585

Type of business: Craft mall

In business since: 1992

Hours: M-F 10-7, Sat 10-5, Sun 12-5

Description of business: A 10,500 sq. ft. craft and antique mall.

Types of products: Hand crafted items and antiques

Categories: Fine crafts, wearable art, jewelry, miniatures/dollhouses, wooden crafts, paper products, stained glass items, needlework crafts, hand blown glass items, home decor, figurines, dolls/stuffed animals/toys, pottery/ceramics, nature crafts/floral, leather crafts, baskets, sculpture

Price range: $1-150 (crafts)

Advertising/Promotion: Local radio and newspapers; *Country Pleasures, Brag About Washington*, Olympia's visitors guide.

Spaces available: 150. $2' \times 4'$; $3' \times 4'$; $4' \times 4'$

Cost of space: $71.50, $77.00 and $82.50

Application process: For consideration, provide photos.

Contract: Length of contract is 8 months. Craftsperson is paid twice monthly.

Out-of-town requirements: Accepts work by local or out-of-town craftspeople. Free booth set up and remote stocking.

Craftsperson's responsibilities: Crafter must get crafts to location. A sales staff operates the mall.

Additional information: Located off of I-5, across from Costco's.

HOOSIER CRAFT GALLERY

Martin Mathews
1401 Walnut Ave.
Frankfort, IN 46041

Phone: (317)659-4606; (800)950-3255

Fax: (317)659-1059

E-mail: mwire@holli.com

Type of business: Craft mall

In business since: 1993

Hours: M-Sat 7AM-8PM, Sun 12-4

Description of business: Huge variety of candles, furniture, framed prints, hot foods, Southwest, antique reproductions, bird houses, clothing, Coca Cola. Store uses various consumer items to attract customers for craft items and gifts.

Categories: Fine crafts, wearable art, jewelry, miniatures/dollhouses, wooden crafts, paper products, stained glass items, needlework crafts, hand blown glass items, home decor, figurines, dolls/stuffed animals/toys, pottery/ceramics, nature crafts/floral, leather crafts, baskets, recycled crafts, sculpture

Price range: No item less than $2.95

Advertising/Promotion: Store promotions, billboards, TV, newspaper. $20,000/year budget.

Spaces available: 280. Full range of sizes.

Cost of space: $20-180 per month, plus 5% of sales.

Application process: For consideration, provide photos or slides, sample of work, catalog/promotional materials or written description of work. Store may request more info if needed.

Contract: Length of contract is 6 months. Pay first and last month rent as deposit. Craftsperson paid monthly.

Out-of-town requirements: Accepts work by local or out-of-town craftspeople. $15 first set up, $10 per box restock; may be adjusted per nature of merchandise, size of box, etc.

Craftsperson's responsibilities: Crafter must get crafts to location. Crafter must keep track of stock. Store can do set up if needed. Merchandise is sold by store staff.

KNICK KNACKS CRAFT AND ANTIQUE MALL

215 W. Camp Wisdom Rd. #8
Duncanville, TX 75116
Phone/Fax: (214)283-9007
Type of business: Craft and antique mall
In business since: 1992
Description of business: Colonial style mall complete with red brick and white columns with carpeted, climate controlled interior. Beautiful store layout that avoids the "warehouse"

craft mall look. Over 20,000 sq. ft. of the finest crafts and antiques in America.

Types of products: Hand crafted items and antiques

Categories: Wearable art, jewelry, miniatures/dollhouses, wooden crafts, paper products, stained glass items, needlework crafts, hand blown glass items, home decor, figurines, dolls/stuffed animals/toys, pottery/ceramics, nature crafts/floral, baskets

Price range: 25¢-$250

Advertising/Promotion: Trade magazines: *Where It's At, Antiquing Texas, Neighbors & Friends, Crafters Supply*; plus billboards. $40,000/year budget.

Spaces available: 300. 3'×3' to 8'×8' booths.

Cost of space: $55-250. There are no commissions on sales.

Application process: Call the above number and ask for Kathy or Cheryl.

Contract: Length of contract is 6 months or a year. Craftsperson is paid twice a month.

Out-of-town requirements: Accepts work by local or out-of-town craftspeople. Free remote service is offered.

Craftsperson's responsibilities: Crafter must get crafts to location. Monthly report sent with payment. Crafter usually sets up display, but we will gladly set up for out-of-town craftspeople.

MADE BY HAND CRAFT MALL I

Jerri Siddall
4938 S. Staples
Corpus Christi, TX 78411
Phone: (512)991-6555
Type of business: Craft and antique mall
In business since: 1991
Hours: M-Sat 10-6, Sun 12-5
Description of business: Made By Hand Craft Malls offer modern, well located retail stores providing sales outlets for hundreds of artists and craftsmen. Customers enjoy the huge selection of quality American made merchandise at reasonable prices. Professional staff will assist with any questions you may have. At Made By Hand, we belive in creating a positive environment for the growth and success of our employees and vendors.

Types of products: Hand crafted items and antiques and collectibles

Categories: Fine crafts, wearable art, jewelry, miniatures/dollhouses, wooden crafts, paper products, stained glass items, needlework crafts, hand blown glass items, home decor, figurines, dolls/stuffed animals/toys, pottery/ceramics, nature crafts/floral, leather crafts, baskets, sculpture

Price range: $2-300

Advertising/Promotion: Local newspaper, craft magazines, Yellow Pages, TV and radio

Spaces available: 325-440. 3'×4' booths and larger; these include peg board partitions. Sizes go from 3'×4' to 4'×12' and larger spaces upon request.

Cost of space: $38 for end-cap, $60 for 3'×4' booth, up to $180 for 3'×12' or 4'×12'; other prices available upon request.

Application process: For consideration, contact stores and provide description of work.

Contract: Length of contract is month to month or up to 6 month leases. Nominal start up fee. 8% service charge for operating expenses. There are no credit card or check handling charges, Made By Hand incurs those costs. We do not charge security deposits. Craftsperson is paid twice a month.

Out-of-town requirements: Accepts work by local or out-of-town craftspeople. Vendor is required to supply hooks, shelves and any display pieces.

Craftsperson's responsibilities: Crafter must get crafts to location, keep track of stock and set up display. Out-of-town vendors do not have to be here to set up. They send a picture or description of display. Accounts are issued to vendors to put on price tags. Item is entered in their account at time of purchase. Print-out of items sold is provided with payment on the 1st and 15th of each month.

Additional information: There is a "Cooperative Staffing Program" of 5 hours each month. Vendors assist in the store, straighten booths, and other small projects. There is a $15 charge if vendor chooses not to work. Please see listings below for other locations.

MADE BY HAND CRAFT MALL II

Brenda Dyson

12311 Nacogdoches #108

San Antonio, TX 78217

Phone: (210)656-5091

Type of business: Craft and antique mall

In business since: 1991

Hours: M-Sat 10-6, Sun 12-5

Description of business: Please see above listing for more information.

MADE BY HAND CRAFT MALL III

3307 Wurzbach

San Antonio, TX 78238

Phone: (210)647-1128

Type of business: Craft and antique mall

In business since: 1991

Hours: M-Sat 10-6, Sun 12-5

Description of business: Please see above listing for more information.

PAT'S ART—A BROZOS CRAFT MALL

Pat Blackwell

1003 S. University Parks Dr.

Waco, TX 76706

Phone: (817)756-3854

Type of business: Craft mall

In business since: 1993

Hours: T-Sat 10-6, Sun 1-5

Description of business: A friendly Texas gift shop, custom orders welcome.

Types of products: Hand crafted items and stained glass supplies

Categories: Fine crafts, wearable art, jewelry, wooden crafts, paper products, stained glass items, needlework crafts, hand blown glass items, home decor, figurines, dolls/stuffed animals/toys, pottery/ceramics, nature crafts/floral, leather crafts, baskets, recycled crafts, sculpture

More about products: We are located in the tourist area of Waco, Texas, thus we sell a lot of souvenirs and locally made items.

Price range: $1-1,000

Advertising/Promotion: Local newspapers, radio, visitor display racks in various locations

Spaces available: Small shelves 8″ wide by 3′, up to booths 4′ × 6′

Cost of space: Shelves start at $15 per month and go up to $150 per month

Application process: For consideration, provide sample of work.

Contract: Length of contract is 3 months (starting contract). If sales per month reach 4 times amount of rent paid, 10% is taken from all over the 4 times amount. Craftsperson is paid once a month (after the 15th).

Out-of-town requirements: Accepts work by local or out-of-town craftspeople. For credit card sales, 4% is taken.

Craftsperson's responsibilities: Crafter must get crafts to location. Items may be mailed or shipped in. Crafter must keep track of stock. Crafters have a choice of setting up displays or having us do it for them. Each person is given an ID number and craftspeople are given copies of all items sold during the month.

Additional information: Painting classes and stained glass classes available.

POTOMAC CRAFTSMEN GALLERY

Marty Martin

Torpedo Factory, Studio 18

105 North Union St.

Alexandria, VA 22314

Phone: (703)548-0935

Fax: (703)683-5786

Type of business: Co-op

In business since: 1974

Hours: M-F 10-4, Sat-Sun and holidays 11-5

Description of business: The goal of the Potomac Craftsmen Gallery is to provide gallery space for the work of the DC area's finest fiber artists. Exhibitors must be members of the Potomac Craftsmen Guild and the Potomac Craftsmen Gallery, which is a cooperative venture.

Types of products: Hand crafted items only.

Categories: Wearable art, jewelry, paper products, needlework crafts, home decor, dolls/stuffed animals/toys, nature crafts/floral, baskets, sculpture

More about products: All work in the gallery is juried and must be composed of at least 50 percent fiber or composed using fiber techniques.

Price range: $10-1,000

Advertising/Promotion: Ads in *American Style* magazine. Listings in *Alexandria Guide*, *Galleries* magazine, *Smithsonian Craft Show* guide. Brochures provided by us to three commonwealth of Virginia Welcome Centers. $1,600/year budget.

Spaces available: One gallery with an exhibition area of 496.71 sq. ft.

Cost of space: Members of the Potomac Craftsmen Gallery must pay membership fees annually ($18/Potomac Craftsmen Guild, $30/Potomac Craftsmen Gallery).

Contract: Commissions are paid monthly.

Out-of-town requirements: Accepts work by local craftspeople only.

Craftsperson's responsibilities: Crafter must get crafts to location. The craftsperson must bring work to the gallery on jurying day (usually first Monday of month). Merchandise is sold by members of the gallery. Each member must work one day each month in gallery.

POLLY REILLY'S BOUTIQUE

Polly Reilly

16 Bismark Way, P.O. Box 478

Dennis, MA 02638

Phone: (580)385-2619 home; (508)233-4680 boutique

Type of business: Craft boutique, open twice a year

In business since: 1968

Hours: Open 4 weeks in November, M-Sat 10-5, Th 10-9; 3 weeks prior to Easter, Sun 1-5

Description of business: A hand craft boutique including antique furniture. Unusual and quality items appealing to all ages. Boutique is held on the 2nd floor of Andrea's Furniture Store, 540 S. Ave., Westfield NJ.

Types of products: Hand crafted items and gift items that mesh with hand crafts

Categories: Wearable art, jewelry, wooden crafts, paper products, stained glass items, needlework crafts, hand blown glass items, home decor, dolls/stuffed animals/toys, pottery/ceramics, nature crafts/floral, ornaments at Christmas

Price range: $1-450

Advertising/Promotion: Invitations are designed for each boutique (customers self-address their envelope at each boutique for the following one). We also advertise in local newspaper. $1,000/year budget.

Spaces available: Boutique is set up like a shop. Crafters do not stay to sell their items.

Application process: For consideration, provide sample of work with prices.

Contract: Length of contract is 2 months. 25% commission with a $35 entry fee plus a donation of a wrapped gift for the Cancer Society raffle for each boutique. Craftsperson is paid at end of boutique.

Out-of-town requirements: Accepts work by local or out-of-town craftspeople. Craftspeople who live out of town pay UPS or U.S. mail charges.

Craftsperson's responsibilities: Crafter must get crafts to location. Will keep track of stock with a phone call. Central checkout is provided.

SENTIMENTAL JOURNEY ANTIQUE AND CRAFT MALL

Sharon Porter
421 W. I-30 @ Beltline
Garland, TX 75043
Phone: (214)240-7073
Fax: (214)240-7251
Type of business: Antique and craft mall with tea room
In business since: 1994
Hours: M-W, F-Sat 10-3, Th 10-8, Sun 1-5
Description of business: Craft and antique mall with a 3½ star rated "opal tea room"
Types of products: Hand crafted items and collectibles, furniture, gifts, antiques
Categories: Fine crafts, wearable art, jewelry, miniatures/dollhouses, wooden crafts, paper products, stained glass items, needlework crafts, figurines, dolls/stuffed animals/toys, pottery/ceramics, nature crafts/floral
Price range: $5-100
Advertising/Promotion: Newspapers. $1,200/year budget.
Spaces available: 14. 2′×4′, 2′×6′, 2′×8′, 4′×4′
Cost of space: $60-90
Application process: For consideration, provide sample of work.
Contract: Length of contract is 6 months. 5% of sales go to company for credit

card and check processing. Craftsperson is paid twice monthly.

Out-of-town requirements: Accepts work by local or out-of-town craftspeople. Crafters responsible for shipping. Store will stock small booths at no cost, but larger booths may require a small fee.

Craftsperson's responsibilities: Crafter must get crafts to location, keep track of stock and set up display. Mall provides central checkout. There are certain items (cards, candles) that are to be sold by store only.

SONFLOWER'S ARTS & CRAFTS GALLERY

Yvonne
1006 N. Old SR 49
Chestertown, IN 46304
Phone: (219)929-4333
Fax: (219)929-1358
Type of business: Craft mall
In business since: 1994
Hours: M-Sat 10-5, Sun 12-4 (closed Tuesday January-March)
Description of business: We cater to the American crafter and do not compete with our own retail gift items. We try to be sure the artist/crafter actually makes their own product and we limit the types of crafts in the store.
Types of products: Hand crafted items and Wisconsin Wilderness bottled and bagged food items
Categories: Fine crafts, wearable art, jewelry, miniatures/dollhouses, wooden crafts, paper products, stained glass items, needlework crafts, hand blown glass items, home decor, dolls/stuffed animals/toys, pottery/ceramics, nature crafts/floral, leather crafts, baskets, recycled crafts
Price range: $1-1,000
Advertising/Promotion: Northwest Indiana newspapers, Northeast Illinois newspapers, Chicago Suburbs South, radio, billboards, mass mailings, SAC.
Spaces available: 275. Wall and/or booth spaces, (some walls have 1½ ft. floor space) from 2′×4′ to 5×10
Cost of space: $25-145 plus 3.5¢ per dollar charge fee and 2¢ per dollar check insurance fee. 10% handling fee on sales at month's end.
Application process: For consideration, provide photos and sample of work.

Contract: Length of contract is 6 months to 1 year. 30 day written notice prior to 1st of month, $5 electric fee, must stay within juried limits. Craftsperson paid monthly.

Out-of-town requirements: Accepts work by local or out-of-town craftspeople. Extra charge depends on what they want done; $10-90 for peg board, etc.

Craftsperson's responsibilities: Crafter must get crafts to location, keep track of stock and set up display unless prearranged. They can paint, wallpaper, carpet, whatever they want to make it their own. Full staff of very personable and well trained clerks. Must be pleasant to the sweet dispositioned staff.

Additional information: We have an easy on-off access from the Indiana toll road 80-90 (⅛ north of toll road) 3½ miles south of 94 on old 49 which runs parallel to the new 49. Only one hour from downtown Chicago.

THE TREASURE CACHÉ, INC.

Robin Nicholas
33 West Whitman Rd., Suite 110
Huntington Station, NY 11746
Phone: (800)969-5969; (516)271-4500
Fax: (516)427-3221
E-mail: info@treasurecache.com
Website: http://www.treasurecache.com
Type of business: Indoor mall specialty gift store
In business since: 1992
Hours: Mall hours
Description of business: The Treasure Caché operates specialty gift stores featuring the finest hand crafted gift, decorative and holiday merchandise from America's most talented artisans and crafters situated in regional and super regional indoor malls and high traffic resort areas. The company's showrooms offer successful crafters the highest possible retail sales potential.
Types of products: Hand crafted items only.
Categories: Fine crafts, jewelry, miniatures/dollhouses, wooden crafts, stained glass items, hand blown glass items, home decor, dolls/stuffed animals/toys, pottery/ceramics, nature crafts/floral, baskets

More about products: Moderately priced, high quality creations

Price range: $10-50

Advertising/Promotion: All major craft industry publications, Internet, mall promotions. $150,000/year budget.

Spaces available: 150-175/store. Positioning in America's premier indoor regional and super regional malls.

Cost of space: From $55-75/month plus a percentage of retail sales.

Application process: For consideration, provide photos, sample of work, catalog/promotional materials and written description of work.

Contract: Length of contract is 4-6 months. Craftsperson is paid monthly.

Out-of-town requirements: Accepts work by local or out-of-town craftspeople. Craftsperson will be assigned the next, most appropriate space for his/her items. Craftsperson is responsible for shipping costs. There are no other additional charges.

Craftsperson's responsibilities: Crafter must get crafts to location. All inventory and sales are tracked by Treasure Caché. Local craftspeople are responsible for stocking display space, out-of-towners are not. Merchandise is sold at a retail store in the mall with a regular staff. We require high quality, proven merchandise from successful crafters capable of high volume.

YOUR HEART'S DESIRE

Judylee Koenig
1009 Tiller Ave.
Beachwood, NJ 08722

Phone: (908)244-8736; (908)255-5115 (during boutique hours)

Type of business: Seasonal boutique

In business since: 1984

Hours: Before Easter, 4th of July and in the fall, 10-5 daily

Description of business: A seasonal boutique running 3 times a year. 100 crafters from all over the US are represented.

Types of products: Hand crafted items only.

Categories: Miniatures/dollhouses, wooden crafts, paper products, stained glass items, needlework crafts, home decor, dolls/stuffed animals/toys, pottery/ceramics, nature crafts/floral, baskets

More about products: Country and Victorian crafts

Price range: $1-500

Advertising/Promotion: Send postcards to a mailing list of over 6,000; advertise in 4-6 local newspapers. $2,000/year budget.

Spaces available: Allow 100 crafters to participate. Set up crafts in a store-like manner: by theme, color, etc.

Cost of space: $35 plus 25% commission.

Application process: For consideration, provide photos.

Contract: Craftsperson is paid 3 weeks after close of boutique.

Out-of-town requirements: Accepts work by local or out-of-town craftspeople. Ship via UPS. Returns will be done same way and dollar amount deducted from check.

Craftsperson's responsibilities: Crafter must get crafts to location.

Resources for Selling Through the Mail

CATALOG COMPANIES

DRAGON STAINED GLASS

C.J. Godwin
62 Main St.
Norway, ME 04268
Phone: (207)743-7663
In business since: 1978
Description of catalog: We offer a fine line of stained glass functional gifts, a unique line of our own designed 3D angels (numbered, a limited quantity of 25 each year). A hand painted selection of ceramic angels and Santas. Crystal jewelry, engraved hangings and candles.
Distribution: By mail and at craft shows, state fairs and festivals. 250-700 released yearly.
Types of products: Handmade items only.
Categories: Fine crafts, jewelry, stained glass items, home decor, figurines, pottery/ceramics, nature crafts/floral
More about products: We seek hand crafted items only, must not be production or imports. We seek only Christmas related products but will consider other products of quality.
Price range: $25-200
Business policy: We buy crafts at wholesale and sell them resale through the catalog. We manufacturer 90% of our own work. We buy crafts outright.
Buys: From the craftspeople who query us if we like their work and it fits our theme; at wholesale shows for hand crafted items; at wholesale gift shows; at retail craft shows; crafts people working (set ups) in malls.
For consideration: Provide photos or slides (5), sample of work.

ENGLISH BASKETRY WILLOWS/BASKETS BY BONNIE GALE

Bonnie Gale
RD 1, Box 124A
South New Berlin, NY 13843
Phone: (607)847-8264
Fax: (607)847-6634
In business since: 1983
Description of catalog: Besides selling imported basketry willows, specific willow basketry books and tools, the catalog also sells the traditional willow baskets made by Bonnie Gale.
Distribution: By mail and telephone request. Released once a year.
Types of products: Also sells imported basketry willows, willow basketry books and tools.
Categories: Baskets
More about products: A full range of traditional willow baskets, including fishing creels, backpacks, laundry baskets, shopping baskets and bushel baskets. Custom square baskets also available for designer kitchen drawers.
Price range: $10-195
Buys: From the craftspeople who query us if we like their work and it fits our theme.
For consideration: Provide photos or slides (5), written description of work.

FROM THE HANDS OF KANSAS

Larry Childs
700 SW Harrison, Suite 1300
Topeka, KS 66603
Phone: (913)296-4027
Fax: (913)296-5263
In business since: 1993
Description of catalog: A listing of quality consumer products from Kansas. Listing gives name, contact and description of the products.
Distribution: By mail.
Types of products: All items found on a specialty shop shelf.
Categories: Fine crafts, wearable art, jewelry, miniatures/dollhouses, wooden crafts, paper products, stained glass items, needlework crafts, hand blown glass items, home decor, figurines, dolls/stuffed animals/toys, pottery/ceramics, nature crafts/floral, leather crafts, baskets, recycled crafts, sculpture
Price range: $5-500
Business policy: We are an advertising vehicle only. We include the craftsperson's contact information for ordering purposes.
For consideration: Provide photos or slides, catalog/promotional materials, written description of work. Craftsperson must live in the state of Kansas.

HISTORIC DEERFIELD MUSEUM STORE

Irene Friedman
79 Old Main St., Box 24
Deerfield, MA 01342
Phone: (413)774-5581
Fax: (413)773-7415
In business since: 1958
Description of catalog: 8 page black and white catalog primarily distributed to members of museum.
Distribution: 1,500-2,000 mailed out to members of museum, 50,000 inserted in free advertising paper which is distributed in about 200 locations in Massachusetts.
Categories: Fine crafts, wearable art, jewelry, miniatures/dollhouses, wooden crafts, paper products, stained glass items, needlework crafts, hand blown glass items, home decor, figurines, dolls/stuffed animals/toys, pottery/ceramics, leather crafts, baskets, books
Price range: 75¢-$1,700
Business policy: We buy crafts at wholesale and sell them resale through the catalog. Occasionally we take items on consignment. We buy crafts outright.
Buys: From the craftspeople who query us if we like their work and it fits our theme; from reps or craft brokers; at wholesale shows for hand crafted items; at retail craft shows; at wholesale gift shows
For consideration: Provide photos or slides, sample of work, written description of work.

CUSTOM-MADE CATALOGS AND PROMOTIONAL MATERIALS

ALTERNATIVE MEDIA GROUP

Kevin Van Gundy

P.O. Box 1952

Grand Junction, CO 81502

Phone: (970)242-6030

In business since: 1984

Description of products: The Alternative Media Group is a full-service advertising agency that specializes in servicing the promotional needs of professional arts and crafts people.

Additional information: Call us first, for a free initial consultation and/or estimate.

DYNAMIC FOCUS PHOTOGRAPHY

Brian Ramey

1179 Tasman Dr.

Sunnyvale, CA 94089-2228

Phone: (408)734-2515

Fax: (408)734-3152

In business since: 1974 (under current studio name since 1991)

Description of products: Dynamic Focus Photography is a full-service crafts, commercial and advertising studio serving the professional fine arts and crafts community nationwide. We offer top quality, personalized service, and competitive prices based on over 20 years experience. We specialize in studio and location photography for jury selection, promotional materials, catalogs, gallery advertising, magazine ads, portfolios and booth displays. We offer complete b&w and color lab services.

Photos: We take photos of the craftsperson's work for inclusion in the promotional materials. Craftsperson must provide us with slides or photos of the work to be included.

Words: We will work with craftsperson to write advertising copy.

Cost: Price lists for studio services and popular promotional materials are available upon request. To best serve our clients' needs, all photography charges are based on studio production time and materials used for each project. Quotes will gladly be provied for studio services or printed advertising materials before any project is started.

Samples: Free

Additional information: Brian Ramey, owner/photographer, received his BFA degree from San Francisco State University School of Art in 1972. In 1974, he started his professional photography career in "Silicon Valley" specializing in the commercial/advertising field where his studio is still located. Member of: A.C.C., P.P. of A., B.B.B., Sunnyvale C. of C.

GRACE PHOTO

Patrick Grace

P.O. Box 145

York Harbor, ME 03911

Phone: (207)363-4665

In business since: 1972

Description of products: Color post cards (500 minimum order) of craftspersons, products for advertising or self promotion. I am a jobber and do not print cards in house. I cannot reprint a previously printed (screened) card. Copyrighted photos must have photographer's release.

Photos: Craftsperson must provide us with slides or photos of the work to be included.

Words: Client may supply camera-ready copy especially if copy is complicated or uses different type fonts, logos, etc.

Minimum order: 500 cards

Cost: Standard post cards: 500 cards $280; 1 photo on front, 50 words in black ink on back: Helvetica type face. 1,000 cards $315. Other sizes available. Delivery time 4 weeks. Full payment due with order.

Samples: Available for SASE

Additional information: Sales tax should be added to orders from ME, CA, FL, MS, NY, SC and VA. Color separations remain at printer and are not returnable to client.

CHAPTER ELEVEN

Places to Sell Wholesale

RETAIL STORES, GALLERIES AND OTHER MARKETS

ABC CANTON KIDS SHOP
Linda
Rt. 44, P.O. Box 386
Canton, CT 06019-0386
Phone: (860)693-9221
Type of business: Retail store selling hand crafted items
Description of business: A specialty baby and toddler retailer of furniture, equipment, toys, gifts and accessories. The focus is on wood or natural, non-toxic products with old fashioned quality and lifetime play value. We carry the hard-to-find necessities and accessories; unique, educational playthings for up to ages 8 to 10. No clothing, no "country."
Types of products: Handmade items and furniture, doll furniture
Categories: Wooden crafts, home decor, dolls/stuffed animals/toys
Price range: Varies
Business policy: We take work on consignment and buy crafts outright.
Buys: From the craftspeople who query us if we like their work and it fits our theme; at wholesale shows for hand crafted items; at wholesale gift shows; at wholesale toy, doll and teddy bear shows; at retail craft shows
Advertising/Promotion: Local newspapers, fliers, Yellow Pages, newsletters, direct mail
Application process: Queries are accepted from local/regional and out-of-town craftspeople. For consideration, provide catalog/promotional materials, photos only, sample of work, written description of work.
Additional information: We may either purchase wholesale or establish consignment percentage, generally 60/40, or lease space to crafters with other sales arrangement. We prefer to be flexible on an individual and product basis. Ask about area exclusivity and crafter anonymity. We will try to not duplicate products of like design.

AMERICAN ARTISAN, INC.
Nancy Saturn
4231 Harding Rd.
Nashville, TN 37205
Phone: (615)298-4691
Fax: (615)298-4604
In business since: 1971
Type of business: Retail store selling hand crafted items
Description of business: The American Artisan is a contemporary craft gallery. The owner, Nancy Saturn, selects work from all over the country in every medium: clay, glass, fiber, metal and wood.
Types of products: Handmade items only
Categories: Fine crafts, wearable art, jewelry, wooden crafts, paper products, stained glass items, hand blown glass items, pottery/ceramics, leather crafts, baskets, sculpture
Price range: $15-3,000
Business policy: We buy crafts outright.
Buys: From the craftspeople who query us if we like their work and it fits our theme; at wholesale shows for hand crafted items
Advertising/Promotion: *Nashville Scene, Quest Informant, Key Magazine*, radio. $50,000/year budget.
Special programs: Sponsors the Annual American Artisan Festival
Application process: Queries are accepted. For consideration, provide photos or slides (5), catalog/promotional materials, written description of work, résumé.
Additional information: We feature a bridal registry.

AMERICAN CRAFTS GALLERY
Jeanne Dombcik, Jennifer Douglas and Mary Urbas
13010 Larchmere Blvd.
Cleveland, OH 44120
Phone: (216)231-2008
Fax: (216)231-2009
In business since: 1962
Type of business: Retail store and gallery selling hand crafted items
Description of business: Among the largest and oldest craft galleries in the US. Located in a historic landmark powerhouse building, American Crafts represents artists from across the United States and specializes in handmade, contemporary American crafts. The two level gallery holds 5 shows yearly in its lower level pedestal galleries and has a showroom on the main level.
Types of products: Handmade items only
Categories: Fine crafts, wearable art, jewelry, wooden crafts, stained glass items, hand blown glass items, home decor, toys, pottery/ceramics (functional and decorative), baskets, sculpture, furniture, accessories
Price range: $10-10,000
Business policy: We buy crafts outright, take work on consignment and commission work from craftspeople.
Buys: At wholesale shows for hand crafted items; at retail craft shows. The gallery actively networks and shares resources with other galleries and artists.
Advertising/Promotion: Direct mail 5 times a year (7,300 list), *Art News Gallery Guide*, radio 6-7 times/year, *The Connection* (eastern suburban paper), an occasional magazine ad
Special programs: Ceramic Invitational (spring); Art in Garden (May); Special exhibit (summer); Furniture/Fiber (October); Holiday Invitational (November-December).
Application process: Queries are accepted from local/regional and out-of-town craftspeople. If in town, call ahead for appointment. For consideration, provide photos or slides, catalog/promotional materials, sample of work, written description of work, references (other places selling work), résumé, price list, SASE.

AMERICAN HAND PLUS

Dennis Garrett
2906 M St. NW
Washington, DC 20007
Phone/Fax: (202)965-3273
In business since: 1968
Type of business: Gallery
Description of business: Unique design and craft gallery specializing in fine American studio ceramics, glass, jewelry and lighting. Also shows contemporary international design objects for the home and office.
Types of products: Handmade items and international design items
Categories: Fine crafts, jewelry, hand blown glass items, home decor, pottery/ceramics
More about products: We specialize in contemporary ceramics and glass with emphasis on the vessel.
Price range: $20-2,000
Business policy: We buy crafts outright and take work on consignment.
Buys: From the craftspeople who query us if we like their work and it fits our theme; at wholesale shows for hand crafted items; at wholesale gift shows
Advertising/Promotion: American Craft for special shows
Application process: Queries are accepted from regional and out-of-town craftspeople. Exclusive DC representation required. For consideration, provide photos or slides, catalog/promotional materials, price list and SASE.

ARIANA GALLERY

Anne Kuffler
119 S. Main St.
Royal Oak, MI 48067
Phone: (810)546-8810
Fax: (810)546-6194
In business since: 1987
Type of business: Gallery
Description of business: The Ariana Gallery of Contemporary Arts and Crafts is run by professional art consultant and artist Ann E. Kuffler. The gallery is located in the retail business center of Royal Oak, Michigan, an upper middle class suburb of Detroit. Royal Oak is well known for its historic homes, art theaters, fine restaurants, coffee houses, boutiques and a unique selection of quality art galler-

ies. The Ariana Gallery occupies 3,100 square feet in a historic building that dates back to 1926. The gallery offers artists a vehicle to display their work in an atmosphere of warmth and elegance. Artists from all over the world are showcased. The gallery participates annually in a Teapot show as well as a Glass show among a variety of ever-changing shows that keep Ariana fresh and distinct. The Ariana Gallery also seeks to expand it's philosophy and not be defined by the typical notion of an Arts and Crafts gallery. This philosophy was displayed during the opening of their Dr. Kevorkian show which proved a most successful exhibition. In the future, Ariana plans to continue representing and presenting to the public the more unusual and sometimes controversial examples of artists and their work.
Types of products: Handmade items only
Categories: Fine crafts, wearable art, jewelry, wooden crafts, hand blown glass items, home decor, pottery/ceramics, recycled crafts, sculpture
Price range: $20-10,000
Business policy: We buy crafts outright, display work on consignment and commission work from craftspeople.
Buys: At wholesale shows for hand crafted items; at wholesale apparel shows; through slide registries; from reps or craft brokers; at wholesale gift shows; at retail craft shows; contact guilds; contact artists who appear in professional magazines, e.g., *Ceramics, American Craft, Metal.*
Advertising/Promotion: Local newspapers and magazines, professional magazines. $15,000/year budget.
Special programs: Annual teapot show, annual glass show, annual garden show
Application process: Queries are accepted from local/regional and out-of-town craftspeople. For consideration, provide photos or slides, catalog/promotional materials, sample of work, written description of work and methods used in production, résumé, artist statement, SASE.
Additional information: The Ariana Gallery prides itself on being flexible and open to new or cutting edge opportunities. This philosophy encour-

aged us to show the quilts of Ludmila Uspenskaya who is a Russian artist never seen in this country before and whose work loosely fits the "quilt" definition.

ARTISAN SHOP & GALLERY

Lynn Hansen
248 R.P. Coffin Rd.
Long Grove, IL 60047
Phone: (847)821-8835
Fax: (847)821-8836
In business since: 1968
Type of business: Retail store selling hand crafted items
Description of business: Upbeat, upscale, eclectic. Whimsical works and functional art in a contemporary setting. Also features a children's corner as well as kaleidoscopes for "adult children." Emphasis placed upon quality works by professionals. American craftspeople, artists and designers only.
Types of products: Handmade items and other products
Categories: Fine crafts, jewelry, wooden crafts, paper products, stained glass items, hand blown glass items, home decor, dolls/stuffed animals/toys, pottery/ceramics, recycled crafts
Price range: $5-1,000
Business policy: We buy crafts outright.
Buys: From the craftspeople who query us if we like their work and it fits our theme; at wholesale shows for hand crafted items
Application process: Queries are accepted from local/regional and out-of-town craftspeople. For consideration, provide photos or slides, catalog/promotional materials, written description of work. Include SASE if photos/slides are to be returned.

ARTS & ARTISANS, LTD.

Jeanine Hoffmann
36 S. Wabash Ave., Suite 604
Chicago, IL 60603
Phone: (312)855-9220; (312)641-0088
Fax: (312)855-0994
In business since: 1988
Type of business: Gallery
Description of business: Represent over 250 craft lines chosen on the basis of quality, uniqueness and value. Feature contemporary works, both functional

and decorative, limited edition and production items. Own and operate 4 other retail craft outlets in downtown Chicago and are always seeking new and exciting works.

Types of products: Handmade items only

Categories: Fine crafts, jewelry, wooden crafts, stained glass items, hand blown glass items, home decor, dolls/stuffed animals/toys, pottery/ceramics, sculpture, metal sculpture

Price range: $10-1,000

Business policy: We buy crafts outright.

Buys: From the craftspeople who query us if we like their work and it fits our theme; at wholesale shows for hand crafted items; from reps or craft brokers; at wholesale gift shows; at retail craft shows

Advertising/Promotion: Listings with Convention & Tourism Bureau publications, direct mailings to customers 6 times per year, donations to charity groups, occasional radio, hotel visitor guides. 2% of sales/year budget.

Special programs: Each month, we feature an artist or a group of craft works (e.g., glass paperweights) and promote with a discount sale.

Application process: Queries are accepted from local/regional and out-of-town craftspeople. For consideration, provide photo or slide (1), catalog/promotional materials, sample of work, written description of work, price information (wholesale), artist bio if available.

Additional information: Two retail locations in downtown Chicago: 108 S. Michigan Ave. (across from Art Institute) and 132 N. LaSalle St. (across from City Hall).

THE ARTWORKS
Gloria Fischer, Susan Cridge and Judy Wilson
3677 College Rd. #3
Fairbanks, AK 99709
Phone: (907)479-2563
In business since: 1976
Type of business: Gallery
Description of business: The Artworks carries prints, paintings, pottery, jewelry, sculpture and fiber work by Alaskans and others. We also offer framing services. In assembling our varied collection, we look for quality, workman-

ship and aesthetically pleasing original designs. Located close to the University of Alaska, the gallery attracts both residents and tourists who enjoy its upbeat, open and friendly atmosphere and knowledgeable staff.

Types of products: Handmade items and some manufactured jewelry and giftware

Categories: Fine crafts, jewelry, wooden crafts, paper products, hand blown glass items, pottery/ceramics, sculpture

Price range: $10-300

Business policy: We buy crafts outright and take work on consignment.

Buys: From the craftspeople who query us if we like their work and it fits our theme; at wholesale shows for hand crafted items; from reps or craft brokers; at wholesale gift shows

Advertising/Promotion: Local radio, newspaper, direct mail, tourist brochure placement, *The Milepost*

Application process: Queries are accepted from local/regional and out-of-town craftspeople. For consideration, provide catalog/promotional materials, photos, sample of work, written description of work.

BENET INC.
Bonnie Pike
247 Washington St.
Stoughton, MA 02072
Phone: (617)341-3909
Fax: (617) 344-4758
In business since: 1967
Type of business: Retail store selling hand crafted items
Description of business: A gallery of American hand craft decorative accessories.
Types of products: Handmade items only
Categories: Fine crafts, wooden crafts, paper products, stained glass items, home decor, figurines, pottery/ceramics, baskets, recycled crafts, sculpture
Price range: $20-500
Business policy: We buy crafts outright, take work on consignment and commission work from craftspeople.
Buys: From the craftspeople who query us if we like their work and it fits our theme; at wholesale shows for hand crafted items; at wholesale gift shows; from reps or craft brokers.

Advertising/Promotion: Yellow Pages, local newspapers, new homeowner packs, register receipt advertising

Application process: Queries are accepted from local/regional and out-of-town craftspeople. Crafter responsible for shipping. For consideration, provide photos or slides, catalog/promotional materials, sample of work, written description of work.

BETWEEN FRIENDS
Linda Payne, Debbie McClure and Delaine Turner
Laguna Hills Malls, #1500
Laguna Hills, CA 92653
Phone: (714)859-1445; (714)859-2412
Fax: (714)859-7021
In business since: 1985
Type of business: Retail store selling hand crafted items
Description of business: Between Friends is a 6,000 sq. ft. country store featuring a full line of unique hand crafted gifts and decorations.
Types of products: Handmade items and collectibles, cards, candles
Categories: Wearable art, jewelry, wooden crafts, paper products, needlework crafts, home decor, dolls/stuffed animals/toys, pottery/ceramics, nature crafts/floral
Price range: $1-100
Business policy: We buy crafts outright and take work on consignment.
Buys: From the craftspeople who query us if we like their work and it fits our theme; at wholesale shows for hand crafted items; at wholesale gift shows, from reps or craft brokers, at retail craft shows.
Advertising/Promotion: Direct mail, fliers, newspapers
Application process: Queries are accepted from local/regional and out-of-town craftspeople. For consideration, provide photos.

BIRDSNEST GALLERY
Barbara Entzminger
12 Mt. Desert St.
Bar Harbor, ME 04609
Phone: (207)288-4054
In business since: 1972
Type of business: Gallery
Description of business: The Birdsnest Gallery is Bar Harbor's oldest fine art

gallery, featuring regional and nationally known artists working in oil, watercolor, graphics and sculpture, from realism to impressionism to contemporary.

Types of products: Handmade items only

Categories: sculpture

More about products: Sells sculpture in wood, stone, marble or limited edition bronze castings, fine bird carvings and decoys.

Price range: $200-10,000

Business policy: We take work on consignment. We commission work from craftspeople. Artwork on consignment mostly.

Buys: From the craftspeople who query us if we like their work and it fits our theme; through slide registries; at retail craft shows

Advertising/Promotion: Local papers, press releases, Bar Harbor Chamber of Commerce. Budget varies.

Special programs: We have 10 feature shows for specific sculptors and painters.

Application process: Queries are accepted from local/regional and out-of-town craftspeople. Call for appointment after sending résumé (biography), slides and/or photos of work. For consideration, provide photos or slides (6 or more), catalog/promotional materials, written description of work, résumé.

Additional information: The Birdsnest Gallery is seasonal, open May 15 through October 30.

THE BLUE RABBIT LTD.

Sharon Gunderson
5210 E. Arapahoe Rd.
Littleton, CO 80122

Phone: (303)843-9419

Fax: (303)843-0813

In business since: 1990

Type of business: Retail store selling hand crafted items

Description of business: Specialize in traditional American folk art—no country. Hand crafted in USA; we buy wholesale.

Types of products: Handmade items and some important items for lower price points

Categories: Fine crafts, home decor, dolls/stuffed animals/toys, pottery/ceramics, baskets

Price range: $20-300

Business policy: We buy crafts outright.

Buys: From the craftspeople who query us if we like their work and it fits our theme; at wholesale shows for hand crafted items; at wholesale gift shows; from reps or craft brokers

Advertising/Promotion: *The Country Register* for Colorado, local newspaper and local radio. $7,000-10,000/year budget.

Special programs: Hold open houses twice a year

Application process: Queries are accepted from local/regional and out-of-town craftspeople. For consideration, provide photos or slides, catalog/promotional materials, sample of work, written description of work, and price list.

BOHEMIA RIVER GALLERY

Allaire duPont
P.O. Box 642
Chesapeake City, MD 21915

Phone: (410)885-2194; (410)755-6996

Fax: (302)378-1170

In business since: 1992

Type of business: Retail store selling hand crafted items

Description of business: A unique mix of local Eastern shore artwork and imported handcrafts.

Types of products: Handmade items only

Categories: Fine crafts, wearable art, jewelry, wooden crafts, stained glass items, home decor, pottery/ceramics, baskets, garden accessories

Price range: $1-400

Business policy: We buy crafts outright and commission work from craftspeople.

Buys: From the craftspeople who query us if we like their work and it fits our theme; at wholesale gift shows.

Advertising/Promotion: Local papers and mailing list. Budget varies.

Application process: Queries are accepted from local/regional and out-of-town craftspeople. Call above number. For consideration, provide photos or slides, written description of work.

BROOKE POTTERY

Gloria Brooke
223 N. Kentucky Ave.
Lakeland, FL 33801

Phone: (941)688-6844

Fax: (941)683-4759

E-mail: perkb@aol.com

In business since: 1988

Type of business: Retail store selling hand crafted items

Description of business: We emphasize high quality, functional artwork including pottery, glass, jewelry and wood. Also include decorative work for home and office. We work toward developing productive relationships with artists and customers.

Types of products: Handmade items and cookbooks

Categories: Fine crafts, wearable art, jewelry, wooden crafts, hand blown glass items, home decor, pottery/ceramics, leather crafts, baskets

More about products: Prefer information tags attached to the work to have the artist or studio name only—no addresses or phone numbers.

Price range: $6-1,000

Business policy: We buy crafts outright and take work on consignment.

Buys: From craftspeople who query us if we like their work and it fits our theme; at wholesale shows for hand crafted items; through slide registries; from reps or craft brokers; at retail craft shows; personal networking.

Advertising/Promotion: Local newspapers, tourist monthly magazine, National Public Radio, local and nearby large cities, TV, newsletter

Special programs: A cat show every other year, a teapot show every other year, as well as other similar events.

Application process: Queries are accepted from local/regional and out-of-town craftspeople. For consideration, provide photos or slides, catalog/promotional materials, sample of work.

Additional information: We are very customer oriented. We require exclusivity in the 338-zip code area.

BROOKFIELD CRAFT CENTER

Judith T. Russell
P.O. Box 122
Brookfield, CT 06804

Phone: (203)775-4526

Fax: (203)740-7815

E-mail: brkfldcrft@aol.com

In business since: 1954

Type of business: Retail store selling hand crafted items

Description of business: The shop at BCC sells originally designed, hand-made work, both functional and decorative, produced by American craft artists.

Types of products: Handmade items and books on crafts

Categories: Fine crafts, wearable art, jewelry, wooden crafts, stained glass items, hand blown glass items, pottery/ceramics, leather crafts, baskets, carved birds

Price range: $10-1,000

Business policy: We take work on consignment.

Buys: From the craftspeople who query us if we like their work and it fits our theme; at wholesale shows for hand crafted items; at retail craft shows

Advertising/Promotion: A quarterly publication listing classes and information on the shop is sent to a mailing list of 18,000. Send numerous press releases to local and national publications and place some display advertising during the December holidays.

Special programs: From mid-November through Christmas Eve, quadruple on inventory for annual holiday craft sale and exhibition. Approximately 8,000 people attend this event.

Application process: Queries are accepted from local/regional and out-of-town craftspeople. For consideration, provide photos or slides (3-5), catalog/promotional materials.

THE BROWSING BARN

Carol Corso

34 Newton Rd.

Plaistow, NH 03865

Phone: (603)382-6146

In business since: 1988

Type of business: Gallery

Description of business: Over 80 artisans' hand crafted work is on display in a wide selection of holiday decorations and gifts. Emerging American talents as well as well known professionals' creations are showcased. Focus is on hand crafted Christmas collectibles.

Types of products: Handmade items and Christmas related decorations, ornaments, tree toppers and skirts, angels, santas, snowmen, nutcrackers and smokers, gifts, floral arrangements, nativities and creches

Categories: Fine crafts, jewelry, miniatures/dollhouses, wooden crafts, paper products, stained glass items, hand blown glass items, home decor, dolls/stuffed animals/toys, pottery/ceramics, nature crafts/floral, baskets

Price range: $4-250

Business policy: We buy crafts outright, take work on consignment and commission work from craftspeople.

Buys: From the craftspeople who query us if we like their work and it fits our theme; at wholesale shows for hand crafted items; at wholesale gift shows

Advertising/Promotion: Newspaper ads in local and Boston newspapers, radio ads, fliers to mailing list. $1,500/year budget.

Special programs: Santa visits and a singing choir group.

Application process: Queries are accepted from local/regional and out-of-town craftspeople. By appointment only. For consideration, provide photos or slides, sample of work, written description of work, price list and SASE.

Additional information: Open weekends 9-5, Columbus Day through Christmas.

CAJUN COUNTRY STORE, INC.

Annie Wilson

401 E. Cypress

Lafayette, LA 70501

Phone: (318)233-7977; (800)252-9689

Fax: (318)233-0764

In business since: 1985

Type of business: Retail store selling hand crafted items

Description of business: A large authentic country store in a 1930s warehouse with an extensive inventory of Louisiana products. Local craftsmen, artists and musicians are featured.

Types of products: Handmade items and all Louisiana products—books, gift baskets, cookbooks, T-shirts, souvenirs and art prints.

Categories: Fine crafts, jewelry, wooden crafts, stained glass items, dolls/stuffed animals/toys, pottery/ceramics, sculpture

More about products: Hand crafted products by Louisiana artists including small novelties to cypress furniture for outdoor or indoor, musical instruments; also music tapes and CDs.

Price range: $3-3,000

Business policy: We buy crafts outright.

Buys: From the craftspeople who query us if we like their work and it fits our theme; at wholesale gift shows; from reps or craft brokers

Advertising/Promotion: Advertise through the tourism industry both local and statewide, including brochures, tourist info stops and tourist magazines, local newspapers, hotel directories, direct mail pieces, catalog (does not list crafts). $5-6,000/year budget.

Special programs: Have artists/craftsmen in store during special events (festivals, Christmas, etc.)

Application process: Queries are accepted from local/regional craftspeople only. For consideration, provide photos, sample of work, written description of work.

Additional information: Open 10-6, 7 days (except major holidays). Catalog available. Visa, MasterCard, Discover, American Express accepted.

THE CALLA LILLY

Steve Gauwitz

5901 North Prospect Rd.

Peoria, IL 61614

Phone: (309)693-2988

Fax: (309)693-9013

In business since: 1986

Type of business: Retail store selling hand crafted items

Description of business: An upscale gift shop and gallery. Carry a wide range of crafts, with the exception of clothing.

Types of products: Handmade items and "commercial" items with the hand crafted look

Categories: Fine crafts, jewelry, wooden crafts, stained glass items, hand blown glass items, home decor, dolls/stuffed animals/toys, pottery/ceramics, nature crafts/floral, leather crafts, baskets, sculpture, kaleidoscopes

Price range: $5-800

Business policy: We buy crafts outright.

Buys: From the craftspeople who query us if we like their work and it fits our theme; at wholesale shows for hand crafted items; at wholesale gift shows

Application process: Queries are accepted from local/regional and out-of-town craftspeople. For consideration, provide catalog/promotional materials, sample of work, written description of work.

CASCABEL LTD.

Arlene Kolbert
10 Chase Rd.
Scarsdale, NY 10583
Phone: (914)725-8922
Fax: (914)725-4409
In business since: 1990
Type of business: Retail store selling hand crafted items
Description of business: Cascabel is a home accessory and gift shop that specializes in American crafts. We also carry a large selection of silver and vermeil jewelry hand crafted by American artisans such as Terry Logan, Thomas Mann, Bruce Anderson, Charis Craven, Olga Ganoudis. We are located in a suburb of New York City and cater mostly to local clientele. Some other unique items are metal sculptures by Bill Finks and Judy Bomberger, candlesticks by David Bowman, wood boxes and pens by many artisans, ceramics by Jill Rosenwald, John Shedd, Hudson Valley Pottery, Suze Lindsay, Norman Bacon, Carol McFarlan and many more. A large selection of handblown perfume bottles and glassware. We are known for our exquisite gift wrapping and personal service.
Types of products: Handmade items and imported handcrafts and gift type items
Categories: Fine crafts, jewelry, paper products, hand blown glass items, home decor, pottery/ceramics, leather crafts
More about products: The items have to have a certain look that compliments the earthy feel of the store.
Price range: $10-500
Business policy: We buy crafts outright.
Buys: From the craftspeople who query us if we like their work and it fits our

theme; at wholesale shows for hand crafted items; at wholesale gift shows; at wholesale apparel shows; from reps or craft brokers

Advertising/Promotion: Local paper, Westchester section of the *New York Times*, $10,000/year budget.

Special programs: We have had jewelry shows and expect to do some specialty shows in the fall: teapots metalwork.

Application process: Queries are accepted from local/regional and out-of-town craftspeople. For consideration, provide photos or slides (5), catalog/promotional materials, sample of work, references: kinds of craft shops that currently carry work.

Additional information: "It's hard to sell pottery and certain items because there are so many local retail craft shows in the area." Cascabel ships anywhere in the USA and Canada and offers a bridal and personal registry.

CASUAL CAT

Cindy Doyle
112 Rt. 101A
Amherst, NH 03031
Phone: (603)882-1443
Fax: (603)889-7251
E-mail: doylecindy@aol.com
In business since: 1985
Type of business: Retail store selling hand crafted items
Description of business: The Casual Cat offers a unique collection of artwork, fine crafts, jewelry, pottery, and a large selection of gift items. The Casual Cat also offers Custom Picture Framing. We carry a large selection of frames and mats. All the work is done on premises and most pieces are completed in 7 days or less. We also offer next day framing on in-stock frames and matting.
Types of products: Handmade items only
Categories: Fine crafts, jewelry, wooden crafts, paper products, stained glass items, hand blown glass items, pottery/ceramics, leather crafts, recycled crafts, sculpture
Price range: $5-500
Business policy: We buy crafts outright and take work on consignment.
Buys: From the craftspeople who query us if we like their work and it fits our theme; at wholesale shows for hand

crafted items; from reps or craft brokers

Advertising/Promotion: Newspapers, *NH Home Magazine*, TV. $6,000/year budget.

Application process: Queries are accepted from local/regional and out-of-town craftspeople. Must call for an appointment. For consideration, provide photos or slides, catalog/promotional materials.

Additional information: Open T-Sat.

CELEBRATION OF AMERICAN CRAFTS

Creative Arts Workshop
80 Audubon St.
New Haven, CT 06510
Phone: (203)562-4927
Fax: (203)562-2329
In business since: 1968
Type of business: Gallery
Description of business: Celebration of American Crafts is an exhibition and sale of contemporary fine crafts by more than 400 American artists. Holiday shoppers and fine craft collectors from Connecticut and neighboring states have the opportunity to see and choose among many one-of-a-kind items.
Types of products: Handmade items only
Categories: Fine crafts, wearable art, jewelry, miniatures/dollhouses, wooden crafts, paper products, stained glass items, hand blown glass items, dolls/stuffed animals/toys, pottery/ceramics, baskets, sculpture, furniture
Price range: $5-3,000
Business policy: We take work on consignment.
Buys: From craftspeople who query us if we like their work and it fits our theme; at wholesale shows for hand crafted items; call for entries
Advertising/Promotion: Crafts magazines and journals, local and regional media
Special programs: Opening reception, sponsor parties and receptions, artist talks and seminars
Application process: Queries are accepted from local/regional and out-of-town craftspeople. Write for a prospectus. Deadline is June. For consideration, provide slides (3-6), sample of work, written description of work, résumé and SASE for return of slides.

Additional information: The Celebration attracts over 5,000 visitors from all over the Northeast and media coverage is extensive. The Celebration opens in early November and continues through December 24.

CHESTNUT STREET GALLERY, INC.
Lynn Frazer
3413 Nicholasville Rd.
Lexington, KY 40503
Phone: (606)273-7351
Fax: (606)276-1596
In business since: 1981
Type of business: Retail store selling hand crafted items
Description of business: A 1,500-sq.-ft. showroom in Kentucky's largest indoor mall, features a group of collectibles and American handcrafts.
Types of products: Handmade items and prints and collectibles
Categories: Fine crafts, jewelry, wooden crafts, stained glass items, hand blown glass items, home decor, figurines, dolls/stuffed animals/toys, pottery/ceramics, nature crafts/floral, baskets
Buys: From the craftspeople who query us if we like their work and it fits our theme; at wholesale shows for hand crafted items; at wholesale gift shows; at retail craft shows; from reps or craft brokers
Advertising/Promotion: Daily newspaper, newsletter, TV, radio, postcards. 8% of gross sales/year budget.
Application process: Queries are accepted from local/regional and out-of-town craftspeople. For consideration, provide photos, catalog/promotional materials, written description of work, wholesale price list.

THE CLAY PIGEON
Tom Forte
601 Ogden St.
Denver, CO 80218
Phone: (303)832-5538
Fax: (303)832-2128
In business since: 1970
Type of business: Gallery
Description of business: The Denver area is rich in natural resources necessary to the potter's art. Because of this, the region supports many fine craftspeople. The Clay Pigeon opened its doors with the philosophy of bringing quality ceramics to the public at reasonable prices and revitalizing the ancient tradition of handmade functional items. It has given regional potters working predominately in stoneware and porcelain an enthusiastic outlet for their work. Owners Tom and Peggy Forte, are dedicated artisans devoted to their ideals and a policy of pleasing their customers. The shop is known for its quality and personal care.
Types of products: Handmade items only
Categories: Pottery/ceramics
More about products: Mostly high-temp pottery, slab, coil and thrown work
Price range: $10-500
Business policy: We take work on consignment. We commission work from craftspeople.
Buys: From the craftspeople who query us if we like their work and it fits our theme
Advertising/Promotion: Newspapers, direct mail
Special programs: On-going one person shows 10-12 times each year
Application process: Queries are accepted from local/regional and out-of-town craftspeople. For consideration, provide slides, catalog/promotional materials, written description of work.

THE CLAY PLACE
Elvira L. Peake
5416 Walnut St.
Pittsburgh, PA 15232
Phone: (412)682-3737
Fax: (412)681-1226
In business since: 1973
Type of business: Retail store selling hand crafted items and gallery
Description of business: The Clay Place sells functional and decorative ceramics and sculpture and occasionally glass, enamel on copper and polymer jewelry. Located in a small shopping area near the Carnegie Museum, the shop and galleries include 1,500 sq. ft. for display on the second level of a modern brick building with atrium and elevator. Monthly one-person exhibits showcase work by national and international artists.
Types of products: Handmade items and books, equipment, supplies for clay and sculpture
Categories: Hand blown glass items, pottery/ceramics, sculpture, fine clay crafts
Price range: $15-3,500
Business policy: We buy crafts outright and take work on consignment.
Buys: From the craftspeople who query us if we like their work and it fits our theme; at wholesale shows for hand crafted items
Advertising/Promotion: Direct mail, local newspapers and magazines: *American Ceramics, American Craft, Ceramics Monthly*
Application process: Queries are accepted from local/regional and out-of-town craftspeople. For consideration, provide sample of work.

THE CLAY POT
Tara Silberberg
162 Seventh Ave.
Brooklyn, NY 11215
Phone: (718)788-6564
Fax: (718)965-1138
In business since: 1968
Type of business: Retail store selling hand crafted items
Description of business: Serving the NYC area for over 28 years, The Clay Pot today represents the works of over 600 craft artists. The slant on works sold is functional table top, gifts for all ages, and a vast range of jewelry from hip fashion to classic gold. Over the past decade, The Clay Pot has become a major source of handmade wedding bands and engagement rings in the NYC area, through extensive advertising "The Clay Pot is the place to get that special ring." The Gallery is visited by over 100,000 urbanites a year looking for the best in quality and design that the USA crafts artist has to offer.
Types of products: Handmade items and wedding bands, engagement rings
Categories: Fine crafts, jewelry, hand blown glass items, home decor, pottery/ceramics
Price range: $3-10,000
Business policy: We buy crafts outright and commission work from craftspeople.
Buys: At wholesale shows for hand crafted items; at wholesale apparel

shows; at wholesale gift shows; from reps or craft brokers

Advertising/Promotion: New York Times Sunday and magazine, *New York Magazine, The Village Voice.* $78,500/year budget.

Application process: Queries are accepted from local/regional and out-of-town craftspeople. For consideration, provide photos or slides, catalog/promotional materials, written description of work, SASE, price list.

CLOWNS' BAZAAR

M. Deanna Wagoner
9 Broad St.
Charleston, SC 29401
Phone: (803)723-9769
In business since: 1986
Type of business: Non-profit fair trade showcase
Description of business: The Clowns' Bazaar is a non-profit public corporation for skills development and marketing of crafts made by disadvantaged artisans. We promote fair trade practices to enhance the lives of economically and socially challenged craft producers.
Types of products: Handmade items only
Categories: Fine crafts, wearable art, jewelry, miniatures/dollhouses, wooden crafts, paper products, stained glass items, needlework crafts, hand blown glass items, home decor, figurines, dolls/stuffed animals/toys, pottery/ceramics, nature crafts/floral, leather crafts, baskets, recycled crafts, sculpture, musical instruments
More about products: All crafts must be made by senior citizens (over 65) physically or mentally challenged people or economically and socially disadvantaged people.
Price range: $1-150
Business policy: We buy crafts outright, take work on consignment and commission work from craftspeople.
Buys: From the craftspeople who query us if we like their work and it fits our theme; through Christian Missions and fair trade organizations, Elder Craft
Advertising/Promotion: Newspaper, tourist guidebooks, maps, newsletter. $3,000/year budget.
Application process: Queries are ac-

cepted from local/regional and out-of-town craftspeople. For consideration, provide photos, written description of work, and an explanation of the disability that keeps craftsperson from participating in the open market.
Additional information: Part of a world wide network to provide opportunities for the less advantaged people of the world by marketing their arts and crafts to their advantage rather than for our own profit.

COMMON WEALTH GALLERY

Rick Davidson
Hyatt Regency, 313 Fourth Ave.
Louisville, KY 40202
Phone: (502)589-4747; (502)589-4758
In business since: 1980
Type of business: Gallery
Description of business: We currently represent American craft artists from all over the United States. Specializing in affordable art, exquisite gifts. Unusual clocks, jewelry and sparkling designs in hand crafted glass have been our trademarks for over 15 years. The Common Wealth Gallery has one of the largest collections of kaleidoscopes and serves a diverse clientele including corporate accounts and well-known celebrities.
Types of products: Handmade items and pre-recorded CDs and cassettes, and unusual greeting cards.
Categories: Fine crafts, wearable art, jewelry, wooden crafts, paper products, stained glass items, hand blown glass items, home decor, figurines, dolls/stuffed animals/toys, pottery/ceramics, sculpture
More about products: All items are hand crafted in the United States. The items we sell are juried crafts and must possess strong design and/or functional characteristics.
Price range: $2-several thousand
Business policy: We buy crafts outright.
Buys: From the craftspeople who query us if we like their work and it fits our theme; at wholesale shows for hand crafted items; at retail craft shows.
Advertising/Promotion: Local tourist publications, art auctions for public TV, mailers to our extensive mailing list
Special programs: Two large seasons:

Christmas and late April, early May for the Kentucky Derby visitors
Application process: Queries are accepted from local/regional and out-of-town craftspeople. Please do not call. We prefer to be contacted via mail. For consideration, provide sample of work upon request, catalog/promotional materials, photos, and complete bio including where work is currently available. Do not accept items that are being sold in retail stores, i.e., department stores, etc.
Additional information: While the Common Wealth does not *demand* exclusivity, we are most interested in those craft artists who realize and value the importance of keeping their work "special" and not over-exposed.

J COTTER GALLERY

Jim Cotter
P.O. Box 385
Vail, CO 81657
Phone: (970)476-3131
Fax: (970)827-4222
In business since: 1970
Type of business: Gallery
Description of business: A gallery of contemporary designer jewelry, featuring designs by leading artists from the United States and Europe.
Types of products: Handmade items only
Categories: Jewelry, sculpture
Price range: $50-30,000
Business policy: We take work on consignment.
Buys: From the craftspeople who query us if we like their work and it fits our theme
Advertising/Promotion: Vail Gallery Guide, Vail/Beaver Creek catalogue, *Metalsmith Magazine*
Application process: Queries are accepted from local/regional and out-of-town craftspeople. Out-of-town craftspeople should contact the gallery at the above address. For consideration, provide photos or slides.

COUNTRY PLEASURES OF ESSEX

Connie Connor
58 S. Main St.
Essex, CT 06426
Phone: (860)767-0060
Fax: (860)767-3906
E-mail: qcne50c@prodigy.com

Website: http://essexct.com

In business since: 1985

Type of business: Retail store selling hand crafted items

Description of business: At Country Pleasures, everything is "special," even the large carved rooster outside the blue shuttered door bring smiles to the browsers as they are warmly greeted by owner Connie Connor. Finding the right mix in gifts is always a challenge for any gift shop, but every few days a craftsperson who's work is extraordinary seems to find his or her way into this unique shop. At Country Pleasures you will find crafts of more than 300 artisans featured in an upscale country setting at this unique shop in one of New England's most picturesque villages. Gifts, handcrafted in America, is the specialty here.

Types of products: Handmade items and Koosed Primitives caarvings and watercolors, Cat's Meow Village collectibles featuring local pieces

Categories: Fine crafts, jewelry, miniatures/dollhouses, wooden crafts, stained glass items, hand blown glass items, home decor, figurines, dolls/stuffed animals/toys, pottery/ceramics, baskets, sculpture

Price range: $10-800

Business policy: We buy crafts outright and commission work from craftspeople.

Buys: From the craftspeople who query us if we like their work and it fits our theme; at wholesale shows for hand crafted items; occasionally a rep

Advertising/Promotion: Tourist magazines and publications, World Wide Web, *Mystic Coast & Country Tourist Guide*, store brochure in Welcome Centers, merchant brochure in centers, inns, etc. $2,000/year budget.

Special programs: Artist signings of pieces at Christmas and other special events during year

Application process: Queries are accepted from local/regional and out-of-town craftspeople. For consideration, provide photos (1 per item), sample of work, catalog/promotional materials, written description of work, sample of color like paint swatch, material swatch, etc. to see colors available.

Additional information: During the holidays, a special Connecticut blended tea is served to customers along with the homemade cookies or English lemon bread, a coveted recipe passed down from the owner's grandmother, whose roots go back to Old Sturbridge Village. Store hours M-Sat 10-5 and from Fall through Christmas 7 days a week 9:30-5:30.

THE COUNTRY STUDIO

Lynn McClurg

590 Georgetown Rd.

Hadley, PA 16130

Phone: (412)253-2493

In business since: 1972

Type of business: Gallery

Description of business: The Country Studio art gallery and gift shop features quality original, American art and fine crafts by artists and craftspeople from the local area and across the country. The "country" name reflects the gallery's rural location rather than the type of work that it carries, as the works suit traditional, contemporary and country decors.

Types of products: Handmade items only

Categories: Fine crafts, jewelry, wooden crafts, paper products, stained glass items, hand blown glass items, stuffed animals/toys, pottery/ceramics, baskets, rubber stamps, candles, weaving

More about products: We do not accept pressed or jiggered pottery.

Price range: $1-400

Business policy: We buy crafts outright and take work on consignment.

Buys: At wholesale shows for hand crafted items; at retail craft shows; and sometimes from the craftspeople who query us if we like their work and it fits our theme.

Special programs: Annual shows: 1,001 Pots and the Holiday Show

Application process: Accepts queries from local/regional and out-of-town craftspeople. For consideration, call first.

COUNTRY WORKS

Sherry Mintz

7038 Little Rd.

New Port Richey, FL 34653

Phone: (813)844-7940

In business since: 1991

Type of business: Retail store selling hand crafted items

Description of business: Country Works is located in a little, old, five room frame house with all the charm and coziness of the original early Florida home that it is. It features the talents of more than 25 local and out of state crafters.

Types of products: Handmade items and potpourri, wire, candles

Categories: Wooden crafts, home decor, dolls/stuffed animals/toys, pottery/ceramics, baskets

Price range: $1-500

Business policy: We buy crafts outright.

Buys: From the craftspeople who query us if we like their work and it fits our theme; at wholesale shows for hand crafted items; at wholesale gift shows; at wholesale toy, doll and teddy bear shows; at retail craft shows; from reps or craft brokers

Advertising/Promotion: Local newspapers and magazines. $500/year budget.

Application process: Queries are accepted from local/regional and out-of-town craftspeople. For consideration, provide sample of work.

Additional information: Shop hours are M-F 10-5, Sat 10-4.

COZY NOTIONS

Traci J. Callan

1233 E. First St.

Meridian, ID 83642

Phone: (208)884-0580

Fax: (208)884-0269

In business since: 1994

Type of business: Retail store selling hand crafted items

Types of products: Handmade items and greeting cards, gift bags, candles, etc.

Categories: Fine crafts, wearable art, jewelry, wooden crafts, paper products, stained glass items, needlework crafts, home decor, figurines, dolls/stuffed animals/toys, pottery/ceramics, nature crafts/floral, baskets, recycled crafts

Price range: $2-200

Business policy: We buy crafts outright.

Buys: From the craftspeople who query us if we like their work and it fits our theme; at wholesale shows for hand crafted items; at wholesale gift shows

Advertising/Promotion: Local media, newspaper ads, merchant association, trade publications. Budget varies.

Application process: Queries are accepted from local/regional and out-of-town craftspeople. For consideration, provide catalog/promotional materials, photos, written description of work.

THE CRABNET

Rita and Doug Lambert
925 Decatur St.
New Orleans, LA 70116
Phone: (504)522-3478
In business since: 1981
Type of business: Retail store selling hand crafted items
Description of business: Located in the historic French Quarter, The Crabnet offers a wide array of wildlife art and gifts. Both the sportsman and wildlife enthusiast will enjoy this unique gallery of American-made products.
Types of products: Handmade items and manufactured wildlife gifts, limited edition prints, clothing with wildlife theme
Categories: Fine crafts, wearable art, jewelry, wooden crafts, home decor, pottery/ceramics, nature crafts/floral, sculpture
More about products: All items must have a wildlife theme and be realistic in detail.
Price range: $5-5,000
Business policy: We take work on consignment. Artists must agree to sell work at 50% off their retail price and give net 30 days billing.
Buys: From the craftspeople who query us if we like their work and it fits our theme; at wholesale gift shows; from reps or craft brokers
Advertising/Promotion: New Orleans Tourist Information Shopping Guide, Louisiana Tax Free Shopping Guide (for International visitors), printed shopping bag, word of mouth. $100/year budget.
Application process: Queries are accepted from local/regional and out-of-town craftspeople. For consideration, provide sample of work. Call first for an appointment. Sent samples will not be returned.
Additional information: We specialize in artwork produced by Louisiana residents and natives.

CRADLE OF THE SUN

Elaine
1546 Polk St.
San Francisco, CA 94109
Phone: (415)567-9091
E-mail: cradlesun@aol.com
In business since: 1977
Type of business: Retail store selling hand crafted items and art and stained glass
Description of business: Gift shop sells only glass items. Two locations.
Types of products: Handmade items and Tiffany-style lamps, window hangings, perfume bottles, etc.
Categories: Stained glass items, hand blown glass items
Price range: $20-1,000
Business policy: We buy crafts outright and take work on consignment.
Buys: From the craftspeople who query us if we like their work and it fits our theme; at wholesale shows for hand crafted items; at wholesale gift shows
Advertising/Promotion: San Francisco Visitor's Guide, Yellow Pages. $4,000/year budget.
Application process: Queries are accepted from local/regional and out-of-town craftspeople. For consideration, provide photos, brochure, wholesale price list.

THE CRAFT ABOUT STORE

Debbie Nita
227½ Ridge Rd.
Munster, IN 46321
Phone: (219)836-8861
In business since: 1993
Type of business: Retail store selling hand crafted items
Description of business: The store caters to local as well as out-of-state crafters. It is located in the heart of Munster, IN, on busy Ridge Road, about 40 miles southeast of Chicago.
Types of products: Handmade items only
Categories: Fine crafts, wearable art, jewelry, miniatures/dollhouses, wooden crafts, paper products, stained glass items, needlework crafts, home decor, pottery/ceramics, nature crafts/floral, leather crafts, baskets, recycled crafts

Price range: $1-80
Business policy: Carry a mix of space rental, consignment and crafts bought at wholesale
Buys: From the craftspeople who query us if we like their work and it fits our theme; at wholesale shows for hand crafted items; rental and consignments
Advertising/Promotion: Local newspapers with ads, press releases, stories, *Craft Marketing News.* 5% of gross sales/year budget.
Special programs: Hold store "events," open house every other month
Application process: Queries are accepted from local/regional and out-of-town craftspeople. Crafts are taken in on a 60% (to crafter) consignment basis. For consideration, provide photos, written description of work.

THE CRAFT GALLERY

Dori Young
424 Main St.
Sanford, ME 04073
Phone: (207)324-1408
In business since: 1992
Type of business: Retail store selling hand crafted items
Description of business: The Craft Gallery is a gift shop with a large variety of items. The focus is on hand crafted gifts, but we sell many mass produced items as well. The theme is country, but it is not exclusive. We try to cater to the needs of customers who are buying gifts and home decor.
Types of products: Handmade items and candles, Dreamsicles, wire and more
Categories: Jewelry, miniatures/dollhouses, wooden crafts, paper products, stained glass items, home decor, figurines, dolls/stuffed animals/toys, pottery/ceramics, nature crafts/floral, baskets
Price range: $2-100
Business policy: We buy crafts outright.
Buys: From the craftspeople who query us if we like their work and it fits our theme; at wholesale shows for hand crafted items; at wholesale gift shows; from reps or craft brokers
Advertising/Promotion: Local newspaper, storefront displays
Application process: Queries are accepted from local/regional and out-of-

town craftspeople. For consideration, provide catalog/promotional materials.

Additional information: We would like the crafters to understand that there are many reasons their work may be refused. Best of luck to all.

DEDHAM WOMEN'S EXCHANGE

Sue Carter and Dale Cabot
445 Washington St.
Dedham, MA 02026
Phone: (617)326-0627
In business since: 1914
Type of business: Retail store selling hand crafted items
Description of business: A gift shop carrying about half consigned and half commercial items. All proceeds go to charity, all connected with children—day care programs, high school scholarships, etc.
Types of products: Handmade and commercial items
Categories: Fine crafts, wooden crafts, stained glass items, needlework crafts, home decor, dolls/stuffed animals/toys, nature crafts/floral
More about products: Also sell baby dresses, sweaters, painted items, holiday decorations
Price range: $5-100
Business policy: We take work on consignment.
Buys: From the craftspeople who query us if we like their work and it fits our theme; at wholesale shows for hand crafted items; at retail craft shows
Advertising/Promotion: At craft fairs and in storefront windows, and have a table at children's theater
Application process: Queries are accepted from local/regional and out-of-town craftspeople. Out-of-town craftspeople must pay postage. For consideration, provide photos, sample of work, written description of work.

ABRAM DEMAREE HOMESTEAD

Mary Crain, president
252 Schraalenburg Rd.
Haworth, NJ 07641
Phone/Fax: (201)385-7309
Type of business: House filled with crafts/gifts
In business since: 1979
Hours: Th-F 10-9, Sat-Sun 10-5

Description of business: A national historic site: 1720 stone house, 1780 Dutch barn, 1780 Blacksmith shop and greenhouse filled with 1 million handmade crafts to delight you.
Types of products: Hand crafted items and gifts, art, flowers, plants
Categories: Fine crafts, wearable art, jewelry, wooden crafts, stained glass items, needlework crafts, hand blown glass items, home decor, figurines, dolls/stuffed animals/toys, pottery/ceramics, nature crafts/floral, leather crafts, baskets, recycled crafts, sculpture
Price range: $1-500
Business Policy: We buy crafts outright.
Buys: From the craftspeople who query us if we like their work and it fits our theme; at wholesale shows for hand-crafted items.
Advertising/Promotion: *The Record Newspaper* every week
Application process: Queries are accepted from local/regional and out-of-town craftspeople. For consideration, provide photos (4), sample of work and catalog/promotional materials.

DESIGNWEAR

Jo Ann Lesnett
218 E. Pine St. #4
Lakeland, FL 33801
Phone: (941)682-8921
In business since: 1990
Type of business: Retail store selling hand crafted items
Description of business: Designwear, located in Lakeland's Antiques District, specializes in clothing and jewelry by artists but also carries some gift items. It is an upscale shop representing 100 artists such as Laurel Burch, Lunch at the Ritz and many talented Florida artists.
Types of products: Handmade items only
Categories: Fine crafts, wearable art, jewelry, home decor, pottery/ceramics
Price range: $5-550
Business policy: We buy crafts outright and take work on consignment.
Buys: From the craftspeople who query us if we like their work and it fits our theme; at wholesale shows for hand crafted items; at wholesale apparel shows; at retail craft shows; from reps or craft brokers

Advertising/Promotion: *Ledger*, a local newspaper, *Here Abouts*, a colorful tourist magazine, cable TV
Special programs: Available
Application process: Queries are accepted from local/regional and out-of-town craftspeople. For consideration, provide photos or slides (3-5), catalog/promotional materials, sample of work, written description of work.

DIANNES

Tracy and Dianne Heffron
54 Hartford Turnpike
Vernon, CT 06066
Phone: (860)647-7074
In business since: 1982
Type of business: Retail store selling hand crafted items
Description of business: We feature artists who work in all types of materials in all forms from jewelry to gifts. Diannes strives for customer service, offering custom bridal jewelry and gifts for the wedding party. Diannes is always changing and offers something new every time one visits.
Types of products: Handmade items only
Categories: Fine crafts, wearable art, jewelry, hand blown glass items, home decor, sculpture
More about products: Products are required to be high quality, not in price, but of time and effort.
Price range: $10-500
Business policy: We buy crafts outright.
Buys: At wholesale shows for hand crafted items; at wholesale gift shows; from reps or craft brokers
Advertising/Promotion: Word of mouth, mailing lists
Special programs: An open house every November to thank customers; a formal tea in the spring and Trunk Shows.
Application process: Queries are accepted from local/regional and out-of-town craftspeople. For consideration, provide photos, sample of work, catalog/promotional materials, written description of work.

A DIFFERENT DRUMMER, INC.

Mary Ann Bloom and Barbara Spessard
2 Town Square
Hollidaysburg, PA 16648
Phone: (814)696-4141
Fax: (814)695-6858

In business since: 1983

Type of business: Retail store selling hand crafted items

Description of business: A retail store selling only hand crafted gifts all made in America. These gifts include collectibles, jewelry, porcelain, glass, metal and fiber for all ages. Each item is created by craftspersons from more than 47 different states.

Types of products: Handmade items only

Categories: Fine crafts, jewelry, wooden crafts, stained glass items, needlework crafts, hand blown glass items, home decor, figurines, dolls/stuffed animals/toys, pottery/ceramics, leather crafts, sculpture

Price range: $1.45-500

Business policy: We buy crafts outright.

Buys: From the craftspeople who query us if we like their work and it fits our theme; at wholesale shows for hand crafted items; from reps or craft brokers

Advertising/Promotion: Radio, *Altoona Mirror* newspaper, Blair County Convention and Tourist Bureau, Hollidaysburg Community Partnership, Bedford Folliage Periodical. $2,000 year/budget.

Special programs: Woman's Club presentations, display for a special tour—Altoona Symphony, auctions for nonprofit organizations, Sergio Lub

Application process: Queries are accepted from local/regional and out-of-town craftspeople. For consideration, provide catalog/promotional materials, sample of work, written description of work.

DISCOVERIES GALLERY

Douglas Fisher

P.O. Box 1552

Reading, PA 19603

Phone: (610)372-2595; (610)373-4131

Fax: (610)373-0730

In business since: 1980

Type of business: Gallery

Description of business: A complete inventory of US crafts from 600 artists. Specialize in decorative accessories. Range is from jewelry to sculptures to furniture represented in all mediums. Approximately 2,500 sq. ft. of display with a constantly changing inventory.

Types of products: Handmade items only

Categories: Fine crafts, jewelry, wooden crafts, paper products, stained glass items, hand blown glass items, home decor, figurines, dolls/stuffed animals/toys, pottery/ceramics, nature crafts/floral, leather crafts, baskets, recycled crafts, sculpture

Price range: $25-25,000

Business policy: We buy crafts outright.

Buys: From the craftspeople who query us if we like their work and it fits our theme; at wholesale shows for hand crafted items

Advertising/Promotion: Radio, newspaper and cultural programs

Special programs: Annual open house with 2 or 3 artists represented. We also set-up our tent and take a representative group of merchandise for nonprofit social events (i.e., hospital garden parties, opera benefits, etc.). We share the profit.

Application process: Queries are accepted from local/regional and out-of-town craftspeople. For consideration, provide photos or slides (3).

DIVINITY'S SPLENDOUR GLOW

Renuka O'Connell

311 Broadway

Arlington, MA 02174

Phone: (617)648-7100

In business since: 1979

Type of business: Retail store selling hand crafted items

Description of business: Located in a town center, we have a beautiful store with skylights, fountain and a lot of light. We carry gifts for all ages in a varied price range. The products that do the best are wall items, pottery, ceramics, wood, jewelry, mobiles, baby items, candles and glass. We like to receive information about affordable gifts, especially unique adornments for the home.

Types of products: Handmade items and artful wares that have been offset printed

Categories: Wearable art, jewelry, wooden crafts, stained glass items, hand blown glass items, home decor, figurines, dolls/stuffed animals/toys, pottery/ceramics, nature crafts/floral, leather crafts, recycled crafts, sculpture

Price range: $3-95

Business policy: We buy crafts outright and take work on consignment.

Buys: From the craftspeople who query us if we like their work and it fits our theme; at wholesale shows for hand crafted items; at wholesale gift shows; at retail craft shows; from reps or craft brokers

Advertising/Promotion: Local newspaper, mailing list. 2% of gross sales/year budget.

Special programs: Educational workshops free of charge in stained glass, beading, painting, pottery

Application process: Queries are accepted. For consideration, provide photos, catalog/promotional materials, sample of work.

DRAGON'S DEN

C.J. Godwin

P.O. Box 2525

Elkins, WV 26241

Phone: (304)637-4318

In business since: 1978

Type of business: Retail store selling hand crafted items

Description of business: Sell high quality, US-made (no mass production) crafts related to Christmas, Easter and other major holidays.

Types of products: US handmade items only

Categories: Fine crafts, jewelry, miniatures/dollhouses, wooden crafts, stained glass items, hand blown glass items, figurines, dolls, pottery/ceramics, baskets, candles

Price range: $5-1,000

Business policy: We buy crafts outright, take work on consignment and commission work from craftspeople.

Buys: From the craftspeople who query us if we like their work and it fits our theme; at wholesale shows for hand crafted items; at wholesale gift shows; at retail craft shows; from reps or craft brokers

Advertising/Promotion: Newpapers, block ads, local TV, Consumer Channel, free papers, i.e., *Thrifty Nickle*, *Uncle Henry's*. Budget varies.

Special programs: Try to do 4-6 craft shows a year

Application process: Queries are accepted from local/regional and out-of-town craftspeople. For consideration, provide photos or slides (3-5), catalog/promotional materials, sample of work.

DON DRUMM STUDIOS & GALLERY

Lisa Drumm
437 Crouse St.
Akron, OH 44311
Phone: (330)253-6268
Fax: (330)253-4014
In business since: 1960
Type of business: Gallery
Description of business: Don Drumm Studios and Gallery has a two-building, nine-showroom complex of retail space. Represent the works of over 500 professional artists and craftspeople. Primarily interested in contemporary design and always looking for new and interesting work to bring to the area.
Types of products: Handmade items only in Main Gallery. An additional store next to the main store sells a variety of interesting imports and uniquely designed commercial products along with the handmade products.
Categories: Fine crafts, jewelry, wooden crafts, paper products, stained glass items, hand blown glass items, dolls/stuffed animals/toys, pottery/ceramics, sculpture
Price range: $1-2,000
Business policy: We buy crafts outright and take work on consignment.
Buys: From the craftspeople who query us if we like their work and it fits our theme; at wholesale shows for hand crafted items; from reps or craft brokers
Advertising/Promotion: Newspaper, radio, direct mail, area magazines, area theater and concert, etc., programs
Special programs: Three major shows each year—spring, fall and holiday
Application process: Queries are accepted from local/regional and out-of-town craftspeople. For consideration, provide photos or slides, catalog/promotional materials and SASE. Please be sure that all are properly marked with identification—selling price (retail or wholesale and marked as such on price list, etc.). Craftspeople who would like to show their work in person must call for an appointment.

EASY STREET

Marsha and Terry Moore
8 Francis St.
Annapolis, MD 21401
Phone: (410)263-5556
In business since: 1979
Type of business: Gallery
Description of business: Features fine American crafts, specializing in art glass, stained glass, kaleidoscopes, etc.
Types of products: Handmade items only
Categories: Fine crafts, jewelry, stained glass items, hand blown glass items, home decor, pottery/ceramics, kaleidoscopes
Price range: $15-1,600
Business policy: We buy crafts outright.
Buys: From the craftspeople who query us if we like their work and it fits our theme; at wholesale shows for hand crafted items; at wholesale gift shows; at retail craft shows; from reps or craft brokers
Advertising/Promotion: Hotel books, local magazines
Application process: Call for an appointment. For consideration, provide catalog/promotional materials, written description of work.

ELDER CRAFTSMEN SHOP

1742 Sansom St.
Philadelphia, PA 19103
Phone: (215)665-9330
In business since: 1959
Type of business: Retail store selling hand crafted items
Description of business: Men and women over 55 from across the US sell their hand crafted items in this nonprofit shop.
Types of products: Handmade items only
Categories: Fine crafts, wearable art, jewelry, miniatures, wooden crafts, paper products, stained glass items, needlework crafts, hand blown glass items, home decor, figurines, dolls/stuffed animals/toys, pottery/ceramics, leather crafts
More about products: Products include hand-knitted and crocheted sweaters and afghans, Raggedy Anns and Andys and handmade quilts.
Price range: $3-300
Business policy: We take work on consignment, return 50% of the selling price of an item to its maker *after* it is sold.
Buys: From the craftspeople who query us if we like their work and it fits our theme; at retail craft shows; through ads in senior publications
Advertising/Promotion: Celebrate Age Exposition at Philadelphia Convention Center annually, occasional ads in centercity/downtown publications, TV news show "human interest" spot and newspaper articles about the shop
Special programs: We offer Live and Learn Teaching program, open to all ages. Classes are held periodically to help preserve the traditional crafts and hand crafting skills, so that these arts will be passed on to future generations.
Application process: Queries are accepted from local/regional and out-of-town craftspeople. Out-of-town craftspeople send photos first, then ship UPS or mail to shop if accepted for consignment. For consideration, provide photos, sample of work. Call for appointment to meet with Director or Board members, of if accepted and long distance, an application and regulation sheet will be mailed to craftsperson's home.
Additional information: Store hours M-F 10-4:45; open Sat 10-5 before Christmas only.

EVERGREEN FINE CRAFTS

Sharon Silvestrini
21 Boston St.
Guilford, CT 06437
Phone: (203)453-4324
In business since: 1983
Type of business: Retail store selling hand crafted items
Description of business: Evergreen Fine Crafts is located on the historic Guilford green. They represent the works of over 200 professional American craftspeople. Contemporary jewelry, functional and decorative ceramics, woodworks, and art glass are featured.
Types of products: Handmade items only
Categories: Fine crafts, jewelry, wooden crafts, paper products, hand blown glass items, pottery/ceramics, leather crafts
Price range: $5-375
Business policy: We buy crafts outright

and take work on consignment.

Buys: From the craftspeople who query us if we like their work and it fits our theme; at wholesale shows for hand crafted items; at wholesale gift shows

Advertising/Promotion: Direct mail

Application process: Queries are accepted from local/regional and out-of-town craftspeople. For consideration, provide photos or slides, sample of work.

Additional information: Store hours M-Sat 10-5 and Sun 12-4.

FABRIC ADDICT, INC.

Mary Beth Woods
P.O. Box 620
Nashville, IN 47448
Phone: (812)988-4993
In business since: 1987
Type of business: Retail store selling hand crafted items

Description of business: An excellent resource for fabrics, buttons, patterns and interested in "country clothing" such as vests, jumpers. The shop is located in southern Indiana tourist town of 300 shops. Also have a basket accessory corner to dress handmade baskets. The shop right now is 80% for the do-it-yourself people.

Types of products: Handmade items and quilting supplies, fabrics, patterns, clothing and basket accessories.

Categories: Wearable art, needlework crafts, dolls/stuffed animals/toys, pottery/ceramics, leather crafts, baskets, primitive dolls, quilted wallhangings and quilts (traditional patterns)

Price range: $3-350

Business policy: We take work on consignment.

Buys: From the craftspeople who query us if we like their work and it fits our theme.

Advertising/Promotion: Nashville (Brown County) Chamber of Commerce has a regular mailing that includes an almanac of merchants and advertises for shops. These have been mailed worldwide. Being a "tourist" town, most advertising is done for the whole town to promote traffic sales to all shops. $500/year budget, promotions vary.

Application process: Queries are ac-

cepted from local/regional and out-of-town craftspeople. For consideration, provide photos, catalog/promotional materials.

FAIR HAVEN WOODWORKS

Elizabeth Orsini
72 Blatchley Ave.
New Haven, CT 06513
Phone: (203)776-3099
Fax: (203)772-4153
In business since: 1980
Type of business: Retail store selling hand crafted items

Description of business: Fair Haven Woodworks features two floors of furniture designed and hand crafted by local and Vermont craftspeople, and furnishings and gifts as eclectic and unique as anything you could find in SoHo or Cambridge.

Types of products: Handmade items and quality hardwood furniture, gifts and accessories for the home

Categories: Fine crafts, wooden crafts, paper products, stained glass items, home decor, toys, pottery/ceramics, nature crafts/floral, baskets, recycled crafts, furniture

More about products: We specialize in Shaker, Mission and Arts and Crafts style furniture and contemporary "takes" on these styles in addition to complementary styles—Japanese tansu, iron and granite pieces for instance. Carry many lamps, Galbraith paper, Noguchi, Frank Lloyd Wright/Mission styles.

Price range: $25-400

Business policy: We buy crafts outright and take work on consignment.

Buys: From the craftspeople who query us if we like their work and it fits our theme; at wholesale shows for hand crafted items; at wholesale gift shows; from reps or craft brokers

Advertising/Promotion: Connecticut Magazine, New York Times Connecticut section (Sunday), Connecticut Law Tribune, New Haven Arts monthly newspaper. $30,000/year budget.

Application process: Queries are accepted from local/regional and out-of-town craftspeople. For consideration,

provide photos, sample of work, catalog/promotional materials.

FARMINGTON VALLEY ARTS CENTER

Sally Bloomberg
25 Arts Center Lane
Avon, CT 06001
Phone/Fax: (860)678-1867
In business since: 1986
Type of business: Retail store selling hand crafted items and gallery

Description of business: We carry contemporary and traditional crafts in a variety of medium. Jewelry, wood, clay, glass, pewter, clothing accessories make up the collection meant to provide a wide range of gift possibilities. We try to carry a lot of Connecticut artists. A part of a nonprofit arts center that has an educational program housed in an old dynamite factory in a beautiful wooded setting.

Types of products: Handmade items and cards and stationery

Categories: Fine crafts, wearable art, jewelry, wooden crafts, paper products, stained glass items, hand blown glass items, home decor, dolls/stuffed animals/toys, pottery/ceramics, baskets, recycled crafts, pewter, iron work

More about products: Mostly functional and wearable, a full range of gifts

Price range: $5-350

Business policy: We take work on consignment.

Buys: From the craftspeople who query us if we like their work and it fits our theme; at wholesale shows for hand crafted items; at wholesale gift shows; at retail craft shows; from reps or craft brokers

Advertising/Promotion: City newspaper, theatre playbills. Also there is a newsprint magazine for the whole area for services and tag sales used year-round.

Special programs: Four gallery shows per year; annual holiday exhibit and sale with candlelight opening; Open Arts Day event for entire Arts Center; Empty Bowl, an annual fundraiser event for the food bank.

Application process: Queries are accepted from local/regional and out-of-town craftspeople. Artist pays shipping to shop, gallery pays return shipping. For consideration, provide photos or slides, catalog/promotional materials, written description of work.

Additional information: We are seriously committed to a professional consignment relationship. We are responsible for any damaged or missing goods and work to make it a successful experience for our artists. References gladly given.

FLORIDA CRAFTSMEN GALLERY

Suzanne Wismer
501 Central Ave.
St. Petersburg, FL 33701-3703
Phone: (813)821-7391
Fax: (813)822-4294
In business since: 1986
Type of business: Retail store and gallery selling hand crafted items
Description of business: Florida Craftsmen Gallery is a showcase for contemporary craftwork by Florida artists. The exhibition space focuses on changing thematic exhibitions of national and regional scope. Offering a wide range of work, the gallery appeals to serious collectors as well as those looking for unusual gifts.
Types of products: Handmade items only
Categories: Fine crafts, wearable art, jewelry, wooden crafts, paper products, stained glass items, hand blown glass items, pottery/ceramics, baskets, sculpture
More about products: Artist must be member of Florida Craftsmen ($35 annual individual membership) and work must pass Standards Review, held bimonthly.
Price range: $4-3,000
Business policy: We work on consignment. We commission work from craftspeople through clients. Work is on loan for special exhibitions with an opportunity to sell. Our commission is 45%.
Buys: From the craftspeople who query us if we like their work and it fits our theme; through slide registries; also solicits work through membership newsletter.
Advertising/Promotion: Local: arts reviews, newspapers, theatre guides, downtown arts association, chamber of commerce. National: magazines, occasionally. $2,000/year budget.
Special programs: Visiting artist public lectures, opening receptions, design/decorator lecture-receptions and corporate party receptions
Application process: Queries are accepted from local/regional craftspeople only who are members of Florida Craftsmen. See the organization's listing on page 187 to learn how to become a member. For consideration, provide photos or slides (5), catalog/promotional materials, sample of work, written description of work, résumé and sample price sheet.

THE FREEWHEEL POTTERY

Phil Bresler
7 Tinker St.
Woodstock, NY 12498
Phone: (914)679-7478
Fax: (914)679-6764
In business since: 1968
Type of business: Retail store selling hand crafted items
Description of business: The store specializes in moderately priced American crafts and particularly features products of exotic woods. We also sell quality international crafts with an emphasis on silver jewelry.
Types of products: Handmade items only
Categories: Fine crafts, wearable art, jewelry, miniatures/dollhouses, wooden crafts, paper products, stained glass items, hand blown glass items, home decor, figurines, dolls/stuffed animals/toys, pottery/ceramics, nature crafts/floral, leather crafts, baskets, recycled crafts, sculpture
Price range: $5-300
Business policy: We buy crafts outright.
Buys: From the craftspeople who query us if we like their work and it fits our theme; at wholesale shows for hand crafted items; at wholesale gift shows; at wholesale apparel shows; from reps or craft brokers
Advertising/Promotion: $400/year budget.
Application process: Queries are accepted from local/regional and out-of-town craftspeople. For consideration, provide photos or slides, catalog/promotional materials, sample of work.

FUSION FINE CRAFTS

John Allcorn
121 E. Tarpon Ave.
Tarpon Springs, FL 34689
Phone: (813)934-9396
Fax: (813)938-8836
In business since: 1985
Type of business: Retail store selling hand crafted items
Description of business: A 1,500 sq. ft. fine crafts store dedicated to presenting American fine crafts. They have developed a reputation for fairness and service with customers and artisans.
Types of products: Handmade items and books, art cards and music
Categories: Fine crafts, wearable art, jewelry, wooden crafts, stained glass items, hand blown glass items, pottery/ceramics, leather crafts
Price range: $10-400
Business policy: We buy crafts outright.
Buys: From the craftspeople who query us if we like their work and it fits our theme; at retail craft shows; from reps or craft brokers
Advertising/Promotion: Local publications and mailings. $3,000/year budget.
Application process: Queries are accepted from local/regional and out-of-town craftspeople. For consideration, provide photos or slides, catalog/promotional materials, sample of work.
Additional information: We are uncompromisingly committed to our customers and artisan, growing *with* our artisans as they grow. We therefore select only a few additional artisans each year but welcome queries.

G. WHIZ

Jan Cunningham
724 W. Northwest Hwy.
Barrington, IL 60010
Phone: (847)304-0255
In business since: 1989
Type of business: Retail store selling hand crafted items
Description of business: A unique store specializing in unusual hand crafted imaginative gifts and artisan jewelry. Conservative area with value oriented buyers. No country, no contemporary. Looking to work with flexible artists

whose items "fly" out of retail stores. Special areas for teachers, music, golf, bath, pre-teen, tennis, cats, dogs and holidays.

Types of products: Handmade items, unique gift items, cards

Categories: Fine crafts, jewelry, wooden crafts, paper products, hand blown glass items, home decor, nature crafts/floral, recycled crafts

More about products: Unique and unusual, yet conservative

Price range: $5-150

Business policy: We buy crafts outright.

Buys: From the craftspeople who query us if we like their work and it fits our theme; at wholesale shows for hand crafted items; at wholesale gift shows; at retail craft shows; from reps or craft brokers

Advertising/Promotion: Direct mail newsletter 2-3 times per year, ads in local newspapers and magazines every month, miscellaneous ad events. 10% of sales/year budget.

Special programs: Open House with artists on site, special sales, holiday events

Application process: Queries are accepted by mail only from local/regional and out-of-town craftspeople. Must not be carried by another store in town. For consideration, provide photos (3), non-returnable sample of work, written description of work, catalog/promotional materials, price list.

Additional information: Our store carries an unusual mix of product. We fall between a gift store and a gallery. Unique, imaginative and unusual are our trademarks.

GALLERY/SHOP AT WESLEYAN POTTERS

Maureen LoPresti
350 South Main St. (Rt. 17)
Middletown, CT 06457
Phone: (860)344-0039
In business since: 1982
Type of business: Retail store selling hand crafted items and gallery
Description of business: The Gallery/Shop operates under the auspices of Wesleyan Potters, Inc., a nonprofit craft education center run as a cooperative by about 100 members and offering classes in pottery, weaving, basketry and jewelry. The Gallery/

Shop features contemporary American hand crafts made both by members and invited outside craftspeople.

Types of products: Handmade items only

Categories: Fine crafts, wearable art, jewelry, wooden crafts, paper products, stained glass items, hand blown glass items, leather crafts, baskets

More about products: Work must be made in the US by the craftsman, not mass produced, and must be able to do business with that craftsman on an individual basis (no reps).

Price range: $3-300

Business policy: We take work on consignment after jurying.

Buys: From the craftspeople who query us if we like their work and it fits our theme; at wholesale shows for hand crafted items and from ads in the *Crafts Report.*

Advertising/Promotion: Advertise in a quarterly brochure mailed out by Wesleyan Potters listing classes, Gallery/Shop exhibitions and special events, select magazine ads within Connecticut, *Art New England* display ads, calendar listings in newspapers, news releases with photos for exhibits, and display ads in local newspapers

Special programs: Ten exhibitions are held each year, among them a student exhibition, a faculty exhibition, a spring wedding gift show and other select exhibition in clay, fiber, etc. Annual exhibit and sale held for two weeks each fall following Thanksgiving, is one of New England's oldest and finest juried craft events.

Application process: Queries are accepted from local/regional and out-of-town craftspeople. For consideration, provide photos (8-12), catalog/promotional materials, written description of work.

THE FANNY GARVER GALLERY

Jack Garver
230 State St.
Madison, WI 53703
Phone: (608)833-8000; (608)256-6755
In business since: 1972
Type of business: Gallery
Description of business: The Fanny Garver Gallery features contemporary crafts and fine art: paintings, drawings, graphics and sculpture.

Types of products: Handmade items only

Categories: Fine crafts, jewelry, wooden crafts, stained glass items, hand blown glass items

Price range: $25-2,000

Business policy: We buy crafts outright and take work on consignment.

Buys: From the craftspeople who query us if we like their work and it fits our theme; at wholesale shows for hand crafted items; at wholesale gift shows

Advertising/Promotion: Direct mail, print. $25,000/year budget.

Special programs: One show a month, 11 per year. May feature one artist or a group of artists, or a theme.

Application process: Queries are accepted from local/regional and out-of-town craftspeople. Out-of-town craftspeople may have to pay shipping. For consideration, provide photos or slides (12).

GEODE LTD.

Walter Glenn
3393 Peachtree Rd.
Atlanta, GA 30326
Phone: (404)261-9346
Fax: (404)261-9397
In business since: 1974
Type of business: Gallery
Description of business: A jewelry-only gallery representing over 50 artists.

Types of products: Handmade items only

Categories: Jewelry

More about products: We sell only karat gold, sterling silver one-of-a-kind jewelry with precious and semi-precious stones.

Price range: $30-5,000

Business policy: We take work on consignment and commission work from craftspeople.

Buys: From the craftspeople who query us if we like their work and it fits our theme; at wholesale shows for hand crafted items; through slide registries; from reps or craft brokers

Advertising/Promotion: Printed matter in specialty formats

Special programs: Wine and cheese artist receptions

Application process: Queries are accepted from local/regional and out-of-town craftspeople. For consideration, provide photos or slides, catalog/promotional materials, sample of work.

GIMCRACKS

Lucile Krasnow
1513 Sherman Ave.
Evanston, IL 60201
Phone: (847)475-0900
Fax: (847)475-0912
In business since: 1985
Type of business: Retail store selling hand crafted items
Description of business: A gallery of American crafts and ethnic objects including furniture, lighting, jewelry, textiles, gifts and home accessories.
Types of products: Handmade items and frames, candlesticks
Categories: Fine crafts, wearable art, jewelry, wooden crafts, paper products, hand blown glass items, home decor, pottery/ceramics, baskets, sculpture
Price range: $10-1,000
Business policy: We buy crafts outright and take work on consignment.
Buys: From the craftspeople who query us if we like their work and it fits our theme; at wholesale shows for hand crafted items; at wholesale gift shows; at retail craft shows; from reps or craft brokers
Advertising/Promotion: Magazines, mailers
Application process: Queries are accepted from local/regional and out-of-town craftspeople. For consideration, provide photos or slides, SASE.

GOLDEN HOBBY SHOP

630 S. Third St.
Columbus, OH 43206
Phone: (614)645-8329
In business since: 1971
Type of business: Retail store selling hand crafted items
Description of business: Located in the 1864 Third Street School building, the Golden Hobby Shop is operated as a nonprofit consignment shop for individuals 55 years of age and older who reside in Franklin County. The shop is owned by the Columbus Recreation & Parks Department. Ten rooms house magnificent crafts from magnets to fabulous quilts.
Types of products: Handmade items only
Categories: Fine crafts, wearable art, jewelry, miniatures/dollhouses, wooden crafts, paper products, stained glass items, needlework crafts, home decor, figurines, dolls/stuffed animals/toys, pottery/ceramics, nature crafts/floral, leather crafts, baskets
More about products: Everything brought in on consignment must be made from new materials.
Price range: 25¢-$600
Business policy: We take work on consignment.
Advertising/Promotion: *Ohio Magazine*, Actor's Summer Theatre playbill, Lion's Roar, German Village special events programs. $1,000/year budget.
Special programs: Annual Christmas Open House with demonstrations, refreshments, entertainment.
Application process: Queries are accepted from local/regional craftspeople only. Consignors must be 55 years of age or older and live in Franklin County. Make an appointment to bring items in for consignment.
Additional information: Hours are M-Sat 10-5, Sun 1-5.

GREENFIELD HERB GARDEN

Arlene Shannon
P.O. Box 9
Shipshewana, IN 46565
Phone: (219)768-7110
In business since: 1985
Type of business: Retail store selling hand crafted items
Description of business: An upscale gardening/nature shop with functional gardening items.
Types of products: Handmade items and general gardening and nature-related gifts
Categories: Nature crafts/floral
Price range: $10-200
Business policy: We buy crafts outright.
Buys: From the craftspeople who query us if we like their work and it fits our theme; at wholesale shows for hand-crafted items; at wholesale gift shows; at retail craft shows
Application process: Queries are accepted from local/regional and out-of-town craftspeople. For consideration, provide photos (2-3), sample of work (if personal visit), catalog/promotional materials.

HANDMADE AND MORE

Marge Schenck and Carla Webb
6 N. Front St.
New Paltz, NY 12561
Phone: (914)255-6277
Fax: (914)255-0625
In business since: 1974
Type of business: Retail store selling hand crafted items
Description of business: An eclectic gift store featuring hand crafted items from around the neighborhood, country and world. Handmade and More carries jewelry, pottery, glassware, house and garden items, toys, cards, etc.
Types of products: Handmade items and imported crafts and mass produced items that look handmade.
Categories: Fine crafts, jewelry, wooden crafts, paper products, stained glass items, hand blown glass items, home decor, pottery/ceramics, leather crafts, baskets, recycled crafts
Price range: $6-150
Business policy: We buy crafts outright and take work on consignment.
Buys: From the craftspeople who query us if we like their work and it fits our theme; at wholesale shows for hand crafted items; at wholesale gift shows; from reps or craft brokers
Advertising/Promotion: Newspapers, radio, regional tourist magazines, direct mail. $30,000/year budget.
Application process: Queries are accepted from local/regional and out-of-town craftspeople. For consideration, provide photos or slides (1), catalog/promotional materials.
Additional information: We pride ourselves on customer service. We gift wrap free, offer UPS shipping and layaway service. We're open every day and offer extended hours at holiday time.

HANDWORKS, GALLERY OF AMERICAN CRAFTS

Glenn Johnson
161 Great Rd.
Acton, MA 01801
Phone: (508)263-1707
In business since: 1978
Type of business: Gallery
Description of business: Handworks Gallery exhibits an ever changing se-

lection of beautiful works by professional American artists/craftspeople in its sunny space. Inspiration and imagination spark an immediate response, thoughtful design and fine craftsmanship ensure that that appeal will endure. Artists' background information and explanations of the processes involved add to the customers' appreciation and is an important part of the whole.

Types of products: Handmade items only

Categories: Fine crafts, wearable art, jewelry, wooden crafts, stained glass items, hand blown glass items, dolls/stuffed animals/toys, pottery/ceramics, leather crafts, baskets, sculpture, quilts, weavings

Price range: $8-6,000

Business policy: We buy crafts outright and take work on consignment.

Buys: From the craftspeople who query us if we like their work and it fits our theme; at wholesale shows for hand crafted items; from reps or craft brokers

Advertising/Promotion: Direct mail to customers, newspapers

Special programs: Garden Sculpture show, Wood show, Fiber show, Expressions of Love (Valentine's Day)

Application process: Queries are accepted from local/regional and out-of-town craftspeople. Call first for an appointment and short phone interview. For consideration, provide photos or slides, catalog/promotional materials, written description of work.

HANDWORKS SENIOR CRAFT COOPERATIVE

Mystic Valley Elder Services, Inc.
177A Pleasant St.
Malden, MA 02148
Phone: (617)324-3331
In business since: 1977
Type of business: Consignment store for elderly and disabled
Description of business: Handworks Senior Craft Cooperative is a nonprofit program accepting crafted goods from those 60 years of age and older as well as disabled individuals.
Types of products: Handmade items only
Categories: Fine crafts, wooden crafts, needlework crafts, home decor, dolls/stuffed animals, hand-knitted baby clothes, afghans and sweaters

Price range: $3-85

Business policy: We take work on consignment.

Buys: From the craftspeople who query us if we like their work and it fits our theme

Advertising/Promotion: Public access TV and radio and in local newspapers. Nonprofit, no charge for advertising.

Application process: Queries are accepted from local/regional and out-of-town craftspeople who are 60 years of age or older, or disabled. For consideration, make an appointment to show sample of work.

Additional information: Our mission is to keep senior citizens busy.

HANSON GALLERIES

Donna Milstein, Larry Williams and Amy Schilder
800 W. Sam Houston Pkwy. N., E-118
Houston, TX 77024
Phone: (713)984-1242
Fax: (713)984-1680
In business since: 1977
Type of business: Galleries
Description of business: Two craft galleries specializing in American fine crafts with 500 artists.
Types of products: Handmade items only
Categories: Fine crafts, jewelry, wooden crafts, paper products, stained glass items, hand blown glass items, home decor, pottery/ceramics, leather crafts, sculpture
Price range: $3-3,000
Business policy: We buy crafts outright and take work on consignment.
Buys: From the craftspeople who query us if we like their work and it fits our theme; at wholesale shows for hand crafted items; at wholesale gift shows; at retail craft shows
Advertising/Promotion: Direct mail, newspaper, weekly publication, performing arts programs, guest informant. 4% sales/year budget.
Application process: Queries are accepted from local/regional and out-of-town craftspeople. For consideration, provide photos or slides, catalog/promotional materials, written description of work, wholesale prices/consignment terms.

HEARTLAND GALLERY

Holly Plotner
Village at West Lake
701 Capital of Texas Hwy. S., Suite 880
Austin, TX 78746
Phone: (512)347-1720
In business since: 1984
Type of business: Retail store selling hand crafted items
Description of business: This small contemporary store, located in Brodie Oaks II shopping center, sells a huge array of fine quality American crafts including gift items, personal adornments and home/office accessories. Over 200 local and national artisans supply functional and decorative items.
Types of products: Handmade items only
Categories: Fine crafts, jewelry, wooden crafts, paper products, stained glass items, needlework crafts, hand blown glass items, home decor, figurines, dolls/stuffed animals/toys, pottery/ceramics, sculpture
Price range: $1.75-1,000
Business policy: We buy crafts outright and take work on consignment.
Buys: From the craftspeople who query us if we like their work and it fits our theme; at wholesale shows for handcrafted items; at retail craft shows
Advertising/Promotion: Direct mail, local print media (newspapers, magazines, tabloids), local NPR radio station. 2.5% sales/year budget.
Application process: Queries are accepted from local/regional and out-of-town craftspeople. For consideration, provide photos or slides, catalog/promotional materials, written description of work, price list.
Additional information: Heartland offers gift wrapping, shipping and bridal registry services. Hours are M-Sat 10-6, Th 10-9, Sun 12-5. Christmas season M-Sat 10-9.

HEARTSONG POTTERY & GIFTS

Shara Fain
HC 62 Box 768
Deer, AR 72628-9405
Phone: (501)428-5269
In business since: 1984
Type of business: Retail store selling hand crafted items.
Description of business: A remote shop

off scenic highway 7, surrounded by National Forest, carrying gifts for a wide variety of styles, price ranges and ages from knickknacks to gallery quality art. Pottery is handmade on site.

Types of products: Handmade items only

Categories: Fine crafts, wearable art, jewelry, wooden crafts, paper products, stained glass items, needlework crafts, hand blown glass items, home decor, figurines, dolls/stuffed animals/toys, pottery/ceramics, nature crafts/floral, leather crafts, baskets, recycled crafts, sculpture

Price range: Wide variety

Business policy: We buy crafts outright (and barter occasionally).

Buys: From the craftspeople who query us if we like their work and it fits our theme; catalogue orders; barter with local artisans

Advertising/Promotion: Chamber of Commerce, state and national ads, local newspaper, mailings, giveaways in shop and word of mouth.

Special programs: Christmas open house each year between Thanksgiving and Christmas

Application process: Queries are accepted from local/regional and out-of-town craftspeople. For consideration, provide sample of work.

Additional information: Please do not put us on any mailing lists or include us in mailings. Thank you.

HIGHLIGHT GALLERY

Clyde Jones
P.O. Box 1515
Mendocino, CA 95460
Phone: (707)937-3132
In business since: 1979
Type of business: Retail store selling hand crafted items and gallery
Description of business: A 3,800-sq.-ft. gallery featuring only fine, high quality handmade craft and art.
Types of products: Handmade items only
Categories: Fine crafts, jewelry, wooden crafts, hand blown glass items, home decor, pottery/ceramics, sculpture
More about products: All work must be made in the US and be of high quality.
Price range: $5-12,000
Business policy: We buy crafts outright, take work on consignment and com-

mission work from craftspeople.

Buys: From the craftspeople who query us if we like their work and it fits our theme; at wholesale shows for hand crafted items

Advertising/Promotion: Local publications and direct mailings

Special programs: Six shows a year

Application process: Queries are accepted from local/regional and out-of-town craftspeople. Items must be exclusive in our regional area. For consideration, provide photos or slides, catalog/promotional materials, written description of work, SASE.

Additional information: Highlight has a reputation for showing quality. Best known for fine furniture but also present other craft as well as paintings and sculpture.

HILLYER HOUSE

Katherine Reed
207 E. Scenic Dr.
Pass Christian, MS 39571
Phone: (601)452-4810
In business since: 1970
Type of business: Retail store selling hand crafted items
Description of business: Hillyer House represents 175 talented Americans who create jewelry, pottery, blown glass and watercolors.
Types of products: Handmade items only
Categories: Jewelry, hand blown glass items, pottery/ceramics, watercolors
Price range: $15-125
Business policy: We buy crafts outright.
Buys: From the craftspeople who query us if we like their work and it fits our theme; at wholesale shows for hand crafted items; American Artisan shows
Advertising/Promotion: We only advertise in our brochure; 10,000 are distributed every 3 months along the Mississippi Gulf Coast.
Special programs: Artist demonstrations.
Application process: Queries are accepted from local/regional and out-of-town craftspeople. For consideration, provide catalog/promotional materials, photos, sample of work, and artist bio and photo which we frame for display by each artist's collection.

HODGELL GALLERY

Kate O'Connell
46 Palm Ave. South
Sarasota, FL 34236
Phone/Fax: (941)366-1146
In business since: 1976
Type of business: Gallery
Description of business: Hodgell Gallery represents 50 contemporary, regional, national and international artists. Carry a wide variety of works with an emphasis on fine art glass and large abstract paintings.
Types of products: Handmade items only
Categories: Hand blown glass items, sculpture, fine art glass
Price range: $40-20,000
Business policy: We take work on consignment.
Buys: From the craftspeople who query us if we like their work and it fits our theme; through slide registries; from reps or craft brokers
Advertising/Promotion: Local Arts Review, *Glass* Magazine, *Art News*, local newspaper, mail 1,400 invitations to show openings
Application process: Queries are accepted from local/regional and out-of-town craftspeople. For consideration, provide photos or slides, résumé, size of work, media, price of works.
Additional information: Carry a wide array of one-of-a-kind fine art pieces.

THE HOPE GALLERY

Hope Davis
595 Piedmont Ave., Suite 102-C
Atlanta, GA 30308
Phone: (404)892-0534
Fax: (404)636-2235
E-mail: luluhope@ix.netcom.com
In business since: 1993
Type of business: Gallery
Description of business: Hope Gallery sells contemporary art by local, national and international artists.
Types of products: Handmade items and paintings
Categories: Fine crafts, wearable art, jewelry, hand blown glass items, pottery/ceramics, recycled crafts, sculpture
Price range: $10-4,000
Business policy: We take work on consignment.
Buys: From the craftspeople who query

us if we like their work and it fits our theme; at wholesale shows for hand crafted items; at retail craft shows; through slide registries; from reps or craft brokers

Advertising/Promotion: Local magazines and newspapers. $900/month budget.

Special programs: Artist openings every 6 weeks, special group theme shows and holiday shows

Application process: Queries are accepted from local/regional and out-of-town craftspeople. For consideration, provide photos or slides (5-15), catalog/promotional materials, written description of work, retail price range, SASE.

HUDSON RIVER GALLERY

Pat Lawrence
217 Main St.
Ossining, NY 10562
Phone: (914)762-5300
Fax: (914)941-3838
In business since: 1985
Type of business: Gallery
Description of business: Hudson River Gallery has an eclectic collection of art in various media. The gallery is housed in a landmark building built in 1870 in the historic district of Ossining. Located on a heavily trafficked road (Route 9), easily accessible to Westchester County and New York City.
Types of products: Handmade items only
Categories: Fine crafts, wearable art, jewelry, wooden crafts, paper products, stained glass items, hand blown glass items, pottery/ceramics, sculpture
Price range: $10-1,500
Business policy: We buy crafts outright.
Buys: From the craftspeople who query us if we like their work and it fits our theme; at wholesale shows for hand crafted items; at wholesale gift shows; at retail craft shows; from reps or craft brokers; also travel and purchase directly from studios.
Advertising/Promotion: Cable TV, local newspapers, local guides to the Hudson Valley and Westchester, Yellow Pages. $15,000/year budget.
Application process: Queries are accepted from local/regional and out-of-

town craftspeople. For consideration, provide photos or slides (6), catalog/promotional materials, written description of work.

HYACINTH CONTEMPORARY CRAFTS

Sara Quart
40-04 Bell Blvd.
Bayside, NY 11361
Phone: (718)224-9228
In business since: 1981
Type of business: Retail store selling hand crafted items
Description of business: We show the work of over 600 different American artists and small companies. It is the largest selection under one roof in the area.
Types of products: Handmade items and frames, cards, incense
Categories: Fine crafts, jewelry, wooden crafts, paper products, stained glass items, hand blown glass items, home decor, pottery/ceramics, recycled crafts, metal crafts, candles
More about products: American Indian jewelry, forged iron, many fantasy items
Price range: $5-1,500
Business policy: We buy crafts outright and commission work from craftspeople.
Buys: From the craftspeople who query us if we like their work and it fits our theme; at wholesale shows for hand crafted items; at wholesale gift shows; from reps or craft brokers
Advertising/Promotion: Newspapers, word of mouth and occasionally in *NY Times Magazine, Elle* magazine. $2,000/year budget.
Special programs: One function is animal rescue work. A number of rescued cats waiting for adoption are always walking around the store.
Application process: Queries are accepted from local/regional and out-of-town craftspeople. For consideration, provide photos, catalog/promotional materials, written description of work or call the store at the number above.

IDEA FACTORY

Kenneth Ford
838 Chartres St.
New Orleans, LA 70116
Phone: (504)524-5195; (800)524-IDEA
In business since: 1974

Type of business: Retail store selling hand crafted items
Description of business: The Idea Factory represents some of the finest woodcraft in the US. A wonderful selection of wooden toys, boxes, kitchen and desk accessories and sculpture. Offers hand craft wood signs, designs and logo reproductions on the premises.
Types of products: Handmade items only
Categories: Wooden crafts, toys, sculpture
More about products: All made of wood
Price range: $1-1,000
Business policy: We buy crafts outright.
Buys: At wholesale shows for hand crafted items; at wholesale gift shows
Advertising/Promotion: Tourist magazines and Yellow Pages. $2,000-3,000 year/budget.
Application process: Queries are accepted from local/regional and out-of-town craftspeople. For consideration, provide photos or slides, catalog/promotional materials, sample of work, written description of work, price list.

IMAGE GALLERY & GIFTS

Nancy and Gene Ware
3330 W. 26th St., #1
Erie, PA 16506
Phone: (814)838-8077
In business since: 1982
Type of business: Gallery
Description of business: Fine art and photography gallery featuring hand crafted gifts.
Types of products: Handmade items and art, photography and framing
Categories: Fine crafts, jewelry, stained glass items, hand blown glass items, figurines, pottery/ceramics, nature crafts/floral, baskets, sculpture
Price range: $20-500
Business policy: We buy crafts outright, take work on consignment and commission work from craftspeople.
Buys: From the craftspeople who query us if we like their work and it fits our theme; at wholesale shows for hand crafted items; at wholesale gift shows; at retail craft shows
Advertising/Promotion: Direct mail, newspapers. $10,000/year budget.
Application process: Queries are accepted from local/regional and out-of-

town craftspeople. For consideration, provide photos or slides, catalog/promotional materials, sample of work.

THE INDIAN CRAFT SHOP

Susan Pourian

Dept. of the Interior, 1849 C St. NW, Room 1023

Washington, DC 20240

Phone: (202)208-4056

Fax: (202)208-6950

In business since: 1938

Type of business: Museum gift shop

Description of business: The Indian Craft Shop has been located inside the Department of the Interior since 1938. We represent quality and authenticity in American Indian arts and crafts from over 40 US tribal areas. Crafts included are pottery, jewelry, kachinas, sandpainting sculpture, Alaskan carvings, rugs, dolls, fetishes, basketry, drums and more. We have established national recognition in representing authenticity in the variety of crafts included.

Types of products: Handmade items only

Categories: Jewelry, miniatures, pottery, baskets, sculpture

More about products: All items must be handmade by an American Indian artist (must be enrolled or have tribal affiliation documentation). Tribal areas restricted within US border.

Price range: $4-6,000

Business policy: We buy crafts outright.

Buys: From the craftspeople who query us if we like their work and it fits our theme; at wholesale shows for hand crafted items; from reps or craft brokers

Advertising/Promotion: Washington, DC guide books, *Washington Post*, *American Indian Art* magazine, gallery guides

Special programs: Educational events including lectures/presentations on craft areas, promotional shows highlighting selected artists and/or craft areas

Application process: Queries are accepted from all American Indian artists within US border. For consideration, provide samples or photos of work with a prior phone call arranging such.

INTERIORS & EXTRAS

Nancy Hirsch Lassen

324 Metairie Rd.

Metairie, LA 70005

Phone: (504)835-9902; (504)835-9903

Fax: (504)835-9913

In business since: 1986

Type of business: Retail shop with interior design studio

Description of business: We offer eclectic art, furniture, accessories and jewelry. We have 5,000 sq. ft. of fine crafts, original art, and a staff of 5 interior designers to put everything together. We're set in an old home in an upscale suburb of New Orleans. We have off-street parking under 5 100-year-old oak trees.

Types of products: Handmade items and furniture, gifts, upholstery, accessories, wallpaper, fabrics, lamps, etc.

Categories: Fine crafts, wearable art, jewelry, paper products, needlework crafts, hand blown glass items, home decor, pottery/ceramics, nature crafts/floral, baskets, recycled crafts, sculpture

Price range: $5-5,000

Business policy: We buy crafts outright, take work on consignment and commission work from craftspeople.

Buys: From the craftspeople who query us if we like their work and it fits our theme; at wholesale shows for hand crafted items; at wholesale apparel shows; at wholesale gift shows; at retail craft shows; from reps or craft brokers

Advertising/Promotion: ¼ page color ads at least once a month in *Gambit*, a local free newspaper, direct mail to mailing list of 2,000 and occasionally advertise in *New Orleans Magazine* and *The Times Picayune* newspaper. $10,000/year budget.

Special programs: As designers, we do special events each year as charity fund-raisers.

Application process: Queries are accepted from local/regional and out-of-town craftspeople. For consideration, provide photos or slides, catalog/promotional materials, prefers photos with a description, first. If the product looks interesting, they will request more information.

INTERNATIONAL GALLERY

643 G St.

San Diego, CA 92101

Phone: (619)235-8255

In business since: 1984

Type of business: Retail store selling hand crafted items

Description of business: We feature fine contemporary American crafts, African and Melanesian tribal art, including ritual masks, sculpture, and basketry; and textiles from North Africa and Central Asia.

Types of products: Handmade items only

Categories: Fine crafts, jewelry, wooden crafts, hand blown glass items, home decor, pottery/ceramics, baskets, recycled crafts

Price range: $10-1,000

Business policy: We buy crafts outright and take work on consignment.

Buys: From the craftspeople who query us if we like their work and it fits our theme; at wholesale shows for hand crafted items.

Advertising/Promotion: Direct mail

Application process: Queries are accepted from local/regional and out-of-town craftspeople. For consideration, provide photos or slides (12), catalog/promotional materials, written description of work, résumé, where shown and SASE.

IOWA ARTISANS GALLERY

Christiane Knorr

117 E. College St.

Iowa City, IA 52240

Phone: (319)351-8686

In business since: 1984

Type of business: Gallery

Description of business: Iowa Artisans Gallery is a retail sales gallery showcasing contemporary fine crafts and selected fine art by Midwestern artists. Founded by twelve crafts artists, the Gallery is currently run by five of its original founders. Media include ceramics, metal, fiber, glass, wood, and selected prints, paintings and photography.

Types of products: Handmade items only

Categories: Fine crafts, jewelry, paper products, hand blown glass items, pottery/ceramics

Price range: $3-2,000

Business policy: We buy crafts outright

and take work on consignment.

Buys: From the craftspeople who query us if we like their work and it fits our theme; at wholesale shows for hand crafted items; at wholesale gift shows; at retail craft shows

Advertising/Promotion: Newspaper, direct mail, TV, radio. 4% of total income/year budget.

Special programs: We sponsor regular rotating special exhibits as well as featured artist displays and participation in 3 Gallery Walks annually. Also present educational slide shows on fine crafts to interested organizations, free of charge.

Application process: Queries are accepted from local/regional and out-of-town craftspeople. For consideration, provide photos or slides (8), catalog/promotional materials, written description of work, price list.

Additional information: Hours are M 10-9, T-F 10-7, Sat 10-5:30, Sun 12-4.

J & M JEWELRY

Judith Pollock
P.O. Box 2938
Breckenridge, CO 80424
Phone: (970)453-5637
In business since: 1991
Type of business: Retail store selling hand crafted items

Description of business: J & M Jewelry is primarily a fine designer jewelry shop selling 14k gold and sterling silver contemporary work. Sells rings and pendants with gemstones (only gold) and lots of unique earrings and bracelets in gold and silver. Not interested in other metals and costume-type jewelry.

Types of products: Handmade items and 14k gold charms

Categories: Jewelry

More about products: 14k gold (mostly) and sterling silver and vermeil designer jewelry. Particularly looking for ski, snow and/or mountain motifs.

Price range: $10-1,000, average $100

Business policy: We buy crafts outright.

Buys: From the craftspeople who query us if we like their work and it fits our theme; at wholesale shows for hand crafted items; from reps or craft brokers; wholesale jewelry shows

Advertising/Promotion: Local 4-color tourist magazines. $6,000/year budget.

Application process: Queries are accepted from local/regional and out-of-town craftspeople. For consideration, provide catalog/promotional materials. No slides or samples.

JOIE DE VIVRE

Linda Given
1792 Massachusetts Ave.
Cambridge, MA 02140
In business since: 1984
Type of business: Retail store selling hand crafted items

Description of business: Joic dc Vivrc is a small eclectic gift store selling a wide range of items intended to amuse or delight both children and grown-ups.

Types of products: Handmade items and books, hats, postcards, snow globes, puppets

Categories: Fine crafts, wearable art, jewelry, miniatures/dollhouses, wooden crafts, paper products, hand blown glass items, home decor, dolls/stuffed animals/toys, pottery/ceramics, recycled crafts

More about products: Looking for whimsical, sophisticated items, nothing cutesy.

Price range: $10-600

Business policy: We buy crafts outright.

Buys: From the craftspeople who query us if we like their work and it fits our theme; at wholesale shows for hand crafted items, at wholesale gift shows, at wholesale toy, doll and teddy bear shows; from reps or craft brokers

Application process: Queries are accepted from local/regional and out-of-town craftspeople. For consideration, provide photos, catalog/promotional materials, written description of work, wholesale information, and information regarding time it takes to receive orders, etc.

JUBILEE GALLERY

Richard Lorenz
121 W. Court Ave.
Jeffersonville, IN 47130
Phone: (812)282-9997
In business since: 1980
Type of business: Gallery

Description of business: The gallery deals mostly in hand crafted items from around the country. Always looking for artists with unique crafts to sell.

Types of products: Handmade items and manufactured items such as picture frames

Categories: Fine crafts, wearable art, jewelry, wooden crafts, stained glass items, hand blown glass items, pottery/ceramics

Price range: $10-200

Business policy: We buy crafts outright and take work on consignment.

Buys: From the craftspeople who query us if we like their work and it fits our theme; at wholesale shows for hand crafted items; at wholesale gift shows; from reps or craft brokers

Advertising/Promotion: Fliers at art shows, newspaper

Application process: Queries are accepted from local/regional and out-of-town craftspeople. For consideration, provide catalog/promotional materials, photos, sample of work, written description of work.

JUST DUCKY

Victoria Chandler
P.O. Box 1252
Nashville, IN 47448
Phone: (812)988-8017
In business since: 1989
Type of business: Retail store selling hand crafted items

Description of business: Started the business mainly to sell Victoria's creations.

Types of products: Handmade items and cards, pewter, candles, jewelry

Categories: Miniatures/dollhouses, wooden crafts, home decor, dolls/stuffed animals/toys, leather crafts, baskets

More about products: We have to be able to retail merchandise at a reasonable price. We have mainly ceramic items and florals, which Victoria makes herself.

Price range: 50¢-$50

Business policy: We prefer a commission of 50/50 to cover overhead.

Buys: At wholesale shows for hand crafted items; from reps or craft brokers

Advertising/Promotion: Local newspaper magazine

Application process: Queries are accepted from local/regional and out-of-town craftspeople. All shipping costs are the craftsperson's responsibility. For consideration, provide photos or slides, catalog/promotional materials.

Additional information: Nashville is a tourist town and variety is definitely the key. We are in competition with several craft malls so it is necessary to keep prices low. We do not accept any crafts that resemble Victoria's handmade items.

KATYDIDS

Kathleen and Bill Fesq
6 E. Main St.
Mendham, NJ 07945
Phone: (908)832-7901; (201)543-1770
Fax: (908)832-6232
In business since: 1981
Type of business: Retail store selling hand crafted items
Description of business: A romantic collection of sophisticated gifts, designer accessories and one of a kind hand crafts.
Types of products: Handmade items and some commercial products
Categories: Wearable art, jewelry, wooden crafts, stained glass items, needlework crafts, home decor, dolls/ stuffed animals/toys, pottery/ceramics, nature crafts/floral, baskets, home furnishings
Price range: $10-700
Business policy: We buy crafts outright and take work on consignment.
Buys: From the craftspeople who query us if we like their work and it fits our theme; at wholesale shows for hand crafted items; at wholesale apparel shows; at wholesale gift shows; at wholesale toy, doll and teddy bear shows; at retail craft shows; from reps or craft brokers
Advertising/Promotion: Mailing list, local newspapers
Application process: Queries are accepted from local/regional and out-of-town craftspeople. For consideration, provide photos or slides, sample of work.

KEEP IN TOUCH

Ron Isaacson and Lori Goodman, buyers
1504 Sherman Ave.
Evanston, IL 60201
Phone: (847)864-3456
Fax: (847)864-2815
In business since: 1994
Type of business: Retail store selling specialty cards/gifts/handmade paper
Description of business: Keep In Touch is a unique specialty store created by the owners of Mindscape Gallery (see page 143) with a focus on handmade cards, paper products, limited edition artist designed works with functional applications.
Types of products: Handmade items and limited edition, high quality cards, papers, specialty items.
Categories: Wearable art, paper products, handmade journals, small gift items
Price range: $1-50
Business policy: We buy crafts outright and commission work from craftspeople.
Buys: From the craftspeople who query us if we like their work and it fits our theme; at wholesale shows for hand crafted items; at wholesale gift shows; at retail craft shows; stationery shows
Advertising/Promotion: Local daily newspaper ads. $10,000/year budget.
Application process: Queries are accepted from local/regional and out-of-town craftspeople. For consideration, provide photos or slides, catalog/promotional materials, sample of work, written description of work. Send samples with return packaging and postage or send photos and price lists.
Additional information: Keep In Touch also sells office and desk related items such as pens, book marks, sealing wax, rubber stamps, boxes, bags, etc. Prefers to stock only handmade limited production items in these categories.

KRAFTERS OUTLET OF CALIFORNIA INC., #2

Carl Yocum
P.O. Box 9594
Fresno, CA 93793
Phone: (209)645-4016
Fax: (209)645-0803
In business since: 1991
Type of business: Retail store selling hand crafted items
Description of business: Krafters Outlet is a treasure trove of unique hand crafted items that take your breath away. Stocked to overflowing, there are more than 10,000 items to choose from. Local customers shop regularly to purchase one-of-a-kind pieces and visitors to cities where our stores are located are thrilled when they can get unusual gifts for people back home, and at bargain prices too! Krafters Outlet, with its distinctive country facade is distinguished from other such stores in the area. The first Krafters Outlet now has three stores with more on the drawing board. Customers fall in love with the atmosphere because the stores are not a big commercial place. Crafters find Krafters Outlet is a wonderful place to display and sell their crafts. Many crafters are represented at Krafters Outlet, both local and out of state.
Types of products: Handmade items and country items, unique, unusual items
Categories: Wearable art, wooden crafts, paper products, home decor, figurines, dolls/stuffed animals/toys, pottery/ceramics, nature crafts/floral
More about products: Most hand craft items purchased are from local crafters who can fill individual special orders for size, color, etc.
Price range: 99¢-$499
Business policy: We buy crafts outright, take work on consignment and commission work from craftspeople. We rent space to good crafters.
Buys: From the craftspeople who query us if we like their work and it fits our theme; at wholesale shows for hand crafted items; at wholesale gift shows; from reps or craft brokers
Advertising/Promotion: Direct mail from customer list, newspaper, radio, TV, fliers
Application process: Queries are accepted from local/regional and out-of-town craftspeople. We stock and merchandise and provide weekly sales to crafters who request it. For consideration, provide photos (1 of each item/ or a group picture), sample of work.
Additional information: Currently we have 3 stores and have plans for add-

ing more between San Francisco and Los Angeles in the future. We are a family corporation with extensive marketing and sales experience. See the following listings for other locations.

KRAFTERS OUTLET OF CALIFORNIA INC., #4

Carl Yocum
P.O. Box 9594
Fresno, CA 93793
Phone: (209)522-3883
Fax: (209)522-5021
In business since: 1991
Type of business: Retail store selling hand crafted items
Description of business: See the above listing for more information.

KRAFTERS OUTLET OF CALIFORNIA INC., #5

Carl Yocum
P.O. Box 9594
Fresno, CA 93793
Phone: (805)871-4289
Fax: (805)871-4349
In business since: 1991
Type of business: Retail store selling hand crafted items
Description of business: See the above listing for more information.

LAKEVIEW MUSEUM SALES GALLERY

Joyce Spurr, manager
1125 West Lake Ave.
Peoria, IL 61614
Phone: (309)686-7000
Fax: (309)686-0280
In business since: 1965
Type of business: Museum gift shop
Description of business: A 1,300-sq.-ft. facility that services an immediate market area of 350,000. We carry art and science-related items of museum quality. Specialize in fine crafts of original and one-of-a-kind designs. While we emphasize local and regional fine crafts, we do carry artists of national reputation from other areas.
Types of products: Handmade items and 2-dimensional visual arts (oil, acrylic, pastels, watercolor, gauche, pencil, mixed media, woodcuts, etc.) and books by local writers
Categories: Fine crafts, wearable art,

jewelry, wooden crafts (carvings, vases, bowls), hand blown glass items, pottery/ceramics, baskets, sculpture
More about products: Items that coincide with exhibitions and collections are preferred—planetarium, 18th-21st-century American art, Illinois folk art (heavy on coverlets and Illinois River decoys), West African art, rocks/minerals and entomology.
Price range: $5-1,000
Business policy: We take work on consignment.
Buys: From the craftspeople who query us if we like their work and it fits our theme; at wholesale shows for hand crafted items; at retail craft shows.
Advertising/Promotion: Print media, radio, TV and membership newsletter. Attends local business expos and is listed in area and state tourist brochures. $5,000/year budget.
Application process: Queries are accepted from local/regional and out-of-town craftspeople. Artist is responsible for shipping both ways and must make an appointment for personal deliveries and pickups. For consideration, provide photos or slides (5), sample of work. Unsolicited and non-preapproved merchandise will not be returned unless the artist pays for return postage. Consignment percentage is 35%. A contract must be signed before approved items will be displayed in the gallery showroom.
Additional information: The non-craft product line coincides with exhibitions and collections, emphasizing education. Store hours T 10-5, W 10-8, Th-Sat 10-5, Sun 1-5.

LANGMAN GALLERY

Joann Blackman/Suzane Langeman
Willow Grove Park
Willow Grove, PA 19090
Phone: (215)657-8333
Fax: (215)657-8334
In business since: 1972
Type of business: Gallery
Description of business: A 2,000 sq. ft. gallery located in an upscale suburban mall. Shows both fine crafts and fine art. A part of the gallery is dedicated to changing monthly exhibits. While much of the work is from the leading

craft artists in the US, we are very interested in new artists whose work is truly outstanding.
Types of products: Handmade items only
Categories: Fine crafts, jewelry, hand blown glass items
Price range: $50-5,000
Business policy: We buy crafts outright and take work on consignment.
Buys: From the craftspeople who query us if we like their work and it fits our theme; at wholesale shows for hand crafted items
Advertising/Promotion: Direct mail (invitations for shows), magazine ads (*Gallery Guide, Philadelphia Magazine*), cable TV. $12,000-15,000/year budget.
Application process: Queries are accepted from local/regional and out-of-town craftspeople. For consideration, provide photos or slides with SASE.

LILL STREET GALLERY

Laurie Shaman
1021 W. Lill
Chicago, IL 60614
Phone: (312)477-6185
Fax: (312)477-5065
In business since: 1975
Type of business: Gallery
Description of business: Lill Street is the Midwest's largest clay facility with a focus on contemporary, functional and sculptural ceramics by emerging and established artists. The gallery also features glass, jewelry, frames and other hand crafted objects.
Types of products: Handmade items only
Categories: Jewelry, wooden crafts, paper products, hand blown glass items, dolls/stuffed animals/toys, pottery/ceramics
Price range: $20-3,500
Business policy: We buy crafts outright and take work on consignment.
Buys: From the craftspeople who query us if we like their work and it fits our theme; at wholesale shows for hand crafted items; at wholesale gift shows; from reps of craft brokers
Advertising/Promotion: *Chicago Tribune, The Reader*, exhibition postcard mailings, gallery guide, local listings, occasional radio promotion
Special programs: Gallery 1021, is an enclosed space adjacent to the main

gallery, featuring select, fine ceramics from artists nationwide, as well as annual theme shows such as the Coffee and Teapot Invitational.

Application process: Queries are accepted from local/regional and out-of-town craftspeople. For consideration, provide photos or slides, catalog/promotional materials, price list, artist bio, résumé.

LITTLE SWITZERLAND

Nancy Atkinson
P.O. Box 502
Jasper, AR 72641
Phone: (800)510-0691; (501)446-2693
In business since: 1991
Type of business: Retail store selling hand crafted items
Description of business: Crafts are high quality and not found in every store up and down the highway.
Types of products: Handmade items only
Categories: Fine crafts, wearable art, jewelry, miniatures/dollhouses, wooden crafts, paper products, stained glass items, needlework crafts, hand blown glass items, home decor, figurines, dolls/stuffed animals/toys, pottery/ceramics, nature crafts/floral, leather crafts, baskets, recycled crafts, sculpture
More about products: Will not duplicate items that one crafter already has in the shop
Price range: 80¢-$400
Business policy: We take work on consignment.
Buys: From the craftspeople who query us if we like their work and it fits our theme
Advertising/Promotion: Jasper/Newton Co. Chamber of Commerce, Harrison Chamber of Commerce, Ozark Mountain Region Tourism Assoc., Arkansas State tour guide. Budget varies.
Application process: Queries are accepted from local/regional and out-of-town craftspeople. For consideration, provide photos, sample of work, catalog/promotional materials.
Additional information: Monthly inventory reports are mailed to each crafter who has sales or changes on their reports.

MAURINE LITTLETON GALLERY

1667 Wisconsin Ave., NW
Washington, DC 20037
Phone: (202)333-9307
Fax: (202)342-2004
In business since: 1985
Type of business: Gallery
Description of business: Maurine Littleton Gallery brings to Washington, DC sculptural works in glass and ceramics by the most renowned artists working in those media. The gallery exhibits prints, drawings and paintings by its artists as well as innovative prints made from glass plates.
Types of products: Handmade items only
Categories: Glass, ceramic, sculpture
Price range: $200-150,000
Business policy: We take work on consignment.
Advertising/Promotion: Sculpture Objects and Functional Art (SOFA), Chicago and Miami
Application process: Queries are accepted from local/regional and out-of-town craftspeople. For consideration, provide slides, catalog/promotional materials, résumé, recommendations.

THE LONE MOOSE FINE CRAFTS

Sherry and Ivan Rasmussen
78 West St., on the Waterfront
P.O. Box 956
Bar Harbor, ME 04609-0956
Phone: (207)288-4229 (seasonal); (207)288-9428 (home)
E-mail: lmoose@acadia.net
In business since: 1976
Type of business: Retail store selling fine crafts and gallery
Description of business: The island's oldest "Made in Maine" gallery.
Types of products: Handmade items only
Categories: Fine crafts, wearable art, jewelry, miniatures (wheel-thrown), paper products, stained glass items, home decor (fine furniture), pottery, baskets, sculpture, studio buttons, hand painted silk
Price range: $1.50-5,000
Business policy: We buy crafts outright, take work on consignment and commission work from craftspeople.
Buys: From the craftspeople who query us if we like their work and it fits our theme; at retail craft shows; and through referrals

Advertising/Promotion: In *Galleries of Bar Harbor*, *Acadia Weekly*, Cable Visitors Channel, Chamber of Commerce Guide Book, local newspapers, performing arts programs, *Down East* magazine, etc.; varies year to year
Special programs: Seasonal gallery (early summer to late fall, 4½-5 months) July and August special shows. Also sponsors craft classes from time to time and tests market for new craftspeople
Application process: Queries are accepted from Maine craftspeople only. For consideration, provide photos or slides, catalog/promotional materials, written description of work.

MAINE'S MASSACHUSETTS HOUSE GALLERIES

Ernest and Valerie Schoeck
P.O. Box 210
Lincolnville, ME 04849
Phone: (207)789-5705
Fax: (207)789-5707
In business since: 1949
Type of business: Gallery
Description of business: Maine's Massachusetts House Galleries was established as an outlet for artists and craftspeople on the coast of Maine. Has two buildings occupying over 6,000 sq. ft. with rock and sculpture gardens surrounding both.
Types of products: Handmade items and items from small manufacturers around the world
Categories: Fine crafts, wearable art (children's), jewelry, miniatures (toy soldiers), wooden crafts, paper products, stained glass items, hand blown glass items, home decor, figurines, dolls/stuffed animals/toys, pottery/ceramics, nature crafts/floral, leather crafts, baskets, recycled crafts, sculpture
More about products: We sell only quality products usually done in the traditional way but like to try anything that is well-made and priced intelligently.
Price range: $5.50-25,000
Business policy: We usually take work on consignment; smaller work is usually purchased.
Buys: From the craftspeople who query us if we like their work and it fits our theme; at wholesale shows for hand

crafted items; at wholesale gift shows; at wholesale toy, doll and teddy bear shows; from reps or craft brokers

Advertising/Promotion: Direct mail to customers and produces a brochure for local distribution. $12,000/year budget.

Special programs: Several shows a year both general and for individual artists.

Application process: Queries are accepted from local/regional and out-of-town craftspeople. For consideration, provide photos or slides, catalog/promotional materials.

Additional information: Gallery is open March through January.

MANN GALLERY

Nancie Mann
39 Newbury St. #208
Boston, MA 02116
Phone: (617)696-6666
Fax: (617)696-6667
In business since: 1990
Type of business: Gallery
Description of business: A gallery showcasing upscale, high-end, superior quality, one-of-a-kind work by people with an art background or theatre related experience. Especially interested in 3-dimensional figurative work.
Types of products: Handmade items and small editions (5-25) in resin
Categories: Fine crafts, jewelry, miniatures/dollhouses, home decor, figurines, dolls, sculpture
Business policy: We buy crafts outright, take work on consignment and commission work from craftspeople.
Buys: From the craftspeople who query us if we like their work and it fits our theme; at wholesale shows for hand crafted items; at wholesale gift shows; at wholesale doll shows; at retail craft shows; through slide registries; from reps or craft brokers
Advertising/Promotion: Art gallery guide, *Contemporary Art Doll* magazine, Newbury Street guide. Budget varies.
Application process: Queries are accepted from local/regional and out-of-town craftspeople. For consideration, provide photos or slides, catalog/promotional materials, sample of work, written description of work.

Additional information: We are always looking for artists capable of doing dressed sculpture, characters and fantasy figures, etc. We welcome inquiries and submission of photos. Crafters are invited to drop in and see what is in the gallery to help artists be familiar with this new art genre.

NANCY MARGOLIS GALLERY

Nancy Margolis and Mary Zanoni
367 Fore St.
Portland, ME 04101
Phone: (207)775-3822
Fax: (207)773-2294
In business since: 1974
Type of business: Retail store selling hand crafted items and gallery
Description of business: The gallery features American functional ceramics; one-of-a-kind art pieces by American and European artists; unusual, fun jewelry; and contemporary classic gold and silver, hand blown glass and special exhibits of baskets and textiles.
Types of products: Handmade items only
Categories: Fine crafts, wearable art, jewelry, wooden crafts, paper products, hand blown glass items, pottery/ceramics, baskets, sculpture
Price range: $5-5,000
Business policy: We buy crafts outright and take work on consignment.
Buys: From the craftspeople who query us if we like their work and it fits our theme; at wholesale shows for hand crafted items; at retail craft shows
Advertising/Promotion: *American Craft Magazine* and local newspapers and publications
Special programs: Annual summer exhibits (July 1-Labor Day), annual holiday exhibits (November 1-January 1) and wedding band exhibit (March)
Application process: Queries are accepted from local/regional and out-of-town craftspeople. For consideration, provide photos or slides (6-12), catalog/promotional materials, written description of work, SASE.

NANCY MARKOE FINE AMERICAN CRAFTS GALLERY

Nancy Markoe
3112 Pass A Grille Way
St. Pete Beach, FL 33706

Phone: (813)360-0729
Fax: (813)360-8750
In business since: 1985
Type of business: Gallery
Description of business: Nancy Markoe Fine American Crafts Gallery represents over 350 artists in all media from all over the country. Recipient of 1995 *Niche* Award—top 100 American Craft Galleries in the country. Located on a resort beach, there is a large repeat local clientele, and a large tourist clientele. Staff is well trained to be enthusiastic and informative, giving a lot of personal attention.
Types of products: Handmade items only
Categories: Fine crafts, wearable art, jewelry, wooden crafts, paper products, stained glass items, hand blown glass items, home decor, pottery/ceramics
More about products: 85% is functional pottery. All jewelry is fine metal.
Price range: $3-4,000
Business policy: We buy crafts outright.
Buys: From the craftspeople who query us if we like their work and it fits our theme; at wholesale shows for hand crafted items; at retail craft shows
Advertising/Promotion: *St. Pete Times* newspaper, many neighborhood newspapers, tourist publications
Application process: Queries are accepted from local/regional and out-of-town craftspeople. For consideration, provide photos or slides (4), catalog/promotional materials

THE MELTING POT

Skip MacLaren
P.O. Box 845
Mendocino, CA 95460
Phone: (707)937-0173
In business since: 1972
Type of business: Retail store selling hand crafted items
Description of business: "More than a Gallery," The Melting Pot is a source for fine American crafts; kaleidoscopes and decorative accessories, all media, representing over 250 artists.
Types of products: Handmade items only
Categories: Fine crafts, jewelry, stained glass items, hand blown glass items, home decor, pottery/ceramics, leather crafts, baskets

Price range: $20-2,000

Business policy: We buy crafts outright.

Buys: From the craftspeople who query us if we like their work and it fits our theme; at wholesale shows for hand crafted items; at wholesale gift shows; at retail craft shows; from reps or craft brokers

Special programs: Features ongoing programs representing American craft artists

Application process: Queries are accepted from local/regional and out-of-town craftspeople. For consideration, provide photos or slides, catalog/promotional materials, sample of work.

A MERRY-GO-ROUND OF FINE CRAFTS

Alison Walton Meslin

319 Main St. S.

Woodbury, CT 06798

Phone: (203)263-2920

In business since: 1991

Type of business: Retail store selling hand crafted items and gallery

Description of business: Specialize in high-quality, unique hand-crafted treasures, all made by Connecticut artisans. Creations are included in many of the artistic displays throughout the seven rooms of an 1837 house.

Types of products: Handmade items only

Categories: Fine crafts, wearable art, jewelry, miniatures/dollhouses, wooden crafts, paper products, stained glass items, needlework crafts, hand blown glass items, home decor, figurines, dolls/stuffed animals/toys, pottery/ceramics, nature crafts/floral, leather crafts, baskets, sculpture

Price range: $3-3,000

Business policy: We take work on consignment. Artisans pay low monthly fee with a low mark up

Buys: From the craftspeople who query us if we like their work and it fits our theme

Advertising/Promotion: Local papers, direct mail (10,000), tourist guides. 5% of sales/year budget.

Special programs: Summer festival, June; anniversary celebration, November; weekend demonstrations

Application process: Queries are accepted from local/regional and out-of-town craftspeople. For consideration,

provide sample of work, make a personal visit.

JAMES MEYER COMPANY

Mary Herzenberg and Elise Craner

441 Market St.

Williamsport, PA 17701

Phone: (717)326-4874; (800)326-9391

Fax: (717)326-9480

In business since: 1970

Type of business: Retail store selling hand crafted items and workshop manufacturing gold jewelry

Description of business: Since 1970, we have been promoting and selling the works of American craftspeople. Whether these pieces are fashioned from wood, clay, glass, metal or fiber, they are part of the revival of American Craftsmanship which is taking place today. We select those pieces that demonstrate beauty, usefulness and that intangible quality perhaps best expressed as the "joy of life."

Types of products: Handmade items only

Categories: Fine crafts, jewelry, wooden crafts, stained glass items, hand blown glass items, home decor, pottery/ceramics, leather crafts

More about products: Fine craftsmanship, good design and integrity must be shown in each piece.

Price range: $2.50-25,000

Business policy: We buy crafts outright.

Buys: From the craftspeople who query us if we like their work and it fits our theme; at wholesale shows for hand crafted items; at retail craft shows

Advertising/Promotion: Annual mail order catalog, selling our jewelry and a few other featured craftsmen

Application process: Queries are accepted from local/regional and out-of-town craftspeople. For consideration, provide photos or slides, catalog/promotional materials.

Additional information: The shop space is divided into three areas: American crafts found in the home (pottery, blown glass, decorative yet functional metal objects, wooden wares, etc.); jewelry made by craftspersons throughout the USA including gold jewelry (with precious stones) which is manufactured by 4 artists in the third area of the shop.

MINDSCAPE GALLERY

Ron Isaacson and Deborah Farber

1506 Sherman Ave.

Evanston, IL 60201

Phone: (847)864-2660

Fax: (847)864-2815

In business since: 1973

Type of business: Gallery

Description of business: Mindscape represents emerging and established craftspeople. The 16,000 sq. ft. gallery is the oldest and largest consignment gallery in the Midwest, currently representing over 500 functional and nonfunctional artists with limited series and one-of-a-kind artforms.

Types of products: Items are 90% handmade works, 10% artist-designed production pieces.

Categories: Fine crafts, wearable art, jewelry, paper products, hand blown glass items, home decor, pottery/ceramics, sculpture

More about products: Unique artist designed contemporary artforms only.

Price range: $5-20,000

Business policy: We buy crafts outright, take work on consignment and commission work from craftspeople.

Buys: From the craftspeople who query us if we like their work and it fits our theme; at wholesale shows for hand-crafted items; at wholesale gift shows; at wholesale apparel shows; at retail craft shows; through slide registries. A formal jury system has been established to review potential artists for representation.

Advertising/Promotion: Direct mail, local, regional and national advertising, special exhibitions, featured artist programs, educational forums and events. $100,000/year budget.

Special programs: Bodyscapes, wearable art shows; Adornments, jewelry shows; A Gather of Glass, glass focus forums; and Table topics, functional pottery shows. All are nationally advertised.

Application process: Queries are accepted from local/regional and out-of-town craftspeople. Write to request jury packet. Mention media and include SASE. Formal jury review by media 5 times per year.

Additional information: The majority of

work is on consignment. In 1995 the gallery was voted one of the top 10 galleries in the US by *Niche* magazine. Reviews artists annually for technique, quality, integrity and design sense.

MIRABELLE

Glynda Gister
910 Whalley Ave.
New Haven, CT 06515
Phone: (203)387-3699
In business since: 1992
Type of business: Retail store selling handcrafted items
Description of business: A children's shop that sells handmade clothing and toys.
Types of products: Handmade items and clothing, books, dolls, toys, shoes, sweaters, coats, mittens, etc.
Categories: Wooden crafts, paper products, needlework crafts, dolls/stuffed animals/toys
Price range: $5-60
Buys: From the craftspeople who query us if we like their work and it fits our theme; at wholesale shows for handcrafted items; at wholesale gift shows; at wholesale toy, doll and teddy bear shows; from reps or craft brokers
Advertising/Promotion: Local newspapers
Application process: Queries are accepted from local/regional and out-of-town craftspeople. For consideration, provide sample of work.

MODERN LIFE DESIGNS

668 Post St.
San Francisco, CA 94109
Phone: (415)441-7118
In business since: 1980
Type of business: Gallery
Description of business: At the present Modern Life Designs carries only Douglas & Kathy Brett's work. We make original pieces in gold and silver. Kathy does animal motifs in a represental fashion. Douglas does figurative oriented work that is modern and abstract in a soft geometric style. Our philosophy is to create unique images in concept and design, yet classical in style and high in quality.
Types of products: Handmade items only

Categories: Jewelry, hand blown glass items
Business policy: We buy crafts outright and take work on consignment.
Buys: From the craftspeople who query us if we like their work and it fits our theme
Advertising/Promotion: Tourist books
Application process: Queries are accepted from local/regional and out-of-town craftspeople. For consideration, provide photos or slides, catalog/promotional materials, sample of work, written description of work.

MOONSTONES GALLERY

Robert Unger
2531 Village Lane, Unit J
Cambria, CA 93428
Phone/Fax: (805)927-4678
Website: http://www.online.com/Moonstone Gallery/
In business since: 1981
Type of business: Retail store selling handcrafted items
Description of business: Contemporary American craft gallery looking for well crafted items made with imagination and care. Moonstones Gallery is located on the central coast of California, near Big Sur. It is a nature oriented resort area that attracts customers looking for quality art and craft items infused with a sense of imagination and spirit.
Types of products: Handmade items and kaleidoscopes, kinetic sculptures
Categories: Fine crafts, wearable art, jewelry, wooden crafts, paper products, stained glass items, hand blown glass items, home decor, dolls/stuffed animals/toys, pottery/ceramics, leather crafts, baskets, sculpture
Price range: $10-3,000
Business policy: We buy crafts outright and test market work on consignment.
Buys: From the craftspeople who query us if we like their work and it fits our theme; at wholesale shows for handcrafted items; at wholesale gift shows; from reps or craft brokers
Advertising/Promotion: Local newspapers, magazines, $7,500/year budget.
Application process: Queries are accepted from local/regional and out-of-town craftspeople. For consideration,

provide photos or slides, catalog/promotional materials, sample of work, written description of work.

MUSEUM OF THE AMERICAN QUILTER'S SOCIETY

Ruby Armstrong
215 Jefferson St.
Paducah, KY 42001
Phone: (502)442-8856
Fax: (502)442-5448
In business since: 1991
Type of business: Museum gift shop
Description of business: The shop features an extensive selection of fine crafts from around the country, including glass, pottery, wood, notecards, a wide range of jewelry, miscellaneous other items plus over 300 different books on quilts and textiles. Good design and quality techniques and materials emphasized in purchases. Inventory provides much to choose from for tourists, regional people shopping for gifts, and visiting quiltmakers. Note: quilts are not offered for sale, and only a limited number of textile items are sold.
Types of products: Handmade items and books, regional foods
Categories: Fine crafts, wearable art, jewelry, wooden crafts, paper products, stained glass items, needlework crafts, hand blown glass items, dolls/stuffed animals/toys, pottery/ceramics, leather crafts, baskets
More about products: Good design and workmanship are required.
Price range: $1-600
Business policy: We buy crafts outright.
Buys: From the craftspeople who query us if we like their work and it fits our theme; at wholesale shows for hand crafted items; at retail craft shows
Advertising/Promotion: Group tour magazines, newspapers, referred to in editorial copy about museum
Application process: Queries are accepted from local/regional and out-of-town craftspeople. For consideration, provide photos or slides, catalog/promotional materials, written description of work, wholesale price list, minimum order information.

MUSEUM SHOP, LTD.
Vicky Kornemann
20 N. Market St.
Frederick, MD 21701
Phone: (301)695-0424
Fax: (301)698-5242
In business since: 1962
Type of business: Retail store selling hand crafted items, gallery and museum gift shop
Description of business: Present crafts as the art they are, in a sophisticated gallery setting with bios of the artists. Fine art includes originals by Whistler, Pennell, Arms, Miro and others and Japanese ukiyo-e. Therefore, the crafts selected are high-quality but must also be a good value. Entire staff are artists/craftspeople.
Types of products: Handmade items and museum reproduction jewelry and decorative objects, greeting cards, music, reproduction sculpture
Categories: Fine crafts, wearable art, jewelry, wooden crafts, paper products, hand blown glass items, home decor, pottery/ceramics, nature crafts/floral, sculpture
Price range: Up to $2,000
Business policy: We buy crafts outright and take work on consignment. Currently looking for crafts on consignment.
Buys: At wholesale shows for hand crafted items.
Advertising/Promotion: Cable TV advertising, direct mail to our own clients and in our newsletter, tourist brochures.
Application process: Queries are accepted from local/regional and out-of-town craftspeople only if they consign. For consideration, provide photos with SASE for return.

NEW MORNING GALLERY
John E. Cram
7 Boston Way
Asheville, NC 28803
Phone: (704)274-2831
Fax: (704)274-2851
In business since: 1972
Type of business: Gallery
Description of business: New Morning Gallery started as a small shop for high quality crafts and has grown into a 6,000 sq. ft. showcase of "Art for Living." The Gallery, located in Historic Biltmore Village, has become a destination for those seeeking a fresh mix of functional and sculptural pottery, fine art glass, furniture, jewelry and other handmade objects.
Types of products: Handmade items only
Categories: Fine crafts, jewelry, wooden crafts, stained glass items, hand blown glass items, pottery/ceramics, recycled crafts
Price range: $10-3,000
Business policy: We buy crafts outright.
Buys: From the craftspeople who query us if we like their work and it fits our theme; at wholesale shows for hand crafted items
Advertising/Promotion: Gallery brochure, "This Week" magazine, direct mail. $60,000/year budget.
Special programs: Annual village Art & Craft Fair
Application process: Queries are accepted from local/regional and out-of-town craftspeople. For consideration, provide photos or slides, catalog/promotional materials, written description of work, SASE, artist bio, price list.

NORFOLK SENIOR CENTER
Shop Manager
924 W. 21st St.
Norfolk, VA 23517
Phone: (804)625-5857
Fax: (804)625-5858
E-mail: mjquale@eniac.seas.upenn.edu.
*In business since:*1967
Type of business: Senior center gift shop
Description of business: The gift shop has been an integral part of Norfolk Senior Center for many years. The shop provides the membership with a place to sell hand crafted items on consignment, thus augmenting their often-times limited financial resources. The shop is located just inside the main lobby entrance, where items are attractively displayed by a manager and many dedicated volunteers. When demand is high on an item, special orders may be placed with the crafter, if they indicate a willingness to work from orders.
Types of products: Handmade items only
Categories: Fine crafts, wearable art, jewelry, miniatures/dollhouses, wooden crafts, paper products, stained glass items, needlework crafts, hand blown glass items, home decor, figurines, dolls/stuffed animals/toys, pottery/ceramics, nature crafts/floral, leather crafts, baskets, sculpture
Price range: $1.25-50
Business policy: We accept work on consignment. Crafters must be members of Norfolk Senior Center (membership open to anyone 55 years and over).
Buys: From the craftspeople who query us if we like their work and it fits our theme
Advertising/Promotion: Our publication *PrimeTime*, and through the area's daily newspaper.
Application process: Queries are accepted from local/regional and out-of-town craftspeople. Must have pre-approval before sending items. For consideration, provide photos or slides (2-6), sample of work (local applicants), written description of work.
Additional information: Many of the consignees also exhibit in the Center's annual Senior ArtFest, an annual event open to the public for participating as an artist and viewing the exhibits. The items entered are offered for sale if the exhibitor desires.

NORTH AMERICAN NATIVE AMERICAN INDIAN INFORMATION AND TRADE CENTER
Fred Snyder
P.O. Box 27626
Tucson, AZ 85726
Phone: (520)622-4900; (520)295-1350
Fax: (520)292-0779
In business since: 1969
Type of business: Retail store selling hand crafted items
Description of business: Unique museum quality authentic American Indian crafts, both contemporary and traditional. The gift shop and American Indian expositions include 2,700 Indian artists from 410 tribal nations in Canada and the US. We market worldwide through 14 gift shops owned by co-op members, supply 160 museum gift shops, and participate in over 50 American Indian shows each year.
Types of products: Handmade items and

note cards, music, herbs, books, newspapers all relating to American Indians

Categories: Wearable art, jewelry, miniatures, wooden crafts, paper products, pottery, baskets, beadwork, quillwork, rugs

Price range: $5-25,000

Business policy: We buy crafts outright.

Buys: From the craftspeople who query us if we like their work and it fits our theme; at Indian festivals

Advertising/Promotion: *NY Times Magazine*, direct mail, display advertising. $100,000/year budget.

Special programs: November: Native American Month Social Pow Wow and Indian Market; January: New Years Competition Pow Wow and Indian Market; February: Tucson American Indian Exposition; and June-September: Visit American Indian events with store

Application process: Queries are accepted from local/regional and out-of-town Native American craftspeople. For consideration, provide photos, sample of work, written description of work.

Additional information: We have co-established an Indian Information Center in Belgium.

NORTHPORT CRAFTERS GALLERY

Ed Leonard
106 Main St.
Northport, NY 11768

Phone: (516)757-1603

In business since: 1981

Type of business: Retail store selling hand crafted items

Description of business: Northport Crafters Gallery features items from 150 of America's crafters.

Types of products: Handmade items only

Categories: Jewelry, wooden crafts, pottery/ceramics, leather crafts, furniture

Price range: $5-300

Buys: At wholesale shows for hand crafted items; from reps or craft brokers

Advertising/Promotion: Local newspapers: *Northport Observer, Record, Long Islander* and *Long Island* magazine

Application process: Queries are accepted from local/regional and out-of-town craftspeople. For consideration, provide catalog/promotional materials.

OBSIDIAN GALLERY

Elouise Rusk
4340 N. Campbell #90
Tucson, AZ 85718

Phone: (520)577-3598

Fax: (520)577-9018

In business since: 1985

Type of business: Gallery

Description of business: The finest contemporary crafts can be found at Obsidian Gallery. The emphasis is on traditional craft media: clay, fiber, metal, glass and wood. The works reflect regional themes and evoke the charm of Southwestern culture. Prominent and emerging artists—local/regional and national—are represented.

Types of products: Handmade items only

Categories: Fine crafts, wearable art, jewelry, wooden crafts, paper products, hand blown glass items, home decor, pottery/ceramics, baskets, recycled crafts, sculpture, art dolls

Price range: $8-2,750

Business policy: We buy crafts outright and take work on consignment.

Buys: From the craftspeople who query us if we like their work and it fits our theme; at wholesale shows for hand crafted items; at retail craft shows

Advertising/Promotion: *American Craft Magazine, Tucson Guide Quarterly, Desert Leaf, Ornament Magazine, Art Life*, mailings. $12,000/year budget.

Special programs: Four-five opening receptions/year for exhibitions featuring specific artists. In addition, other shows are advertised. Probably 10-12 different features per year.

Application process: Queries are accepted from local/regional and out-of-town craftspeople. Very selective and are only looking for specific things to fill in. Only the best. For consideration, provide photos or slides (6), catalog/promotional materials, written description of work, SASE for return of materials.

THE OBVIOUS PLACE, INC.

12 N. Section St.
Fairhope, AL 36532

Phone: (334)928-1111

In business since: 1988

Type of business: Retail store selling hand crafted items

Description of business: The Obvious Place, Inc. is a retail gift and craft store known for unusual merchandise of good quality at reasonable prices. It is located in Fairhope, a top-rated retirement and living community.

Types of products: Handmade items and prints, frames, T-shirts, kitchen items, cooking books, toys, African masks, toys and door accessories

Categories: Jewelry, stained glass items, hand blown glass items, pottery/ceramics, baskets

Price range: $5-500

Business policy: We buy crafts outright.

Buys: From the craftspeople who query us if we like their work and it fits our theme; at wholesale gift shows; at retail craft shows

Advertising/Promotion: Yellow Pages, Fairhope Retail Merchants Association, local civic activities

Application process: Queries are accepted from local/regional and out-of-town craftspeople. For consideration, provide photos, sample of work, written description of work, catalog/promotional materials, price list.

THE OCTAGON CENTER FOR THE ARTS

Alissa Hansen
427 Douglas Ave.
Ames, IA 50010

Phone: (515)232-5331

Fax: (515)232-5088

In business since: 1971

Type of business: Museum gift shop

Description of business: The Octagon Shop sells handmade and one-of-a-kind items made by local, regional and nationally known artisans.

Types of products: Handmade items and some wholesale catalog items

Categories: Fine crafts, wearable art, jewelry, miniatures/dollhouses, wooden crafts, paper products, stained glass items, needlework crafts, hand blown glass items, home decor, figurines, dolls/stuffed animals/toys, pottery/ceramics, nature crafts/floral, sculpture

More about products: Many items are made in Iowa or the Midwest, including pottery, jewelry, stationery, fiber work, which are the most popular.

Price range: 50¢-$1,300

Business policy: We take work on consignment.

Buys: From the craftspeople who query us if we like their work and it fits our theme; at wholesale shows for hand crafted items; at wholesale gift shows; at retail craft shows

Advertising/Promotion: Local newspapers: *The Daily Tribune, The Iowa State Daily, The Campus Reader* and *The Advertiser*, radio. $3,800/year budget.

Special programs: A holiday open house every November featuring artist demonstrations and booksigners.

Application process: Queries are accepted from local/regional and out-of-town craftspeople. Please call or write to receive a copy of our consignment contract and/or send photos or slides, catalog/promotional materials, sample of work, written description of work.

Additional information: Store hours M 1-8, T-Sat 10-5:30.

ON A WHIM GALLERY

BJ & Bonnie
12000 SE Dixie Hwy.
Hobe Sound, FL 33455

Phone: (561)546-1155

Fax: (561)546-5215

In business since: 1991

Type of business: Retail store selling hand crafted items

Types of products: Handmade items and books

Categories: Wearable art, jewelry, wooden crafts, stained glass items, needlework crafts, hand blown glass items, home decor, figurines, dolls/stuffed animals/toys, pottery/ceramics, nature crafts/floral, leather crafts, baskets, recycled crafts, sculpture

Price range: $3-150

Business policy: We take work on consignment.

Buys: From the craftspeople who query us if we like their work and it fits our theme; at wholesale shows for hand crafted items; at retail craft shows

Advertising/Promotion: *Craft Magazine*, newspaper, area promotion, fliers

Application process: Queries are accepted from local/regional and out-of-town craftspeople. Out-of-town craft-

ers pay shipping. For consideration, provide catalog/promotional materials or photos.

OOP!

297 Thayer St.
Providence, RI 02906

Phone: (401)751-9211

Fax: (401)751-9055

In business since: 1990

Type of business: Retail store selling hand crafted items

Description of business: Fun, whimsical, eclectic, clever, contemporary gift gallery.

Types of products: Handmade items and mix of gifts

Categories: Fine crafts, jewelry, wooden crafts, paper products, hand blown glass items, home decor, dolls/stuffed animals/toys, pottery/ceramics, nature crafts/floral, baskets, recycled crafts, sculpture

Price range: 50¢-$5,000

Business policy: We buy crafts outright.

Buys: From the craftspeople who query us if we like their work and it fits our theme; at wholesale shows for hand crafted items; at wholesale apparel shows; at wholesale gift shows; at wholesale toy, doll and teddy bear shows; at retail craft shows; through slide registries; from reps or craft brokers

Advertising/Promotion: *Providence Phoenix, Providence East Side Monthly, Art New England*. $10,000/year budget.

Special programs: Sponsors the annual Thayer St. Art Festival

Application process: Queries are accepted from local/regional and out-of-town craftspeople. For consideration, provide photos or slides (4), catalog/promotional materials, sample of work.

Additional information: Nominated one of the top 100 craft galleries in the USA.

THE OPULENT OWL

Lori and Kevin Nery
195 Wayland Ave.
Providence, RI 02906

Phone: (401)521-6698

Fax: (401)521-0157

In business since: 1978

Type of business: Retail store selling hand crafted items

Description of business: Upscale retailer selling gifts, jewelry, tableware, decorative accessories, stationery, children's clothing and toys, kitchenware. We operate 3 stores: The Opulent Owl, Mattapoisett, MA; The Sitting Duck, Marion, MA; The Sitting Duck for Kids, Marion, MA. All displaying an eclectic assortment of affordable gifts.

Types of products: Handmade items and stationery, clothing, kitchenware

Categories: Fine crafts, wearable art, jewelry, paper products, stained glass items, hand blown glass items, home decor, stuffed animals/toys, pottery/ceramics, leather crafts

Price range: $1-500

Business policy: We buy crafts outright.

Buys: From the craftspeople who query us if we like their work and it fits our theme; at wholesale shows for hand crafted items; at wholesale gift shows; from reps or craft brokers; from permanent showrooms

Advertising/Promotion: *American Style Magazine, Rhode Island Monthly*, newspaper, radio and TV

Application process: Queries are accepted from local/regional and out-of-town craftspeople. For consideration, provide photos, sample of work, catalog/promotional materials. Call for an appointment.

Additional information: Selected as a "Top 100 Retailer of American Craft" by *Niche Magazine*, 1995. Selected "Best of Rhode Island" 1996.

ORIEL CONTEMPORARY CRAFT GALLERY

Joyce Beaupre
17 College St.
South Hadley, MA 01075

Phone: (413)532-6469

E-mail: oriel3@aol.com.

In business since: 1989

Type of business: Gallery

Description of business: Oriel is a gallery of American crafts featuring over 250 artists. Located directly across from Mt. Holyoke College and within 10 miles of 5 higher learning institutions; therefore, we have all price points.

Types of products: Handmade items only

Categories: Fine crafts, wearable art, jewelry, wooden crafts, paper products, stained glass items, hand blown glass items, home decor, pottery/ceramics, leather crafts, sculpture

Price range: $10-1,000

Business policy: We buy crafts outright.

Buys: From the craftspeople who query us if we like their work and it fits our theme; at wholesale shows for hand crafted items; at retail craft shows; from reps or craft brokers

Advertising/Promotion: TV, local newspapers, press releases for special events/openings. 5% of gross sales/year budget.

Application process: Queries are accepted from local/regional and out-of-town craftspeople. For consideration, provide photos, catalog/promotional materials, written description of work.

OZARK NATIVE CRAFT ASSOCIATION CONSIGNMENT SHOP

22733 N. Hwy. 71

Winslow, AR 72959

Phone: (501)634-3791

In business since: 1970

Type of business: Retail store selling hand crafted items

Description of business: Twelve rooms filled with quality items hand crafted by members of the Ozark Native Craft Association.

Types of products: Handmade items only

Categories: Fine crafts, wearable art, jewelry, miniatures/dollhouses, wooden crafts, paper products, needlework crafts, home decor, figurines, dolls/stuffed animals/toys, pottery/ceramics, nature crafts/floral, baskets, recycled crafts, sculpture, quilts

Price range: 10¢-$600

Business policy: We take work on consignment (a yearly $35 membership with a 30% commission).

Buys: From the craftspeople who query us if we like their work and it fits our theme

Advertising/Promotion: Brochures in all ports of entry and state parks. Included in a magazine that goes to all motels, hotels in area. A non-for-profit organization, so funds are limited.

Special programs: We have a school of sculpture and woodcarving located in the upper part of the building. We also have an art studio and quilters who meet once a week.

Application process: Queries are accepted from local/regional craftspeople only. For consideration, provide written description of work.

PANACHE CRAFT GALLERY

Judy Kerr

2910 E. Sixth Ave.

Denver, CO 80206

Phone: (303)321-8069

In business since: 1977

Type of business: Gallery

Description of business: Panache is one of Denver's oldest craft galleries. We select our artists on the basis of their mastery (and especially their style) of the media they work in and how it complements the mix of crafts presently showing. Customers are looking for items for their homes and offices, gifts and jewelry and wearable art for themselves.

Types of products: Handmade items only.

Categories: Fine crafts, wearable art, jewelry, hand blown glass items, home decor, pottery/ceramics, sculpture

More about products: Looks for beautifully done crafts—contemporary, colorful and showing a unique perspective.

Price range: $5-1,000

Business policy: We take work on consignment.

Buys: From the craftspeople who query us if we like their work and it fits our theme

Advertising/Promotion: Mailings of cards and newsletters to our customer list, advertise in *Colorado Homes & Lifestyles* magazine and cooperate with Cherry Creek North Arts Association for gallery stroll newspaper and radio advertising. $5,000/year budget.

Special programs: The Cherry Creek Arts Association sponsors 4 major art walks a year and also 3 summer "Visions" walks. Features gallery artists with special shows at those times.

Application process: Queries are accepted from local/regional and out-of-town craftspeople. Out-of-town artists pay for shipping to gallery; gallery pays for return postage. For consideration, provide photos or slides, catalog/promotional materials, sample of work if possible, written description of work.

PARADOX ART GALLERY

Susan Griggs Allen

109 Southgate Plaza

Sarasota, FL 34239

Phone: (941)362-3715; (941)365-0435

In business since: 1993

Type of business: Retail store selling hand crafted items

Description of business: Paradox Art Gallery is located in a high-traffic, upscale shopping plaza. Prime customers are between 30 and 55 years old and in the middle- to upper-income brackets. Paradox also works directly with interior designers on custom commission works.

Types of products: Handmade items and 10% very contemporary manufactured items, pens, clocks, notecards.

Categories: Fine crafts, wearable art, jewelry, wooden crafts, paper products, stained glass items, hand blown glass items, home decor, pottery/ceramics, sculpture

More about products: Sells contemporary crafts with an avant garde flair, whimsical—never boring. Nothing country, but some with a folk-art feel, fine details.

Price range: $12-2,000

Business policy: We take work on consignment.

Buys: From the craftspeople who query us if we like their work and it fits our theme; at wholesale shows for hand crafted items; at retail craft shows; from reps or craft brokers

Advertising/Promotion: Local art newspaper, direct mail, mall's marquee. $5,000/year budget.

Special programs: Monthly open house and artist showings, art classes and apprenticeships available.

Application process: Queries are accepted from local/regional and out-of-town craftspeople. From out-of-town craftspeople accepts jewelry mostly. No breakables or large shipments. Artists pay shipping. For consideration, provide photos (6 or more), catalog/promotional materials, written description of work.

OWEN PATRICK GALLERY

James Gilroy and Gary Pelkey
4345 Main St.
Philadelphia, PA 19127
Phone: (215)482-9395
Fax: (215)483-1307
In business since: 1989
Type of business: Gallery
Description of business: A gallery of contemporary art and design.
Types of products: Handmade items and studio designed functional art and furniture
Categories: Fine crafts, hand blown glass items, home decor, pottery/ceramics
Price range: $40-2,000
Business policy: We buy crafts outright, take work on consignment and commission work from craftspeople.
Buys: From the craftspeople who query us if we like their work and it fits our theme; at wholesale shows for hand crafted items; at wholesale gift shows
Advertising/Promotion: Magazines, newspapers and direct mail
Special programs: 2-4 one person exhibitions each year
Application process: Queries are accepted from local/regional and out-of-town craftspeople. For consideration, provide photos or slides (10), catalog/promotional materials, résumé, SASE.

THE PEORIA ART GUILD

1831 N. Knoxville
Peoria, IL 61603
Phone: (309)685-7522
Fax: (309)685-7446
E-mail: peoriaart@aol.com
In business since: 1969
Type of business: Retail store and gallery selling hand crafted items
Description of business: The Peoria Art Guild exists to serve the artists and the community through the exhibition and sale of contemporary art work to provide education and to promote appreciation of visual arts.
Types of products: Handmade items only.
Categories: Jewelry, stained glass items, hand blown glass items, sculpture, ceramics, wooden crafts

Price range: $2-5,000
Business policy: We take work on consignment.
Buys: From the craftspeople who query us if we like their work and it fits our theme
Advertising/Promotion: Local publications, radio
Special programs: Annual fine art fair and digital photography show
Application process: Queries are accepted from local/regional and out-of-town craftspeople. For consideration, provide photos or slides (8-10), sample of work.

PER TE INC.

Marilyn Gulotta
1000 Central Ave.
Woodmere, NY 11598
Phone: (516)295-5045
Fax: (516)295-5074
In business since: 1980
Type of business: Retail store selling hand crafted items
Description of business: Per te, which means "for you" in Italian, is a gallery, a gift shop and a studio. A gallery with art glass and ceramics by contemporary artists. A gift shop with costume jewelry, fashion and decorative home accessories. A studio where we design, custom paint and decorate just about anything.
Types of products: Handmade items and mass produced items that have a hand crafted character
Categories: Fine crafts, jewelry, hand blown glass items, home decor, dolls/stuffed animals/toys, pottery/ceramics, nature crafts/floral, leather crafts, baskets
Price range: $20-500
Business policy: We buy crafts outright.
Buys: At wholesale shows for hand crafted items; at wholesale gift shows; from reps or craft brokers
Advertising/Promotion: Local newspapers, bridal magazines
Application process: Queries are accepted from local/regional and out-of-town craftspeople. For consideration, provide photos or slides, catalog/promotional materials, sample of work.

PLAIN AND FANCY ORIGINALS/ "COUNTRY JUNQUE"

Suanne Shirley
1540 North State Rd. 135
Nashville, IN 47448
Phone: (812)988-4537
Fax: (812)988-4549
In business since: 1987
Type of business: Bed & breakfast gift shop
Description of business: "Country Junque" was developed initially for the bed and breakfast guests, but is open to the public Fri 12-6, Sat-Sun 10-6. The shop is sometimes available by appointment.
Types of products: Handmade items and antiques.
Categories: Fine crafts, wearable art, jewelry, miniatures/dollhouses, wooden crafts, paper products, stained glass items, needlework crafts, home decor, figurines, dolls/stuffed animals/toys, pottery/ceramics, nature crafts/floral, leather crafts, baskets, recycled crafts
More about products: All items are locally crafted. No items from outside Brown County are considered.
Price range: $2-100
Business policy: We buy crafts outright and take work on consignment.
Buys: From the craftspeople who query us if we like their work and it fits our theme
Advertising/Promotion: Direct mail, signage
Application process: Queries are accepted from local/regional craftspeople only. For consideration, provide sample of work.

PM GALLERY

Maria Galloway
726 N. High St.
Columbus, OH 43215
Phone: (614)299-0860
In business since: 1980
Type of business: Gallery
Description of business: The oldest gallery in the Short North, a renovated urban area just north of downtown Columbus. We carry the work of approximately 150 artists and artisans from around the country.
Types of products: Handmade items only.

Categories: Fine crafts, jewelry, wooden crafts, paper products, stained glass items, hand blown glass items, pottery/ceramics, iron/metal work, kaleidoscopes

Price range: $2-1,000

Business policy: We buy crafts outright and take work on consignment.

Buys: From the craftspeople who query us if we like their work and it fits our theme; at wholesale shows for hand crafted items; at retail craft shows; from reps or craft brokers

Advertising/Promotion: Local print media, public and private radio, joint promotions in visitors guides, theatre programs, press releases for special events or shows. 4% of gross sales/year budget.

Special programs: The Gallery Hop takes place the first Saturday of every month. Every business in the area is open late, some have refreshments, music, etc. It's the second most attended arts event in the city.

Application process: Queries are accepted from local/regional and out-of-town craftspeople. For consideration, provide photos (6 or less, note dimensions), written description of work, catalog/promotional materials, price list, terms, conditions of exclusivity.

POOPSIE'S

Sue Landen

107 S. Main St.

Galena, IL 61036

Phone: (815)777-1999

Fax: (815)777-9991

In business since: 1993

Type of business: Retail store selling hand crafted items

Description of business: A 3,000 sq. ft. shop in a small historic town which attracts a large volume of tourists and weekend residents. Shop carries a variety of unusual and interesting items, with a bias toward the contemporary.

Types of products: Handmade items and books, cards, records, some toys, some factory-made accessories.

Categories: Fine crafts, wearable art, jewelry, wooden crafts, paper products, stained glass items, needlework crafts, hand blown glass items, home decor, dolls/stuffed animals/toys, pot-

tery/ceramics, nature crafts/floral, recycled crafts, sculpture

More about products: Need predictable quality and consistency, reliable reordering, careful packing, costing which enables us to move volume!

Price range: $3-2,000

Business policy: We buy crafts outright.

Buys: From the craftspeople who query us if we like their work and it fits our theme; at wholesale shows for hand crafted items; at wholesale gift shows; at retail craft shows; from reps or craft brokers

Advertising/Promotion: Regional tourist-oriented publications, local newspapers, public service advertising, billboard, some direct mail.

Application process: Queries are accepted from local/regional and out-of-town craftspeople. For consideration, provide photos, catalog/promotional materials, written description of work.

Additional information: Particularly interested in unusual items that make a good impulse gift purchase with retail under $50. *Niche* magazine named Poopsie's in it's 1996 Top 100 Craft Retailers issue.

POSNER FINE ART

Judith L. Posner

940 Westmount Dr., Suite 204

W. Hollywood, CA 90069

Phone: (310)260-8858

Fax: (310)260-8860

In business since: 1993

Type of business: We sell to companies to place in stores

Description of business: Posner Fine Art sells retail and wholesale through offices and trade shows.

Types of products: Handmade items only

Categories: Fine crafts, wearable art, jewelry, pottery/ceramics, sculpture.

Price range: Up to $1,000

Business policy: We take work on consignment

Buys: From the craftspeople who query us if we like their work and it fits our theme; at wholesale gift shows; through slide registries

Advertising/Promotion: *Decor Magazine, Art Business News,* mailings. $200-500 per month/budget.

Application process: Queries are accepted from local/regional and out-of-

town craftspeople. For consideration, provide photos, catalog/promotional materials, SASE.

Additional information: We are always looking for the unusual.

THE POTTER ETC.

Faith Matheus

Box 305

Jerome, AZ 86331

Phone: (520)634-9425

In business since: 1976

Type of business: Retail store selling hand crafted items

Description of business: A retail gift shop selling hand crafted items including batik, musical instruments, wind chimes, handwoven clothing and silk accessories

Types of products: Handmade items and books of the area (Arizona).

Categories: Fine crafts, wearable art, jewelry, paper products, home decor, figurines, pottery/ceramics, nature crafts/floral, baskets, sculpture

Price range: $5-150

Business policy: We prefer to buy outright but sometimes do consignment on higher priced items.

Buys: From the craftspeople who query us if we like their work and it fits our theme; at wholesale shows for hand crafted items; at wholesale gift shows; at retail craft shows

Application process: Queries are accepted from local/regional and out-of-town craftspeople. For consideration, provide photos or slides, catalog/promotional materials, sample of work if possible; this is best.

Additional information: Jerome is an old copper mining town. It is situated high on a mountain in northern Arizona (5,000 ft.). It is a small town where many artists and writers have settled and is visited by over 1 million tourists each year.

PRAIRIE PEACOCK

Gayle Keiser

53 S. Seminary St.

Galesburg, IL 61401

Phone: (309)342-4900

In business since: 1988

Type of business: Gallery

Description of business: Specializing in American artcraft including jewelry, pottery (clayware, porcelain and raku), glass, woods, metals, 2-dimensional art and custom framing done in the store.

Types of products: Handmade items only

Categories: Fine crafts, wearable art, jewelry, wooden crafts, paper products, stained glass items, hand blown glass items, home decor, figurines, toys, pottery/ceramics, nature crafts, baskets, sculpture.

Price range: $5-400

Business policy: We buys crafts outright. Carry on consignment; 60% to artist of agreed upon retail price.

Buys: From the craftspeople who query us if we like their work and it fits our theme; at wholesale shows; at retail craft shows; through slide registries; from reps or craft brokers

Advertising/Promotion: We advertise and do direct mailing for special events in the store and at Christmas time. Otherwise advertising is done continuously for this store and others in specialty shopping area where located. TV advertising on regional basis quite successfully. $50,000/year budget.

Special programs: Feature individual artist when Seminary Street merchants do special promotions 4 times/year.

Application process: Queries are accepted from local/regional and out-of-town craftspeople. In town is consignment only. Out of town is consignment or wholesale depending on nature of their work and time of year. For consideration, provide photos or slides, catalog/promotional materials, sample of work.

Additional information: We draw from a regional market and have a multi state clientele. Nice welcoming atmosphere with New Age music and antique display fixture combined with gallery area.

THE PRESTON COLLECTION INC.

Gayle Thetford
305 Preston Royal
Dallas, TX 75230
Phone: (214)373-6065
Fax: (214)692-6589
In business since: 1980

Type of business: Retail store selling hand crafted items

Description of business: A gift store offering custom framing and bridal register, collectibles and decorative accessories. We are always looking for something unique and exclusive to Dallas.

Types of products: Handmade items and Dept. 56 Villages, Waterford, Crabtree & Evelyn, Gail Pittman Pottery

Categories: Fine crafts, wearable art, jewelry, paper products, stained glass items, home decor, figurines, dolls/stuffed animals/toys, pottery/ceramics, nature crafts/floral, leather crafts, baskets, recycled crafts.

Price range: $17.95-250

Business policy: We buy crafts outright and take work on consignment.

Buys: From the craftspeople who query us if we like their work and it fits our theme; at wholesale shows for hand crafted items; at wholesale gift shows

Advertising/Promotion: Newspapers, mailing list, catalogue, special events, personal appearances by artists

Application process: Queries are accepted from local/regional and out-of-town craftspeople. For consideration, provide photos, catalog/promotional materials, sample of work.

THE PROMENADE GALLERY

Kathy West
204 Center St.
Berea, KY 40403
Phone: (606)986-1609
In business since: 1986
Type of business: Gallery

Description of business: The Promenade is a spacious gallery full of fine American hand crafts. Primarily represents regional artists and craftsmen and about 65% of the work comes from Kentucky. We feature excellent-quality production and one-of-a-kind pieces from whimsical folkart to exquisite miniature oak baskets to beautiful accent furniture pieces. Just about every medium is represented. We are always looking for unusual and interesting things to intrigue and entice customers. Located on the historic Berea College Square, in Berea.

Types of products: Handmade items only.

Categories: Fine crafts, jewelry, miniatures, wooden crafts, paper products, stained glass items, hand blown glass items, pottery/ceramics, nature crafts/floral, leather crafts, baskets, recycled crafts, sculpture

More about products: Must be top quality, contemporary and traditional, prefer work that is innovative, unusual, with excellent design.

Price range: $1-2,000

Business policy: We buy crafts outright, take work on consignment and commission work from craftspeople.

Buys: From the craftspeople who query us if we like their work and it fits our theme; at wholesale shows for hand crafted items; at retail craft shows

Advertising/Promotion: Berea Guide, and other cooperative advertising opportunities through Berea Tourism

Application process: Queries are accepted from local/regional and out-of-town craftspeople. For consideration, provide photos or slides, catalog/promotional materials, written description of work.

QUAINT CORNER

Joyce Schechter
4026 Westheimer
Houston, TX 77027
Phone: (713)961-4898
Fax: (713)961-5668
In business since: 1974

Type of business: Retail store selling hand crafted items

Types of products: Handmade items and frames, sterling engravables, sachets, oils, potpourri, books.

Categories: Fine crafts, jewelry, paper products, hand blown glass items, dolls/stuffed animals/toys, pottery/ceramics, nature crafts/floral, baskets

Price range: $10-1,000

Business policy: We buy crafts outright.

Buys: From the craftspeople who query us if we like their work and it fits our theme; at wholesale shows for hand crafted items; at wholesale gift shows; at retail craft shows; from reps or craft brokers

Advertising/Promotion: Direct mail, newspaper, radio

Application process: Queries are accepted from local/regional and out-of-town craftspeople. For consideration, provide photos or slides, catalog/promotional materials, sample of work, written description of work

Additional information: We provide engraving on metals and offer a bridal registry.

QUARTER MOON DESIGNS

Ellis Shallbetter
918 Royal St.
New Orleans, LA 70116
Phone: (504)524-3208
Fax: (504)529-5223
E-mail: quartermoon@accesscom.net
Website: http://www.quartermoon.com
In business since: 1984
Type of business: Gallery
Types of products: Handmade items only.
Categories: Fine crafts, wearable art, jewelry
More about products: Specialize in wearables, prefer regional artists
Price range: $20-1,000
Business policy: Determined on an individual basis.
Buys: From the craftspeople who query us if we like their work and it fits our theme
Advertising/Promotion: Local publications, tour guide books, the Internet. Budget varies.
Application process: Queries are accepted from local/regional craftspeople only. For consideration, provide photos or slides, written description of work.
Additional information: Please see the listing below for a second location.

QUARTER MOON EAST

Ellis Shallbetter
146 Main St.
Bay St. Louis, MS 39520
Phone: (504)524-3208
Fax: (504)529-5223
E-mail: quartermoon@accesscom.net
In business since: 1984
Type of business: Gallery
Description of business: Please see the above listing for more information.

THE QUEST

Claire G. Cirz
38 Main St.
Chester, NJ 07930
Phone: (908)879-8144
In business since: 1989

Type of business: Retail store selling hand crafted items
Description of business: The Quest is a gallery of contemporary American hand crafts. Specializes in functional crafts designed by over 250 of America's nationally known and newly discovered artists.
Types of products: Handmade items and miscellaneous items such as lamp oil for handblown oilites, music played in store, jewelry cleaning cloths.
Categories: Fine crafts, wearable art, jewelry, wooden crafts, paper products, stained glass items, hand blown glass items, home decor, pottery/ceramics, leather crafts, recycled crafts
More about products: All work must be contemporary and hand crafted in the USA or Canada.
Price range: $5-600
Business policy: We buy crafts outright.
Buys: From the craftspeople who query us if we like their work and it fits our theme; at wholesale shows for hand crafted items
Advertising/Promotion: *New Jersey Country Roads*, *New Jersey Monthly* magazines, direct mailings 4 times/year to customer list, (newsletter and postcard mailings). $12,000/year budget.
Application process: Queries are accepted from local/regional and out-of-town craftspeople. For consideration, provide photos or slides, catalog/promotional materials, written description of work. No reps.

RAGAZZI'S FLYING SHUTTLE

JoAnn and Anna Williams
607 First Ave.
Seattle, WA 98104
Phone: (206)343-9762; (206)343-9829
Fax: (206)343-3101
In business since: 1982
Type of business: Retail store selling hand crafted items
Description of business: The Northwest's largest collection of high quality American crafts—specializing in contemporary apparel, jewelry and accessories of over 150 artists.
Types of products: Handmade items only.
Categories: Wearable art, jewelry, wooden crafts, home decor

More about products: All work must be of the highest quality, and store requires a regional exclusive to represent or handle the product.
Price range: $25-2,000
Business policy: We buy crafts outright and take work on consignment.
Buys: From the craftspeople who query us if we like their work and it fits our theme; at wholesale shows for hand crafted items; at wholesale apparel shows; from reps or craft brokers
Advertising/Promotion: mailers to clients, *American Craft*, *Metalsmith*, *Where Magazine*. $25,000/year budget.
Special programs: Hosts quarterly shows for gallery artists, annual invitational, participate in regional fashion shows.
Application process: Queries are accepted from local/regional and out-of-town craftspeople. For consideration, provide photos or slides (6), catalog/promotional materials. By mail only, must include complete package of slides, price list, artist bio and return mailer if want package returned. Do not send actual work.

RAINBLUE GALLERY

Mike and Verdeen Morgan
1205 Johnson Ferry Rd. #117
Marietta, GA 30068
Phone: (770)973-1091
In business since: 1976
Type of business: Gallery
Description of business: A retail American hand crafted pottery shop specializing in functional and decorative works from about 200 local and regional artists.
Types of products: Handmade items only.
Categories: Fine crafts, wooden crafts, paper products, stained glass items, hand blown glass items, pottery/ceramics
Price range: $5-400
Business policy: We buy crafts outright.
Buys: From the craftspeople who query us if we like their work and it fits our theme; at wholesale shows for hand crafted items
Advertising/Promotion: Word of mouth, direct mail
Special programs: Holiday Open House
Application process: Queries are ac-

cepted from local/regional and out-of-town craftspeople. For consideration, provide photos, written description of work. No phone calls please.

THE RED OAK

Trisha Riex
P.O. Box 98
Bishop Hill, IL 61419
Phone: (309)927-3539
In business since: 1970
Type of business: Retail store selling hand crafted items
Description of business: The Red Oak operates a gift shop and luncheonbörd in the restored Swedish communal village of Bishop Hill, a national historic landmark. We seek quality crafts to add to our line. We are particularly interested in new and unusual items to compliment our merchandise.
Types of products: Handmade items and quality gifts of a general appeal.
Categories: Fine crafts, jewelry, wooden crafts, paper products, stained glass items, needlework crafts, hand blown glass items, home decor, dolls/stuffed animals/toys, pottery/ceramics, nature crafts/floral, leather crafts, baskets, recycled crafts
Price range: $10-200
Business policy: We buy crafts outright and take work on consignment.
Buys: From the craftspeople who query us if we like their work and it fits our theme; at wholesale shows for hand crafted items; at wholesale gift shows
Advertising/Promotion: Local and regional publications (newspapers, visitors guides), some radio and TV. Some Swedish publications. $5,000/year budget.
Special programs: Occasional shows
Application process: Queries are accepted from local/regional and out-of-town craftspeople. For consideration, provide photos or slides, catalog/promotional materials, sample of work, written description of work.

RIVERWORKS CRAFT GALLERY

Brenda Bowers
105 E. River St.
Savannah, GA 31401
Phone: (912)236-2012
Fax: (912)236-9883
In business since: 1979

Type of business: Retail store selling hand crafted items
Description of business: An outstanding collection of fine crafts and contemporary gifts by over one hundred American craftspeople. Located on historic River Street.
Types of products: Handmade items only.
Categories: Fine crafts, wearable art, jewelry, stained glass items, hand blown glass items, figurines, pottery/ceramics, baskets, sculpture
Price range: $25-700
Business policy: We buy crafts outright and take work on consignment.
Buys: From the craftspeople who query us if we like their work and it fits our theme; at wholesale shows for hand crafted items; at wholesale gift shows; from reps or craft brokers
Advertising/Promotion: Featured in free local calendars, River Street brochure distributed locally
Application process: Queries are accepted from local/regional and out-of-town craftspeople. For consideration, provide photos, catalog/promotional materials. Please contact Brenda Bowers for an appointment.

ROOKIE-TO GALLERY

Bob and Karen Altaras
P.O. Box 606
Boonville, CA 95415
Phone: (707)895-2204
In business since: 1986
Type of business: Gallery
Description of business: Feature a large selection of high-quality work by contemporary artists and craftspeople.
Types of products: Handmade items only.
Categories: Fine crafts, wearable art, jewelry, wooden crafts, paper products, hand blown glass items, home decor, pottery/ceramics, leather crafts, baskets, sculpture, metalwork
Business policy: We buy crafts outright and take work on consignment.
Buys: From the craftspeople who query us if we like their work and it fits our theme; at wholesale shows for hand crafted items; at wholesale gift shows; at retail craft shows
Advertising/Promotion: Local tourist publications, and local publications, at

least 4 mailings to extensive mail list per year.
Special programs: Three to four shows each year featuring an individual or groups of artists.
Application process: Queries are accepted from local/regional and out-of-town craftspeople. For consideration, provide photos or slides, catalog/promotional materials, sample of work, written description of work.
Additional information: We are always looking for new work to show in the gallery. Original conception and high quality of craftsmanship are the primary criteria along with value. We also appreciate some kind of point-of-sale tag or other information on artist and special techniques.

ROUTE 5, INC.

Donald and Lois Funk
380 Wayne Ave.
Chambersburg, PA 17201-3717
Phone: (717)263-0327
Fax: (717)263-7141
In business since: 1974
Type of business: Retail store selling hand crafted items
Description of business: Route 5 features American-made finished crafts of high quality. Eclectic, but contemporary and likes functional crafts. Form follows function; appreciates clean, simple design.
Types of products: Handmade items only.
Categories: Fine crafts, jewelry, wooden crafts, stained glass items, hand blown glass items, home decor, stuffed animals/toys, pottery/ceramics, nature crafts, leather crafts, sculpture
Price range: $10-700
Business policy: We buy crafts outright.
Buys: At wholesale shows for hand crafted items and at wholesale gift shows
Advertising/Promotion: TV and cable, radio, brochures, targeted marketing. $25,000/year budget.
Application process: Queries are accepted from local/regional and out-of-town craftspeople. Crafters must be full-time with lines proven to retail at a 2.2 markup. For consideration, provide photos or slides (6), catalog/promotional materials.

Additional information: Route 5 was nominated as a top 100 craft gallery in the USA in 1995 by *Niche* magazine. It was voted Best Gift Shop in the Cumberland Valley 1993, 1994, 1995 and 1996 by readers of *Public Opinion* newspaper.

RUNNING RIDGE GALLERY

Barbara Grabowski and Ruth Farnham
640 Canyon Rd.
Santa Fe, NM 87501
Phone: (505)988-2515
Fax: (505)988-7692
In business since: 1976
Type of business: Gallery
Description of business: Fine art and crafts gallery specializing in ceramics, glass, fiber, sculpture and jewelry.
Types of products: Handmade items only.
Categories: Fine crafts, jewelry, wooden crafts, hand blown glass items, pottery/ceramics, sculpture
Price range: $12-12,000
Business policy: We buy crafts outright and take work on consignment.
Buys: From the craftspeople who query us if we like their work and it fits our theme; at wholesale shows for hand crafted items; at wholesale gift shows
Advertising/Promotion: Locally and *American Craft* magazine. Budget varies.
Application process: Queries are accepted from local/regional and out-of-town craftspeople. Presentation information will not be returned without SASE. Jury process takes 3 months. Provide photos or slides, catalog/promotional materials, written description of work, SASE.

ST. ARMANDS WOODERY

Shelby Cowles
8 N. Blvd. of the Presidents
Sarasota, FL 34236
Phone: (941)388-1406
In business since: 1983
Type of business: Gallery
Description of business: Unique hand crafted wood sculptures, home decor and specialty items. Gallery quality and custom work available. Most are one of a kind.
Types of products: Handmade items and some reproductions.

Categories: Fine crafts, jewelry, miniatures, wooden crafts, home decor, nature crafts, sculpture
Price range: $20-3,000
Business policy: We take work on consignment and commission work from craftspeople.
Buys: From the craftspeople who query us if we like their work and it fits our theme; at wholesale shows for hand crafted items; at wholesale gift shows; at retail craft shows; from reps or craft brokers; referrals
Advertising/Promotion: *Sarasota Magazine*, *The Art Review*, local papers
Special programs: Juried Art Show each October
Application process: Queries are accepted from local/regional and out-of-town craftspeople. Some work is purchased outright. If taken on consignment payment is made first of month following sale. For consideration, provide photos or slides, catalog/promotional materials, written description of work, any visual available is acceptable along with pricing of individual pieces.

SALISBURY ART & FRAMING

Marilyn Bookmyer
213 North Blvd.
Salisbury, MD 21801
Phone: (410)742-9522
In business since: 1972
Type of business: Gallery
Description of business: Specialize in fine art, custom framing and contemporary crafts by American artists.
Types of products: Handmade items only.
Categories: Fine crafts, jewelry, wooden crafts, paper products, stained glass items, hand blown glass items, home decor, pottery/ceramics, nature crafts/floral, baskets, sculpture
Price range: $10-1,000
Business policy: We buy crafts outright, take work on consignment and commission work from craftspeople.
Buys: From the craftspeople who query us if we like their work and it fits our theme; at wholesale shows for hand crafted items; at wholesale gift shows; at retail craft shows; from reps or craft brokers

Advertising/Promotion: Newspapers, radio, direct mail
Special programs: Shows featuring particular artists
Application process: Queries are accepted by mail from local/regional and out-of-town craftspeople. For consideration, provide photos or slides, catalog/promotional materials, written description of work. Occasionally a sample of work may be requested.

SALMON FALLS ARTISANS SHOWROOM

Lynne Shulda
1 Ashfield St., P.O. Box 176
Shelburne Falls, MA 01370
Phone: (413)625-9833
In business since: 1986
Type of business: Gallery
Description of business: Salmon Falls Artisans Showroom is a quality gallery representing representing over 185 of the region's craftspeople and artists. Setting is a restored post-and-beam grainery building called Salmon Falls Marketplace, set on a knoll overlooking the historic Bridge of Flowers and Glacial Potholes. Some artists are nationally and internationally known.
Types of products: Handmade items only.
Categories: Fine crafts, wearable art, jewelry, wooden crafts, paper products, stained glass items, hand blown glass items, dolls/stuffed animals/toys, pottery/ceramics, leather crafts, baskets, sculpture
More about products: Our quality hand crafted items are regionally made (65 mile radius).
Price range: $1.50-10,000
Business policy: We take work on consignment, commission work from craftspeople and buy some crafts outright.
Buys: From the craftspeople who query us if we like their work and it fits our theme
Advertising/Promotion: Radio, newspapers, visitor guides, *Yankee Magazine*, concert programs and postcards/direct mail. About $10,000/year budget.
Special programs: Features furniture shows, blown glass (Josh Simpson), lighting and sculpture

Application process: Queries are accepted from local/regional and out-of-town craftspeople. Out-of-town craftspeople have to be within a 65-mile radius. For consideration, provide photos or slides, sample of work.

SANDWICH GLASS MUSEUM
P.O. Box 103
Sandwich, MA 02563
Phone: (508)888-0251
Fax: (508)888-4941
In business since: 1907
Type of business: Museum gift shop
Description of business: Sell American-made hand crafted glass items
Types of products: Handmade items only.
Categories: Fine crafts, jewelry, stained glass items, hand blown glass items
Price range: $5-500
Business policy: We buy crafts outright.
Buys: From the craftspeople who query us if we like their work and it fits our theme; at wholesale shows for hand crafted items; at wholesale gift shows
Application process: Queries are accepted from local/regional and out-of-town craftspeople. For consideration, provide photos or slides, sample of work.

SASSAFRAS RIDGE
Ed Lawrence
10 Abbott Way
Piedmont, CA 94618
Phone: (510)654-6272
Fax: (510)836-2132
In business since: 1982
Type of business: Retail store selling hand crafted items
Description of business: Boutique selling hand-crafted items from rural America.
Types of products: Handmade items and roll-top desks and clocks.
Categories: Fine crafts, wooden crafts, needlework crafts, home decor, dolls/stuffed animals/toys, baskets
Price range: $2-500
Business policy: We buy crafts outright.
Buys: From the craftspeople who query us if we like their work and it fits our theme; at wholesale shows for hand crafted items; at wholesale gift shows
Application process: Queries are accepted from local/regional and out-of-

town craftspeople. For consideration, provide photos, sample of work.

SAYWELL'S
Marcie and Jerry Saywell
326 Main St.
Wakefield Village, RI 02879
Phone: (401)783-0630
In business since: 1987
Type of business: Gallery
Description of business: Saywell's is a multi-media gallery with an emphasis on wood and pottery. Represents more than 300 American artisans who are professionals in their field.
Types of products: Handmade items and cards, machine woven items.
Categories: Fine crafts, jewelry, wooden crafts, stained glass items, hand blown glass items, home decor, pottery/ceramics, baskets
More about products: All products offered are by full-time craftspeople, most of whom have juried credentials.
Price range: Up to $1,000
Business policy: We buy crafts outright.
Buys: From the craftspeople who query us if we like their work and it fits our theme; at wholesale shows for hand crafted items; from reps or craft brokers. We also travel to find items.
Application process: Queries are accepted from local/regional and out-of-town craftspeople. Letter inquiries from out-of-town craftspeople. Please—no phone calls. For consideration, provide photos (1), sample of work, written description of work, catalog/promotional materials, artist biography.

JOEL SCHWALB GALLERY
Joel Schwalb
12 South Broadway
Nyack, NY 10960
Phone: (914)358-1701
E-mail: js4ausmith@aol.com
In business since: 1975
Type of business: Retail store selling hand crafted items
Description of business: The Joel Schwalb Gallery features over 80 jewelry designers including custom designs by Joel Schwalb, designer and goldsmith.
Types of products: Handmade items only.

Categories: Fine crafts, wearable art, jewelry, wooden crafts, stained glass items, hand blown glass items, home decor, pottery/ceramics, sculpture, metal objects
Price range: $25-5,000
Business policy: We buy crafts outright.
Buys: From the craftspeople who query us if we like their work and it fits our theme; at wholesale shows for hand crafted items; at wholesale gift shows; from reps or craft brokers
Advertising/Promotion: Newspapers, guide books and direct mail. $5,000/year budget.
Application process: Queries are accepted from local/regional and out-of-town craftspeople. For consideration, provide photos or slides, catalog/promotional materials, written description of work.

THE SEEKERS COLLECTION & GALLERY
Lynda Adelson
4090 Burton Dr.
Cambria, CA 93428
Phone: (805)927-4352; (800)841-5250
Fax: (805)927-5984
E-mail: glassart@ix.net.com
Website: http://www.seekersglass.com
In business since: 1981
Type of business: Gallery
Description of business: Seekers is a gallery with one of the largest collections of museum cquality, contemporary American studio glass to be found anywhere in the world. Exhibits orginial works by more than 175 of America's leading studio glass artists. Each one of a kind, signed piece is the work of an individual American artist/designer. Occupies two floors at the corner of Burton Drive and Center Street, in Cambria's historic East Village.
Types of products: Handmade items only.
Categories: Fine crafts, wearable art, jewelry, stained glass items, hand blown glass items, home decor, pottery/ceramics, sculpture
Price range: $10-30,000
Buys: From the craftspeople who query us if we like their work and it fits our theme; at wholesale shows for hand crafted items; at wholesale gift shows.
Advertising/Promotion: Local tourist

publications. $10,000/year budget.

Application process: Queries are accepted from local/regional and out-of-town craftspeople. For consideration, provide photos or slides, written description of work, price list.

Additional information: Store hours Sun-F 10-10.

SHOOT THE MOON AND SHOOT THE MOON II

Dinorah Spalding
P.O. Box 1382
Kennebunkport, ME 04046
Phone: (207)967-2755; (207)967-5484
In business since: 1990
Type of business: Gallery
Description of business: These are 2 different contemporary craft galleries. Each store represents different artists.
Types of products: Handmade items only.
Categories: Fine crafts, wearable art, jewelry, wooden crafts, paper products, stained glass items, hand blown glass items, home decor, figurines, dolls/stuffed animals/toys, pottery/ceramics, nature crafts/floral
More about products: No country crafts
Price range: $20-1,000
Business policy: We buy crafts outright and take work on consignment.
Buys: From the craftspeole who query us if we like their work and it fits our theme; at wholesale shows for hand-crated items; at wholesale gift shows; from reps or craft brokers
Advertising/Promotion: Local paper, *Down East Magazine*, TV. $2,000 budget.
Application process: Queries are accepted from local/regional and out-of-town craftspeople. For consideration, provide photos or slides, SASE.

THE SHOP AT THE GUILFORD HANDCRAFT CENTER

Patricia Seekamp
P.O. Box 589
Guilford, CT 06437
Phone: (203)453-5947
Fax: (203)453-6237
In business since: 1965
Type of business: Retail store selling hand crafted items
Description of business: The shop fea-

tures quality American handcrafted gifts tastefully displayed in a friendly atmosphere. It is open year round and is part of a craft center with classes in fine arts and crafts, and a gallery that presents 7 different shows throughout the year.
Types of products: Handmade items only.
Categories: Fine crafts, jewelry, wooden crafts, hand blown glass items, pottery/ceramics, baskets, hand woven pieces, forged metal
Price range: Up to $300
Business policy: We take work on consignment. We consign crafts at a 60%/40% agreement.
Advertising/Promotion: Local newspapers, local radio, cards in the tourist information racks at the highway rest areas. Very small budget.
Special programs: "Artistry, a Holiday Festival of Crafts" is held in our gallery every November and December. The work of over 400 craftspeople is exhibited.
Application process: Queries are accepted from local/regional and out-of-town craftspeople. A jury meets monthly to review possible work. For consideration, provide photos or slides, written description of work and selling price, including 40% commission.

SHOP AT THE MANCHESTER INSTITUTE

Linda Randazzo
148 Concord St.
Manchester, NH 03104
Phone: (603)623-0313; (603)669-2731
Fax: (603)641-1832
In business since: 1979
Type of business: Museum gift shop
Description of business: The shop at the Manchester Institute features fine hand crafts, related books and art supplies. The Manchester Institute is an art school offering certificates in photography, painting and sculpture.
Types of products: Handmade items and art supplies and art and craft books.
Categories: Wearable art, jewelry, wooden crafts, paper products, needlework crafts, hand blown glass items, figurines, pottery/ceramics, baskets

Price range: $5-200
Business policy: We buy crafts outright.
Buys: From the craftspeople who query us if we like their work and it fits our theme; at wholesale shows for hand crafted items; at wholesale gift shows; at retail craft shows; from reps or craft brokers
Advertising/Promotion: Newspaper, newsletter to membership
Special programs: We feature craftspeople, sometimes in the theme or media being shown in our gallery
Application process: Queries are accepted from local/regional and out-of-town craftspeople. For consideration, provide photos, catalog/promotional materials.

SIGNATURE DESIGNS

Debra Kornhauser
5 W. Main St.
Moorestown, NJ 08057
Phone/Fax: (609)778-8657
In business since: 1980
Type of business: Retail store selling hand crafted items
Description of business: A contemporary American craft gallery carrying only quality work by American artists in various media. Featuring works for both men and women, home or office.
Types of products: Hand made items only
Categories: Fine crafts, wearable art, jewelry, wooden crafts, paper products, stained glass items, needlework crafts, hand blown glass items, home decor, pottery/ceramics, table linens
Price range: $50-100
Business policy: We buy crafts outright.
Buys: From the craftspeople who query us if we like their work and it fits our theme; at wholesale shows for hand crafted items; from reps or craft brokers.
Advertising/Promotion: Mailing list of customers, store window displays, local newspaper ads, press releases. $10,000-12,000/year budget.
Application process: Queries are accepted from local/regional and out-of-town craftspeople. For consideration, provide catalog/promotional materials, written description of work, price list.

SIGNET GALLERY

Penny Bosworth
212 Fifth St. NE, P.O. Box 753
Charlottesville, VA 22902
Phone/Fax: (804)296-6463
In business since: 1979
Type of business: Gallery
Description of business: Siget Gallery represents the work of 300 of this country's foremost jewelers, clothing designers, potters, woodworkers and glass blowers. The collection is wide and varied. The *New York Times* said " . . .where craft becomes art," *The Washington Post* " . . . don't miss Signet Gallery."
Types of products: Handmade items only.
Categories: Fine crafts, wearable art, jewelry, hand blown glass items, pottery/ceramics, leather crafts
Price range: $10-5,000
Business policy: We buy crafts outright.
Buys: From the craftspeople who query us if we like their work and it fits our theme; at wholesale shows for hand-crafted items; at retail craft shows.
Advertising/Promotion: TV, visitor's guides, newspaper and direct mail. Budget varies.
Application process: Queries are accepted. For consideration, provide photos or slides, SASE.
Additional information: Store hours are M-Sat, 11-5

SILVER WORKS & MORE

Cara and Jim Connelly
715 Massachusetts St.
Lawrence, KS 66044
Phone: (913)842-1460
In business since: 1985
Type of business: Gallery
Description of business: A gallery of fine jewelry and crafts. Emphasizes quality and good designs.
Types of products: Handmade items only.
Categories: Fine crafts, jewelry, wooden crafts, paper products, hand blown glass items, pottery/ceramics
More about products: Jewelry is gold, sterling silver and mixed metal.
Price range: $10-3,000
Business policy: We buy crafts outright and take work on consignment.

Buys: From the craftspeople who query us if we like their work and it fits our theme; at wholesale shows for hand crafted items.
Advertising/Promotion: Direct mail, TV (area), local newspaper. $3,000-5,000/year budget (depends on show schedule)
Special programs: Group shows: ceramic box show; metal show of 3 different metalsmiths; jewelers graduating from University of Kansas
Application process: Queries are accepted from local/regional and out-of-town craftsepeople. Out-of-town craftspeople call and set up appointments. For consideration, provide photos or slides (5-10), written description of work, SASE.

SKERA GALLERY

Harriet Rogers
221 Main St.
Northampton, MA 01060
Phone: (413)586-4563
In business since: 1974
Type of business: Gallery
Description of business: Skera Gallery celebrates the uniqueness of American handcraft. We specialize in hand woven, dyed and pieced clothing and fabrics. We are one of the many fine craft galleries of Northampton.
Types of products: Handmade items only.
Categories: Fine crafts, wearable art, jewelry, wooden crafts, paper products, stained glass items, hand blown glass items, home decor, dolls/stuffed animals/toys, pottery/ceramics, sculpture
Price range: $3-12,000
Business policy: We buy crafts outright, take work on consignment and commission work from craftspeople.
Buys: From the craftspeople who query us if we like their work and it fits our theme; at wholesale shows for hand crafted items; at wholesale gift shows; at retail craft shows; from reps or craft brokers
Advertising/Promotion: Local newspaper, direct mail, *American Craft Magazine*, TV, radio. $10,000/year budget.
Special programs: 4-5 one person or

theme exhibits per year; also fashion shows
Application process: Queries are accepted from local/regional and out-of-town craftspeople. Call ahead for appointment. For consideration, provide photos (5-6), catalog/promotional materials, SASE.

THE SOCIETY OF ARTS & CRAFTS

Beth Ann Gerstein
175 Newbury St.
Boston, MA 02116
Phone: (617)266-1810
Fax: (617)266-5654
In business since: 1897
Type of business: Gallery
Types of products: Handmade items only.
Categories: Fine crafts, wearable art, jewelry, wooden crafts, paper products, stained glass items, needlework crafts, hand blown glass items, pottery/ceramics, baskets, sculpture
Price range: $2-20,000
Business policy: We take work on consignment and commission work from craftspeople.
Buys: From the craftspeople who query us if we like their work and it fits our theme; at wholesale shows for hand crafted items; at retail craft shows
Advertising/Promotion: *Gallery Guide, Art New England, Penorama, Quick Guide,* mailing list
Special programs: Offers outreach programs for Boston public school students, cash grants to craft artists, lectures, symposium, artist slide registry for furniture artists, video library and annual exhibits.
Application process: Queries are accepted from local/regional and out-of-town craftspeople. For consideration, provide photos or slides (10-20), catalog/promotional materials, written description of work, résumé.
Additional information: The mission of the Society of Arts & Crafts is to support excellence in crafts by encouraging diversity in the creation, collection and conservation of the work of craft artists and by educating and promoting public appreciation of fine craftsmanship.

THE SOFT TOUCH ARTISTS COLLECTIVE GALLERY

Robin Lewis
1580 Haight St.
San Francisco, CA 94121
Phone: (415)863-3279
Fax: (415)695-0243
In business since: 1975
Type of business: Retail store selling hand crafted items and gallery
Description of business: The Soft Touch is an artist owned collective store and gallery supporting and encouraging local artists. Nestled in the Haight Ashbury for 20 years, we are Bay Area artists creating wearable art, soft sculpture, unusual clothing, unique jewelry and clocks, and delightful accessories and miniatures to amuse ourselves and you. It's a gallery for women and men and children of all ages.
Types of products: Handmade items only.
Categories: Fine crafts, wearable art, jewelry, miniatures, paper products, stained glass items, hand blown glass items, home decor, dolls/stuffed animals/toys, recycled crafts, sculpture, hats, costumes, lots of different clocks, scarves, purses, gloves, paintings, photography, etc.
Price range: $10-1,000
Business policy: We take work on consignment.
Buys: From craftspeople who query us if we like their work and it fits our theme; at wholesale shows for hand crafted items; at retail craft shows
Advertising/Promotion: Word of mouth, local papers, college papers, campus bulletin boards, local art shops, cafés, mailing list of great customers. Very limited budget.
Special programs: Monthly shows by specific artists in upstairs gallery and sometimes have group shows with a call to other artists
Application process: Queries are accepted from local/regional and out-of-town craftspeople. Helps if they know a person in the area to deal with their inventory or are committed to be on top of keeping inventory current. For consideration, provide photos or slides, catalog/promotional materials, written description of work.

Additional information: Although we are predominually a Bay Area local artist shop we make exceptions for wonderful work we really like. So check us out.

SONGBIRD SILVERWORKS

Norman Saunders
300 N. First Ave.
Sandpoint, ID 83864
Phone: (208)265-4313
In business since: 1983
Type of business: Retail store selling hand crafted items
Description of business: We buy hand-made silverwork, leatherwork, moccasins, knives, horse track, etc. at wholesale.
Types of products: Handmade items only.
Categories: Jewelry, leather crafts
Price range: $10-500
Business policy: We buy crafts outright, take work on consignment and commission work from craftspeople.
Buys: From the craftspeople who query us if we like their work and it fits our theme; from reps or craft brokers
Application process: Queries are accepted from local/regional and out-of-town craftspeople. For consideration, provide photos or slides (3-5), sample of work, written description of work.
Additional information: Sandpoint is a heavy year-round tourist town—lake in summer, skiing in winter. It is located 60 miles from the Canadian border.

STARSHINE

Betsy Wheeler
362 Boston Post Rd.
Westbrook, CT 06498
Phone: (860)399-5149
In business since: 1981
Type of business: Gallery
Description of business: Starshine is a handcraft gallery featuring the work of roughly 30 different artists from throughout the US. Owner and leather designer Betsy Wheeler works on the premises. The main theme of the gallery focuses on the Southwest.
Types of products: Handmade items only.
Categories: Wearable art, jewelry, pottery/ceramics, baskets, sculpture

Price range: $1.50-800
Business policy: We buy crafts outright and take work on consignment.
Buys: From the craftspeople who query us if we like their work and it fits our theme.
Advertising/Promotion: Yellow Pages, newspapers
Special programs: Periodic 1 or 2 person shows
Application process: Queries are accepted from local/regional and out-of-town craftspeople. For consideration, provide photos or slides (5), catalog/promotional materials, written description of work.

STEAMBOAT ART COMPANY

Julie Orton and Deanel Sandoval
903 Lincoln Ave.
Steamboat Springs, CO 80487
Phone: (970)879-3383
Fax: (970)879-5818
In business since: 1978
Description of business: Retail store selling hand crafted items
Type of business: The Steamboat Art Company showcases handcrafts from all around the world, specializing in crafts and decorative accessories from the Rocky Mountain region. The selection is electic in style.
Types of products: Handmade items and cards, bath products, music, limited edition prints, candles, throws.
Categories: Fine crafts, jewelry, wooden crafts, paper products, stained glass items, hand blown glass items, home decor, pottery, nature crafts/floral, leather crafts, baskets, recycled crafts, sculpture
More about products: Looking for products with a regional feel, reflecting the Rocky Mountain area and lifestyle. Products reflecting the natural environment are desirable.
Price range: $5-5,000
Business policy: We buy crafts outright and take work on consignment.
Buys: From the craftspeople who query us if we like their work and it fits our theme; at wholesale shows for hand crafted items; at wholesale gift shows; at retail craft shows; from reps or craft brokers
Advertising/Promotion: Local news-

paper, radio, magazine, tourist guides. $20,000/year budget.

Application process: Queries are accepted from local/regional and out-of-town craftspeople. For consideration, provide photos or slides, catalog/promotional materials.

Additional information: We are a seasonal business with strong traffic December through March and June through September. Store hours M-Sat 10-10, Sun 10-9.

THE STEIN GALLERY

Anne Stein
20 Milk St.
Portland, ME 04101
Phone: (207)772-9072
In business since: 1974
Type of business: Gallery
Description of business: Feature the work of 75 emerging and nationally recognized comtemporary American glass artists creating dramatic one-of-a-kind pieces as well as eclectic functional and decorative work.
Types of products: Handmade items only.
Categories: Jewelry, hand blown glass items
Price range: $50-7,500
Business policy: We buy crafts outright and take work on consignment.
Buys: From the craftspeople who query us if we like their work and it fits our theme; at wholesale shows for hand crafted items; through slide registries; at retail craft shows; at studio visits
Advertising/Promotion: American Craft Magazine and *Glass Magazine,* local media and direct mail
Application process: Queries are accepted from local/regional and out-of-town craftspeople. For consideration, provide photos or slides (at least 3), catalog/promotional materials, résumé, background, price information.

STUDIO V

Jack Garber
672 N. Dearborn
Chicago, IL 60610
Phone: (312)440-1937
E-mail: studiov@crome.com
Website: http://www.crome.com/studiov
In business since: 1975

Type of business: Retail store selling hand crafted items
Description of business: Studio V is an eclectic gift shop specializing in 20th century design items. Some themes are: art glass, airplanes, garden, lamps, scarves, hats & ties, cufflinks, martinis, books and so much more.
Types of products: Handmade items and antique telephones, antique jewelry, books.
Categories: Wearable art, jewelry, wooden crafts, stained glass items, hand blown glass items, home decor, dolls/stuffed animals/toys, sculpture, cast and worked metal
More about products: Fun and/or useful are the key ideas
Price range: $6-1,250
Business policy: We buy crafts outright and take work on consignment.
Buys: From the craftspeople who query us if we like their work and it fits our theme; at wholesale shows for hand crafted items; at wholesale gift shows
Application process: Queries are accepted from local/regional and out-of-town craftspeople. Call for appointment. For consideration, provide photos, sample of work, catalog/promotional materials, written description of work.

SUN UP, INC.

Nancy S. Klotz
95 Watch Hill Rd.
Westerly, RI 02891
Phone: (401)596-0800; (401)596-8464
Fax: (401)596-8421
In business since: 1977
Type of business: Gallery
Description of business: Sun Up Gallery of fine American crafts and clothing is located in scenic Rhode Island along a waterfront. Sun Up is known for the best Rhode Island has to offer in pottery, jewelry and fashion foward clothing for women with an artistic flair. Sun Up has recently added a home furnishings cottage, making the one stop shopping experience complete.
Types of products: Handmade items and women's clothing.
Categories: Fine crafts, wearable art, jewelry, wooden crafts, stained glass items, hand blown glass items, home

decor, dolls/stuffed animals/toys, pottery/ceramics, recycled crafts, sculpture
More about products: Always looking for outdoor sculptures, clothing, jewelry and lamps
Price range: $5-5,000
Business policy: We buy crafts outright, take work on consignment and commission work from craftspeople.
Buys: At wholesale shows for hand crafted items; at wholesale gift shows; at wholesale apparel shows; at retail craft shows
Advertising/Promotion: R.I. Monthly Magazine, New London Day, Conn Magazine, Providence Journal, Mystic Coast and Country Magazine, direct mail. $50,000/year budget.
Special programs: Sculpture show, clock show, fashion show, trunk show
Application process: Queries are accepted from local/regional and out-of-town craftspeople. No phone queries please. For consideration, provide photos or slides (10), catalog/promotional materials, written description of work.
Additional information: Sun Up was incorporated as a single destination business. Gardens, extensive inventory, friendly service, something for everyone.

THE SUQ

Denise Browning
1155 E. 58th St.
Chicago, IL 60637
Phone: (312)702-9509; (312)702-9510
Fax: (312)702-9853
E-mail: dbrowning1@uchicago.edu
In business since: 1967
Type of business: Museum gift shop
Description of business: Museum shop that deals with crafts from ancient Near East, Egypt, Mesopotamia, Israel, Syria, Turkey, Afghanisan and Central Asia. Crafters create exact reproductions or use same technique or materials as ancient Near East, for example, lapis, carnelian, malachite, myrrh, filigree, granulation, pottery slips, basket weaving and textiles.
Types of products: Handmade items and books, games, incense, reproductions from molds.
Categories: Fine crafts, wearable art,

jewelry, wooden crafts, paper products, needlework crafts, hand blown glass items, home decor, figurines, pottery/ceramics, leather crafts, baskets, sculpture

Price range: 50¢-$150

Business policy: We buy crafts outright.

Buys: At wholesale shows for hand crafted items; at wholesale gift shows

Special programs: We have 2-3 exhibitions a year.

Application process: Queries are accepted from local/regional and out-of-town craftspeople. For consideration, provide photos or slides, sample of work.

Additional information: The store is staffed by volunteers. The museum is an academic institution connected with the University of Chicago.

SUSAN'S CORNER

Susan Kute
1581 Bardstown Rd.
Louisville, KY 40205
Phone: (502)458-1712
In business since: 1986
Type of business: Retail store selling hand crafted items
Description of business: Specialize in unique gift items and hand made Kentucky crafts. The shop is located in one of Louisville's most unusual shopping and restaurant districts, and is open year-round. Although our space is limited, we have a wide assortment of gifts. Basket supplies and classes are also available.
Types of products: Handmade items and antiques and collectibles, table lace, flags and poles and gift bags.
Categories: Fine crafts, wearable art, wooden crafts, stained glass items, needlework crafts, home decor, dolls/stuffed animals/toys, pottery/ceramics, nature crafts/floral, baskets, recycled crafts
Price range: $1-75
Business policy: We take work on consignment and when sold, pay crafter monthly
Buys: From the craftspeople who query us if we like their work and it fits our theme; at wholesale gift shows
Advertising/Promotion: Direct mail to previous customers, in high-traffic

storefront and participate in local business promotions. Very minimal budget.
Special programs: Bardstown Road Aglow is a special area promotion on the first Saturday of December. We have demonstrations and music and refreshments.
Application process: Queries are accepted from local/regional craftspeople only. For consideration, provide sample of work in person on Thursdays only.

SUSI'S A GALLERY FOR CHILDREN

Susi Cooper
348 Huron Ave.
Cambridge, MA 02138
Phone: (617)876-7874
Fax: (617)969-3872
E-mail: susi@susigallery.com
In business since: 1989
Type of business: Gallery
Description of business: Susi's offers a variety of whimsical, colorful art, including furniture, clocks, mobiles, clothing, paintings, prints and frames. All the work shown is handmade by artists from all over the country.
Types of products: Handmade items only.
Categories: Fine crafts, wearable art, jewelry, wooden crafts, home decor, dolls/stuffed animals/toys, pottery/ceramics, recycled crafts
More about products: Always interested in looking at new artwork. Our only requirement is the work has color, whimsy and is made to last.
Price range: $10-1,000
Business policy: We take work on consignment.
Buys: From the craftspeople who query us if we like their work and it fits our theme; at wholesale shows for hand crafted items
Advertising/Promotion: Mailing list
Special programs: We have 4 shows per year.
Application process: Queries are accepted from local/regional and out-of-town craftspeople. For consideration, provide photos or slides, catalog/promotional materials, written description of work.

TATIANA LTD.

Wendy Queen
Providence Church
Glenelg, MD 21737
Phone: (410)442-1144; (301)854-6289
Fax: (301)854-5291
In business since: 1972
Type of business: Gallery
Description of business: Fine arts gallery and studio of artist, Tatiana, in a historic American gothic church building.
Types of products: Handmade items only.
Categories: Fine crafts, jewelry, hand blown glass items
Price range: $20-3,000
Business policy: We buy crafts outright and commission work from craftspeople.
Buys: From the craftspeople who query us if we like their work and it fits our theme; at wholesale shows for hand crafted items; at wholesale gift shows; from reps or craft brokers
Advertising/Promotion: Direct mail, *Galleries Magazine, Smithsonian Craft Show Magazine,* local symphony program. $19,000/year budget.
Special programs: Valentine's Day Show, May Event (theme show), seconds sale in August, holiday champagne opening weekend before Thanksgiving
Application process: Queries are accepted from local/regional and out-of-town craftspeople. Visit the gallery and be certain whether it's appropriate. Then make an appointment to show samples of work.
Additional information: My own ceramic pieces are often large with gold and platinum lusters. My own work is represented, in addition to my own gallery, in seven major showrooms across the country. Located 35 minutes from downtown Baltimore. Store hours Sat-Sun 11-5, weekdays by appointment.

TELLURIDE GALLERY OF FINE ART

Will Thompson
Box 1900
Telluride, CO 81435
Phone: (970)728-3300
In business since: 1985

Type of business: Gallery

Description of business: Known for its excellence in fine art and contemporary craft. The Smithsonian and Seattle Art Museum have borrowed work for their exhibitions from this gallery. We also feature work by contemporary jewelry designers who are the vanguard of the art jewelry movement.

Types of products: Handmade items only.

Categories: Fine crafts, wearable art, jewelry

Price range: $22-16,000

Business policy: We take work on consignment.

Buys: Usually from SOFA show or contacts from museum shows.

Advertising/Promotion: *Telluride Magazine, Metalsmith Magazine, Ornament Magazine, American Craft Magazine* and *Art and Antiques Magazine*

Application process: Queries are accepted from local/regional and out-of-town craftspeople. For consideration, provide photos or slides, catalog/promotional materials, written description of work, SASE if craftsperson wishes materials to be returned.

TERRY'S COUNTRY SHOPPE

Terry
1049 Queen St.
Southington, CT 06489
Phone: (860)793-9388
Fax: (860)793-9001
In business since: 1983
Type of business: Retail store selling hand crafted items and furniture

Description of business: Terry's features American-made gifts, home furnishing, decorating accessories, many one-of-a-kind hand made gifts and collectibles. Terry's ships worldwide.

Types of products: Handmade items and furniture, collectibles

Categories: Fine crafts, miniatures/dollhouses, wooden crafts, needlework crafts, home decor, figurines, dolls/stuffed animals/toys, pottery/ceramics, nature crafts/floral, baskets

More about products: Country, no jewelry

Price range: $1-1,000

Business policy: We buy crafts outright.

Buys: From the craftspeople who query us if we like their work and it fits our theme; at wholesale shows for hand crafted items; at wholesale gift shows; at wholesale toy, doll and teddy bear shows; at retail craft shows; from reps or craft brokers

Advertising/Promotion: Radio, TV, newspapers. $35,000/year budget.

Application process: Queries are accepted from local/regional and out-of-town craftspeople. Call for appointment. For consideration, provide sample of work, catalog/promotional materials, written description of work.

TO LIFE!

Amy Hoffmann
36 S. Wabash Ave., Suite 604
Chicago, IL 60603
Phone: (312)855-9220
Fax: (312)855-0994
In business since: 1988
Type of business: Gallery

Description of business: There are two "To Life!" craft galleries in the heart of downtown Chicago. Both feature full media in themes related to life, music and good living. Objects are both functional and decorative, including whimsical. Lots of jewelry with flora and fauna themes. These are upbeat, fun environments, with merchandise to match and enhance the feel!

Types of products: Handmade items only.

Categories: Fine crafts, jewelry, wooden crafts, paper products, stained glass items, hand blown glass items, home decor, figurines, dolls/stuffed animals/toys, pottery/ceramics, nature crafts/floral, leather crafts, sculpture

Price range: $10-500

Business policy: We buy crafts outright.

Buys: From the craftspeople who query us if we like their work and it fits our theme; at wholesale shows for hand crafted items; at wholesale gift shows; at retail craft shows; from reps or craft brokers

Advertising/Promotion: Chamber of Commerce and hotel visitor's guides; direct mailings to customers 6 times per year; some newspaper and radio advertising. 2% of sales/year budget.

Special programs: Features an "artist of the month" with promotional discount.

Application process: Queries are accepted from local/regional and out-of-town craftspeople. For consideration, provide photos or slides, catalog/promotional materials, sample of work, written description of work, price information (wholesale) and artist background.

Additional information: To Life! has 2 locations in downtown Chicago: 333 N. Michigan Ave. and 224 S. Michigan Ave. (across from the Art Institute).

TOMLINSON CRAFT COLLECTION I

Ginny Tomlinson, Anne Dawson and Beth Roder
711 W. 40th St.
Baltimore, MD 21211
Phone: (410)338-1572
Fax: (410)467-7029
In business since: 1972
Type of business: Retail store selling hand crafted items

Description of business: Contemporary American craft store

Categories: Fine crafts, jewelry, wooden crafts, paper products, stained glass items, hand blown glass items, pottery/ceramics, leather crafts, sculpture

More about products: Contemporary crafts, not country

Price range: $5-1,000

Business policy: We buy crafts outright and take work on consignment for special exhibitions.

Buys: From the craftspeople who query us if we like their work and it fits our theme; at wholesale shows for hand crafted items; at wholesale gift shows; at retail craft shows; from reps or craft brokers

Advertising/Promotion: Radio, newspaper, direct mail

Application process: Queries are accepted from local/regional and out-of-town craftspeople. For consideration, provide photos or slides, sample of work, price list.

Additional information: Please see the listing below for a second location.

TOMLINSON CRAFT COLLECTION II

435 York Rd.
Towson Commons
Towson, MD 21204
Phone: (410)823-1297
Type of business: Retail store selling hand crafted items
Additional information: Please see the listing above for more information.

TOPS

Robert and Dawn Walker
23410 Civic Center Way C-1
Malibu, CA 90265
Phone: (310)456-8677; (310)456-6002
Fax: (310)456-6738
In business since: 1983
Type of business: Retail store selling hand crafted items
Description of business: Tops is a functional art emporium with a magical, colorful, whimsical atmosphere. We feature jewelry and a wide range of creative home furnishing, such as lamps, clocks, mirrors, beds, tables, chairs, candlesticks, tableware, rugs, etc. Will occasionally accept work whose only function is to evoke awe and delight.
Types of products: Handmade items and manufactured gift cards and frames
Categories: Fine crafts, jewelry, wooden crafts, paper products, stained glass items, hand blown glass items, home decor, dolls/stuffed animals/toys, pottery/ceramics, leather crafts, baskets, recycled crafts, sculpture
Price range: $10-10,000
Business policy: We take work on consignment and commission work from craftspeople for special orders.
Advertising/Promotion: Local advertising
Application process: Queries are accepted from local/regional and out-of-town craftspeople. Will pay shipping back if items are not sold. For consideration, provide photos or slides, catalog/promotional materials, sample of work, written description of work, SASE.

A TOUCH OF EARTH

Lianne Lurie and Paul Pittman
6580 Richmond Rd.
Williamsburg, VA 23188
Phone: (757)565-0425
In business since: 1977

Type of business: Gallery
Description of business: This American craft gallery offers a collection of fine crafts and art by regional as well as nationally prominent contemporary working American artists.
Types of products: Handmade items and photography and watercolors
Categories: Fine crafts, wearable art, jewelry, wooden crafts, paper products, stained glass items, hand blown glass items, pottery/ceramics
More about products: The store's focus is on hand crafted pottery.
Price range: $5-1,000
Business policy: We buy crafts outright and take work on consignment.
Buys: From the craftspeople who query us if we like their work and if it fits our theme; at wholesale shows for hand crafted items
Special programs: Feature a different craft person each month throughout the year. In the fall and winter, we have talented local musicians performing on weekends.
Application process: Quries are accepted from local/regional and out-of-town craftspeople.

TRADITIONS

Brenda Oler
18 S. 19th St.
Richmond, IN 47374
Phone: (317)935-0553
In business since: 1987
Type of business: Retail store selling hand crafted items
Description of business: Interior design and gift shop featuring home accessories, unusual gift items and hand crafted items.
Types of products: Handmade items and fabric, wallcoverings
Categories: Fine crafts, wearable art, jewelry, paper products, needlework crafts, home decor, pottery/ceramics, nature crafts/floral, baskets
Business policy: We buy crafts outright and take work on consignment.
Buys: From the craftspeople who query us if we like their work and it fits our theme; at wholesale shows for hand crafted items; at wholesale apparel shows
Advertising/Promotion: Symphony and civic theatre programs, direct mail

Special programs: Decorator Show House
Application process: Queries are accepted from local/regional and out-of-town craftspeople. For consideration, provide catalog/promotional materials, photos, sample of work.

TRIPLE OAK GIFT SHOP

Annalee Hampton
HC 30, Box 95
Pelsor, AR 72856
Phone: (501)294-5290
In business since: 1990
Type of business: Retail store selling hand crafted items
Description of business: Antique craft shop of gifts by Arkansas's foremost craftsmen, including white oak baskets made in the shop
Types of products: Handmade items only.
Categories: Fine crafts, wearable art, wooden crafts, needlework crafts, home decor, furniture
Price range: $1-500
Business policy: We buy crafts outright.
Buys: From the craftspeople who query us if we like their work and it fits our theme; at retail craft shows
Application process: Queries are accepted from local/regional craftspeople only. For consideration, provide photos or slides, sample of work, written description of work.
Additional information: Store hours are M-Sat 8-5 and Sun 1-5:30. Wheelchair accessible; RVs and buses welcome; Visa and MasterCard accepted.

TWINING WEAVERS AND CONTEMPORARY CRAFTS, LTD.

Sally Bachman
135 Paseo Del Pueblo Norte
Taos, NM 87571
Phone: (505)758-9000
Fax: (505)751-3814
In business since: 1978
Type of business: Retail store selling hand crafted items and weaving studio
Description of business: An eclectic collection of contemporary crafts from around the world reflecting our interests in other countries and cultures. Local and regional crafts are also represented, and a portion of our hand-

woven rugs and pillows are provided on the premises.

Types of products: Handmade items only.

Categories: Fine crafts, wearable art, jewelry, wooden crafts, home decor, dolls/stuffed animals/toys, pottery/ceramics, leather crafts, baskets

Price range: $5-3,000

Business policy: We buy crafts outright and take work on consignment.

Buys: From the craftspeople who query us if we like their work and it fits our theme; at wholesale shows for hand crafted items; at wholesale gift shows; at wholesale toy, doll and teddy bear shows; at retail craft shows; from reps or craft brokers

Advertising/Promotion: Customer contact through referrals by local bed & breakfasts

TWIST I

30 NW 23rd Place
Portland, OR 97210
Phone: (503)224-0334
Fax: (503)241-3581
In business since: 1979
Type of business: Gallery
Description of business: Twist is an American craft gallery featuring fine design, art jewelry, furniture and lighting. This exciting and creative shopping experience features found objects, assemblages, neon sculptures, custom gold wedding sets and funky candles.

Types of products: Handmade items only.

Categories: Fine crafts, jewelry, hand blown glass items, pottery/ceramics, recycled crafts, sculpture

Price range: $5-10,000

Business policy: We buy crafts outright and take work on consignment.

Buys: At wholesale shows for hand crafted items; from reps or craft brokers

Advertising/Promotion: Direct mail. $40,000/year budget.

Application process: Queries are accepted from local/regional and out-of-town craftspeole. For consideration, provide photos or slides, sample of work.

Additional information: Please see the listings below for other locations.

TWIST II

700 SW Fifth
Portland, OR 97204
Type of business: Gallery
Description of business: Please see the above listing for more information.

TWIST III

296 E. Fifth Ave. 8-6
Eugene, OR 97401
Type of business: Gallery
Description of business: Please see the above listing for more information.

VERMONT ARTISAN DESIGNS

Greg Worden
106 Main St.
Brattleboro, VT 05301
Phone: (802)257-7044
Fax: (802)257-3049
In business since: 1970
Type of business: Retail store selling hand crafted items and gallery

Description of business: Vermont Artisan Designs is one of Vermont's oldest and largest contemporary craft galleries. The shop and gallery feature the work of more than 300 American craftspeople, most of whom are from Vermont or New England. Potters, jewelers, glassblowers, blacksmiths, woodworkers, fabric artists and fine artists are all featured in a beautiful Main Street setting.

Types of products: Handmade items only.

Categories: Fine crafts, wearable art, jewelry, miniatures/dollhouses, wooden crafts, paper products, stained glass items, hand blown glass items, home decor, dolls/stuffed animals/toys, pottery/ceramics, leather crafts, baskets, sculpture

Price range: $1-5,000

Business policy: We buy crafts outright, take work on consignment and commission work from craftspeople.

Buys: From the craftspeople who query us if we like their work and it fits our theme; at wholesale shows for hand crafted items; at wholesale gift shows; through slide registries; at retail craft shows; from reps or craft brokers

Advertising/Promotion: Local and area newspapers, radio, TV, *American Style*, *Vermont Life*, *Vermont Magazine*, and other regional publications. Budget varies.

Special programs: First Friday of each month includes a reception for artist or craftsperson of the month. Changing exhibits monthly. Bridal registry offered as well as wish list. Personal shopping service available.

Application process: Accepts queries from local/regional and out-of-town craftspeople. For consideration, provide photos or slides (6-12), sample of work, written description of work, artist bio, other places work shows, price, whether or not made by the individual or by others in studio.

Additional information: Open 7 days a week.

THE VERMONT SHOP

Robin and Thomas Burke
P.O. Box 2535
Edgartown, MA 02539
Phone: (508)627-8448
In business since: 1980
Type of business: Retail store selling hand crafted items

Description of business: The Vermont Shop was created to market the fine work of Vermont artisans on the island of Martha's Vineyard. Substantial annual growth, accelerated by a 1986 move to larger retail space, has resulted in a current offering of the work of over 250 of America's top craftspeople, from coast-to-coast and border-to-border. As one of Edgartown's finest gift shops, the emphasis continues on unique handmade products by individual artisans. Today, at its charming location on the corner of Winter and Summer streets in Edgartown on the island of Martha's Vineyard, the Vermont Shop enjoys a reputation for integrity from both its ever expanding customer base and the creative, talented artisans who make the lovely things offered in the store.

Types of products: Handmade items and functional and decorative gifts for the home.

Categories: Fine crafts, jewelry, wooden crafts, stained glass items, hand blown glass items, home decor, figurines, pottery/ceramics, leather crafts, sculpture

Price range: $20-400

Business policy: We buy crafts outright.

Buys: At wholesale shows for hand crafted items; at wholesale gift shows; from reps or craft brokers

Advertising/Promotion: Local newspapers

Application process: Queries are accepted from local/reginal and out-of-town craftspeople. For consideration, provide photos or slides, catalog/promotional materials, written description of work, price list.

VESPERMANN GALLERY

Seranda Vespermann and Tracey Lofton
2140 Peachtree Rd.
Atlanta, GA 30309
Phone: (404)350-9698
Fax: (404)350-0046
In business since: 1984
Type of business: Gallery
Description of business: A contemporary gallery specializing in glass artists from throughout the country. The gallery also features custom corporate gifts designed and fabricated by glass artists throughout the country.

Types of products: Handmade items only.

Categories: Fine crafts, wearable art, jewelry, hand blown glass items, sculpture

More about products: Specialize in glass: perfume bottles, paperweights, jewelry, vases, platters, sculptures, salt and pepper shakers, etc.

Price range: $20-20,000

Business policy: We buy crafts outright, take work on consignment and commission work from craftspeople.

Buys: From the craftspeople who query us if we like their work and it fits our theme; at wholesale shows for hand crafted items

Advertising/Promotion: Local magazines and newspapers, craft magazines, direct mail

Special programs: 6 shows a year including an annual jewelry show, as well as an annual perfume bottle show

Application process: Queries are accepted from local/regional and out-of-town craftspeople. For consideration, provide photos or slides, catalog/promotional mateials, résumé.

A VICTORIAN GARDEN

Kelly Bradley
618 Silas Deane Hwy.
Wethersfield, CT 06109
Phone: (860)563-8414
Fax: (860)563-1647
E-mail: bradlk@torrington.com
In business since: 1988
Type of business: Retail store selling hand crafted items
Description of business: A full service florist offering angels, flowers, gifts, gargoyles and more.

Types of products: Handmade items and flowers/arrangements, statuary, sun dials

Categories: Fine crafts, stained glass items, hand blown glass items

More about products: No "country" crafts

Price range: $10 and up

Business policy: We take work on consignment.

Buys: From the craftspeople who query us if we like their work and it fits our theme; at wholesale shows for hand crafted items; at wholesale gift shows; at retail craft shows

Advertising/Promotion: Newspaper, radio, direct mail. 6% of gross sales/year budget.

Application process: Queries are accepted from local/regional and out-of-town craftspeople. For consideration, provide photos or slides, written description of work.

Additional information: Signings and mini art shows are welcomed.

VISTA FINE CRAFTS

Sherrie Posternak
P.O. Box 2034
Middleburg, VA 20118
Phone: (540)687-3317
In business since: 1988
Type of business: Retail store selling hand crafted items
Description of business: Contemporary American hand crafted gifts in all media for women, men, children, the home and garden.

Types of products: Handmade items and acoustic music CDs and tapes

Categories: Fine crafts, wearable art, jewelry, wooden crafts, hand blown glass items, home decor, dolls/stuffed animals/toys, pottery/ceramics

Price range: $1.50-300

Business policy: We buy crafts outright and take work on consignment.

Buys: From the craftspeople who query us if we like their work and it fits our theme; at wholesale shows for hand crafted items; at wholesale gift shows; from reps or craft brokers

Advertising/Promotion: Direct mail postcards and newsletters, ads in regional and local publications. $5,000/year budget.

Special programs: 2 yearly theme exhibits

Application process: Queries are accepted from local/regional and out-of-town craftspeople. Call for appointment or to receive information. For consideration, provide photos or slides (5-10), catalog/promotional materials.

MARALYN WILSON GALLERY, INC.

Maralyn Wilson and Cathleen Cooper
2010 Cahaba Rd.
Birmingham, AL 35223
Phone: (205)879-0582
Fax: (205)870-3022
In business since: 1973
Type of business: Gallery
Description of business: The Maralyn Wilson Gallery, just over the hill from downtown Birmingham in English Village, continues to provide fine art, crafts, custom framing and art consulting to Birmingham as it has for over twenty years. Today, the Gallery has two distinct atmospheres: the White Gallery which features fine crafts, and the Black Gallery which displays paintings and sculpture. The Gallery provides conservation framing and art consulting to private collectors and corporations. In selecting art for corporations, Maralyn and her staff choose pieces that best convey a company's image.

Types of products: Handmade items and cards and stationery, gourmet foods.

Categories: Fine crafts, wearable art, jewelry, wooden crafts, paper products, hand blown glass items, home decor, pottery/ceramics, sculpture

Price range: $2-25,000

Business policy: We buy crafts outright, take work on consignment and commission work from craftspeople.

Buys: From the craftspeople who query us if we like their work and it fits our theme; at wholesale shows for hand crafted items; through slide registries

Advertising/Promotion: Local publications and newspapers

Special programs: Shows every 6 weeks. Typically, we are devoted to a fixed group of regular artists.

Application process: Queries are accepted from local/regional and out-of-town craftspeople. For consideration, provide photos or slides (5), catalog/promotional materials. Do not bring samples of work to the gallery unless invited.

WINDOW SHOPPING, INC.

Bill Nichols
433 Albert Ave.
Shreveport, LA 71105
Phone: (318)869-4527
Fax: (318)747-8900
In business since: 1976
Type of business: Retail store selling handcrafted items
Description of business: A collection of hard-to-find, one-of-a-kind, unique hand crafted gifts. Featured crafts are wood, glass (both leaded and blown) and pottery. Corporate accounts welcomed.
Types of products: Handmade items only.
Categories: Fine crafts, wearable art, jewelry, wooden crafts, paper products, stained glass items, hand blown glass items, home decor, pottery/ceramics, nature crafts/floral, leather crafts, baskets, sculpture
More about products: Large assortment of blown glass holiday ornaments
Price range: $20-200
Business policy: We buy crafts outright.
Buys: From the craftspeople who query us if we like their work and it fits our theme; at wholesale shows for hand crafted items; at wholesale gift shows; at retail craft shows
Advertising/Promotion: Direct mail, visitors guides, crafts magazines. $2,000/year budget.
Application process: Queries are accepted from local/regional and out-of-town craftspeople. For consideration, provide catalog/promotional materials.

Additional information: We are the area's most experienced dealer in fine crafts.

WORCESTER CENTER FOR CRAFTS' GALLERY GIFT STORE

Melissa Figuerido
25 Sagamore Rd.
Worcester, MA 01605
Phone: (508)753-8183, ext. 3005
Fax: (508)797-5626
Type of business: Gallery, gift shop
Description of business: The Gallery Gift Store has been a feature of the Worcester Center for crafts for over 35 years. In that time, the management has consistently strived to maintain the highest qulaity of crafts. We are constatnly searching for new and different craftspeople to add to our client list. The setting of the Gallery Gift Store enhances the appearance of crafts displayed on pedestals and shelving in this 3,500 sq. ft. space. Full-spectrum lighting accurately shows the colors of the items. The Gallery Gift Store atracts sophisticated craft-knowledgeable clientele throughout the year, especially during the May and November craft fairs and during the holidays.
Types of products: Handmade items only.
Categories: Fine crafts, wearable art, jewelry, paper products, stained glass items, hand blown glass items, pottery/ceramics
More about products: All products are original, handmade in US
Price range: $5-300
Business policy: We buy crafts outright.
Buys: From the craftspeople who query us if we like their work and it fits our theme; at wholesale shows for hand crafted items; at wholesale gift shows; from reps or craft brokers
Advertising/Promotion: Local paper, *Worcester Magazine*; mailings: postcards, fliers. $10,000/year budget.
Application process: Queries are accepted from local/regional and out-of-town craftspeople. For consideration, call or provide photos or slides, written description of work.

THE WORKS GALLERY

Liz Duggan, Ruth Snyderman and Bruce Hoffman
303 Cherry St.
Philadelphia, PA 19106
Phone: (215)922-7775
Fax: (215)238-9351
In business since: 1965
Type of business: Gallery
Description of business: Our goal is to supply to the public the finest array of crafts available today. Nothing less than excellence in design and craftsmanship is exhibited in the gallery. The focus is on jewelry, ceramics and fiber, however glass, furniture, wood and mixed media are also represented.
Types of products: Handmade items only.
Categories: Fine crafts, jewelry, hand blown glass items, pottery/ceramics, baskets, sculpture
Price range: $50 and up
Business policy: We buy crafts outright, take work on consignment and commission work from craftspeople.
Buys: From the craftspeople who query us if we like their work and it fits our theme; at wholesale shows for hand crafted items; at retail craft shows
Advertising/Promotion: Mailings, advertise in *American Craft, Metalsmith, Ornament, American Ceramics*
Special programs: There are 5 major exhibitions annually.
Application process: Queries are accepted from local/regional and out-of-town craftspeople. Artist is responsible for all shipping and insurance to the gallery. For consideration, provide slides (10-20), catalog/promotional materials, written description of work, bigoraphy, material description, wholesale price list, special shipping needs.

WORLDLY GOODS

Vinc Mellen and Marty Choboy
37 Congress St.
Portsmouth, NH 03801
Phone: (603)436-9311
Fax: (603)427-0081
In business since: 1986
Type of business: Retail store selling hand crafted items
Description of business: A retail store specializing in contemporary and tra-

ditional American hand crafts with a concentration on functional and whimsical pieces. The inventory consists of pottery, glassware, woodworking, jewelry and everything in between.

Types of products: Handmade items only.

Categories: Fine crafts, wearable art, jewelry, wooden crafts, paper products, hand blown glass items, home decor, dolls/stuffed animals/toys, pottery/ceramics, baskets

Price range: $10-500

Business policy: We buy crafts outright.

Buys: From craftspeople who query us if we like their work and it fits our theme; at wholesale shows for hand crafted items; at wholesale gift shows; at retail craft shows; from reps or craft brokers

Advertising/Promotion: Locally in print media. $1,500/year budget.

Special programs: Two large, month long sales that generate heavy traffic and sales during off seasons.

Application process: Queries are accepted from local/regional and out-of-town craftspeople. N/30 method of payment. For consideration, provide catalog/promotional materials, written description of work.

ZEPHYR GALLERY, INC.

Toby Quitel

19 N. Main St.

New Hope, PA 18938

Phone: (215)862-9765; (215)794-8771

In business since: 1991

Type of business: Gallery

Description of business: Whimsical, creative, colorful galleries featuring art jewelry, art to wear, functional and decorative objects of cut in glass ceramics, wood and metal.

Types of products: Handmade items only.

Categories: Fine crafts, wearable art, jewelry, wooden crafts, hand blown glass items, home decor, dolls, pottery/ceramics, recycled crafts

Price range: $25-2,00

Business policy: We buy crafts outright and take work on consignment.

Buys: From the craftspeople who query us if we like their work and it fits our

theme; at wholesale shows for hand crafted items; at wholesale gift shows; at wholesale apparel shows

Advertising/Promotion: Newspapers

Special programs: Seasonal trunk shows, craft demonstrations

Application process: Queries are accepted from local/regional and out-of-town craftspeople. For consideration, provide catalog/promotional materials, photos, sample of work, written description of work.

Additional information: Second location at Peddler's Village, Lahasker, PA.

CRAFT BROKERS AND REPRESENTATIVES

ACCESSORY RESOURCE GALLERY/ ACCESSORY BRAINSTORMS

Joan Lefkowitz

7 W. 36th St.

New York, NY 10018

Phone: (212)971-7300

Fax: (212)714-2881

In business since: 1983

Area: Nationwide

Sells: To retail stores; to catalogs and other direct mail markets

Description of services: They are a permanent NY showroom representing production jewelry and fashion accessory lines and inventions.

Types of products: Will represent more than one craftsperson selling the same type of item.

Categories: Wearable art, jewelry, stained glass items, leather crafts, recycled crafts, fashion accessories and costume jewelry

Price range: $2-40

Advertising: Advertising to the trade, telephone solicitation, mailers.

Cost/Payment policies: Commission, not paid up front. Paid by manufacturer.

For consideration: Provide catalog/promotional materials and photos.

AMERICRAFT, THE GIFT BROKERS, INC.

Robert Cabral

Stillwaters, 210 Lockes Village Rd.

Wendell, MA 01379

Phone: (508)544-7330

Fax: (508)544-2771

E-mail: 73672.307@compuserve.com

In business since: 1978

Area: Nationwide

Sells: To catalogs and other direct mail markets, at wholesale gift shows

Description of services: Americraft is a link between production craft/manufacturers and the mail order catalog industry. Using a proprietary information management system, products are promoted directly to key catalog buyers. We are especially successful with personalized merchandise and products with a strong folklore or historical context. Americraft is not for start ups, production must exceed $1,000/week of selected items.

Types of products: Hand crafted items and sandblasted slate, stone, ceramics; lasered wood, glass; computer-print color personalization, etc. All quality, personalized merchandise.

Categories: Wooden crafts, stained glass items, home decor, pottery/ceramics, lawn/garden accents. Personalized merchandise (names of customers) for all ages and markets. Target grandparents, homeowners.

Price range: Retail $20-75

Special requirements: No beginners. We are looking for products tested in retail shows and ready for mass markets.

Advertising: Direct sales to catalogs and magazines

Cost/Payment policies: Commissions only. Craftsperson paid per sales.

For consideration: Provide photos, written description of work, wholesale price and production capabilities. Do not call first.

ARTEMIS, INC.

Sandra Tropper

4715 Crescent St.

Bethesda, MD 20816

Phone: (301)229-2058

Fax: (301)229-2186

In business since: 1990

Area: Washington DC-Baltimore corridor including Northern Virginia

Sells: To private clients, corporations and through the design trade

Description of services: I work with artists, craftsmen and clients (both private and corporate) to mate artwork with buyers, taking into consideration environment, budget, tastes and needs. This often involves commissions and special projects for craftspeople and artists.

Types of products: Hand crafted items and artwork including paintings, sculpture and limited edition prints. Will represent more than one craftsperson selling the same type of item.

Categories: Fine crafts, wooden crafts, stained glass items, needlework crafts, hand blown glass items, home decor, pottery/ceramics, baskets, sculpture, hand made or artist made paper fabrications. Larger, more sculptural work.

Price range: $100-10,000

Special requirements: I want a constant price to the public established by craftsperson and his/her dealers. Percentages to be negotiated by the individuals.

Cost/Payment policies: A percentage of the retail price. Craftsperson is paid at time of sale.

For consideration: Provide photos or slides, catalog/promotional materials, written description of work and background of craftsperson.

B K ENTERPRISES

Brenda Kain
3833 Schaefer #E
Chino, CA 91710
Phone: (909)628-1291
Fax: (714)996-0214
In business since: 1986
Area: TX, GA, IL, CA, WA, KS, PA
Sells: At wholesale shows for hand crafted items; at wholesale gift shows
Description of services: Sales representation at major wholesale trade shows for products hand made in the USA
Types of products: Hand crafted items only. Will represent more one craftsperson selling the same type of item.
Categories: Wearable art, wooden crafts, paper products, needlework crafts, figurines, dolls/stuffed animals/toys, pottery/ceramics, nature crafts/floral, recycled crafts, sculpture
Price range: $3-60
Advertising: Trade show directories
Cost/Payment policies: Commission on orders shipped
For consideration: Provide catalog/promotional materials and sample of work.

ETCO, INC.

Eitan Toker
6100 4th Ave. S., #218-219-221
Seattle, WA 98108
Phone: (206)762-1707; (206)762-1708; (800)729-1707
Fax: (206)762-1361
In business since: 1977
Area: WA, OR, ID, MT, AK
Sells: To retail stores
Description of services: Manufacturer's representative
Types of products: Hand crafted items and others.
Categories: Fine crafts, hand blown glass items, figurines, pottery/ceramics, sculpture
Price range: Varies
Special requirements: Need to have a catalog
Advertising: We have a showroom at the Seattle Gift Center.
Cost/Payment policies: 15-20% commission.
For consideration: Provide catalog/promotional materials.

JERRY S. KAYE ASSOCIATES

6433 Topanga Canyon Blvd., #102
Canoga Park, CA 91303-2621
Phone: (818)347-2894 (best time to call is LA time: 7-8:30AM)
In business since: 1976
Area: CA, NV, AZ
Sells: To retail stores; at wholesale gift shows
Description of services: Largest "full-time" road "rep" group in California—specializing in handcraft, accessories and home decor. We call on gift outlets, country stores, art stores, collectible shops, florists, drug stores and card shops.
Types of products: Specialize in country crafts and home accessories. Will not represent more than one craftsperson selling the same type of item.
Categories: Fine crafts, wearable art, jewelry, miniatures/dollhouses, wooden crafts, paper products, stained glass items, needlework crafts, hand blown glass items, home decor, figurines, dolls/stuffed animals/toys, pottery/ceramics, nature crafts/floral, leather crafts, baskets, recycled crafts, sculpture

Price range: Wholesale $2-200
Advertising: Word of mouth from other retailers
Cost/Payment policies: 15-20% commission. Paid after artisan gets paid.
For consideration: Provide photos only, catalog/promotional materials, written description of work, price list.
Additional information: There are 10 people on the road selling these handmade items.

KEMP KRAFTS

Richard T. Kemp
288 Flynn Ave. #20
Burlington, VT 05401-5374
Phone: (802)862-4418
E-mail: rtkemp@aol.com
In business since: 1983
Area: Nationwide
Sells: To retail stores; to catalogs and other direct mail markets
Description of services: A telemarketing group. Catalogs are sent to regular accounts; businesses are gift stores, craft stores, zoos and nature centers. A telephone call is made to follow up on a mailing. With this method of marketing, travel time is greatly reduced. Able to reach outlets in the entire country.
Types of products: Hand crafted items and posters, greeting cards, books, candy. Will represent more than one craftsperson selling the same type of item.
Categories: Jewelry, wooden crafts, paper products, home decor, toys
Price range: $15-150
Advertising: Craft publication and direct mail
Cost/Payment policies: A commission of 10-20% once a month. Craftsperson paid once a month.
For consideration: Provide catalog/promotional materials, photos, written description of work, 8½" × 11" color sheets are the best.

LAUGHLIN'S COUNTRY PRIDE

Linda Laughlin
7326 Winsford Lane
Sylvania, OH 43560
Phone: (419)885-5266
Fax: (419)885-5277
In business since: 1986

Area: OH, PA, IL, MO

Sells: To retail stores; to catalogs and other direct mail markets; at wholesale shows for hand crafted items; at wholesale gift shows

Description of services: Laughlin's Country Pride specializes in Cottage Industry manufacturers. 10 years experience of marketing at the wholesale gift shows. We are always on the look-out for unique, quality, reasonably priced country/traditional decor lines to market in wholesale gift shows. We have references and are buyer and manufacturer friendly. Would be delighted to take a look at any products. Large or small manufacturers are all considered.

Types of products: Hand crafted items only. Will represent more than one craftsperson selling the same type of item.

Categories: Fine crafts, wooden crafts, home decor, dolls/stuffed animals, pottery/ceramics

Price range: $2.50-25

Advertising: *Craft Supply Magazine* and show directories

Cost/Payment policies: I work on a booth fee and 15% commission basis. Commission check is paid to rep once a month. Orders are written COD.

For consideration: Provide photos and sample of work.

FRANK LENNOX ASSOCIATES, INC.

Frank Lennox
3813 Lindy Lane
Weidman, MI 48893
Phone: (517)644-5053
Fax: (517)644-5162
In business since: 1958
Area: MI
Sells: To retail stores; at wholesale shows for hand crafted items; at wholesale gift shows

Description of services: I sell to over 1,500 retail stores in Michigan including gift shops, souvenir stores, Hallmark shops, floral, garden and hardware stores and other specialty stores. I also count inventory, advise on display and advertising and help with promotions.

Types of products: Hand crafted and other items. Will not represent more than one crafter selling the same type of item.

Categories: Fine crafts, miniatures/dollhouses, wooden crafts, paper products, stained glass items, home decor, figurines, pottery/ceramics, nature crafts/floral

Price range: All price ranges

Special requirements: Need catalog or color photos, samples for road and showroom

Advertising: MAGS, Northville, MI, permanent show building. North Michigan Gift Show, Harbor Springs, MI and Great Lake Gift Show, Mackinaw City, MI.

Cost/Payment policies: 15% commission. Net 30 days from customer.

For consideration: Provide catalog/promotional materials, photos, sample of work.

LINEWORKS, INC.

Jerry Freundlich
1786 Bellmore Ave.
Bellmore, NY 11710-5522
Phone: (516)783-9741
Fax: (516)781-7913
E-mail: lineworks@aol.com
In business since: 1985
Area: NY, NJ, Eastern PA, DE
Sells: To retail stores; to catalogs and other direct mail markets; at wholesale gift shows; at wholesale toy, doll and teddy bear shows

Description of services: Broad-based, diverse road coverage to the specialty retail markets

Categories: Home decor, figurines, dolls/stuffed animals/toys, pottery/ceramics, baskets, garden accessories

Price range: All price ranges

Special requirements: Workable catalog is required.

Advertising: Catalog mailings

Cost/Payment policies: Commission

For consideration: Provide catalog/promotional materials.

THE MISSING LINK

Georgia Schorr
6100 Fourth Ave. S #450
Seattle, WA 98108
Phone: (206)767-7597
Fax: (206)767-7594
In business since: 1984
Area: AK, WA, OR, ID, MT (USA); British Columbia, Alberta (Canada)

Sells: To retail stores; to catalogs and other direct mail markets; at wholesale shows for hand crafted items; at wholesale gift shows; wholesale garden shows

Description of services: Craft rep in the Northwest, understanding the capabilities and limitations of the craftsperson in the retail world. Represent over 20 fine, handmade lines in every price range, and in every type of store or gallery. Customers look to us for new, exciting talent and constantly visit showroom to seek out new items. We also have 7 full-time road reps.

Types of products: Books, toys, children's accessories, greeting cards, journals, chimes, bird houses/feeders, glass, frames, journals, mugs, folk art, posters, T-shirts, tote bags, sculpture, puzzles, candles, magnets. Will represent more than one craftsperson selling the same type of item only if there are substantial differences in design.

Categories: Fine crafts, wearable art, jewelry, wooden crafts, paper products, stained glass items, hand blown glass items, home decor, dolls/stuffed animals/toys, pottery/ceramics, nature crafts/floral, leather crafts, baskets, recycled crafts, sculpture

Price range: $1.50-7,000

Special requirements: Need a good catalog; not necessarily in color, but clearly representing the line.

Advertising: A magazine that has a circulation of 20,000+; our building advertises in national trades; we do mail quarterly to our own accounts.

Cost/Payment policies: Commission. Paid monthly, on paid accounts. Craftsperson paid by the retailer—each order—COD or net 30 days.

For consideration: Provide photos or slides, catalog/promotional materials, sample of work.

HAL MORGAN & ASSOCIATES

Hal Morgan
P.O. Box 472, 255 Woody Hill Rd.
Hope Valley, RI 02832
Phone: (401)539-7298
Fax: (401)539-7597
In business since: 1972
Area: ME, NH, VT, CT, MA, RI

Sells: To retail stores; at wholesale gift shows

Description of services: Area intensive reps ready and able to call on diverse retailers in their limited geographic areas.

Types of products: Artist and craft person manufactured gifts and garden wares

Categories: Fine crafts, miniatures/dollhouses, wooden crafts, paper products, stained glass items, needlework crafts, hand blown glass items, home decor, figurines, dolls/stuffed animals/toys, pottery/ceramics, nature crafts/floral, leather crafts, baskets, recycled crafts, sculpture

Price range: Wholesale $3-60

Special requirements: Crafters must be able to produce in commercial quantity and be able to capitalize their business themselves.

Advertising: Six salespeople on the road

Cost/Payment policies: Commission on invoice (merchandise) amount

For consideration: Provide photos or slides, catalog/promotional materials, sample of work.

NORTHWOODS TRADING CO.

Sharon Olson
13451 Essex Ct.
Eden Prairie, MN 55347
Phone: (612)937-5275
In business since: 1986
Area: MN, ND, SD, IA, WI, IL, MI, PA
Sells: At wholesale gift shows
Description of services: Represents small companies who specialize in folkart with a primitive, whimsical, Americana or country theme in any media. You do not have to be a pro. Will help in any phase of setting up your business. Very flexible to work with. No jewelry or crochet.
Types of products: Hand crafted items only. Will represent more than one craftsperson selling the same type of item.
Categories: Miniatures/dollhouses, wooden crafts, home decor, figurines, dolls/stuffed animals/toys, pottery/ceramics, baskets, sculpture
Price range: $2.75-30
Advertising: Trade show directories
Cost/Payment policies: 15% commission after craftsperson has been paid. Paid

directly by the shop. Craftsperson sets own terms.

For consideration: Provide photos or slides, catalog/promotional materials, price list, SASE.

Additional information: 6 shows attended per year.

PACIFIC NORTHWEST IMAGES, INC.

Bill McSherry
6100 Fourth Ave. S., Suite 350
Seattle, WA 98108
Phone: (206)762-1063
Fax: (206)767-2650
In business since: 1979
Area: WA, OR, ID, AK, MT, WY
Sells: To retail stores; to catalogs and other direct mail markets; at wholesale gift shows
Description of services: They call on gift, country and other retailers in above territory. Have 9 representatives located in their area and are able to offer both road coverage and art showroom, space at their permanent showroom in the Seattle Gift Center.
Types of products: Will represent more than one craftsperson selling the same type of item.
Categories: Miniatures/dollhouses, wooden crafts, home decor, figurines, dolls/stuffed animals/toys
Price range: Wholesale $5-40
Advertising: In showroom and on the road
Cost/Payment policies: Commission; payment not required up front
For consideration: Provide photos or slides, catalog/promotional materials, sample of work, written description of work.

REGAL SALES

Martin L. Oaks
438 E. Beech St.
Long Beach, NY 11561
Phone: (516)889-6112; (516)889-6122
Fax: (516)889-3286
In business since: 1965
Area: Long Island, Brooklyn, Queens, New York City and West Chester, NY
Sells: To retail stores; at wholesale shows for hand crafted items; at wholesale gift shows; at wholesale toy, doll and teddy bear shows
Types of products: Hand crafted items only. Gift/gourmet/garden/miniature

items. Specialize in Christmas and country gifts. Will not represent more than one crafter selling the same type of item.

Categories: Jewelry, miniatures/dollhouses, wooden crafts, paper products, stained glass items, figurines, dolls/stuffed animals/toys, nature crafts/floral, baskets

Price range: $1.45-100

Cost/Payment policies: 15% commission

For consideration: Provide catalog/promotional materials, sample of work.

ROAD RUNNERS

Rudy La Porta
222 Monte Vista Dr.
Napa, CA 94559
Phone: (707)255-2683; (415)343-3145
Fax: (415)343-3248
In business since: 1981
Area: Northern CA, Northern NV, HI
Sells: To retail stores; at wholesale gift shows
Types of products: Hand crafted items and others. Will not represent more than one craftsperson selling the same type of item.
Categories: Jewelry, paper products, home decor, figurines, pottery/ceramics
Price range: $5-50
Cost/Payment policies: 15% commission paid upon shipment
For consideration: Provide catalog/promotional materials, sample of work.

SARM & NASTOVSKI

Blanche Nastovski
1575 Merchandise Mart
Chicago, IL 60654
Phone: (312)527-1688
Fax: (312)527-1601
In business since: 1992
Area: IL, IN, WI, MI, IA, OH, MN, Western PA
Sells: To retail stores; to catalogs and other direct mail markets; at wholesale gift shows; at wholesale apparel shows
Description of services: We are equipped to handle lines who just want to be in a showroom space. We are open daily in the Chicago Merchandise Mart.
Types of products: Hand crafted items and gift related products.
Categories: Fine crafts, wearable art, pa-

per products, home decor, recycled crafts

Price range: All ranges

Advertising: During all major gift shows in the midwest area

Cost/Payment policies: Commission

For consideration: Provide catalog/promotional materials, photos only, sample of work

SANDRA SCIRIA AND ASSOC.

Sandra Sciria
114B E. Lake Rd.
Auburn, NY 13021

Phone: (315)253-6552; (800)5-SCIRIA

Fax: (315)255-9228

In business since: 1984

Area: New England states and NY

Sells: To retail shops

Description of services: We represent quality made in the USA only, country and traditional crafts. Roadwork is the strength of our organization.

Types of products: Hand crafted items and books and cards. Will not represent more than one craftsperson selling the same type of item.

Categories: Fine crafts, jewelry, miniatures/dollhouses, wooden crafts, paper products, home decor, figurines, dolls/stuffed animals/toys, pottery/ceramics, nature crafts/floral

Price range: $1-200

Advertising: On the road newsletters

Cost/Payment policies: Commission. Payment up front is not required. If commission check is 30 days past due, we stop showing the line.

For consideration: Provide catalog/promotional materials, sample of work.

Additional information: We are a very responsible, honest, hard working group—very detailed and organized.

STERLING REPRESENTATION

Lloyd S. Graydon
685 Miramonte Dr.
Santa Barbara, CA 93109

Phone/Fax: (805)962-9787

In business since: 1989

Area: Central CA coasts: Ventura County, Santa Barbara County, San Luis Obispo County and Monterey and Santa Cruz

Sells: To retail stores; retail tourist shops (50% of business)

Description of services: Specializes in items for the tourist trade and general gift items.

Categories: Jewelry, figurines, general gift crafts

Price range: Retail $5-35. Some up to $60 retail.

Cost/Payment policies: Commission on sale. Craftsperson bills stores directly. 15% to 20% commission paid by craftsperson for my services.

For consideration: Provide catalog/promotional materials, photos (a few).

TRADITIONS

Pamela Kline
Box 416
Claverack, NY 12513

Phone: (518)672-5044; 672-5043

Fax: (518)672-4917

In business since: 1982

Area: US, Europe, Japan

Sells: To retail stores; to catalogs and other direct mail markets; at wholesale shows for hand crafted items; at wholesale gift shows; wholesale home textile shows (bidding); wholesale furniture shows

Description of services: Representing historical reproduction textiles, furniture and home accent accessories.

Types of products: Hand crafted items and bed linens, curtains, fabrics, handbags and luggage. Will represent more than one craftsperson selling the same type of item.

Categories: Wooden crafts, needlework crafts, home decor, pottery/ceramics, baskets, textiles

Price range: $10-500

Special requirements: Must have historical background.

Advertising: Trade magazine ads, color postcards

Cost/Payment policies: 15% commission once a month after craftsperson has been paid by retail store. Craftsperson is paid directly by store.

For consideration: Provide catalog/promotional materials, photos only, sample of work, written description of work.

MARTY WASSERBERG & ASSOCIATES

Marty Wasserberg
P.O. Box 367, Glen Alpin Rd.
New Vernon, NJ 07976

Phone: (201)538-2552

Fax: (201)538-8151

In business since: 1961

Area: NY, NJ, Eastern PA

Sells: To retail stores; to catalogs and other direct mail markets; at wholesale shows for hand crafted items; at wholesale gift shows

Description of services: Fourteen salespeople on the road call on gift, drug and boutique stores as well as card shops, independent toy shops and kids' stores. They exhibit at national and international trade shows in New York City 3 times a year.

Categories: Wooden crafts, paper products, stained glass items, home decor, pottery/ceramics, nature crafts/floral, leather crafts, sculpture

Price range: $4.50-50

Cost/Payment policies: 15-20% commission payable the following month after shipment or invoice is sent.

For consideration: Provide catalog/promotional materials, photos only, sample of work.

3

RESOURCES

CHAPTER TWELVE

Business Products

PACKAGING PRODUCTS

ACTION BAG CO.

Nancy Cwynar
501 N. Edgewood Ave.
Wood Dale, IL 60191
Phone: (800)824-2247; (630)766-2881
Fax: (800)400-4451; (630)766-3548
In business since: 1980
Products: A complete line of paper and plastic bags including zipclose, plain polybags and retail handle bags. Featuring an expanded line or packaging products including shrink systems, boxes, bows and related accessories. Printing available in large or small quantities.
Products for: Professional and hobbyist craftspeople
Catalog: Free
Samples: Free
Minimum order: $50

BAGS & BOWS

Marcy Schlecter
33 Union Ave.
Sudbury, MA 01776
Phone: (508)440-8659; (800)225-8155 (orders)
Fax: (800)225-8455
In business since: 1974
Products: Shopping bags, labels, merchandise bags, gift boxes, ribbon, retail signs, bows, tissue paper, polypro film, wrapping paper, custom hot stamping and more.
Products for: Professional and hobbyist craftspeople
Catalog: Free
Samples: Free
Minimum order: $50

BAGSPLUS

Fred Cwynar
640 Country Club Lane, Suite 201A
Itasca, IL 60143-1496
Phone: (630)250-1336
Fax: (630)250-0405
E-mail: bagsplus@aol.com
In business since: 1980

Products: Assorted sizes and styles of zipclose bags, gift totes, paper and plastic retail and cellophane bags. We specialize in small quantity orders.
Products for: Professional and hobbyist craftspeople
Price range: Up to $22
Catalog: Free
Samples: Free
Minimum order: $15

EVERGREEN BAG CO.

Bill Adams
22 Ash St.
East Hartford, CT 06108
Phone: (800)775-3595; (860)282-0319
Fax: (860)289-0081
E-mail: everbag@aol.com
In business since: 1984
Products: An extensive line of shopping bags, gift boxes, tissue paper, wraps and ribbons, as well as polyethylene, polypropylene and cellophane bags in several sizes. Also corrugated shipping boxes, tape and other supplies. Printing and custom solutions are available for all products. Sells partial cases on many items, for those who need a little, and give quantity discounts for those who need a lot. Most orders received by 2:00PM ship the same day.
Products for: Professional and hobbyist craftspeople
Catalog: Free
Samples: Free
Minimum order: $10, or a service charge will be added

GRAPHCOMM SERVICES

Val Mayer
P.O. Box 220
Freeland, WA 98249
Phone: (360)331-5668; (800)488-7436
Fax: (360)331-3282
In business since: 1987
Products: GraphComm Services offers self-adhesive labels, fabric sew-in labels, custom hangtags, tagging equipment and supplies. The company of-

fers fast, friendly service—most items ship in 7 days. Free typesetting; add your logo for small charge. Design assistance available. Convenient toll-free or fax ordering.
Products for: Professional craftspeople
Price range: Vary
Catalog: Free, included with each brochure is a $5 coupon toward the first order.
Samples: Free
Minimum order: Quantity minimum of 1,000 on most items

IMPACT IMAGES

Benny Wilkins
4919 Windplay Dr.
El Dorado Hills, CA 95762
Phone: (916)933-4700; (800)233-2630
Fax: (916)933-4717
E-mail: bwilkins@footnet.com
In business since: 1992
Products: Impact Images provides self sealing Crystal Clear Plastic Bags. These bags are used to package individual pieces for retail sale. On the open end they have an extended flap with an adhesive strip. Once the art has been inserted into the bag the flap is folded over and sealed to the back, much like a self sealing envelope. The result is a professionally packaged piece of art completely protected in crystal clear plastic. These bags have been extremely popular with those that have used them. Sizes range from small 2″ × 3″ bags up to large 32″ × 42″ bags. Most of our customers are the result of referrals from other happy customers. If a picture is worth a thousand words a sample is worth even more.
Products for: Professional and hobbyist craftspeople
Price range: 3¢-$1.25
Catalog: Available
Samples: Available
Minimum order: $25. Bags ordered in multiples of 100 per size.
Additional information: For faster ser-

vice we serve our customers from 2 locations, 1 in California and 1 in Tennessee.

PLASTIC BAGMART

Bob Courtney
554 Haddon Ave.
Collingswood, NJ 08108
Phone: (609)858-0800; (800)360-BAGS
Fax: (609)854-6006
E-mail: rcourt0236@aol.com
In business since: 1985
Products: Plastic bags of all types and sizes: clear bags, zipclose bags, merchandise carryout bags. All sizes of trash bags. Packing materials, shipping materials and white tissue paper.
Products for: Professional and hobbyist craftspeople
Catalog: $3, refunded on order
Samples: Free (if available)
Additional information: Send for a free descriptive price list. We accept Visa and MasterCard. Small orders are our specialty. Next day shipment in most cases.

STERLING NAME TAPE CO.

9 Willow St., P.O. Box 939
Winsted, CT 06098
Phone: (800)654-5210; (860)379-5142
Fax: (860)379-0394
E-mail: colwash@esslink.com
In business since: 1901
Products: Printed satin-polyester garment labels, available one or two colors (your choice out of 12) printed on your choice of white, cream, grey or black background. Care instructions, content, or logos.
Products for: Professional and hobbyist craftspeople
Price range: $19.89/100 with one time $10 plate charge
Catalog: $1
Samples: Available
Minimum order: 100 labels

SHOW EQUIPMENT

AIM FIXTURES & DISPLAYS

Ron Kieselhorst
P.O. Box 718
Franklin, NC 28734
Phone: (704)369-9803; (800)524-9833
In business since: 1977

Products: AIM manufactures a quality modular display system. Unique, versatile, all you add is imagination! All display panels are built with anodized aluminum frames. AIM displays can be built with aluminum diamond shaped mesh inserts, velvet loop fabric over hardfoam board inserts, open bar units or combination units. Shelving can be added or customed designed. 6″ leveler feet are adjustable to uneven surfaces, or longer legs are available to adjust panels to desired heights. A 360 degree slip in-slip out folding hinge allows displays to seperate or accordion fold for easy set up and fast take down. AIM producst are user friendly with fast service and "quality built into every display!"
Products for: Professional and hobbyist craftspeople
Price range: $90-125 per display panel which includes our unique folding hinge and built in leveler feet
Catalog: Free
Additional information: Rush orders (at no extra charge) are available. Accessories may be ordered any time at reasonable prices.

ARMSTRONG PRODUCTS, INC.

Gary Armstrong, Jr.
P.O. Box 979
Guthrie, OK 73044
Phone: (800)278-4279; (405)282-7584
Fax: (405)282-1130
In business since: 1974
Products: Equipment for a lightweight and portable display
Products for: Professional craftspeople
Price range: 3′×6′ panel starts at $107
Catalog: Free

AVANTI DISPLAY

Brian Wilson
1034 Ohio Ave.
Richmond, CA 94804
Phone: (510)233-5950; (800)282-9951
Fax: (510)233-3569
In business since: 1993
Products: A large selection of acrylic risers and plate stands as well as wooden and brass easels.
Products for: Professional craftspeople, craftshops, galleries
Catalog: Free
Minimum order: $50

Additional information: Accepts Visa, MasterCard or C.O.D.

CREATIVE ENERGIES, INC.

Roxanne
1607 N. Magnolia Ave.
Ocala, Fl 34475
Phone: (800)351-8889
Fax: (904)351-9448
In business since: 1988
Products: Light-Dome® canopies are waterproof, fast, easy, one person set ups. Engineered to combine compact size, light weight and maximum strength without compromising long-lasting durability.
Products for: Professional and hobbyist craftspeople
Price range: $389+
Catalog: Free
Samples: Video $5
Additional information: We are a manufacturer selling wholesale to the consumer.

FLOURISH CO.

Bob Billig
5763 Wheeler Rd.
Fayetteville, AR 72704
Phone: (800)296-0049; (501)444-8400
Fax: (501)444-8480
In business since: 1985
Products: Makers of the Protector Canopy, Flourish Co., recently introduced the Archtop Canopy, a top-of-the-line unit with fully zippered sides, wind vents and double-wide skylight. Flouish also offers a huge range of flame-resistant fabrics and fabric products (drapery, table covers, etc.). Exhibitors are invited to call for a customized sampling of fabrics. For those exhibitors who show indoors only, Flourish offers two sturdy indoor booth frames.
Products for: Professional and hobbyist craftspeople
Price range: Canopies $545-745, indoor booth frames from $155, flame-resistant fabric products quoted individually.
Catalog: Free
Samples: Free

FRED'S STUDIO TENTS & CANOPIES, INC.

Fred Tracy, president
7 Trent Lane, P.O. Box 156
Stillwater, NY 12170
Phone: (518)664-4905; (800)998-3687
Fax: (518)664-4379
In business since: 1987
Products: Our tents utilize a 1.163″ galvanized steel tubing framework, 14 gauge anodized steel fittings which are mig and tig welded, side and top tarps made of a poly or vinyl material. The poly and vinyl are all flame retardant (except for the silver/black or silver/white). The tarps all have reinforced binding on all sides with solid brass grommets every 2′.
Products for: Professional and hobbyist craftspeople
Catalog: Free
Additional information: We are in the business of manufacturing, sales, and rentals of tents. We are confident that you will be satisfied.

GALLERY LIGHTING

Rafael Quinones
P.O. Box 18446
Austin, TX 78760
Phone: (800)256-7114
Fax: (800)324-8605
In business since: 1984
Products: We supply support, advice and supplies needed for lighting a show booth the most economical way possible. We offer bulbs, fixtures, support systems and all items needed to present products.
Products for: Professional and hobbyist craftspeople
Price range: Overhead support, 6′ tall is $29.95; upright support 6′ to 8′ is $29.95; support bases are $98.95 a piece. A complete stand system is $127.75.
Catalog: Free
Additional information: We provide free lighting design and will specify exact components and give you a total cost delivered to your door.

GRAPHIC DISPLAY SYSTEMS

Robert E. Tobias
308 S. First St.
Lebanon, PA 17042
Phone: (800)848-3020; (717)274-3954
Fax: (717)274-2710
In business since: 1976
Products: Graphic Display Systems is a unique system designed to accommodate the working artist or institution to display two dimensional work in a professional manner.
Products for: Professional and hobbyist craftspeople
Price range: Display panels range from $65-110
Catalog: Free

'MAGINATION INC.

Marina Kaisor
47A Germay Dr.
Wilmington, DE 19804
Phone: (302)655-4464
Fax: (302)654-0875
E-mail: stands 4@dca.net
In business since: 1992
Products: Offers line of display stands, tools, tables and more. Stack 'n Stands® are collapsible, durable, interchangeable and versatile. Each stand assembles or disassembles in 2 minutes, stacks for shipping or storage within a 2″ height, and will support over 300 lbs. Made of Melamine laminate, the finish is easy to care for. They are available in 6 different heights (12″-42″) and interchange with 8 different sizes of tops/bases (offers in 3 shapes: square, octagon, rectangle). They come in 4 standard colors (white, black, almond, light gray) and a variety of premium colors.
Products for: Professional and hobbyist craftspeple, home and office use.
Price range: $25-125
Catalog: Free

ELAINE MARTIN COMPANY

Customer Service
444 Lake Cook Rd. #1
Deerfield, IL 60015
Phone: (847)945-9445; (800)642-1043 (orders)
Fax: (847)945-9573
In business since: 1977
Products: Specializing in show and display equipment, such as snap joint canopies in flat slant or peak modcls. Also EZUP and KD canopies, the Dome Display Booth, side panels display grids, display panels, indoor booths, fire retardant drapes and table covers, dispaly pedestals, folding tables, director chairs and accessories. We offer a full line of products for the cost conscious to the experienced professional crafter and artisan.
Products for: Professional and hobbyist craftspeople, art shows
Price range: Indoor and outdoor canopies starting under $350 for basic models.
Catalog: Free
Additional information: Custom displays, garage style and heavy duty canopies made to order. Call for quotes.

NEW VENTURE PRODUCTS INC.

Kathy and Steve
14115-B 63rd Way N.
Clearwater, FL 34620-3617
Phone: (813)524-2823; (800)771-7469
Fax: (813)524-3110
In business since: 1990
Products: Showoff™ line of canopy and display products. Roll up commercial display system holds heavy work while leaving lots of extra transport room; lightweight structural aluminum canopy frame; choices in canopy fabric. Also awnings, skylight, banners, sand bags and accessories. The Showoff is a 10′ × 10′ canopy (also available 10′ × 8′ and 10′ × 6′) that has a true round roofline . . . it is waterproof, roomy and comfortable.
Products for: Professional and hobbyist craftspeople
Price range: Canopies $375-1,475; accessories $40 and up
Catalog: Free
Samples: Free
Additional information: We also provide accessories and displays for other canopies.

NEWTON DISPLAY PRODUCTS, INC.

122 Fifth St.
Ft. Myers, FL 33907
Phone: (800)678-8677; (941)936-9199
Fax: (941)936-2242
In business since: 1981
Products: Craft Hut display booths, Interloc display panels in aluminum or steel, panel covers.
Products for: Professional craftspeople
Price range: Craft Huts $725; panels $60-105; covers $25-34

Catalog: Free
Samples: Free

PRO PANELS BY MD ENTERPRISES

Mick Dixon and David Curry
9738 Abernathy
Dallas, TX 75220
Phone: (214)350-5765
In business since: 1988
Products: MD Enterprises manufacturers display panels and show accessories for the professional artist and crafter. Our Pro Panels are lightweight, strong and durable. They come covered by a heavy loop pile, velcro receptive, material that's available in five colors.
Products for: Professional craftspeople
Price range: $98-149
Catalog: Available

SKYCAP CANOPY CO.

Tom Bannon
37 W. 19th St.
New York, NY 10011
Phone: (800)243-9227
Fax: (212)691-0175
E-mail: canopies@aol.com
In business since: 1986
Products: Skycap Canopy Company is a manufacturer and distributor of 6 types of canopies and portable festival tents. In sizes from 7′ × 10′ to 20′ × 40′. All canopies are waterproof and come in a variety of colors and fabrics.
Products for: Professional and hobbyist craftspeople
Price range: Canopies from $140-500
Catalog: Free

THE SOURCE UNLIMITED

Margaret
331 E. Ninth St.
New York, NY 10003
Phone: (212)473-7833
Fax: (212)673-5248
In business since: 1982

Products: Business cards, self-adhesive labels and rubber stamps
Products for: Professional and hobbyist craftspeople
Catalog: $1 (refundable)

A. STEELE

Jon Steele
W12351 Long Lane
Stockholm, WI 54769
Phone: (800)693-3353
Fax: (715)448-2119
In business since: 1983
Products: We provide the craftsperson with a variety of products to assist the mobil business community to conduct business more efficiently, professionally, with the least amount of labor and time. To set up for and to do business, we offer the E-Z Up Instant Shelters, up or down in 60 seconds, tried and proven for 15 years. The Swintec SW 20 battery operated cash register will save you time with each customer, when its time to pay sales tax, or to report your earnings. It automatically adds sales tax and tells how much change to give. The Magliner Convertible Hand Truck-Cart is the Cadillac of all hand trucks.
Products for: Professional and hobbyist craftspeople
Catalog: Available

THE WOOD FACTORY

Bill Gillett
1225 Red Cedar Circle
Fort Collins, CO 80524
Phone: (800)842-9663; (970)224-1999
Fax: (970)224-1949
In business since: 1983
Products: All wood displays by The Wood Factory have been custom-designed to be portable and space efficient, yet naturally attractive. Made of pine and selected hardwood plywood, Wood Factory displays provide a warm, natural look. All models are designed and packaged to be shipped by UPS and most do not require any tools

for assembly. More than seventy different display units are made by The Wood Factory with many options and accessories for increased versatility. Custom and private label designs may be produced in quantity. Wood burning of logos and names is also available.
Products for: Professional craftspeople, stores, in-home use.
Price range: From $11.95 for tabletop displays up to $195 for a 6 foot arch with 3 shelves (arch collapses to 24″)
Catalog: Free

COMPUTER PRODUCTS

RFCANON, INC.

Roy Canon
4711 Shavano Oak, Suite 101
San Antonio, TX 78249-4026
Phone: (210)408-1396; (888)785-0465
Fax: (210)408-0122
E-mail: 74151.3470@compuserve.com
In business since: 1983
Products: RFCanon provides a variety of computer hardware and software as well as free technical support. RFCanon, Inc. produces and markets two computer software products specific to the craft industry: The Craft Tracker™ is an inventory, sales and profit tracking system designed specifically for professional crafters who sell their creations through a variety of different sales localtions, such as craft malls, consignment shops, craft shows, mail order, etc.; The Mall Manager™ is a Point-of-Sale software system for operating and managing multi-merchant craft malls or consignment shops. Both products are easy to use with simple menus and extensive on-line "help" systems.
Products for: Professional craftspeople
Price range: Prices start at $195.
Catalog: Available.

CHAPTER THIRTEEN
Services for Craftspeople

BANKING/ACCOUNTING

ARTS & CRAFTS BUSINESS SOLUTIONS
Guy McDonald
2804 Bishopgate Dr.
Raleigh, NC 27613-7219
Phone: (800)873-1192
Fax: (919)676-7651
In business since: 1991
Business is for: Any business that supports the industry, e.g., craft suppliers, galleries, magazines, etc.
Services provided: Arts and Crafts Business Solutions is a company that works specifically in the arts and crafts marketplace. Imagine a cellular credit card system designed to work in the buildings where your business is conducted, as well as a bankcard service tailored to the needs of this marketplace. The biggest advantage for this group is that individuals no longer negotiate their discount rates and fees with their banks. Our objective is to help each individual make the best choice for their business in credit card processing. Other "Arts Group" benefits now include health benefits, and we are working on product liability insurance for this group.
Cost: $440-2,499, depending on the individual's needs.
Additional information: We care about the advancement of American arts and crafts and donate 5% of net profit each year back to the industry.

INSURANCE

CONNELL INSURORS, INC.
Pat Connell and Sherri Chinnery
P.O. Box 1840
Branson, MO 65615
Phone: (417)334-2000; (800)356-8140
Fax: (417)334-4906
In business since: 1970
Business is for: Professional craftspeople only.
Services provided: We are an independent insurance agency who offers a program designed specifically to meet the liability insurance needs of those crafters selling their merchandise from temporary booths in malls and craft shows.
Cost: The plan provides up to $1 million of liability coverage for any one loss associated with your booth location. The plan also includes product liability protection, once product is sold. Also provides replacement cost coverage up to $2,500 for business personal property. The cost is $425 for one booth and $175 for each additional booth operated simultaneously.

HARBOUR INSURANCE MANAGEMENT
11400 W. Olympic Blvd.
Los Angeles, CA 90064
Phone: (800)477-4930; (310)477-4886
Fax: (310)477-1364
E-mail: harbourins@aol.com
In business since: 1973
Business is for: Professional craftspeople and all artists
Services provided: Specializing in speical event insurance, Harbour insurance Management develops, markets, and underwrites "no hassle" insurance programs for all types of craftspeople. Event promoters, professional crafters, amateur crafters, craft festivals, craft malls, music festivals, conventions, and city celebrations are among the industries served. All facets of special event insurance can be provided; event liability, umbrella liability, liquor liability, automobile liability, bad weather protection, event cancellation, property, workers' compensation, and accident medical coverage. Domestic and foreign coverage is arranged through nationally recognized and licensed insurance companies on a per-event or annual basis. Brochures are available on all programs. Service oriented, all quotations and policies are prepared within a 24 hour period. Additionally, Harbour provides special event risk management consulting as well as bid specification development and implemention. By properly managing an event's insurance and their transfer of risks to others, clients have saved 20-30% on their overall insurance program.
Cost: Premiums are as low as $300 for short term policies and $500 for annual policies.
Additional information: Recent clients include Scottsdale Celebration of Fine Arts, Town of Telluride Special Events, First Night Celebrations Nationwide, San Antonio Festival, and L.A. Fiesta Broadway, among many others.

LEGAL

LOUISIANA VOLUNTEER LAWYERS FOR THE ARTS
Thérèse Wegmann
Arts Council of New Orleans
821 Gravier St., Sixth Floor
New Orleans, LA 70112-1581
Phone: (504)523-1465
Fax: (504)529-2430
E-mail: acno@tmn.com
Business is for: Professional craftspeople and individuals with an arts-related problem whose family/household income is less than $15,000/year; non-profit organizations whose yearly operating budget does not exceed $100,000 are also eligible.
Services provided: The Louisiana Volunteer Lawyers for the Arts (LVLA) is sponsored by the Arts Council of New Orleans and by the Louisiana State Bar Association. It is an organization of legal professionals dedicated to providing artists and arts organizations in Louisiana with free legal advice, representation and information for arts-related problems. The primary functions of the LVLA is to establish professional communication between volunteer attorneys and artists or arts organizations needing legal assistance

for arsts-related problems. Coordination and staff support are provided by the Arts Council of New Orleans. The staff screens each applicant for legal assistance to ascertain the nature of the legal problem, determine that is is related to artistic pursuits, and verify that the applicant is eligible for legal assistance. Applicants who meet these requirements are referred to a volunteer attorney who specializes in the appropriate area of law, so that the volunteer and the artist can establish a confidential attorney/client relationship. Examples of arts-related problems include copyright application or infringement, contract disputes and negotiations, and organizing a non-profit corporation. Applicants may call LVLA to see if their problem qualifies.

Cost: Free except for an application fee ($15 for individuals and $25 for organizations) and any filing fees, expenses or court costs related to the client's matter.

Additional information: Legal questions that require only routine information and no special research may be handled without formal application. In addition, help is available throughout the state of Louisiana. Attorneys from New Orleans, Baton Rouge, Bossier City, Lake Charles, Lafayette, Monroe, Opelousas and Shreveport are among the volunteers.

PHILADELPHIA VOLUNTEER LAWYERS FOR THE ARTS

Dorothy Manou, Executive Director
251 South 18th St.
Philadelphia, PA 19103
Phone: (215)545-3385 ext. 21
Fax: (215)545-0767
In business since: 1978
Business is for: Professional craftspeople and any artist and cultural non-profit organization with arts-related business and legal issues.
Services provided: Philadelphia Volunteer Lawyers for the Arts (PVLA) operates a pro-bono legal referral service providing assistance by volunteer attorneys to artists and area cultural nonprofit organizations with arts related legal problems. PVLA sponsors educational programs and seminars as

well as markets books and pamphlets that offer legal and business advice to artists and nonprofits. PVLA maintains an extensive library of arts related legal materials for public use.

Cost: Legal services are provided free of charge to qualified artists and cultural nonprofits. Qualification is based on the individual's income or the organization's budget and nonprofit status. At present, PVLA asks for a nominal donation (under $20) for individuals who use our full service referral. Our legal-line consultantions are also free of charge.

ST. LOUIS VOLUNTEER LAWYERS & ACCOUNTANTS FOR THE ARTS

Sue Greenberg
3540 Washington
St. Louis, MO 63103
Phone: (314)652-2410
Fax: (314)652-0011
In business since: 1981
Business is for: All disciplines and artists and small arts organizations.
Services provided: Library, speaker's bureau, seminars and publications.

TOLEDO VOLUNTEER LAWYERS FOR THE ARTS

Arnold N. Gottlieb
608 Madison Ave., Suite 1523
Toledo, OH 43604
Phone: (419)255-3344
Fax: (419)255-1329
In business since: 1989
Business is for: Professional craftspeople and artists of all media, non-profit organizations
Services provided: Organization provides low-cost services to artists and arts organizations. Periodic seminars and a lending library are available.
Cost: Sliding scale depending upon ability to pay.

VOLUNTEER LAWYERS FOR THE ARTS

1 E 53rd St., 6th Floor
New York, NY 10022
Phone: (212)319-2787
In business since: 1969
Business is for: Professional craftspeople and all artists: visual, choreographers, musicians, film/videomakers, performers, etc.
Services provided: For more than 25

years, Volunteer Lawyers for the Arts has provided free arts-related legal assistance to artist and arts organizations working in all creative disciplines. With an extensive network of attorneys who donate their time to assist VLA clinets, VLA provides thousands of emerging artists and art organizations in the New York metropolitan area with access to the legal help they need to protect themselves, their art and their livelihoods. VLA provides counseling and representation on a wide variety of arts-related legal topics, including: contracts, copyright and trademark, housing, loft and performance space problems, nonprofit incorporation/tax exemption, labor relations, small claims court advice, tax, wills and trusts and first amendment and other constitutional issues. VLA provides many educational programs designed to help artists and art administrators understand the laws that affect their professional careers, anticipate problems before they arise and avoid legal entanglements. VLA operates the Art Law Line [call (212)319-2910], a legal hotline for artist or arts organizations seeking arts-related legal information. Callers to the Art Law Line receive answers to legal questions, referrals to other legal service providers and arts organizations, and information about VLA publications, seminars and free legal services.

MARKETING, PROMOTING AND CONSULTING

ALTERNATIVE MEDIA GROUP

Kevin Van Gundy
P.O. Box 1952
Grant Junction, CO 81502
Phone: (970)242-6030
In business since: 1984
Business is for: Many kinds of clients but specialize in arts and crafts people.
Cost: Varies
Additional information: A full-service advertising agency that specializes in servicing the promotional needs of professional arts and crafts people.

THE ENTREPRENEURIAL CENTER FOR SMALL BUSINESS DEVELOPMENT

Constance Hallinan Lagan
35 Claremont Ave.
North Babylon, NY 11703
Phone: (516)661-5181
Fax: (516)321-0615
In business since: 1980
Business is for: Professional crafts-people and organizations, associations and individuals who wish to start and/or expand their business.
Services provided: The Entrepreneurial Center provides marketing advice specific to the craft industry in the areas of pricing, publicity, product development, distribution, sales, networking, mail order and stress management through meditation. We service our craft clients in several arenas: individual consults, seminars, publications and audio recordings. Our goal is to motivate craft clients to take action to transform their passion into profitable and professional businesses. Our client base includes sole proprietors, two-person operations, corporations and non-profit organizatons. Clients receive individualized marketing plans, personal attention, customized goal charts and networking opportunities. Our services enable clients to integrate all aspects of their lives, empowering them to achieve happiness and harmony in both their personal and professional lives.
Cost: $200/hour; $800/day; plus expenses (if any)
Additional information: The Entrepreneurial Center has provided programming for dozens of craft groups, including Brookfield Craft Center, Lancaster Craftsmens' Guild, The Michigan Guild of Artists and Artisans, Oregon School of Arts and Crafts, Pacific Northwest College of Art and *The Crafts Report.*

MASSIE'S

Barbara Massie
12 Flathead Dr.
Cherokee Village, AR 72529
Phone: (501)257-3837
Fax: (501)257-2033
E-mail: massies@centuryinter.net
In business since: 1983
Business is for: Professional crafts-people and any person with a home-based business or hoping to have a business.
Services provided: Massie shares her business experiences of over twenty-five years with creative people through writing and speaking. Booth space in malls, participating in craft shows and a degree in business management/accounting gives a solid base from which to share experience.
Cost: Costs vary depending on time needed, travel arrangements, etc. How-to-do business guides start at $5.95.
Additional information: With numerous how-to-do business writings to her credit, Massie has also produced two ribbon bow-making videos. Her popular demonstration classes include gift basket designing and bow-making. Massie is an ACCI Certified Professional Demonstrator (CPD.) She presents business seminars on marketing, pricing and other business related topics at conferences, to groups and to individuals. Her articles appear on the Internet, in *Neighbors & Friends* and other industry publications.

NANCRAFT®

Nancy Mosher
2804 Ryan Place Dr.
Ft. Worth, TX 76110-3127
Phone/fax: (817)921-6005
In business since: 1989
Business is for: Professional crafts-people and for the small sole proprietorship and/or home based business.
Services provided: Private consulting by phone, mail or personal conference can be arranged on a variety of topics on the business aspects of crafting. Topics incude but are not exclusive to bookkeeping and other record tracking, display, product line, advertising, business cards and pricing. Booth critiques of a craft mall space or craft show set up can be by photo or in person. Critique includes discussion of display, productions, pricing, etc. to guide the crafter to more successful sales.
Cost: $35 per hour; ½ hour booth critiques $15
Additional information: Nancy sells some business supplies she has developed specifically for the professional crafter including a bookkeeping ledger, long distance telephone log, craft show schedule organizer and small business signs such as sale sign or payment service available. Write for price list.

INTERNET

AMERICAN CRAFT CONNECTION

Linda C. Brzezinski
P.O. Box 3097
Ann Arbor, MI 48106
Phone/Fax: (313)971-7424
E-mail: daylily@ic.net
Website: http://www.daylilycrafts.com/acc.html
Business is for: Professional crafts-people only.
Services provided: A marketing tool for artists and craftspeople who wish to sell their art or crafts world wide on the computer Internet. The American Craft Connection is linked to hundreds of shopping malls and art/craft related sites on the Internet. Potential customers can view your online catalog 24 hours a day, 7 days a week. All sales are made directly to the artisan. No need to own a computer or have Internet access.
Cost: $100 set-up fee; $125 for 3 months service; $225 for 6 months; $400 for 12 months

CRAFTNET VILLAGE

Chris Larson, sales manager
5910 N. Lilly Rd.
Menomonee Falls, WI 53051
Phone: (414)252-4122; (800)839-0306
Fax: (414)252-3833
E-mail: chrisl@web.craftnet.org
Business is for: Professional crafts-people and craft manufacturers, publishers, designers
Services provided: CraftNet Village Bazaar offers pro-crafters the hottest craft site on the Internet to sell their finished crafts. Each page consists of a color photo of their hand crafted item, descriptive text, ordering information and an e-mail reply box for direct inquiries. Online secure order forms are also available.
Cost: Pages start at $150; each additional

page is $50. Custom sites quoted upon request.

Additional information: This is one of the leading all-craft sites on the Internet, chosen as a top 5% site in 1996.

CUTTING EDGE DISTRIBUTION, INC.

Will Simpson
12414 Alderbrook Dr., Suite 103
Austin, TX 78758
Phone: (512)339-2151
Fax: (512)672-4922
E-mail: cediinfo@cedi.com
Website: http://www.ced.com and http://www.craft.com
In business since: 1993
Business is for: All
Services provided: A full service Internet provider, CEDI offers turn-key or placement only services. We take the time to explain the pluses and minuses of an Internet website. From a small ad on page to a full domained site, Cutting Edge wants to be your World Wide Web provider.
Cost: One time set up starts at around $250; full written quote before starting. Monthly charges start at $60/month (billed quarterly).

WORKSHOPS

Technique

BROOKFIELD CRAFT CENTER

John Russell, Director
P.O. Box 122
Brookfield, CT 06804
Phone: (203)775-4526
Fax: (203)740-7815
E-mail: brkfldcrft@aol.com
Description: Brookfield Craft Center is a nonprofit school that holds approximately 250 different workshops each year in a wide variety of craft media, including ceramics, wood, metal, fibers and glass. Four free catalogs are published each year.
Cost: $110-480
When: New classes offered quarterly.
Where: At Brookfield Craft Center, Route 25, Brookfield, CT

CREATIVE ARTS WORKSHOP

Susan Smith, executive director; Francine Harcourt Caplan, director of public relations and development
80 Audubon St.
New Haven, CT 06510
Phone: (203)562-4927
Fax: (203)562-2329
Description: Nonprofit art school that offers classes in pottery, weaving, jewelry, painting, drawing, sculpture, lampmaking workshops, book arts.
Cost: Ranges from $150 for 12 session classes to $30 for a one-day workshop.
Where: Creative Arts Workshop at the above address

THE GUILFORD HANDCRAFT CENTER, INC.

Susan Tamulevich, registrar
P.O. Box 589, Church St.
Guilford, CT 06437
Phone: (203)453-5947
Fax: (203)453-6237
Description: A school offering both fine arts and craft classes in many media for adults, teens and youth. Workshops and classes range from basketry, weaving and blacksmithing to glass arts, bird carving and clay sculpture.
Cost: $15-205
Instructor's qualifications: Faculty of 44 with various degrees and experience
When: Year-round
Where: At the address above.
Additional information: The Guildford Handcraft Center was incorporated as an educational nonprofit organization in 1967. Our programs are supported by memberships and contributions. Our mission is to provide the public with enrichment in the arts through an inspiring range of programs and creative experiences. Financial Aid is available.

MUDFLAT POTTERY SCHOOL INC.

Lynn Gervens
149 Broadway
Somerville, MA 02145
Phone: (617)628-0589
Description: Mudflat offers a wide variety of classes for adults and children. Classes offered include wheelthrowing, handbuilding, sculpture and technical topics. Special classes and visit-

ing artist workshops are offered each semester.
Cost: $345 for 14 week semester/3 semesters per year
Instructor's qualifications: Most instructors have undergraduate and/or graduate degrees in ceramics, plus teaching experience.
When: Most classes meet once a week for 3 hours. Students can come in for additional practice time at no extra cost.
Where: Mudflat has 2 classrooms (one for wheelthrowing, one for handbuilding) plus 3 separate glaze rooms, located at above address.
Additional information: Mudflat's Open Studio and Sales, held every May and December, showcase the work of studio renters and students and provide an opportunity for friends, family and the community to visit the studios and school.

NORTHERN CLAY CENTER

Ann Kohls, education and studio program director
2375 Unviersity Ave. W
St. Paul, MN 55114
Phone: (612)642-1735
Fax: (612)644-8025
Description: On-going classes and workshops for all experience levels. NCC publishes a quarterly newsletter. Please call for more information and registration information.
Cost: Varies

OREGON COLLEGE OF ART & CRAFT

Shirl Lipkin, workshop coordinator
8245 SW Barnes Rd.
Portland, OR 97225
Phone: (503)297-5544
Fax: (503)297-9651
Description: Fine craft workshops throughout the year offered on weekends fall through spring and week-long in summer, in the following departments: book arts, ceramics, drawing, fibers, metal, photography, wood
Cost: Varies
Instructor's qualifications: Nationally and internationally renowned visiting faculty
When: 10-15 workshops per quarter
Where: In studios on the campus of Ore-

gon College of Art & Craft at the above address

PENNSYLVANIA GUILD OF CRAFTSMEN

Lyn Jackson, executive director
10 Stable Mill Lane
Richboro, PA 18954
Phone: (215)579-5997
Fax: (215)504-0650
Description: Offers intermediate- to professional-level crafts workshops with nationally recognized presenters. The 1996 series included: kaleidoscopes, glass blowing, advanced rubbers and resins, Michael James Pattern, Fred Fenster Pewtersmithing, Bruce Baker slides and jury process, planter mold-making for fine ceramics. Workshops are usually 1-3 days.
Cost: Varies
When: Year-round
Additional information: See the organization's listing on page 189 to learn how to join.

PETERS VALLEY CRAFT CENTER

Jennifer Brooks, registrar
19 Kuhn Rd.
Layton, NY 07851
Phone: (201)948-5200
Fax: (201)948-0011
Description: 2-9 day workshops running June through August in blacksmithing, ceramics, weaving, woodworking, photography, surface design and fine metals. Nationally recognized artist/teachers conduct these workshops for students beginner through advanced.
Cost: $135 for 2 days; $380 for 9 days
Instructor's qualifications: Varies from artist to artist. Many have MFAs and most have at least BAs or many years of producing their own work.
When: Approximately 70 different workshops are taught between June 2-August 31.
Where: At one of our seven studios located in the Peters Valley Craft Center, located within the rural Delaware Water Gap National Recreation area.
Additional information: Peters Valley offers an assistantship program each summer for students to live here and develop their skills further through study and working with the instruc-

tors. The deadline for applications is April 1.

REVERE ACADEMY OF JEWELRY ARTS

Alan Revere
760 Market St., Suite 900
San Francisco, CA 94102
Phone: (415)391-4179
Fax: (415)391-7570
Description: Study with nationally recognized masters and experts. Over 40 short, intensive classes. We have certificate and diploma courses for serious students and working jewelers at all levels.
Cost: Diploma progam(s) are $4,000-7,400 plus tools. Individual classes are $150-800.
Instructor's qualifications: Mr. Revere has been an instructor for over 20 years. The rest of the faculty are all working professionals with many years of experience in the jewelry industry.
When: 3 terms annually. Classes run 1-5 days.
Where: The Historic Phelan Building in downtown San Francisco, located at the above address.

SEGMENTED WOOD TURNINGS

George Radeschi
P.O. Box 1498
Doylestown, PA 18901
Phone: (215)348-5208
Fax: (215)348-4113
Description: Two-day workshops from introductory to advance levels on learning how to design, laminate, measure, cut, join, turn and finish segmented wood. Classes held monthly.
Cost: $200
Instructor's qualifications: Has taught for 20 years. Radeschi has been featured in numerous books and magazines and his work favorably reviewed by critics. His turnings are in several public, corporate and private collections.
When: Monthly on a Saturday and Sunday. Call or write for dates and details.
Where: At Radeschi's studio, 125 Windover Lane, Doylestown, PA
Additional information: Most recently featured in the book *Faceplate Turning-Features, Projects, Practice* published by Guild of Master Craftsmen

Publications and *Design Book Seven*, published by Taunton Press.

SUSAN'S CORNER/BASKET CLASSES

Susan Kute
1581 Bardstown Rd.
Louisville, KY 40205
Phone: (502)458-1712
Description: Beginners are most welcome. Learn to make a complete basket in just 2 evenings. A different basket is made/taught each month. Some favorites are egg, Jerimiah, Suzy, gathering and casserole. Small class size, individual attention, relaxed and fun atmosphere.
Cost: 2 day class $15 plus supplies (usually $10-15)
Instructor's qualifications: Has taught for 5 years. Attends and teaches at state workshops; won 4 ribbons at the 1995 Kentucky State Fair for baskets; sells baskets at local business and craft shows.
When: Once a month usually on Thursday evenings; special classes for groups held on request.
Where: At above address.

GEORGE B. SUTHERLAND PAINTING WORKSHOPS

George B. Sutherland
65 Hidden Brook Dr.
Stamford, CT 06907
Phone: (203)329-0488
Description: With outdoor day trips to a variety of settings, George B. Sutherland teaches the study of light and form from inspiring locations. Daily demonstrations cover basic painting techniques, mixing colors, composition and simple drawing. Students of all levels receive individual instructions and critiques. Classes specialize in watercolor painting, but teach pastels, oils and acrylic painting as well. During these workshops you will be able to gather resource material for many future paintings. Overall, be assured it will be rewarding and enjoyable art experience.
Cost: $200-2,500
Instructor's qualifications: Has taught for 30 years. George B. Sutherland studied illustration and graphic design at Parsons School of Design and then fine arts at the Art Students League in

New York City. A founder of the Stamford Art Association, Mr. Sutherland is a member of the American Watercolor Society, American Artist Professional League, Academic Artist Society of Springfield, MA. He has exhibited his work in more than 150 shows.

When: Workshops are offered April through October, range in length from four to seven days, and are limited to 6-15 students.

Where: In Stamford studio and on location: Giverny, France; Rockport, MA; Mystic Seaport, CT; Portland, ME; Caribbean; Cape Cod, MA; Rutland, VT.

TOUCHSTONE CENTER FOR CRAFTS

Julie Greene
RD 1, Box 783
Farmington, PA 15437
Phone: (412)329-1370
Fax: (412)329-1371
E-mail: tchstone@pennet.com
Description: A multitude of classes covering such areas as painting, drawing, fibers, ceramics, glass, wood, jewelry, blacksmithing and other mediums.
Cost: $150-290 for 5-6 day classes
When: Week-long workshops are M-F 9-4 and Sat 9-12.
Where: The Touchstone Center for Crafts is located 10 miles east of Uniontown, PA (60 miles southeast of Pittsburgh), off Route 40 East on the Elliotsville Road.

TRADITIONAL WILLOW BASKETRY

Bonnie Gale
RD 1, Box 124A
South New Berlin, NY 13843
Phone: (607)847-8264
Fax: (607)847-6634
Description: Offers one-, two- and three-day willow basketry classes for all levels.
Cost: Tuition ranges from $40 to 140. Material costs range from $20 to 68.
Instructor's qualifications: Has taught since 1984. Bonnie Gale, trained with professional European willow basketmakers and has taught traditional willow basketry to major guilds and conventions over the last 12 years. She is an active professional willow basketmaker herself.

When: March-September
Where: At Bonnie Gale's home in upstate New York
Additional information: I teach many different traditional willow basketry classes with the help of international guest instructors.

WESLEYAN POTTERS, INC.

Melissa Schilke
350 S. Main St.
Middletown, CT 06457
Phone/Fax: (800)347-5925
Description: We offer classes in basketry, weaving, jewelry and pottery.
Cost: Generally $100 for 9 weeks
Instructor's qualifications: Staff has taught for 1-10 years
When: Held once a week
Where: At the pottery studios at the above address.

WHEATON VILLAGE

J. Kenneth Leap
1501 Glasstown Rd.
Millville, NJ 08332
Phone: (609)825-6800, ext. 2762
Fax: (609)825-2410
Description: Introduction to Glass Painting is a three day workshop using examples of historic windows as a guide. Students of all skill levels will learn to mix, apply and fire glass based pigments. Traditional techniques covered include tracing, matting, using a badger blender and silver staining. Students will cut out, paint and fire glass during the workshop to create a small panel which they can assemble at home.
Cost: $180 plus $35 materials and firing fee
Instructor's qualifications: Has taught since 1988. BFA Rhode Island School of Design.
When: Twice a year: Spring and Fall
Where: In the Painted Window Stained Glass Studio at Wheaton Village in Millville
Additional information: Wheaton Village also offers other opportunities to learn about glassmaking and other crafts. Information is available on request.

WORCESTER CENTER FOR CRAFTS

25 Sagamore Rd.
Worcester, MA 01605
Phone: (508)753-8183
Fax: (508)797-5626
E-mail: craftctr@usal.com
Description: The Worcester Center for Crafts, organized in 1856, is one of the oldest non-profit institutions for craft education in the United States. Offering the finest in contemporary craft education, the Worcester Center for Crafts features a two-year certificate program of full-time professional training for career-oriented students in clay, fibers, metals and wood. At the same time, classes are offered for adults, teens and children of all levels of ability in a wide variety of craft media. Two galleries devoted exclusively to craft exhibitions, workshops with visiting artists and two annual crafts fairs further expand the Worcester Center for Crafts' mission of craft education.
Cost: Varies
When: Year-round
Where: All classes and workshops are held at the Worcester Center for Crafts at the above address.
Additional information: The department heads are: Tom O'Malley, ceramics; Johanna Evans, fibers; Sarah Nelson, metals; Bob March, wood; Loren Manbeck, refinishing; Peter Faulkner, photography.

Business

BEHIND-THE-SCENES SELLING SECRETS OF PROFESSIONAL ARTISTS & CRAFTSPEOPLE

Kevin Van Gundy
P.O. Box 1952
Grand Junction, CO 81502
Phone: (970)241-8008
Fax: (970)242-6030
Description: Provides inside information in a four hour, hands-on, high-energy, brain-in-gear, example-rich, one-of-a-kind workshop that teaches how to sell more arts and crafts.
Cost: $99
Instructor's qualifications: Has taught since 1986. Show promoting between Salt Lake City and Denver since 1979, he's an artisan and a professionally-

trained international marketing consultant.

When: On demand

Where: Live at your location or by audio album with workbook.

CRAFT BUSINESS INSTITUTE

Linda McCormick

The Rosen Group

3000 Chestnut Ave., Suite 300

Baltimore, MD 21211

Phone: (410)889-2933

Fax: (410)889-1320

Description: Designed for craftspeople, students and recent graduates who want to "learn the art of selling what you make." More than two dozen topics are included in this 3-day conference: product development, pricing, public relations, accounting, wholesaling/retailing and more from industry leaders and retail experts.

Cost: $399

Instructor's qualifications: Faculty includes craft retailers, craft artists, director of TV shopping channels, show promoters, publishers, art directors, art dealerships, gallery owners.

When: Annually

Where: Mt. Washington Conference Center, Baltimore, MD

Additional information: Scholarships are available to craft students and recent graduates. Includes room, meals, attendance at all sessions.

CRAFTS MARKETING WORKSHOPS

Loretta Radeschi

P.O. Box 1498

Doylestown, PA 18901

Phone: (215)348-5208

Fax: (215)348-4113

Description: Workshops from one hour in length on a variety of topics including pricing, developing a marketing plan, selecting craft shows and other outlets, retailing, wholesaling, consignment, booth design, business practices, promotional materials, customer service, publicity.

Cost: From $100

Instructor's qualifications: Has taught since 1989. Author of *This Business of Glass* business guide for artists and retailers; editor and writer of business, feature and profile articles since 1978;

marketer and publicist of high end crafts since 1986.

When: As requested by the sponsoring organization

Where: At sponsoring organization's site

MARKETING YOUR CRAFTS PROFITABLY AND PROFESSIONALLY

Constance Hallinan Lagan

35 Claremont Ave.

North Babylon, NY 11703

Phone: (516)661-5181

Fax: (516)321-0615

Description: This seminar is designed for both novice and experienced craft marketers. Topics include the red tape steps of setting up a business, filing for sales tax authorization certification, addressing insurance concerns, selecting distribution channels (craft fairs, juried shows, galleries, home showings, retail gift shops, catalogs, mail order, department stores, mall pushcarts, boutiques), purchasing supplies wholesale, computing retail/wholesale prices, hiring employees versus independent contractors, and estimating overhead costs. Retailing, wholesaling, consignment and rented shelf space are discussed. Attendees learn what to sell, where to sell it, and how to price it; how to avoid costly mistakes, how to correct past marketing errors and management decisions, and how to increase their profit margin.

Cost: Varies

Instructor's qualifications: Has taught since 1980. Instructor's educational background is in marketing/business management. She is author of *Marketing Your Crafts*; columnist for *The Crafts Report* and *Art 'N' Crafts Show Guide*; professional member of National Speakers Association; director of The Enterpreneorial Center. Sponsors include SBA, USDA, Chamber of Commerce, New York State Dept. of Economic Development and faculty of AWED.

When: Approximately 20-30 times each year

Where: Nationwide

Additional information: Craft industry sponsors include: Fletcher Farm School of Craft & Art, Brookfield Craft Center, The L.A. Mart, Ameri-

can Home Sewing & Craft Association, *The Crafts Report*, Michigan Guild of Artists and Artisans, Mississippi Sewing Guild, National Convergence for Machine Knitters, Montclair Craft Guild, Long Island Craft Guild, Lancaster Designer Craftsmen, Mid-Atlantic Fiber Conference, The Canadian Consulate, Oregon School of Art and Design, Pacific Northwest College of Art.

NANCRAFT®—BUSINESS MANAGEMENT FOR THE PROFESSIONAL CRAFTER

Nancy Mosher

2804 Ryan Place Dr.

Ft. Worth, TX 76110-3127

Phone/Fax: (817)921-6005

Description: The seminar is a 3 hour session covering a variety of topics on the business aspects of crafting. Topics include but are not exclusive to how to start, pricing, display, product line, advertising, business cards with an in depth emphasis on bookkeeping and other record keeping. Short sessions on any one topic listed above may be presented on request.

Cost: Sponsored by NanCraft, $35 per session. Cost varies under other sponsorship.

Instructor's qualifications: Has taught since 1988. BA in elementary education plus over 16 years of crafting and selling at craft shows, craft malls and other means, over 30 years home-based business experience also freelance writer for the hand crafted industry. Active as a volunteer in the craft supply trade industry.

When: Times and frequency vary from year to year; sessions are scheduled by the instructor or by invitation as guest speaker/instructor.

Where: Locations vary—may be presented at trade shows or at conference centers scheduled by presenter or other sponsorship.

Additional information: If a class is not available either at the time or place needed, a private consultation by phone, mail or personal conference can be arranged. Anyone interested in sponsoring a presentation by Nancy should call or write for further information.

CHAPTER FOURTEEN
Trade Organizations

AMERICAN ASSOCIATION OF WOODTURNERS

Mary Redig, administrator
3200 Lexington Ave.
Shoreview, MN 55126
Phone: (612)484-9094
Fax: (612)484-1724
E-mail: 75037.2123@compuserve.com
Established in: 1986
Type of organization: International organization for crafters working in woodturning.
Statement of purpose: To provide education, information and organization to those interested in turning wood.
Membership: Open
Membership fee/Dues: $25 general; $50 general business; $100 supporting
Members: 6,200
Meetings: Once a year. Across the country.
Advantages for members: Quarterly journal, local chapters, annual symposium, educational grants, resource directory.
Publication: American Woodturner
Branches: Contact national office for locations.

AMERICAN CRAFT ASSOCIATION, a professional member category of The American Craft Council (ACC)

Helise Winters, director, 1992-1996
21 S. Eltings Corner Rd.
Highland, NY 12528
Phone: (800)724-0859
Fax: (914)883-6130
Established in: ACA category established in 1991
Type of organization: National organization for craftspeople and craft retailers
Statement of purpose: The association is a member category of the American Craft Council. The Council is a not for profit membership organization founded in 1943 to increase public awareness and education of craft and to provide a variety of services and programs for makers, sellers, educators and lovers of craft.

Membership: Open
Membership fee/dues: $50
Members: 3,100 in this professional member category
Activities/Events: In addition to services, ACA sponsors seminars and workshops which address business and philosophical issues related to the craft community.
Advantages for members: When you join you will gain access to such valuable benefits as discounted health and property/casualty insurance, a credit card acceptance program and wide range of educaton seminars.
Publication: The Voice

THE AMERICAN SEWING GUILD (ASG)

Jean Fristensky
P.O. Box 8568
Medford, OR 97504-0568
Phone: (541)776-7740; (541)772-4059
Fax: (541)770-7041
E-mail: sewasg@aol.com
Established in: 1978
Type of organization: National organization for crafters working in sewing and needle arts.
Statement of purpose: ASG is a nonprofit national organization with a network of chapters throughout the United States. Its purpose is to promote sewing through instruction, guidance and encouragement. As a national consumer organization it is a link with the entire sewing industry.
Membership: Open
Membership fee/Dues: $25 Initial year; $20 renewals
Members: 20,000
Meetings: Chapters provide monthly neighborhood group meetings, chapter meetings/events 4-6 times per year.
Activities/Events: Large consumer "sewing & needleart expsoition," national convention
Publication: Notions
Branches: Write to the above address for locations.

AMERICAN SOCIETY OF ARTISTS (A.S.A.)

American Artisans
P.O. Box 1326
Palatine, IL 60078
Phone: (312)751-2500; (847)991-4748
Established in: 1972
Type of organization: A national organization
Statement of purpose: The American Artisans of the American Society of Artists is a national membership organization which is concerned about you, your ambitions, your artistic talents and even your problems.
Membership: Juried. To apply, please supply photos or slides (5 of work, include one slide/photo of display setup if wish to exhibit/list medium on slide), catalog/promotional materials, written description of work, résumé/show listing.
Membership fee/Dues: $20 initation fee/ $50 yearly dues
Members: 7,000
Activities/Events: Art and craft shows in Illinois and Missouri
Advantages for members: Participate in art and craft/craft shows, access to other benefits. Those who qualify participate in Lecture and Demonstration Service and are "booked" for lectures, demonstrations, workshops/seminars for various organizations. We also send people to judge/jury for other organizations. Various other benefits.
Publication: A.S.A. Artisan

AMERICAN WILLOW GROWERS NETWORK

Bonnie Gale
RD 1, Box 124A
South New Berlin, NY 13843
Phone: (607)847-8264
Fax: (607)847-6634
Established in: 1988
Type of organization: International organization for crafters working in willow, florists/nurseries.
Statement of purpose: The American

Willow Growers Network is a network of people dedicated to the growing and exploration of the great potentials of Salix in an open cooprative manner by the sharing of information, exchanging cuttings and the development of the uses of willow.

Membership: Open

Membership fee/Dues: $7 US; $8 Canada; $10 overseas

Members: 400

Advantages for members: Members fill out an annual survey of their growing and use activities. Members have access to an annual list of cuttings (willow) for sale.

Publication: *The Newsletter of the American Willow Growers Network*

ART GLASS SUPPLIERS ASSOCIATION, INTERNATIONAL (AGSA)

Patty Parrish, executive director
1100-H Brandywine Blvd.
P.O. Box 2188
Zanesville, OH 43702-2188
Phone: (614)452-4541
Fax: (614)452-2552
Established in: 1986

Type of organization: National and international organization for professional, full-time craftspeople (studios) involved in the art glass field and who sell supplies; retailers; wholesalers; manufacturers; manufacturer's reps; publishers.

Statement of purpose: To create awareness, knowledge and involvement, within the art glass trade and outward to the public, for the growth and prosperity of the art glass industry. AGSA is a non-profit trade association.

Membership: Must qualify as a member of the trade. Members are retailers, studios, consultants, designers, teachers who can present a resale tax certificate and two other trade IDs (not business card); manufacturers and publishers who can present any three of the following: business ad, check, credit card, utility invoice, lease, letterhead or copy of current year's invoice to wholesaler. Manufacturers' rep who can present a personalized business card, letter of authorization from a supplier and a business letterhead. Wholesalers and distributors who can present a current catalog plus two other trade IDs (not business card).

Membership fee/Dues: $50-250

Members: 643

Meetings: Twice a year

Activities/Events: International art glass suppliers trade show

Advantages for members: All members benefit from education, newsletter, industry promotions, listing in member directory, rental of member lists, annual trade shows and networking. They also benefit by having a voice and vote.

Publication: *AGSA News*

Additional information: AGSA sponsors, each April, the International Art Glass Month Celebration. The event helps create consumer awareness for art and decorative glass as a hobby and in decorating a home or office.

ARTIST-BLACKSMITHS' ASSOCIATION OF NORTH AMERICA (ABANA)

Central Office
P.O. Box 206
Washington, MO 63090
Phone/Fax: (314)390-2133
E-mail: Round Table: listproc@wugate.wustl.edu
Website: http://www.wuarchive.wustl.edu/edu/arts/blacksmithing/ABANA
Established in: 1973

Type of organization: National organzation for artist blacksmithing, miscellaneous metalwork.

Statement of purpose: ABANA is a nonprofit organization of artist blacksmiths dedicated to promoting the art of blacksmithing through educational avenues.

Membership: Open

Membership fee/Dues: $35 per year

Members: 4,000 +

Meetings: A conference every 2 years on the even year. At alternating sites around the U.S. hosted by chapters. 1998—North Carolina.

Activities/Events: Workshops, regional conferences, biennial international conferences.

Advantages for members: 2 publications with membership (quarterly magazine and quarterly newsletter); discount on plans, back issues, souvenirs; rental privileges for VHS and slide library; free resources such as supplier directory, instructional hand-outs; scholarships; liability group insurance; free classified advertising.

Publication: *Blacksmith's Journal* (magazine), *The Anvil's Ring* (magazine), *The Hammer's Blow* (newsletter)

Branches: Chapter list available through membership package or contacting office.

ASSOCIATION OF CRAFTS & CREATIVE INDUSTRIES (ACCI)

Julie Fox, executive director, 1993-1996
1100-H Brandywine Blvd.
P.O. Box 2188
Zanesville, OH 43702-2188
Phone: (614)452-4541
Fax: (614)452-2552
E-mail: acci.info@creative-industries.com
Website: http://www.creative-industries.com/acci
Established in: 1976

Type of organization: International organization for everyone who buys, sells or services the creative industries including manufacturers, retailers, wholesalers, distributors, manufacturer reps, publishers, professional crafters, consultants, designers and teachers.

Statement of purpose: ACCI is the world's largest trade organization representing the craft supply industry. ACCI's mission is "to establish and advance programs creating a larger market share for the crafts and creative industries." ACCI serves the industry through sponsorship of marketplaces, professional development, industry promotion and a network of resources and information.

Membership: Open. There are specific ID requirements for each membership category.

Membership fee/Dues: $35-125 depending on category

Members: Approx. 6,000

Meetings: Annual meeting held during the ACCI-sponsored International Craft Exposition

Activities/Events: ACCI sponsors the International Craft Exposition, a 2,000-plus booth, wholesale supply show; and The Profesional Crafters Trade Shows, regional marketplaces for the production craftsperson and participates in the U.S. Creative Industries Pavilions in England, Mexico, Australia, Germany and Signapore. ACCI is the originator of National Craft Month, celebrated in March and also sponsors the Create-A-Craft School Grant program to encourage craft activites in schools; Discover Creativity, a multimedia industry promotion displaying the benefits and opportunities of crafting; and the Professional Craft Artisan Program, a business program offering recognition and education for the personal and business growth of professional craft artisans. ACCI also sponsors The Creative Industries Connection, a website for its members, as well as The Creativity Connection website, an information resource on craft projects, ideas and supplies.

Advantages for members: ACCI members receive free admittance to the International Craft Exposition and discounts on educational sessions; can participate in programs such as National Craft Month, Create-A-Craft and Discover Creativity; have access to The Creative Industries Connection on the Internet; receive bimonthly newsletter, plus other publications on trends and consumer buying habits. Other member benefits include travel discounts, bankcard service, bar code/ product label information and group health insurance.

Publication: ACCI News

Branches: In the process of establishing international affiliations in England, Mexico, Australia, Germany

CANADIAN CRAFT & HOBBY ASSOCIATION

Patrice Baron-Parent, executive director
#24 1410 40th Ave. NE
Calagary, Alberta T2E 6L9 Canada
Phone: (403)291-0559
Fax: (403)291-0675
E-mail: cchap@cadvision.com
Established in: 1979
Type of organization: International organization for trade only.
Statement of purpose: We offer a forum for meeting new people, learning new ideas and profiting from the benefits of working together.
Membership: Must provide 2 pieces of business identification. Business iden-

tification we accept: copy of Yellow Page listing; copy of business telephone bill; bona fide business rent receipt; copy of current tax assessment; GST registration; copy of incorportion or trade name registration.
Membership fee/Dues: $110 retail; $215 wholesale
Members: 1,000
Meetings: Annual meeting at Calgary Trade Show. At 1410 Olympic Way SE, Calgary AB, Calgary Roundup Centre
Activities/Events: 2 annual trade shows with an educational conference at each show.
Advantages for members: Free admission to Canada's largest annual industry trade show; revenue generating "National Craft Month"; excellent rates on national Visa and MasterCard program; free subscriptions to industry magazines; membership directory and buyer's guide; group insurance and benefits plan.
Publication: Canadian Craft Trade

THE EMBROIDERERS' GUILD OF AMERICA, INC.

Bonnie Key, office manager
335 W. Broadway, Suite 100
Louisville, KY 40202
Phone: (502)589-6956
Fax: (502)584-7900
E-mail: egahq@aol.com
Established in: 1958
Type of organization: National organization for needlework done by hand.
Statement of purpose: The Embroiderers' Guild of America, Inc., is open to all stitchers, beginner, intermediate and advanced. It is a non-profit, educational, charitable, non-discriminatory organzation founded in 1958 to foster high standards of design, color and workmanship in embroidery, to teach the embroidery arts, to preserve our national needle arts heritage.
Membership: Open
Membership fee/Dues: $24 per year for member at large
Members: 20,000 +
Meetings: Chapters meet monthly; national meeting annually. National meeting held in a different geographic location each year: 1997 New Orleans; 1998 Louisville, KY

Activities/Events: Organization sponsors exhibits on local, regional and national level; region and national seminars; school of advanced study, correspondence courses, community outreach programs, etc.
Advantages for members: Quarterly membership publication, needlework exhibits, study boxes, slide shows, videos, lending library, traveling collection, community outreach, extensive education programs, workshops, seminars, master craftsman program, certification programs.
Publication: Needle Arts Magazine
Branches: 353 chapters. Contact the national headquarters at the above address for information.

FLORIDA CRAFTSMEN INC. (FC)

Michele Tuegel, director 1988-1997
501 Central Ave.
St. Petersburg, FL 33701
Phone: (813)821-7391
Fax: (813)822-4294
Established in: 1952
Type of organization: State-wide organization for craftspeople.
Statement of purpose: The mission of Florida Craftsmen, Inc., a service organization, is to broaden public awareness, understanding and appreciation of fine craft art and to encourage professionalism and high aesthetic standards among artists.
Membership: Open
Membership fee/Dues: $35 individual, $60 family, $75 supporting
Members: 800
Meetings: Quarterly board meetings. Held all over the state, primarily at above address.
Activities/Events: Exhibition and members' gallery; statewide competitive annual exhibition; statewide annual crafts conference
Advantages for members: Quarterly newsletters, informational updates, workshop opportunities, 10% discount on FC gallery purchases, access to slide registry, ongoing craft library, latest in crafts information statewide, scholarship opportunities, area shows and workshops, video library, competitive exhibitions, annual membership directory, marketing opportunities, discount on workshops/seminars.

Publication: Florida Craftsmen News

Branches: Call above number for locations. The state is broken up into 9 areas, each with a craftsmember representative.

GLASS ART SOCIETY (G.A.S.)

Penny Berk, executive director, 1996
1305 Fourth Ave., Suite 711
Seattle, WA 98101-2401
Phone: (206)382-1305
Fax: (206)382-2630
E-mail: Alice 110@aol.com
Established in: 1971
Type of organization: International organization for crafters working in glass.
Statement of purpose: G.A.S. is an international non-profit organizaton founded in 1971 to encourage excellence and to advance the appreciation, understanding and development of the glass arts worldwide. The Society strives to stimulate communication among artists, educators, students, collectors, gallery and museum personnel, art critics, manufacturers and all others interested in and involved with the production, technology and aesthetics of glass. We are dedicated to creating greater public awareness and appreciation of the glass arts.
Membership: Open
Membership fee/Dues: US, Canada, Mexico: $40 individual, $60 family, $15 full-time student. Other countries: $50 invidivudal, $25 full-time student.
Members: 1,600
Meetings: Annual conference. All over USA and occasionally abroad.
Activities/Events: Members and student exhibitons at annual conference, lectures, demonstrations, workshops at conference.
Publication: Glass Art Society Journal (annual) and *GAS News*, a thrice yearly newsletter sent to members.

INTERNATIONAL GUILD OF GLASS ARTISTS (IGGA)

Gerry Phibbs, chair
Tonetta Lake Rd.
Brewster, NY 10509
Phone: (914)278-2152
Fax: (914)278-2481
E-mail: 70544.3642@compuserve.com

Website: http://www.BUNGI.com/glass/IGGA
Established in: 1993
Type of organization: International organzation for crafters working in glass.
Statement of purpose: To faciliate communication among the glass artists, to encourage education and promote excellence in the glass arts.
Membership: Open
Membership fee/Dues: In North America (per year): student/hobbyist $25, individual artist $45, partner artists $55, studio/corporate $150, benefactor/founder $500. Outside North America (per year): student/hobbyist $50, individual artist $90, partner artist $110, studio/corporate $300, benefactor/founder $1,000.
Members: 279 (growing at 123%/year)
Meetings: Annual. At various locations in conjunction with trade shows in different venues.
Activities/Events: Referral service, local chapter grants, local chapters, year-round school planned, book service, online contacts and library.
Publication: Common Ground: Glass
Branches: Contact headquarters at above address.

KENTUCKY CRAFT MARKETING PROGRAM

Fran Redmon, program manager, 1987-present
39 Fountain Place
Frankfort, KY 40601
Phone: (502)564-8076
Fax: (502)564-5696
Website: http://www.state.ky.us/crafts/crfthome.htm
Established in: 1981
Type of organization: State government serving craftspeople, residents of Kentucky only.
Statement of purpose: The Kentucky Craft Marketing Program strives to develop the state's craft industry, create an economically viable environment for craft enterprenuers while preserving the state's craft traditions, and generate greater public awareness through education.
Membership: Juried. Kentucky residents only. To apply, please supply slides

only (5); sample of work (5 samples per entry).
Membership fee/Dues: $10
Members: 407
Meetings: 1-2 annually of craft market advisory committee at above address
Activities/Events: Kentucky Craft Market—the only state-sponsored wholesale/retail show in the USA
Advantages for members: Cooperative advertising; able to exhibit via samples at selected national shows; use of Kentucky Crafted logo; exhibit at Governor's Annual Derby Day Celebration; exhibit/sell at annual craft market; business development and loan program; special events/displays
Publication: Kentucky Crafted: The Newsletter and *Kentucky Crafted Buyer's Guide*

MINIATURES INDUSTRY ASSOCIATION OF AMERICA (MIAA)

Patty Parrish, association manager
1100-H Brandywine Blvd.
P.O. Box 2188
Zanesville, OH 43702-2188
Phone: (614)452-4541
Fax: (614)452-2552
Established in: 1979
Type of organization: International organization for professional, full-time craftspeople involved in the miniatures (artisans); manufacturers; retailers; wholesalers; manufacturer's reps.
Statement of purpose: MIAA is an non-profit, international trade association with a steadfast dedication to promoting miniatures, dolls, dollhouses and collectibles.
Membership: Member must qualify as a member of the trade. Retailers can show a resale tax certificate and two other trade IDs (not business card). Wholesaler can show company letterhead, current catalog and photocopy of invoice to a retailer. Artisan, manufacturer and publisher can show any two of the following: business ad, company check, company credit card, business lease, utility invoice or phone listing. Manufacturer's rep can show a company letterhead, personalized business card and letter of authorization from a supplier.
Membership fee/Dues: $75-500
Members: 424

Meetings: Annual meeting, during the summer trade show

Activities/Events: The International Miniature Collectibles Trade Show, Sheraton New York Hotel, New York, NY; National Dollhouse and Miniatures Trade Show and Convention, Rhode Island Convention Center, Providence, RI.

Advantages for members: All members benefit from education, newsletter, industry promotions, listing in member directory, rental of member lists, annual trade shows and networking. They also benefit with voice, vote.

Publication: MIAA Industry News

Additional information: Each October, MIAA sponsors National Dollhouse and Miniatures Month. The event helps create consumer awareness for dollhouses, dolls, miniatures and collectibles as a hobby.

THE NATIONAL NEEDLEWORK ASSOCIATION (TNNA)

Paige S. Bilotta, executive director
1100-H Brandywine Blvd.
P.O. Box 2188
Zanesville, OH 43702-2188
Phone: (614)455-6773
Fax: (614)452-2552
Established in: 1974
Type of organization: National organization for needlework related suppliers and retailers.
Statement of purpose: Preservation, encouragement and enhancement of the tradition of needlearts and the cultivation of a strong, growing and profitable needlearts industry.
Membership: Specific business identification required. 2 types of memberships: regular—for suppliers; associate—for retailers, etc.
Membership fee/Dues: $250-750 regular members; $35 associate members
Members: 1,220
Meetings: Meetings for members held at trade shows.
Activities/Events: 3 trade shows featuring educational programs and special events such as Fashion Show and Needlepoint Galleria.
Advantages for members: Discounts on educational seminars and special events, discounts on business services

and products, scholarship program and more.
Publication: TNNA Today (quarterly newsletter), available to members only

NATIONAL SOCIETY OF TOLE AND DECORATIVE PAINTERS

Julie Vosberg
393 N. McLean Blvd.
Wichita, KS 67203
Phone: (316)269-9300
Fax: (316)269-9191; (316)269-3535
Established in: 1972
Type of organization: International organization for decorative painters.
Statement of purpose: The purpose of the Society is to act as a central dissemination point for information about activities related to decorative painting; raise and maintain a high standard for the art of decorative painting; and stimulate interest in and appreciation for the art form.
Membership: Open
Membership fee/Dues: $30 individual; $60 business
Members: 28,000
Meetings: Annual meeting and convention and chapter meetings on the local level. Chapter meetings are held all around the country. Annual meeting is held in a different city each year.
Activities/Events: Hold the annual meeting and convention, the largest gathering of decorative painters in the world. Chapters host mini-conventions in various regions throughout the country.
Advantages for members: Networking other decorative artists; teaching and publishing opportunities; educational activities; juried art competition; chapter involvement; special society-wide projects; certification program that recognizes painting excellence.
Publication: The Decorative Painter
Branches: Call the national office at the above number for a list or purchase our annual directory.

NEW ENGLAND NEEDLEWORK ASSOCIATION (NENA)

Louise Anne Leader, coordinator, 1986-present
174 Tower Ave.
Needham Heights, MA 02194

Phone/Fax: (617)449-1717
Established in: 1972
Type of organization: Regional organization for shops working in needlework and knitting.
Statement of purpose: This is a small but vital organization dedicated to presenting to shop owners a broad range of vendor exhibitors selling all types of products relating to the needlework industry.
Membership: Open
Membership fee/Dues: $50 per year for exhibitors
Members: 165
Meetings: 1 meeting per year. At Sturbridge Host Inn and Conference Center, Main St., Sturbridge, MA.
Activities/Events: One 2-day wholesale trade show each year.
Advantages for members: Gives an opportunity for manufacturers, distributors and reps to exhibit their line(s).
Additional information: Shops from all over the US and Canada attend this show to see the latest trends in the needlework and knitting industry.

PENNSYLVANIA GUILD OF CRAFTSMEN (PGC)

10 Stable Mill Trail
Richboro, PA 18954
Phone: (215)579-5997
Fax: (215)504-0650
Type of organization: National organization for craftspeople.
Statement of purpose: The purpose and intent is to promote, encourage and develop one of Pennsylvania's finest resources: crafts. For half a century this guild has served the crafts community through educational opportunities, marketing events, information services, encouragement and fellowship.
Membership: Open
Membership fee/Dues: Varies from chapter to chapter
Meetings: Varies among chapters
Activities/Events: Several major Pennsylvanian crafts festivals.
Advantages for members: Provides jurying opportunities, gallery exhibits and annual workshops offering professional development opportunities.
Publication: Pennsylvania Crafts
Branches: Call or write for information.

Additional information: Twenty chapters, while independent in their activities, are an integral part of the whole PGC, and welcome participation by members from other regions. Membership in the Guild may be "At Large," that is, without any chapter affiliation, or through one or more chapters. Chapters have own dues schedule in addition to state fees.

SNAG, AN ORGANIZATION FOR JEWELERS, DESIGNERS AND METALSMITHS

Robert Mitchell, office manager
5009 Londonderry Dr.
Tampa, FL 33647-9910
Phone: (813)977-5326
Fax: (813)977-8462
E-mail: rmitchel@cftnet.com
Established in: 1968
Type of organization: National organization for crafters working in metal.
Statement of purpose: To promote a favorable and enriching environment in which contemporary metalsmiths practice their art. To provide education of the public on the quality and rich diversity of metalsmithing.
Membership: Open
Membership fee/Dues: $55 per year
Members: 2,500
Meetings: Boad of Directors twice a year; membership at annual conference
Activities/Events: Annual conference; 1997—Albuquerque, NM; 1998—Seattle, WA
Advantages for members: Supports scholarships and fellowships for young artists. Provides workshops/lectures for regional and local metal and craft guilds. Sponsors exhibitions.
Publications: Metalsmith, Exhibition in Print and *SNAG News*

SOCIETY OF AMERICAN SILVERSMITHS (SAS)

Jeffrey Herman, executive director
P.O. Box 3599
Cranston, RI 02910
Phone: (401)461-3156; (401)461-3196
E-mail: slvrsmth@ids.net
Website: http://www.ids.net/~slvrsmth/sashome.htm
Established in: 1989
Type of organization: National organization for crafters working in silver.
Statement of purpose: SAS was founded as the nation's only professional organization solely devoted to the preservation and promotion of contemporary silversmithing—specifically in the areas of holloware, flatware and sculpture. Its Artisan members, those silversmiths both practicing and retired, who now or used to smith as a livelihood, are provided with support, networking and greater access to the market. SAS also educates the public in demystifying silversmithing techniques, silver care, restoration and conservation, and the aesthetic value of this art form through its free consulting service. Another aim is to assist those students who have a strong interest in becoming silver craftsmen. With the aid of SAS, its many supplier discounts, and available workshops throughout the school year, students will be better prepared to start their lives as professional silversmiths upon graduation.
Membership: Open Supporting and Associate memberships; juried Artisan membership. To apply, please supply photos or slides (6), must be of sterling or fine silver (not plated) holloware, flatware and/or sculpture, résumé. Members must be out of school with an established shop or smithing within a company. Firescale, buffing drag lines, pitted solder joints, unintentional file marks and poor construction are unacceptable.
Membership fee/Dues: $20 associate, $40 supporting (US); $45 supporting, $35 Artisan (foreign)
Members: 245
Advantages for members: In addition to an outstanding benefits package of 27 suppliers of discounted goods and services, and the yearly traveling exhibition catalog, all members have free access to the Society's technical and marketing expertise, library, and a referral service that commissions work from its Artisans. The archives contain Artisan résumés, slides, photographs and a maker's mark registry for Artisan identification.
Publication: American Silversmith

VIRGINIA MOUNTAIN CRAFTS GUILD

Kathy Sue Hudson
P.O. Box 1369
Salem, VA 24153
Phone: (540)389-6163
Established in: 1975
Type of organization: State-wide organization for craftspeople.
Statement of purpose: To offer education and training for the arts and crafts community and quality arts and crafts to the general public.
Membership: Open. To achieve Exhibiting Status a member's work must be juried and approved for excellence of workmanship.
Membership fee/Dues: $20
Activities/Events: Scholarship program for college and high school students; educational programs; workshops; sponsors 3 arts and crafts shows a year.

WESTERN STATES CRAFT & HOBBY ASSOCIATION (WSCHA)

Betty Scott, secretary
P.O. Box 1007
Huntington Beach, CA 92647
Phone: (310)430-6038
Established in: 1953 as Southern California Craft & Hobby Association
Type of organization: Regional organization for craftspeople and manufacturers, wholesalers, retailers, manufacturers representatives, teachers/demonstrators, publishers, judges/consultants.
Statement of purpose: To promote the craft and hobby industry. Our focus is education of our industry members and the consumer, in the use of craft product (both new and existing).
Membership: Open
Membership fee/Dues: $30-50
Activities/Events: Quarterly and annual meetings; dates and location vary. Annual public juried craft and hobby show.
Advantages for members: Educational and business programs, product seminars, certified professional demonstrator programs and referrals, consumer product education, industry networking, plus a resource center with a toll-free hotline.
Publication: WSCHA News

CHAPTER FIFTEEN

Craft-Related Publications

PERIODICALS

A.S.A. ARTISAN
American Society of Artists
P.O. Box 1326
Palatine, IL 60078
Editorial: American Society of Artists
Phone: (312)751-2500
In business since: 1972
Type of publication: National, trade publication, published 4 times per year. Newsletter style—black and white.
Description of publication: Publication includes information for and about members of American Society of Artists (and crafts division—American Artisans); articles to help members; listings of shows; competitions across the country; information on supplies; information on awards and other achievements by members; articles on members.
Available: For members only
Circulation: Membership
Target audience: Members of American Society of Artists (and crafts division—American Artisans)
Submissions: No unsolicited manuscripts accepted.
Additional information: See the organization's listing on page 185 to learn how to join.

AMERICANSTYLE MAGAZINE
The Rosen Group
3000 Chestnut Ave., #304
Baltimore, MD 21211
Editorial: Hope Daniels, editor
Advertising: John Stefancik
Phone: Editorial—(410)889-3093
Advertising—(800)642-4314
Subscriptions—(800)642-4314
Fax: (410)243-7089
In business since: 1995
Type of publication: National, consumer publication, published 4 times per year. Magazine style—color.
Description of publication: *Americanstyle* is a quarterly magazine that celebrates contemporary fine art in all its forms. It focuses on the work of America's most talented designers; highlighting craft works that can be admired as much for their technical expertise as for their creativity and symbolism. The magazine explores both decorative and functional works in all media in full-page artist profiles and other feature stories. Each issue contains articles on major collectors and collections of American craft art. Arts destination tours are also part of each quarterly edition, complete with gallery locator maps, and lists of major exhibitions and shows, galleries and museums for the city or region being featured.
Available: By subscription; on newsstand ($5/issue)
Circulation: 125,000
Target audience: Educated collectors of fine art and American craft. Affluent gallery enthusiasts seeking information about contemporary art and craft.
Advertisements: Back cover, quarter page, full page, half page, classified. B&W, four-color and full color. Bind-ins and special gallery exhibition highlights with datebook (state by state listing of gallery exhibitions and events).
Advertising rates: $500-2,400
Direct mail ads: For artists and galleries who sell through catalogs. No direct ads please.
Press kits: Available
Submissions: No unsolicited manuscripts accepted.

ART LOVER'S ART & CRAFT FAIR BULLETIN
American Society of Artists
P.O. Box 1326
Palatine, IL 60078
Editorial: American Society of Artists
Phone: (312)751-2500
In business since: 1977
Type of publication: Local, consumer publication published 4 times per year. Newsletter style—black and white.
Description of publication: Listings of art shows, art and craft shows, craft shows that take place in Illinois—for visitors to those events.
Available: By subscription ($12/year)
Target audience: For those who like to visit art shows, art and craft shows, craft shows that take place in the state of Illinois.
Submissions: No unsolicited manuscripts accepted.

BLACKSMITH'S JOURNAL
P.O. Box 193
Washington, MO 63090
Editorial: Jerry Hoffmann, publisher/editor
Phone: (314)239-7049
Fax: (314)390-2133
In business since: 1990
Type of publication: International, trade publication, published 12 times per year. Loose leaf for 3-ring collection in binders. 1 color, illustrated.
Description of publication: The *Blacksmith's Journal* gets right down to business with thousands of step-by-step illustrations with the most useful and innovative instruction available to artist-blacksmiths today. Published monthly, the *Journal* is a continually growing source of information that subscribers can collect in 3-ring custom binders or color coded binders for each yearly volume.
Available: By subscription ($32/year). Back issues and volumes sold separately.
Circulation: 2,200
Target audience: People interested in artist-blacksmithing technique and design.
Advertisements: No advertising accepted.
Submissions: No unsolicited manuscripts accepted.

BRIDAL CRAFTS
2400 Deven Ave., Suite 375
Des Plaines, IL 60018
Editorial: Julie Stephani, editor

Advertising: Stuart Hochwart, vice president of marketing and sales
Phone: Editorial—(847)635-5800
Advertising—(847)635-5800
Subscriptions—(800)272-3871
Fax: (847)635-6311
E-mail: 72567.1066@compuserve.com
In business since: 1991
Type of publication: International, consumer publication, published 1 time per year. Magazine style—color.
Description of publication: This publication is a unique how-to resource for those who wish to make a wedding special through personalized, handmade fashions and decorations. Published annually, each issue contains large, high-quality color photos, complete step-by-step instructions and full-sized patterns.
Available: On newsstand ($3.95/issue)
Circulation: 50,000
Target audience: A publication for the bride who wants to personalize her wedding, aimed at brides and families/friends of brides.
Advertisements: Back cover, quarter page, full page, half page, classified, other size space ads available. B&W, four-color, full color and two-color. Display and classified; including Bridal Boutique, a "magalogue" of finished, hand crafted goods.
Advertising rates: Display ads range from ⅙ page b&w $320, to full page four-color $1,620, at the one time rate. Classifieds: $1.25/word, 20 word minimum.
Direct mail ads: Fulfillment, etc. is handled case by case.
Press kits: Free
Submissions: Please contact editorial department for written guidelines. Pay is to be determined. All quoted on an individual basis.

THE CRAFT DIGEST

P.O. Box 1245
Torrington, CT 06790
Editorial: Joseph Mehan
Advertising: Harry Langenheim
Phone: Editorial—(860)225-8875
Advertising—(860)489-4723
Subscriptions—(860)225-8875
Fax: Editorial—(860)225-7325; Advertising—(860)496-1830
In business since: 1972

Type of publication: Regional, trade publication, published 12 times per year. Tabloid style—black and white.
Description of publication: Extensive listing of art/craft activities for East Coast, including NY and PA. News by craft media, show reviews, book reviews. Subscription includes membership in Connecticut Guild of Craftsmen.
Available: By subscription ($30/year)
Circulation: 3,500
Target audience: This book has information for all levels, from beginners to professionals.
Advertisements: Quarter page, full page, half page. B&W.
Advertising rates: $25-300
Press kits: Free
Submissions: Query with SASE. Compensation is annual subscription to publication.

CRAFT MARKETING NEWS

P.O. Box 1541, Dept. BP
Clifton, NJ 07015-1541
Editorial: Adele Patti
Advertising: Robert Patti
Phone: (201)773-4215
Subscriptions—(800)831-5606
Fax: (201)815-1235
E-mail: rjp@intac.com
Website: http://www.intac.com/~rjp (search: Front Room)
In business since: 1983
Type of publication: National, trade publication, published 6 times per year. Newsletter style—black and white.
Description of publication: This publication is a bimonthly newsletter providing craft marketing opportunities (craft shops, galleries, craft malls, rent-a-space shops) nationwide. Investigative craft reporters nationwide provide fact-filled reports from across the country. Wholesale sources for supplies, special reports; business articles on selling, keeping books, promotionals.
Available: By subscription ($15.95/year), foreign: $40/year, sample: $4.
Circulation: 2,500
Target audience: The publication is aimed at professional crafters/artisans and gift producers of hand crafted items who need to reach wholesale

markets nationwide. Beginners are welcome.
Advertisements: Quarter page, full page, half page, classified. B&W.
Advertising rates: Vary.
Submissions: Send query letter, content of article and LSASE for return of article if not accepted.
Additional information: Descriptive flier available. Free catalog of other publications: *The Learning Catalog* (formerly known as *The Front Room News*).

THE CRAFT REGISTER

P.O. Box 820
Wichita, KS 67201-0820
Editorial/Advertising: Eric McCluer, publisher
Phone: (316)268-6526
Fax: (316)268-6646
In business since: 1991
Type of publication: Regional, trade publication, published annually plus newsletter update. Books—perfect bound.
Description of publication: These publications are regional directories of craft shows, craftspeople and suppliers for Kansas and Missouri.
Available: By subscription ($21.50/for both); sold at bookstores and craft shows.
Circulation: 8,000
Target audience: Aimed at craft show promoters, exhibitors and attenders.
Advertisements: Back cover, quarter page, full page, half page, classified. B&W, four-color, full color.
Advertising rates: Classified are $17 for three lines, $1 for each extra line. Display ads range from $89 to $1,500
Press kits: Free

CRAFTRENDS/SEW BUSINESS

3761 Venture Dr., Suite 140
Duluth, GA 30136
Editorial: Bill Gardner
Advertising: Dixie McDonald
Phone: Editorial—(770)497-1500
Advertising—(800)448-8819
Subscriptions—(847)647-6916
Fax: (770)497-0144
E-mail: craftrends@aol.com
In business since: 1982
Type of publication: International, trade publication, published 12 times per

year. Magazine style—color.

Description of publication: Magazine for retailers and craftspeople who buy craft, needlework, sewing and floral supplies and re-sell them or use for the manufacturer of hand crafted merchandise.

Available: By subscription ($26/year)

Circulation: 34,000

Target audience: Chain and independent retailers, professional craftspersons

Advertisements: Back cover, quarter page, full page, half page, classified, front cover, ⅓ page, ⅙ page, ¹⁄₁₂ page. B&W, four-color and full color. Call or write for specifications and special advertising sections, media kit available.

Advertising rates: Call or write for rate information.

Press kits: Free

Submissions: Must be business articles, retail store profiles, or commentary designed to help people be better at their business. Submit proposal/outline first. Rates vary.

CRAFTS 'N THINGS

2400 Devon Ave., Suite 375
Des Plaines, IL 60018

Editorial: Julie Stephani, editor

Advertising: Stuart Hochwert, vice president of marketing and sales

Phone: Editorial—(847)635-5800
Advertising—(847)635-5800
Subscriptions—(800)272-3871

Fax: (847)635-6311

E-mail: 72567.1066@compuserve.com

Website: http://www.clapper.com

In business since: 1975

Type of publication: International, consumer publication, published 10 times per year. Magazine style—color.

Description of publication: *Crafts 'n Things* offers over 30 projects per issue, special editorial sections, ideas and tips, sources, and a one-sided pattern section.

Available: By subscription ($19.97/ year); on newsstand ($3.95/issue)

Circulation: 330,000

Target audience: *Crafts 'n Things* is an inspirational idea magazine for the woman who is interested in many aspects of crafting. Her personal world is filled with crafts she has made or purchased, and she often engages in other creative, home-centered activites. She recognizes that crafts enrich the quality of her life.

Advertisements: Back cover, quarter page, full page, half page, classified. Other space ads available. B&W, four-color, full color and two-color. Display and classified ads; special sections such as Crafter's Boutique, a "magalogue" of hand-made finished goods; Crafters Showcase (mail order); Catalog Corner (catalogs); What's New (new products).

Advertising rates: Display ads range from ¹⁄₁₂ page, b&w $515 to full page, four-color, $6,920 at the one time rate. Classified ads are $3.25/word, 20 word minimum.

Direct mail ads: Available

Press kits: Free

Submissions: Please contact editorial department for written guidelines. Pay is quoted on an individual basis.

CRAFTSOURCE, A NATIONAL DIRECTORY OF CRAFTS

421-13 Route 59, Suite 143
Monsey, NY 10952

Contact: Karen Lamberton

Phone/Fax: (914)357-4005

In business since: 1995

Type of publication: National, trade publication, published annually. Book—color.

Description of publication: This is a professional's sourcing guide to professional crafts artisans in all major disciplines and regions of the country. Listings include descriptive material explaining the artisan's work, special techniques, etc., professional affliliations and major awards. Some artisans choose to include a photo of their work.

Available: By mail order ($100)

Target audience: Design and decor professionals, museum and gallery directors, giftware and boutique buyers, art and craft show promoters.

Advertisements: None included at this time.

Advertising rates: Artisan's fee for inclusion in the book $25-150.

Direct mail ads: Available

Press kits: Free

THE CROSS STITCHER

2400 Devon Ave., Suite 375
Des Plaines, IL 60018

Editorial: B.J. McDonald, editor

Advertising: Stuart Hochwert, vice president of marekting and sales

Phone: Editorial—(512)251-3306
Advertising—(847)635-5800
Subscriptions—(800)272-3871

Fax: (847)635-6311

E-mail: 72567.1066@compuserve.com

Website: http://www.craftnet.org/cross-st itcher

In business since: 1983

Type of publication: International, consumer publication, published 6 times per year. Magazine style—color.

Description of publication: *The Cross Stitcher* is an inspirational idea and how-to magazine for cross-stitch enthusiasts. The reader has some experience in cross-stitch and is looking for projects that vary from quick and easy to advanced pieces that are more time consuming. The reader has high expectations of receiving clear, consise instructions and easy to follow charts. They recognize the theraputic value of cross-stitching.

Available: By subscription ($14.97/ year); on newsstand ($3.50/issue)

Circulation: 95,000

Target audience: For the cross-stitcher looking for a broad array of patterns, including projects for kids and projects for "tired eyes."

Advertisements: Back cover, quarter page, full page, half page, classified. Other space ads available; offers special sections. B&W, four-color, full color, two-color. Display and classified, special sections such as The Stitchers Boutique, a "magalogue" section for cross-stitch designs and products; Stitcher Emporium, a shop listing.

Advertising rates: Display ads range from ¹⁄₁₂ page, b&w $285 to full page, four-color, $2,530 at the one time rate. Classified ads are $1.75/word, 20 word minimum.

Direct mail ads: Processed on a case by case basis. Requirements to be individually determined.

Press kits: Free

Submissions: Please contact editorial department for submission guidelines. Pay is individually determined.

DECORATIVE ARTIST'S WORKBOOK

1507 Dana Avenue
Cincinnati, OH 45207
Editorial: Anne Hevener, editor
Advertising: Stephanie Curtis, advertising manager
Phone: Editorial—(513)531-2690
Advertising—(513)745-0964
Subscriptions—(800)333-0888
Fax: (513)531-2902
E-mail: dawedit@aol.com
In business since: 1987
Type of publication: National, consumer publication, published 6 times per year. Magazine style—color.
Description of publication: Decorative Artist Workbook teaches beginning, intermediate and advanced decorative artists how to paint, and how to paint better. Readers learn the processes and techniques of decorative painting firsthand from other artists via step-by-step instructions and illustrations.
Available: By subscription ($19/year); on newstand ($3.99/issue)
Circulation: 85,667
Target audience: Beginning, intermediate and advanced decorative painters.
Advertisements: Back cover, quarter page, full page, half page, classified, ⅓ page, ⅔ page, ⅙ page, ⅒ page, b&w, four-color.
Advertising rates: $290-2,410 for b&w; $150-550 for color; reply cards charged at 50% of earned page rate (cards must be accompanied by an adjacent full page ad).
Press kits: Available
Submissions: Unsolicited manuscripts considered, query first with SASE. $125-250 for features; $85 on average for columns.

DESIGNER SOURCE LISTING

Carikean Publishing
P.O. Box 11771
Chicago, IL 60611-0711
Editorial/Advertising: Maryanne Burgess
Phone: (312)728-6118
Fax: (312)728-7035
In business since: 1985
Type of publication: National, consumer publication, published annually. Book—perfect bound.
Description of publication: The *Designer Source Listing*, updated yearly, is the oldest and best sourcebook for mail order shopping by the sewer and needle crafter. Shop anytime, anywhere without leaving the comfort of home. Find the best in fabrics, notions, machines and over 120 pattern companies, 21 categories in all. Buy a little or a lot at great prices. Using this updated sourcebook saves you time and money.
Available: At bookstores ($17.95), by mail order ($19.95, includes shipping and handling)
Target audience: The hobbyist who sews and crafts for themself and their family, the home based and small shop fashion and crafts designers, dressmakers and home economics teachers.
Advertisements: All ads are free to those selling retail and wholesale sewing and needle crafts supplies by mail. All ads have a description of supplies available by mail, minimum order requirements, methods of sale, i.e., check, money order, credit cards, trade charges, etc. No display ads.
Additional information: Also publishes a newsletter, "Cause I Said Sew!" full of "how-to" tips, a business information section and new sources of books and materials.

DIRECTORY OF ARTISTS, CRAFTERS, ARTISANS

1935 D Waters Edge
Fort Collins, CO 80526
Editorial/Advertising: Patricia Nay
Phone: Editorial—(970)221-4252
Advertising—(800)449-8430
Subscriptions—(800)449-8430
Fax: (970)221-4252
In business since: 1995
Type of publication: National, trade publication, published 2 times per year. Magazine style—black and white. Directory.
Description of publication: This directory is designed to market the work of artists and crafters to gift shops only. There are no articles at this time though the format could change in the future.
Available: By subscription ($5/year); on newsstand ($2/issue). Free to craftspeople and businesses.
Circulation: 5,000
Target audience: Gift shops
Advertisements: Back cover, quarter page, full page, half page, classified, ¹⁄₁₆ page, ⅛. B&W, four-color, full color.
Advertising rates: Directory listing, 200 words including spaces $35; ¹⁄₁₆ page $90; ⅛ page $150; ¼ page $275; ½ page $460; full page $810; color is $75 more per photograph for four-color
Press kits: Free to businesses, $5 to casual inquiries
Submissions: Accepted. Query first. Pay is negotiable.

DIRECTORY OF WHOLESALE REPS FOR CRAFT PROFESSIONALS

13451 Essex Ct.
Eden Prairie, MN 55347
Contact: Sharon Olson
Phone: (612)937-5275
In business since: 1986
Type of publication: National, trade publication, published 1 time per year. Directory—black and white.
Description of publication: The directory gives the information needed to expand a craft business into a full-time profitable business. It includes 100 + sales reps and companies that will sell finished handcrafts to gift shops, country stores, department stores, catalog companies, etc. Information includes: territories, showrooms, temporary shows, accounts, commissions, crafts wanted and who and how to contact each company. Other useful information and how to get started and many helpful hints from the reps themselves.
Available: By subscription ($16.75/year)
Circulation: 500
Target audience: Professional craftspeople who are interested in selling wholesale to shops, galleries, etc.
Advertisements: Not available.
Advertising rates: All listings of reps are free.

ENTREPRENEUR

P.O. Box 57050
Irvine, CA 92619-7050
Editorial: Rieva Lesonsky, editor in chief
Phone: Editorial—(714)261-2325

Advertising—(212)563-3852 and
(714)261-2325
Subscriptions—(800)274-6229
Fax: (714)755-4211
In business since: 1973
Type of publication: National, consumer
publication, published 13 times per
year. Magazine style—color.
Available: By subscription ($19.97/
year); on newsstand ($4/issue)
Circulation: 510,000
Target audience: Small business owners
Advertisements: Display ads and classified. B&W, four-color. Media kits
available.
Submissions: Submit queries only. En-
close SASE. Allow 6-8 weeks for response. No phone calls. Buys first
worldwide rights and pays upon acceptance. Pays $500 for features.

FIBERARTS: THE MAGAZINE OF TEXTILES
50 College St.
Asheville, NC 28801
Editorial: Ann Batchelder
Advertising: Jacqueline Corbett
Phone: Editorial—(704)253-0467
Advertising—(704)688-3575
Subscriptions—(704)253-0467
Fax: (704)253-7952; (704)688-3575
In business since: 1975
Type of publication: International, trade
publication, published 5 times per
year. Magazine style—color.
Description of publication: Readers of
the magazine are intersted in contemporary trends in surface design, weaving, quilting, stitchery, papermaking,
basketry, wearable art, felting and fiber sculpture. Articles provide the
professional and non-professional
textile enthusiasts with the support,
inspiration, useful information and direction to keep her or him interested,
committed and excited.
Available: By subscription ($22/year); on
newsstand ($4.95/issue)
Circulation: 24,900
Target audience: Audience includes professional artists, textile students, fashion designers, museum curators, gallery owners and collectors.
Advertisements: Back cover, quarter
page, full page, half page, classified,
⅙ page, ⅓ page, ⅔ page b&w, four-
color.
Advertising rates: $75-1,550

Press kits: Available
Submissions: Manuscript must be accompanied by color transparencies
(35mm or larger format) that might
accompany it, a separate number-
keyed photo caption sheet and a
SASE. Potential writers should be familiar with the magazine before making a query or submitting an unsolicited manuscript. Pays $60-400 for
accepted articles.

FREE STUFF FOR PEOPLE WHO ENJOY CRAFTING, SEWING & MORE
1954 First St., P.O. Box 6634
Dept. BWL197
Highland Park, IL 60035
Editorial: Barbara Becker
Phone: (847)831-9080
Fax: (847)831-5570
E-mail: bbeckerl@ix.netcom.com
In business since: 1994
Type of publication: National, consumer
publication, published 2 times per
year. Magazine style—black and
white.
Description of publication: Publication
features free and postage only offers
for crafters, including booklets, patterns, samples, project sheets, newsletters, kits and more. Features Christmas, Easter, Halloween, birthday,
graduation and wedding ideas. Perfect
for beginner to advanced crafters.
Great way to try out cross-stitch, sewing, quilting, needlecraft, tole painting
and other crafts.
Available: By subscription ($3).
Target audience: Crafters, sewers, cross-
stitchers, tole painters, quilters, need-
lecrafters
Advertisements: Quarter page, full page,
sponsorships, package inserts. Manufacturers may include product samples, project sheets, etc. (package inserts). Sponsorships of specific
sections (i.e., tole painting) available
for manufacturers.
Advertising rates: Package inserts: $50
per thousand; sponsorships: custom
Direct mail ads: Listing for product,
book, kit or project sheet. Items must
have postage and handling charge of
less than $2
Press kits: $1

GIFT BASKET NEWS
9655 Chimney Hill Lane, Suite 1036
Dallas, TX 75243
Editorial: Margaret Williams
Advertising: Lorna Hall
Phone: (214)690-1917
Fax: (214)690-0350
In business since: 1993
Type of publication: National, trade publication, published yearly. Magazine
style—black and white.
Description of publication: Readers receive information on marketing, business finance and designing of gift baskets. The articles assist readers in
running their businesses more effec-
tively. The magazine is the entrepreneur's choice for the gifts, gift baskets
and home accessories industry.
Available: By subscription ($25/year)
Circulation: 5,000-8,000
Target audience: Store owners in the gift
industry. These store owners include
but are not limited to: florists, balloon
shop owners, gift shops, gift basket retailer, gourmet stores, and specialty
food stores.
Advertisements: Back cover, quarter
page, full page, half page, classified.
B&W, full color, two-color.
Advertising rates: $50-650
Submissions: Must see sample of past articles. No pay. Will give byline.

HANDS ON GUIDE
255 Cranston Crest
Escondido, CA 92025-7037
Editorial/Advertising: Christel Luther
Phone/Fax: (619)747-8206
E-mail: hog92025@aol.com
In business since: 1988
Type of publication: Regional, trade
publication, published 11 times per
year. Tabloid style—black and white.
Description of publication: Event listings for CA, AZ, CO, ID, MT, NV,
NM, OR, UT, WA, WY. Events include small home boutiques to the
largest street fairs, festivals and trade
shows. Listings include date, location,
booth fee and size, promoter name,
address and phone/fax number. Evalu-
ations of shows by vendors.
Available: By subscription ($28/year); on
newsstand ($3/issue)
Circulation: 22,000
Target audience: A publication for craft-

ers, fine artists, exhibitors, vendors and shoppers.

Advertisements: Back cover, quarter page, full page, half page, classified. B&W.

Advertising rates: 2½" × 1" is $3; 5" × 1" is $6; 7½" × 1" is $9; 10" × 1" is $12. Multiply price by inches in height.

Press kits: Free

Submissions: Accepted.

NEIGHBORS & FRIENDS, THE PROFESSIONAL CRAFTERS MARKET

3410 Black Champ Rd.
Midlothian, TX 76065

Editorial: Renée Chase

Advertising: Carol Eades

Phone: (972)938-8890

Fax: (972)938-8788

E-mail: n-f@crafter.com

Website: http://www.crafter.com

In business since: 1991

Type of publication: International, trade publication, published 12 times per year. Magazine style—black and white with spot color.

Description of publication: Neighbors & Friends is a business resource for professional artists and crafters. This monthly magazine includes a list of craft shows, craft malls, supplies and services, and industry art and news. The magazine's area of coverage and distribution includes the entire US and Canada.

Available: By subscription ($21 for shipping and handling costs). Sample issue $2 plus shipping and handling.

Circulation: 40,000

Target audience: The professional artist and crafter.

Advertisements: Back cover, quarter page, full page, half page, classified, front cover with inside project page. B&W, four-color, full color.

Advertising rates: Range of rates available. Supplies and services: $30 month; through front cover and inside project page: $975.

Press kits: Free

Submissions: Publisher reserves the right to edit submitted material. Include a self-addressed stamped envelope for return of material. Pay for each submission is separately evaluated.

THE NETWORK: MARKETING GUIDE FOR ARTISTS, ARTISANS & CRAFTWORKERS

P.O. Box 1248
Palatine, IL 60078-1248

Editorial: Jeanine Black

Advertising: Nancy Godfrey

Phone (847)438-2737

Fax: (847)438-2737

In business since: 1985

Type of publication: National, trade publication, published 4 times per year. Magazine style—black and white.

Description of publication: The Network includes hundreds of Top Show listings and thousands of other great show listings to enable artists, artisans and craftworkers to make wise decision about where to exhibit their work. Art and craft show customers also use the publication to find the shows they want to attend. Other marketing opportunities include art galleries, handcrafted gift shops, county fairs and wholesale shows. Information on various art guilds, classes and other educational opportunities is available in each issue. One feature of *The Network* is it's Information Exchange where subscribers can obtain help to find hard to locate supplies and advice about the production of their art and/ or craft at no charge. Display advertising from craft malls, art and craft material suppliers, show coordinators and services help subscribers find the products and services they need to keep their professional edge.

Available: By subscription ($25/year)

Circulation: 3,000 +

Target audience: Artists, artisans and craftworkers and fine art and craft show customers

Advertisements: Back cover, full page, half page, classified, 1/16 page, 1/3 page. B&W.

Advertising rates: $60-765, depending on size and number of insertions

Submissions: No unsolicited manuscripts accepted.

NICHE MAGAZINE

The Rosen Group,
3000 Chestnut Ave. #304
Baltimore, MD 21211

Editorial: Hope Daniels, editor

Advertising: John Stefancik

Phone: Editorial—(410)889-3093

Advertising—(800)642-4314

Subscriptions—(800)624-4314

Fax: (410)243-7089

In business since: 1986

Type of publication: National, trade publication published 4 times per year. Magazine style—color.

Description of publication: Niche is edited for retailers of contemporary American art and craft; included in these are American fine art/craft gallery owners who sell retail. Artists utilize *Niche* as their wholesale professional journal. The publication is a combination sourcebook of artists and new works, and editorial features on the business of retailing fine craft art, who's who in the industry (artists and show promoters/marketers), how-to articles on marketing and improving retail operations. Regular editorial features include artist profiles and up to date information on industry trends, retail resources, and a classified (reader response) section. A unique offereing in this magazine are regular cagalog-style features called Advertorials, highlighting crafts for sale by artists to retailers.

Available: Distributed to artists and retailers of American craft at top wholesale and trade shows nationwide

Circulation: 20,000-25,000

Target audience: Craft galleries, resort retailers, department store and museum shops, decorative accessories catalogs, professional craftspeople

Advertisements: Back cover, quarter page, full page, half page, classified, advertorials and showcases. B&W, four-color, full color, two-color. Accommodates display (full-functional size pages), bound-in cards and supplements and catalog-style product shots.

Advertising rates: $380-2,090

Direct mail ads: Direct response to advertiser, magazine forwards requests for additional information through a reader-response card. Call sales office for additional information.

Press kits: Available

Submissions: No unsolicited manuscripts accepted.

PACK-O-FUN

2400 Devon Ave., Suite 375
Des Plaines, IL 60018
Editorial: Bill Stephani, editor
Advertising: Stuart Hochwert, vice president, marketing and sales
Phone: Editorial—(847)635-5800
Advertising—(847)635-5800
Subscriptions—(800)272-3871
Fax: (847)635-6311
E-mail: 7256.1066@compuserve.com
Website: http://www.crafnet.org/pack-o-fun
In business since: 1951
Type of publication: International, consumer publication, published 6 times per year. Magazine style—color.
Description of publication: Pack-o-Fun is a one of a kind magazine filled with creative, how-to projects and activites for kids and those working with kids. Reades are looking for "earth-friendly" quick, easy and inexpensive projects to work on together at home or with their groups.
Available: By subscription ($14.97/year); on newsstand ($2.95/issue)
Circulation: 77,000
Target audience: Kids, families, teachers and activity leaders.
Advertisements: Back cover, quarter page, full page, half page, classified. Other space ads available, offers special sections. B&W, four-color, full color, two-color. Display and classified ads; Catalog Corner (catalogs).
Advertising rates: Display ads range from $\frac{1}{12}$ page, b&w $28, to full page, four-color, $1,605 at the one time rate. Classified ads are $1.25/word, 20 word minimum.
Direct mail ads: Processed on a case by case basis. Requirements to be individually determined.
Press kits: Free
Submissions: Please contact editorial department for written guideliens. Pay is determined on an individual basis.

PAINTING

2400 Devan Ave., Suite 375
Des Plaines, IL 60018
Editorial: Beth Browning, editor
Advertising: Stuart Hochwert, vice president, marketing and sales
Phone: Editorial—(407)870-2121

Advertising—(847)635-5800
Subscriptions—(800)272-3871
Fax: (847)635-6311
E-mail: 72567.1066@compuserve.com
Website: http://www.craftnet.org/painting
In business since: 1985
Type of publication: International, consumer publication, published 6 times per year. Magazine style—color.
Description of publication: Painting is an inspirational how-to magazine for the man or woman who is interested in decorative painting. The reader may be a non-painter who has the desire to paint, a "dabbling" craft painter, or a more experienced painter with a variety of skills.
Available: By subscription ($21.95/year); on newsstand ($3.95/issue)
Circulation: 75,000
Target audience: For decorative painters of all skill levels looking for a variety of projects to create for pleasure, to give as gifts, or sell at shows.
Advertisements: Back cover, quarter page, full page, half page, classified. Other size space ads available. B&W, four-color, full color, two-color. Display, classified and special sections such as Artist Ads (for artists only) and Painting Emporium (shop listing).
Advertising rates: Display ads range from $\frac{1}{6}$ page b&w $430 to full page, four-color $2,200, at the one time rate. Classified: $1.25/word, 20 word minimum.
Direct mail ads: Processed on a case by case basis. Requirements to be determined individually.
Press kits: Free
Submissions: Please contact editorial department for guidelines. Pay is quoted on an individual basis.

POPULAR WOODWORKING

1507 Dana Avenue
Cincinnati, OH 45207
Editorial: Steve Shanesy
Advertising: Joe Wood
Phone: Editorial—(513)531-2690, ext. 238
Advertising—(513)531-2690, ext. 314
(513)531-2690, ext. 320
Fax: (513)531-1843
E-mail: wudworker@aol.com

In business since: 1980
Type of publication: National, consumer publication, published 6 times per year. Magazine style—color.
Description of publication: Popular Woodworking provides an average of 15 projects per issue. These shop-tested projects range from intermediate to beginning levels, and take from a few hours to a few weekends to build. Clear instructions, measured drawings, close-up photos and complete cutting lists make building the projects a snap.
Available: By subscription ($19.97/year); on newsstand ($3.99/issue)
Circulation: 200,000
Target audience: Beginning to intermediate level woodworkers who enjoy woodworking as a hobby.
Advertisements: Back cover, quarter page, full page, half page, classified. B&W, four-color, full color.
Advertising rates: $555-8,780 b&w; $395-1,195 color
Press kits: Available
Submissions: Unsolicited manuscripts considered, include project specifications, photograph, SASE. Pay varies.

SAC NEWSMONTHLY

P.O. Box 159
Bogalusa, LA 70429-0159
Editorial: Wayne Smith
Advertising: Sue Martin
Phone: (800)825-3722
Fax: (504)732-3744
In business since: 1986
Type of publication: National, trade publication, published 12 times per year. Tabloid style—black and white.
Description of publication: Listing complete details about arts and crafts shows and fairs and festivals is the primary goal of *SAC*. We try to assure the most complete list of shows of any publication. Also included in every issue are timely news articles relating to subjects of interest to the artists and craftsmen along with features and classified and display advertisement targeted to this audience.
Available: By subscription ($24/year)
Circulation: 36,000
Target audience: People who exhibit at art and craft shows.

Advertisements: Back cover, quarter page, full page, half page, classified. Any size from 2.5″ × 1″ to 10″ × 13″. B&W, one spot color. Advertisements are mainly for sponsors or promoters of art and craft shows. Some ads are for suppliers of T-shirts, wood products, beads, glue, etc.

Advertising rates: $3 per square inch

Submissions: Should address new product information; art and/or craft shows to be held or been held already; book reviews.

STAINED GLASS

6 SW Second St., #7
Lee's Summit, MO 64063

Editorial: Richard Gross, editor

Advertising: Katei Gross, business manager

Phone: (800)438-9581

Fax: (816)524-9405

In business since: 1906

Type of publication: International, trade publication, published 4 times per year. Magazine style—color.

Description of publication: Since 1906, *Stained Glass* has been the official voice of the Stained Glass Association of America. As the oldest, most respected stained glass publication in North America, *Stained Glass* preserves the techniques of the past as well as illustrates the trends of the future. The architectural focus has showcased projects in churches, public buildings, businesses and homes throughout the world with reliable clarity and accuracy.

Available: By subscription ($30/year); on newsstand ($8.50/issue); membership to SGAA

Circulation: 5,500

Target audience: The information provided is of significant value to the professional stained glass studio, and is also of interest to those for whom stained glass is an avocation or hobby. *Stained Glass* is considered the architectural stained glass reference guide for architects, interior designers, restorationists and contractors. The magazine inspires its readers to understand and enjoy the art, craft and business of stained glass.

Advertisements: Quarter page, full page, half page, classified, 1/16 page, 1/3 page catalog ads. B&W, four-color. Regular display ads are priced per size and frequency; classified mart ads are $1 per word; sources of supply listings are limited to business, name, address and phone ($4 per line). Catalog ads included in Winter and Summer issues only. Educational opportunities are listings for schools and instructors ($10 per listing).

Press kits: Free

Submissions: Send article outlines or abstracts. Preferred length 2,500 words. Exceptions made for scholarly or unusual works. Manuscripts should be directly related to the historical, contemporary, architectural, technical, artistic or craft aspects of the stained and decorative glass craft. Manuscripts of general or peripheral interest may be considered. First consideration is given to manuscripts with illustrations. Highly visual art from calls for excellent photographs. Large format transparencies preferred but will accept high quality slides. Payment upon publication. $125 for illustrated articles, $75 for non-illustrated.

TEXTILE TRADER

Rt. 1, Box 2910
Lakemont, GA 30552

Editorial/Advertising: Melanie Deitz

Phone: (706)782-1516

Fax: (706)782-5135

In business since: 1996

Type of publication: Regional, consumer publication published 4 times per year. Newsletter style—black and white.

Description of publication: A publication of classified ad listings for individuals to buy and sell used textile related equipment, including handweaving looms, spinning wheels, knitting machines and associated equipment.

Available: By subscription ($1/issue)

Circulation: 500

Target audience: Handweavers and spinners

Advertisements: Classified

Advertising rates: 50¢ per word

Submissions: No unsolicited manuscripts accepted.

WILDLIFE ART MAGAZINE

4725 Highway 7, P.O. Box 16246
St. Louis Park, MN 55416

Editorial: Rebecca Hakala Rowland

Advertising: Marlene Boggs

Phone: Editorial—(612)927-9056
Advertising—(612)927-9056
Subscriptions—(800)221-6547

Fax: (612)927-9353

In business since: 1982

Type of publication: International, consumer publication, published 6 times per year, plus annual *Art Collector's Yearbook*. Magazine style—color.

Description of publication: *Wildlife Art* is dedicated to exploring pertinent issues in the wildlife art industry and celebrating the artistic beauty and diversity of the genre. Distributed in more than sixty countries, *Wildlife Art* is the largest and most widely recognized journal for information about art and artists depicting the natural world. Filled with features, art show listings, new relase information and columns, this award-winning, high quality publication examines all aspects of wildlife and nature art, spotlighting contemporary artists to modern masters. *The Art Collector's Yearbook*, part of the annual subscription, is a showcase for artist's working in wildlife, nature and landscape genres and is a proven outlet to reach collectors, gallery representatives, publishers, plate and card companies and consumers. All regular issues of the magazine have a classified ad section where readers can obtain hard-to-find or sold out originals, prints and other collectibles; beautiful, full-color ads; and a listing of outstanding wildlife art galleries. *Wildlife Art* has won numerous industry awards for its design, layout and printing, including the Gold Ozzie (the Oscar of the printing industry) in 1995 for its redesign, and the same award in 1994 for its *Yearbook*.

Available: By subscription ($32.95/year); on newsstand ($6.95/issue); regular and back issues sold at wildlife art shows and museums

Circulation: 47,000

Advertisements: Back cover, quarter page, full page, half page, classified. B&W, four-color, full color

Advertising rates: Please write for current rate card, yearbook date sheet, and special advertising sections.

Direct mail ads: Available

Press kits: Free

Submissions: Please write for submission guidelines and future opportunities. Pay varies, based on research and word counts or assignment.

Additional information: The magazine also provides a "Show Report" of international wildlife art shows. Cost is $10. In addition, it publishes an annual "contest report." Cost $5. Send a SASE for both.

BOOKS

BASIC GUIDE TO SELLING ARTS & CRAFTS

P.O. Box 75

Torreon, NM 87061

Editorial: James Dillehay

Phone: Editorial—(505)384-1102

Orders—(800)235-6570

In business since: 1995

Type of publication: Paperback book.

Description of publication: Everything you need to know to make a successful craft business selling what you make. Price your work for profit, increase sales at craft shows, sell to stores, galleries and interior designers, learn what to do when your work isn't selling, many overlooked markets for crafters and every subject indexed to find the exact information you need.

Available: By mail. Cost is $18.45 (includes shipping).

Target audience: Any crafter, experienced or new, wishing to increase sales, boost profits, cut expenses, and develop additional income streams.

CRAFT RETAILING TODAY

c/o Niche Magazine

3000 Chestnut Ave., #304

Baltimore, MD 21211

Phone: (800)642-4314

Fax: (410)889-1320

In business since: 1995

Type of publication: Book.

Description of publication: Craft Retailing Today is a survey of the trends and buying habits of American craft retailers. Statistics compiled by the University of Florida center for retailing education and research for *Niche* magazine. Data includes product, trends, sales averages, customer profiles, advertising and business practices data. Financial statistic include salaries, turnover, productivity.

Available: By phone ($32).

Target audience: Craft retailers and artists needing business statistics for business planning and financing.

CRAFTING AS A BUSINESS

The Rosen Group

3000 Chestnut Ave., #304

Baltimore, MD 21211

Editorial: Wendy Rosen

Phone: Editorial—(410)889-3093

Orders—(410)889-1320

Fax: (410)889-1320

In business since: 1995

Type of publication: Book. 200 pages, 2-color.

Description of publication: Crafting As A Business is a comprehensive guide for making the move from craft hobbyist to crafting as a career. Includes information on product development, designing promotional materials, marketing and PR, retailing vs wholesaling, networking and more.

Available: By mail order ($22).

THE CRAFTS SUPPLY SOURCEBOOK

Betterway Books

1507 Dana Ave.

Cincinnati, OH 45207

Phone: Orders—(800)289-0963

Fax: (513)531-4082

Type of publication: Book. 320 pages.

Description of publication: A comprehensive shop-by-mail guide for craftspeople, with supplies ranging from printing materials and clothing patterns to specialized tools and hard-to-find accessories. The listings include mailing addresses, descriptions of the supplies offered, and leads to more information.

Available: At bookstores ($18.99); by mail order ($22.49, includes shipping and handling)

THE DOLL SOURCEBOOK

Betterway Books

1507 Dana Ave.

Cincinnati, OH 45207

Phone: Orders—(800)289-0963

Fax: (513)531-4082

Type of publication: Book. 352 pages.

Description of publication: A directory of sources for the dolls hobbyists love and the materials they need to make them. It contains more than 750 listings that make suppliers instantly accessible. Artists will find store and mail order retailers, merchants of doll-making supplies, manufacturers who buy artists' designs, shows, organizations, clubs and more!

Available: At bookstores ($22.99); by mail order ($26.49, includes shipping and handling)

HOW TO START MAKING MONEY WITH YOUR CRAFTS

Betterway Books

1507 Dana Ave.

Cincinnati, OH 45207

Phone: Orders—(800)289-0963

Fax: (513)531-4082

Type of publication: Book. 176 pages.

Description of publication: Starting with the basics and exploring all the exciting possibilities, this friendly guide helps hobbyists launch a rewarding crafts business. End-of-chapter quizzes, worksheets, ideas and lessons learned by successful crafters are all included.

Available: At bookstores ($18.99); by mail order ($22.49, includes shipping and handling)

THE TEDDY BEAR SOURCEBOOK

Betterway Books

1507 Dana Ave.

Cincinnati, OH 45207

Phone: Orders—(800)289-0963

Fax: (513)531-4082

Type of publication: Book. 356 pages.

Description of publication: With its 800-plus listings, this is the most complete treasury of bear information around. Bear collectors and artists will find detailed information on retailers, suppliers, artists, manufacturers, shows, appraisers and more in an alphabetized and cross-referenced format that makes it easy to use.

Available: At bookstores ($18.99); by mail order ($22.49, includes shipping and handling)

Did We Miss You?

If you would like to be in the next edition of *Crafts Marketplace*, please type or neatly print your name and address below, and circle the items that best describe your business. You will receive a questionnaire which can be completed for free inclusion in the next edition. Please be patient—there will be about two years between editions!

Name: _____

Address: _____

_____

_____

Phone: _____

I would like to be included in the following chapters of the next edition of *Crafts Marketplace* (please circle your choices):

1. Show producers and promoters (organizers of *more than one* show a year)
2. Show organizers (organizers of *only one* show a year)
3. Direct sales (businesses renting space to crafters, e.g., craft malls, co-ops)
4. Catalog companies that market/sell handmade crafts
5. Resources that produce custom-made catalogs and promotional material
6. Retail businesses selling handmade crafts
7. Craft brokers and representatives
8. Business and instructional products (show equipment, packaging, videos, etc.)
9. Banking, accounting, insurance, legal and other resources/services
10. Classes and workshops
11. Trade organizations
12. Trade and consumer publications

Comments

Tell us what you think about *Crafts Marketplace*! Please type or neatly print your comments in the space provided below, so we can make the next edition even better!

_____

_____

_____

_____

_____

_____

_____

_____

_____

_____

_____

_____

_____

_____

Please send comments and requests for questionnaires to Betterway Books, *Crafts Marketplace*, 1507 Dana Ave., Cincinnati, OH 45207, or fax to (513)531-7107.

Geographic Index

ALABAMA
Craft Shows
Andalusia B.P.W. Arts and Crafts Show, 80
Blackwell, Elise, 56
Fairhope Arts & Crafts Festival, 84
Festival in the Park, 84
National Annual Shrimp Festival, 89

Places to Sell Wholesale
Obvious Place, Inc., The, 146
Wilson Gallery, Inc., Maralyn, 164

ALASKA
Places to Sell Wholesale
Artworks, The, 119

ARIZONA
Craft Shows
Festival of the Arts, 84
Mill Avenue Merchant Association, 66

Places to Sell Wholesale
North American Native American Indian Information and Trade Center, 145
Obsidian Gallery, 146
Potter Etc., The, 150

ARKANSAS
Craft Shows
Arkansas Valley Arts and Crafts Fair, 80
Good Ole Summertime Arts & Crafts Fair, 86

Places to Sell Wholesale
Heartsong Pottery & Gifts, 134
Little Switzerland, 141
Ozark Native Craft Association

Consignment Shop, 148
Triple Oak Gift Shop, 162

Business Products
Flourish Co., 174

Services for Craftspeople
Massie's, 179

CALIFORNIA
Craft Shows
Gilroy Garlic Festival, 85
Harvest Festival, 63
La Jolla Festival of the Arts and Food Faire, 88
Pacific Fine Art Festivals, 69
Stockton Asparagus Festival Arts & Crafts Show, 91
Toledo Event Managing, Linda, 74
Western Exhibitors, 78
Wishing Well Productions, 77

Direct Sales
Artisans Village, 97
Bunny Hutch Gifts, 98
Crafter's Alley, 102
Crafters' Village, The, 105

Resources for Selling Through the Mail
Dynamic Focus Photography, 116

Places to Sell Wholesale
Between Friends, 119
Cradle of the Sun, 126
Highlight Gallery, 135
International Gallery, 137
Kaye Associates, Jerry S., 167
Krafters Outlet of California Inc., 139, 140
Melting Pot, The, 142
Modern Life Designs, 144
Moonstones Gallery, 144
Posner Fine Art, 150

Road Runners, 169
Rookie-To Gallery, 153
Sassafras Ridge, 155
Seekers Collection & Gallery, The, 155
Soft Touch Artists Collective Gallery, The, 158
Sterling Representation, 170
Tops, 162

Business Products
Avanti Display, 174
Impact Images, 173

Services for Craftspeople
Harbour Insurance Management, 177
Revere Academy of Jewelry Arts, 181

Trade Organizations
Western States Craft & Hobby Association (WSCHA), 190

Craft-Related Publications
Entrepreneur, 194
Hands on Guide, 195

COLORADO
Craft Shows
Capitol Hill People's Fair, 81
Olde Fashion Promotions, 69

Direct Sales
Commonwheil Artists Cooperative, 99

Resources for Selling Through the Mail
Alternative Media Group, 116

Places to Sell Wholesale
Clay Pigeon, The, 123
Cotter Gallery, J, 124

J & M Jewelry, 138
Panache Craft Gallery, 148
Steamboat Art Company, 158
Telluride Gallery of Fine Art, 160

Business Products
Wood Factory, The, 176

Services for Craftspeople
Alternative Media Group, 178
Behind-The-Scenes Selling Secrets of Professional Artists & Craftspeople, 182

Craft-Related Publications
Directory of Artists, Crafters, Artisans, 194

CONNECTICUT
Craft Shows
Art & Craft Boutique, 80
Arts & Crafts Festivals, Inc., 55
Coast & Country Shows, 58
Crafts America, 60
Guilford Handcraft Center, 62
Holiday Crafts Festival, 87
Mystic Community Center, 68
North East Promotions, Inc., 68
Rose Productions, Cookie, 71
Wesleyan Potters Annual Exhibit & Sale, 93

Direct Sales
Handcrafter's Haven, 109

Places to Sell Wholesale
ABC Canton Kids Shop, 117
Brookfield Craft Center, 120

General Index

More Great Books for Crafters!

The Crafter's Guide to Pricing Your Work—Price and sell more than 75 kinds of crafts with this must-have reference. You'll learn how to set prices to maximize income while maintaining a fair profit margin. Includes tips on record-keeping, consignment, taxes, reducing costs and managing your cash flow. #70353/$16.99/160 pages/paperback

Selling Your Dolls and Teddy Bears: A Complete Guide—Earn as you learn the business, public relations and legal aspects of doll and teddy bear sales. Some of the most successful artists in the business share the nitty-gritty details of pricing, photographing, tax planning, customer relations and more! #70352/$18.99/160 pages/31 b&w illus./paperback

Painting & Decorating Birdhouses—Turn unfinished birdhouses into something special—from a quaint Victorian roost to a Southwest pueblo, from a rustic log cabin to a lighthouse! These colorful and easy decorative painting projects are for the birds with 22 clever projects to create indoor decorative birdhouses, as well as functional ones to grace your garden. #30882/$23.99/128 pages/194 color illus./paperback

The Best of Silk Painting—Discover inspiration in sophisticated silk with this gallery of free-flowing creativity. Over 100 full-color photos capture the glorious colors, unusual textures and unique designs of 77 talented artists. #30840/$29.99/128 pages/136 color illus.

Painting Houses, Cottages and Towns on Rocks—Turn ordinary rocks into charming cottages, country churches and Victorian mansions! Accomplished artist Lin Wellford shares 11 fun, inexpensive, step-by-step projects that are sure to please. #30823/$21.99/128 pages/398 color illus./paperback

Making Greeting Cards With Rubber Stamps—Discover hundreds of quick, creative, stamp-happy ways to make extra-special cards—no experience, fancy equipment or expensive materials required! You'll find 30 easy-to-follow projects for holidays, birthdays, thank you's and more! #30821/$21.99/128 pages/231 color illus./paperback

Acrylic Decorative Painting Techniques—Discover stroke-by-stroke instruction that takes you through the basics and beyond! More than 50 fun and easy painting techniques are illustrated in simple demonstrations that offer at least 2 variations on each method. Plus, a thorough discussion on tools, materials, color, preparation and backgrounds. #30884/$24.99/128 pages/550 color illus.

How to Make Clay Characters—Bring cheery clay characters to life! The creator of collectible clay "Pippsywoggins" figures shares her fun and easy techniques for making adorable little figures—no sculpting experience required! #30881/$22.99/128 pages/579 color illus./paperback

The Art of Jewelry Design—Discover a colorful showcase of the world's best contemporary jewelers. This beautiful volume illustrates the skilled creative work of 21 production jewelers, featuring a wide variety of styles, materials and techniques. #30826/$29.99/144 pages/300 color illus.

Decorative Painting Sourcebook—Priscilla Hauser, Phillip Myer and Jackie Shaw lend their expertise to this one-of-a-kind guide straight from the pages of *Decorative Artist's Workbook*! You'll find step-by-step, illustrated instructions on every technique—from basic brushstrokes to faux finishes, painting glassware, wood, clothing and much more! #30883/$24.99/128 pages/200 color illus./paperback

Making Books by Hand—Discover 12 beautiful projects for making handmade albums, scrapbooks, journals and more. Only everyday items like cardboard, wrapping paper and ribbon are needed to make these exquisite books for family and friends. #30942/$24.99/108 pages/250 color illus.

Make It With Paper Series—Discover loads of bright ideas and easy-to-do projects for making colorful paper creations. Includes paper to cut and fold, templates and step-by-step instructions for designing your own creations. Plus, each paperback book has over 200 color illustrations to lead you along the way.
Paper Boxes—#30935/$19.99/114 pages
Paper Pop-Ups—#30936/$19.99/96 pages

The Decorative Stamping Sourcebook—Embellish walls, furniture, fabric and accessories—with stamped designs! You'll find 180 original, traceable motifs in a range of themes and illustrated instructions for making your own stamps to enhance any decorating style. #30898/$24.99/128 pages/200 color illus.

Make Jewelry Series—With basic materials and a little creativity you can make great-looking jewelry! Each 96-page paperback book contains 15 imaginative projects using materials from clay to fabric to paper—and over 200 color illustrations to make jewelry creation a snap!
Make Bracelets—#30939/$15.99
Make Earrings—#30940/$15.99
Make Necklaces—#30941/$15.99

Handmade Jewelry: Simple Steps to Creating Wearable Art—Create unique and wearable pieces of art—and have fun doing it! 42 step-by-step jewelry-making projects are at your fingertips—from necklaces and earrings, to pins and barrettes. Plus, no experience, no fancy equipment and no expensive materials are required! #30820/$21.99/128 pages/126 color, 30 b&w illus./paperback

Master Strokes—Master the techniques of decorative painting with this comprehensive guide! Learn to use decorative paint finishes on everything from small objects and furniture to walls and floors, including dozens of step-by-step demonstrations and numerous techniques. #30937/$22.99/160 pages/400 color illus./paperback

The Doll Sourcebook—Bring your dolls and supplies as close as the telephone with this unique sourcebook of retailers, artists, restorers, appraisers and more! Each listing contains extensive information—from addresses and phone numbers to business hours and product lines. #70325/$22.99/352 pages/176 b&w illus./paperback

How to Start Making Money With Your Crafts—Launch a rewarding crafts business with this guide that starts with the basics—from creating marketable products to setting the right prices—and explores all the exciting possibilities. End-of-chapter quizzes, worksheets, ideas and lessons learned by successful crafters are included to increase your learning curve. #70302/$18.99/176 pages/35 b&w illus./paperback

The Art of Painting Animals on Rocks—Discover how a dash of paint can turn humble stones into charming "pet rocks." This hands-on easy-to-follow book offers a menagerie of fun—and potentially profitable—stone animal projects. Eleven examples, complete with material list, photos of the finished piece and patterns will help you create a forest of fawns, rabbits, foxes and other adorable critters. #30606/$21.99/144 pages/250 color illus./paperback

The Crafts Supply Sourcebook, 4th edition—Turn here to find the materials you need—from specialty tools and the hardest-to-find accessories, to clays, doll parts, patterns, quilting machines and hundreds of other items! Listings organized by area of interest—make it quick and easy! #70344/$18.99/320 pages/paperback

The Teddy Bear Sourcebook: For Collectors and Artists—Discover the most complete treasury of bear information stuffed between covers. You'll turn here whenever you need to find sellers of bear making supplies, major manufacturers of teddy bears, teddy bear shows, auctions and contests, museums that house teddy bear collections and much more. #70294/$18.99/356 pages/202 illus./paperback